Language, Media and Economy in Virtual and Real Life

Language, Media and Economy in Virtual and Real Life:

New Perspectives

Edited by

Paola Cotticelli Kurras and Alfredo Rizza

Cambridge Scholars Publishing

Language, Media and Economy in Virtual and Real Life:
New Perspectives

Edited by Paola Cotticelli Kurras and Alfredo Rizza

This book first published 2018

Cambridge Scholars Publishing

Lady Stephenson Library, Newcastle upon Tyne, NE6 2PA, UK

British Library Cataloguing in Publication Data
A catalogue record for this book is available from the British Library

ISBN (10): 1-5275-0580-4
ISBN (13): 978-1-5275-0580-3

CONTENTS

PREFACE

In a globalized world, a company may spread its message to every corner of the globe and reach lots of potential customers by resorting to multimedia advertising. These media can include, but are not limited to, television, radio, newspapers, magazines, websites and mobile digital devices.

Comparing the linguistic and the marketing perspectives in creating and conducting a multimedia campaign is nowadays a primary interest, in order to observe how the different levels (language, music, imagery ...) interplay in the communication process. Branding keeps being one of the crucial elements of contemporary advertising, since brand awareness is often one of the most important factors in the decision process of any consumer.

The present volume collects revised and selected contributions based on papers read in Verona (June 2015) at the conference "Names in the Economy", the 5th of a series that started in Antwerpen in 2006 (s. Kremer & Ronneberger-Sibold 2007) and took place in 2007 in Vienna (s. Wochele, Kuhn, Stegu), and then every two years in Amsterdam (2009 by the Meertens Instituut's colleagues, s. Boerrigter and Nijboer 2012), and in Turku 2011 (s. Sjöblom, Ainiala, Hakala 2013). The "Verona papers" investigate some new methods and approaches in describing and analysing the multimedia channels in the communication realm of economy. Furthermore they offer an overview on new kinds of corpora and data collections that take into consideration commercial, proper and common names not only in everyday life, but also in virtual life settings.

The volume is organised in four parts.

The **first part** ("Names in their context") deals with marketing strategies and campaigns in different countries (Italy, Finland, Germany) and analyses advertising text with a special focus on brand names and on new strategies for advertising.

Dominik **Baumgarten** ("Multimodal representations of brand names in a literary context") aims to bridge the gap between the linguistic approaches on textual as well as pictorial advertising language and the research on hypertexts from a literary point of view.

Unexpected positive effects are reported from city branding: Angelika **Bergien** ("A city called *Otto*: how a marketing campaign became an (un)wanted success") shows what makes city branding successful, and what happens when the residents themselves use the campaign for their own purposes modifying or reinterpreting the slogans.

Oxana **Issers** ("From Siberia - with a smile: naming of dental clinics in the region of Siberia") investigates how new marketing strategies for dental services and clinics spread out in Siberia after the Soviet Union period and led to autonomous linguistic uses and developments.

Irina **Kryukova** and Anton **Kryukov** ("Internet name contests as a new means of advertising name invention in Russia") show how internet name contests are an interesting sector for developing naming strategies.

Antje **Lobin** ("The integration of the brand name in the advertising text") deals with some morphological, syntactic and lexical context in French, Spanish and Italian Nivea e-mail newsletters from 2010 to 2013 and tries to point out dominant patterns in individual languages.

The **second part** ("Names as markers of national/cultural/regional identity") is dedicated to aspects of country identities and to the strategies to highlight them in advertising.

Daiana **Felecan** ("The rhetoric of pseudonyms in virtual language") examines websites and considers that pseudonyms with sexual connotations are predominant on the basis of the fact that virtual space is free and uncensored, with norms of social, moral and verbal behaviour being neutralised.

Marja **Kalske** ("What is 'Europe' and 'European'?") overviews the denotation and the connotations of the label "Europe" and "European" in Finland from the '90s to our present days. The paper shows how they change over time from far ranging positive connotations to more and more neutral (or almost negative) reference to a generic "western world and values".

Solvita **Pošeiko** (" 'Following in the footsteps of names': commercial ergonymia in linguistic landscape of the Baltic countries") shows how the names of local companies create a particular image of their city which differs from that of other cities. This plays an important role in the Baltic states where ergonyms are characterised by the use of national languages.

Marie Antoinette **Rieger** ("Advertising African coffee. Branding strategies between pity and colonial fantasies") describes how nowadays goods from colonial countries (Africa) circulate in the market coming from fair trade. Due to political correctness, the linguistic dimension does not allow to give a complete and fair image of the countries where the products are from.

Tatiana **Sokolova** ("Non-trivial urbanonyms in Moscow commercial space") focuses on names used for travel agencies, beauty salons and shops. Some of them are made to sound foreign to Muscovites: they are typically Italian or Italian like, just to induce customers to associate them with Italian quality (and to justify higher prices for the sellers).

Advertising in Russia has also been examined: Lyaysan **Zamaletdinova** ("Lexis with ethnocultural semantic components in Moscow restaurant naming") explains how the naming strategies of restaurants in Moscow underline the national identity. She investigates two trends in contemporary Russian naming, such as the use of lexis with ethnocultural semantic components (exotic vocabulary, precedent phenomena, and national onyms) and the introduction of creative linguistic techniques.

The **third part** ("Linguistic features and strategies of names") is entirely dedicated to linguistic strategies for naming in very different sectors, so that the articles give an interesting view on modern life.

Some other aspects of the political language are analysed by Massimo **Arcangeli** ("L'economia filtrata dal linguaggio politico. Dal funzionalismo organico della Prima Repubblica al popular chic"). The author describes the changes in the political language in Italy since the 1990s, changes that begun with Berlusconi's economic and financial vocabulary and end up now in the political language of Matteo Renzi. The latter "dematerializes" the political vocabulary in accordance to a strategy that adapts the political language to a branding campaign in order to diffuse ideological values as brand values.

Ilia **Baranov** ("Bank names and success: a statistical approach") analyses the correlation between banks' assets and name properties in order to explore the connections between the customer's perception of goods or services and their names.

Fiorenza **Fischer** and Holger **Wochele** ("From *Reaganomics* to *Renzinomics*. The puzzling word formations of the type <Proper Name> + *-(eco)nomics* in German and Italian") analyse some examples of naming strategies in the current economic and political press in Italy and in Germany. In particular, terms like "Renzinomics" which means and denotes "the financial politic wave by Renzi". From such names a new suffixoid developed, i.e. *–nomics*, which is now building further forms, such as Soccernomics, Humanomics.

Sergey **Goryaev** and Olga **Olshvang** ("A new subcategory in Commercial Proper Names: Internet Plan Names in Russian") analyse internet plans showing a current tendency to give them proper names. Some of them are abbreviated descriptions "Up to 5 Mbit/s", "Suburban 499", or give technical details, e.g. "Limitless", "Online 879", especially in the sphere of private internet providers.

Katharina **Leibring** and Anna **Svedjedal** ("Naming and marketing a job coaching firm – means and strategies") examine a sample of names of companies, which are dealing with job coaching and represent new enterprises in the Swedish advertising in order to find out if they employ new strategies to communicate their knowledge and products.

Janne **Seppälä** ("Car nicknames and their relation to brand") examines several nicknames of some cars, deriving from the brand name (Chevy from Chrevrolet) or from an existing word (Mitsubitchy < bitchy). From the analysis of 3500 Finnish and 600 Estonian car nicknames he argues that, at least in Finland, cars are metaphorically seen as humans, animals, boxes or machines.

Adriana **Stoichitoiu Ichim** ("Current trends in naming Romanian travel agencies") investigates names and patterns in naming travel agencies in the Romanian economic environment from the nineties to our present days. Most frequent strategies evoke shared historical and sociocultural values. Names of travel agencies are revealed to be functional to the westernization of Romania.

Sabine **Wahl** ("*Oh Lord, won't you buy me a Mercedes Benz*?– Brand names in lyrics and music videos") points out an important aspect of the sound context of advertisement. The author collected multilingual song lyrics containing brand names in their title or text, and analysed the influence and interrelation between music and text as multimodal product placement strategy.

Finally, we thank all who made this volume possible: the Department of Culture e Civiltà of the University of Verona, the contributors, the collaborators of the Language Centre, the scientific board, and Cambridge Scholars Publishing for accepting our volume.

Verona, October 2016
Paola Cotticelli Kurras, Alfredo Rizza

References

Boerrigter, R. and Nijboer, H. (eds.) 2012. *Names and language capital. Proceedings Names in the economy III, Amsterdam, 11-13 June 2009.* Amsterdam: Meertens Instituut. Electronic publication: http://depot.knaw.nl/12899/.

Kremer, L and Ronneberger-Sibold, E. (eds.) 2007. *Names in commerce and industry: past and present.* Berlin: Logos.

Sjöblom, Ainiala, T. and Hakala, U. (eds.) 2013. *Names in the economy: Cultural Prospects*. Newcastle: Cambridge Scholars.

PART I:

NAMES IN THEIR CONTEXT

MULTIMODAL REPRESENTATIONS OF BRAND NAMES IN A LITERARY CONTEXT

DOMINIK BAUMGARTEN

Abstract

Literary texts are genuinely known for being an artistic and inspirational expression of the author's imagination. Given the current technical facilities of the 21st century and the ongoing need for cutting-edge innovative advertising, the printed book eventually became a new focus of the marketing industry. This paper puts emphasis on the current usage of literacy for commercial and advertising purposes and on the integration of literacy into brand campaigns.

Introduction

The academic discourse on names in the economy includes the economic positioning of names in a specific context. The phenomena of names and economy are related especially in the case of names that are meant to function in a commercial environment. These so-called brand names have been a common strategy for unifying commercial items ever since the opening of labelled goods to international trade. Ever since brand names have been popular institutions with not only commercial value but also social and cultural meaning, which can be significant for at least a specific period of time:

> With the growth of industry allowing more production and the construction of transcontinental railroads and steamships making possible better distribution, more and more prepacked consumer goods came on the market, ready to be promoted through advertising. Among the first were patent medicines – manufactured remedies that often consisted primarily of alcohol and laudanum (opium). Instead of being shipped to stores in large containers and bottled at the point of sale, these products arrived bottled and ready to be sold to the consumer (Hanson 2014: 265).

The possibility of an overall "commercial turn", an ever-growing omnipresence of advertising in almost every medium, challenges scholars from literary studies and linguistics with the need to investigate advertisements in order to elaborate on their own fields of study. In particular long and complex texts (such as novellas and novels) can contain numerous references to brand names and product placement, which demand further academic investigation. Even though (printed) books are not the advertising industry's main platform for commercial display, the repetitive use of literary advertising in various languages over the last 10 to 15 years justifies a closer look at this interference (Baumgarten 2013a: 131). This article therefore concentrates on the usage of contemporary literature as a platform for showcasing and advertising brand names.

The origins of brand names in literature

Brand names are a part of everyday life and therefore of everyday oral discourse. Whether they establish a setting, like mentioning a supermarket, shop or other specifically named public space, or explicitly referring to items of all kinds, brand names cannot be avoided without losing concreteness. Furthermore, more and more brand names are lexicalized in a way that they are commonly understood as synonyms for an entire product group rather than referring to specific (commercial) brands. For example, the terms *Tempo* or *Uhu* are already accepted as established oral or orthographic representations for tissues or liquid glue without purposefully featuring the product labels or advertisers. Nevertheless, brand names contribute to the specific uniqueness (and customer awareness) of each product:

> A brand name is a word or phrase attached to prepacked consumer goods so that they can be better promoted to the general public through advertising. In a highly mobile society, these standardized, branded products became a source of stability for consumers. The idea of stability coming from a brand-name product has persisted into the 21st century. For example, wherever they are, weary travellers are likely to stop for a meal at a familiar and comfortable landmark such as McDonald's or Pizza Hut (Hanson 2014: 265 f.).

In a literary context, brand names are a rather controversial topic that still seems to be inconsistent with the artistic purpose of independent literature. Other voices claim the creation of a specific aesthetic and poetic fashion that enters literacy by inserting popular phenomena such as advertisements and product placement (Weyand 2013: 4 f.).

The term "product placement" originally arose from the growth of the film industry in the 1920s in Hollywood, where it quickly established itself as a lucrative possibility of dealing with the constantly growing costs of the booming industry. While the integration of sponsored product placement into the narratives (Bomnüter 2014: 63) of current productions, especially in the German market, count for around 2-3 billion Euros of annual turnover, the film industry is benefitting but not necessarily because it relies on this kind of funding. The first appearances of brand names in a literary context, which trace back to the late 19th century, on the other hand were never reported to have any commercial background at all. A growing presence could be seen in American literature from the 1950s onwards, where various novels such as Ian Fleming's *James Bond* featured brand names in an almost film-like way.

Contemporary novels from the 1990s until today consistently deal with various approaches to brand names, product placement and advertising within a literary framework. The term "pop literature" defines a contemporary drift of literary style, which moves away from elitist spheres in favour of a concentration on popular narratives. The characterization of brands and brand names may vary from enthusiastic glorification to severe criticism, always depending on the author's current political self-positioning. There is not one example of an author from 21st century literature, who was officially paid to go against this artistic or even political freedom.

The main change of the meaning of brand names and product placement for the literary industry came with Fay Weldon's 2001 novel *The Bulgari Connection*. British author Weldon was reported to have signed a sponsorship contract with *Bulgari*, which led her to create a whole story around a piece of jewellery by the brand (The Guardian 2001). Weldon's publication brought a blurriness to the border between literacy and advertising that questions the positioning of sponsored novels as still being a part of literary production or as complementing a multimedia advertising campaign. The 2006 novel *Cathy's Book* by Sean Stewart, Jordan Weisman & Cathy Briggs took this development to the next level. Coming from the fields of creating virtual reality games and graphic design, the trio of authors agreed to develop a trilogy of novels to carry a multitude of product placement from the range of their sponsor *Procter&Gamble*. The further investigation will now lead to a closer look at the presentation of brand names in a commercially motivated literary environment.

Brand names and sponsoring

The growing presence of brand names in contemporary novels attracts the advertising industry, which is constantly looking for new and unconventional ways to feature commercial items. This potential opportunity to finance upcoming literary productions, on the other hand, attracts authors. The publishers of the teenage literature series *Mackenzie Blue*, which features the adventures of a youthful clique, advertise new sequels online before the stories are even written. During the writing process potential sponsors are invited to take part in the creative design of the novel's product environment (Jessica 2008). The main innovation in comparison with the previous popular novels before 2000 is the integration of product placement in a literary production without necessarily needing it for narrative reasons. Brand names in novels therefore are not automatically embedded in a framework they initially belong to – on this point, literary product placement matches its filmic origin.

Bigger conglomerates such as *Coca Cola*, *Nestlé* or *Procter&Gamble* each hold broad product ranges with a multitude of diverse products. These corporations come with enormous marketing budgets and an interest in advertising formats, which have the potential to cover many of their own-brands at the same time in order to create an entire product range. Literacy, on the other hand, usually needs an environment and a setting for its narrative – and not in every case can this environment rely solely on the author's imagination and fictional creation. Existing products can help to establish this framework by creating a kind of product environment the reader recognizes from the outside world. Similar to their real-world-equivalent, brand names in novels also have the potential to trigger specific emotions in the reader: while some brands stand for desirable luxury or healthy lifestyle, others may be connoted with a rather cheap or unattractive image. On the other hand, the representation within a novel and the affirmative contextualization of a brand name might help to improve on the product's prestige in real life. Sponsoring therefore becomes particularly attractive in the case of a novel series that already holds a broad readership and a classy reputation. Especially well-respected youth novels can serve as platforms to introduce specific brands to an audience that is just about to develop a proper shopping culture.

Artistic vs. commercial product placement

An important issue for the scientific analysis of commercially motivated product placement in a literary environment is its structural similarity to non-commercial representations. Scholars currently have to trust the reliability of press coverage in order to identify product placement with a sponsorship background.

A possible indication for artistically motivated product placement might be the creative interlacing of brand names into a complex story line and the extensive examination of a specific brand or product. German author Matthias Sachau's 2011 novel *Linksaufsteher* caricatures the current cult around the brand *Apple* (Sachau 2011: 74 f.). Long passages of the novel comment on the so-called *iCult* and create not only a fictional item, the *iBag*, but also an entire fictional product environment including an advertising campaign. In this clear case of artistic product placement the featured product is not only fictional, it is woven into the novel's narrative in a creative and thoughtful manner. This kind of product placement could not easily be changed for other brands, because long passages are particularly designed to feature this specific item.

In artistic publications brand names are usually well suited to the general narrative. They supply the overall plot with a variety of symbolism and are placed precisely so as to create a specific flair or product environment. Individual brands are connoted either as positive or negative, they can carry certain information about the characters, settings or entire plot elements of the novel. Especially pop literature from the 1990s onwards uses brand names and advertising to discuss current social phenomena, often in a very critical and subversive manner. This approach to brands and products does not collaborate well with the aims of the advertising industry (which, of course, always aims to present commercial goods in the most flattering way possible); very rarely does a brand mock its own product range.

Sponsored product placement, on the other hand, is embedded in a literary setting in a way we already discussed in the case of *Mackenzie Blue*. The inherent product placement does not necessarily bond with the literary environment it is set in. As already mentioned in the previous chapter, sponsors are allowed to get involved in the book project at any time of the creative process. This means that specific items may also be inserted at any stage of the development of the story. Even complete issues of the Mackenzie Blue series would change their sponsors from one edition to another and change the entire product series without losing any plot element. Sponsored product placement can possibly embed exactly the same brand names and advertising topics into a literary context as the unsponsored pendant. The main difference to creative and artistic product placement can be seen in the relation between narrative and advertising. The narrative of sponsored novels does not rely on specific product placement to create e.g. an atmosphere or to characterize a person. Moreover, situations are created to best present a brand. These situations are designed in such a general manner that the embedded product placement can easily be changed from one edition of the text to the next.

From 2000 on, an average number of 0.7 product placements per page of an entertaining novel was reported (Baumgarten 2013b: 158). This noteworthy quantity reflects the omnipresence of brand names not only in a literary but also in almost every context. Presumably, every concrete item can be named with a concrete manufacturer of the author's (or sponsor's) choice, and every brand names labels the brand with a specific flair or connotation. Therefore, commercial advertising can be placed at any point of the narrative, which makes this medium even more attractive for advertisers and even less transparent for readers. However, this inseparability is most likely limited to paper publications, which present all their content in one single medium. Whether or not brand names and advertising become more obvious in media combinations will be investigated in the following passages.

Modality, literature and brand names

Multimodality in the print versions of novels is usually restricted and limited to media forms that can be realized as two-dimensional and static. In novels and other book publications the content is realized in the form of text and image. This traditional modality is closely related to print advertisements, which build a key advertising strategy with the longest history in product marketing.

Orthographic representations build the core body of literature. Brand names are represented in writing. As opposed to their representation in print advertisements, brand names within an orthographic narrative are not separated from the rest of the text e.g. by a special typography or other graphic highlighting. In their orthographic form brand names build a complex word field with a constantly growing lexicon. Even though every single name has its own meaning, many brand names may be substituted by one another within a literary framework without losing the initial literary focus. To establish, for example, a character with an exclusive and luxurious taste and lifestyle, authors may mention brand names such as *Chanel* and *Gaultier* to establish the character's product environment, but they might also use *Cartier* or *Prada* without leaving the price category or the connotation of an exclusive and expansive brand on the reader's mind. Even though orthography best features brand names in their traditional form, this representation is the easiest to replace one brand name for another. In case of a changing sponsorship contract authors can easily get in contact with other advertisers.

Visual representations are – apart from comics and similar image-texts – more on the complementary side and in most cases mirror content that has already been realized orthographically. Due to structural similarity illustrations in novels can resemble advertising imagery quite easily. In both cases the visual mirrors a key element or a valuable benefit of the (brand) narrative. In case of an advertisement, the product is usually represented in an attractive manner. Also close-ups of the key features of a product are possible. Illustrations of a literary narrative, on the other hand, pick up a specific moment out of a more complex narrative and highlight a representative outtake. This can be a main character or a specific situation.

Literature, especially in its digital representation, functions as a communicative medium (Ess 2016: 414). Mixed modalities, which combine orthographic and pictorial elements and create new media in-between, are constructed in the same manner as many contemporary print advertisements. Usually, these print advertisements play around with the relation between text and image to create a kind of dialogue that attracts the attention of the future purchaser.

Illustrations in novels potentially do the same, but they can also just represent a certain scenario that has already been introduced orthographically. In case of product placement, sponsored or not, illustrations can also serve as additional displays to best feature the items by presenting them in more than just one medium. Similar to the differentiation between artistic and commercial product placement the reader might be able to identify sponsored product placement by its lack of connection to the literary plot. While artistic illustrations will always pick up significant details from the narrative, sponsored imagery in books – just like print advertisements in newspapers and magazines – may feature brands that are not related to the plot at all.

Nevertheless, the reader would not be able to avoid these advertisements in novels and would automatically perceive them first before he/she gets the chance to judge the relation to the literary plot. This kind of advertising can therefore be seen as a very attractive way of reaching customers.

The expansion of modality in e-books

Whereas the print version of novels is limited to static text and imagery (and in most cases even restricted to a black-and-white colouring), the digital equivalent opens various possibilities for multimedia additions.

Possible (upcoming) e-publications may include, but are not limited to: moving imagery, moving editorials, URLs, hyperlinks, music, jingles, additional gimmicks, etc. An important fact for both authors and advertisers is the option of updating e-books constantly. W. James Potter even counts the computer as the currently most important medium – and therefore as an inevitable part of literary development:

> *Reading literacy*, *visual literacy*, and *computer literacy* are not synonyms for *media literacy*; instead, they are merely components. *Media literacy* includes these specialised abilities as well as something more. If we do not know how to read, we cannot get much out of print media. If we have trouble understanding visual and narrative conventions, we cannot get much out of television or film. And if we cannot use a computer, we are cut off from what is growing into the most important medium (Potter 2005: 22).

Therefore, the combination of all sorts of media does not only gather various representations of more or less the same content, but further creates an entire "media literacy", which attracts the reader's attention via various senses at the same time. This multimedia usage involves the reader in a different way as print publications do, as the perception of a multitude of media simultaneously demands a lot more attention than focusing on one single medium in particular. Potter explains the usage of this media literacy as a very important strategy to trigger the readers' cognitive involvement.

> Media literacy is set of perspectives that we actively use to expose ourselves to the media to interpret the meaning of the messages we encounter. We build our perspective from knowledge structures. To build our knowledge structures, we need tools and raw material. These tools are our skills. The raw material is information from the media and from the real world. Active use means that we are aware of the messages and are consciously interacting with them (Potter 2005: 22).

Amazon holds the patent for advertisements in e-books since 2010, which from that point on informs the public on upcoming literary publications that are at least structurally open for product placement, if not even specifically designed for this purpose. Current press coverage from 2015 in fact points to the company *Landrover* as the first official client to openly advertise in an electronic publication of literature (The Guardian 2014). Expected publications may take huge advantage of the much broader media range e-books provide in comparison to print publications with the same content.

> The representational media: books, paintings, photographs, writing, architecture, interior decorating, gardening, etc. There are numerous media that use cultural and aesthetic conventions to create a "text" of some sort. They are representational, creative. (Fiske 2011: 16).

This extension of the term "text" is traditionally very popular in the advertising industry – and becomes more and more popular for publishers as well. The reader's acceptance of further media as part of a "text" is an important development for both advertisers and writers, because the success of new publications does not solely rely on the technical possibilities but especially on the willingness of potential readers (or consumers). Potter explains the importance of these cognitive media structures and the skill of picking up information from various media (simultaneously):

> Media literacy is set of perspectives that we actively use to expose ourselves to the media to interpret the meaning of the messages we encounter. We build our perspective from knowledge structures. To build our knowledge structures, we need tools and raw material. These tools are our skills. The raw material is information from the media and from the real world. Active use means that we are aware of the messages and are consciously interacting with them (Potter 2005: 22).

Novels as the latest form of advertainment

Beginning with Weldon's controversial novel, the phenomenon of sponsored literature began to grow in the consciousness of the advertising industry. In particular, this means not only the use of novels as potential platforms for advertising, but entire novels themselves as advertisements. Since 2001, press reports constantly comment on the release of sponsored literary publications, which are usually reviewed with closer regard to the sponsoring than focusing on either the content or the literary quality of the publication at hand.

Sponsored novels as part of an advertising or advertainment campaign become more and more attractive for advertisers as the trigger for various levels of involvement on the part of readers. These range from *pre-attention*, on to *focal attention* and finally *understanding* (Angermann 2005: 39 f.). This attention-trilogy by Frank Angermann stages three levels of attention, which range from a very superficial realization of content without further engagement in any deeper structure on to a more precise focus at least on details of content and finally ends with full understanding and uninterrupted attention. Whereas for example print advertisements mainly reach only the first stage, the involvement of a reader in the narrative of an interesting novel can almost automatically be seen as ultimately focused. Furthermore, the coherent structure of a novel does not allow the reader to skip over the advertising parts. As opposed to a TV series, which includes advertising breaks, books do not specifically mark e.g. certain pages or highlight product placement. The reader automatically has to read the entire body of text of a novel attentively in order not to miss any important plot elements. Therefore, it is impossible to mentally blend out advertising parts of the texts. According to the individual choice of genre, certain readers might even expect literary advertising as a common part of the overall literary artwork – similar to the already socially accepted advertising block in cinemas:

> The overlap between advertising and art is, however, no invention of the 20th century. This goes back even further all the way to the beginning of modern advertising and thus marks the advent of the newly established discipline known as graphic design or visual communication (Klein 2014: 64).

The narratives of novels may possibly deal with any issue round about advertising, whether they address the topic from a positive or negative perspective. But the traditional literary examination of advertising comments rather on the specifics of e.g. consumerism, product cult and product culture or pop culture in general. It is not common to use novels as vehicles for advertising, especially because literacy is traditionally known as a medium of elitist and independent culture.

According to Potter it is exactly this unusual combination of well-known and respected culture and product marketing that attracts the advertising industry. This is justified by the constant pressure on advertisers to come up with a multitude of new and unique ideas for entertaining advertising platforms. These platforms are necessary displays for every new product, especially when cross-promotion needs to be complemented with further advertising strategies:

> There are times when it is not possible to present a message in an environment that will attract an audience of the full size wanted. In this situation, the company must do cross-promotion. [...] Starting a new magazine (as with any new media vehicle) will usually require a high degree of investment to place a promotion for a particular new message in front of an existing audience. For example, a television network must create an audience for its new shows, so it will place a promo for the new program in an existing show (Potter 2009: 78).

Product placement in books will in the rarest cases feature other literary publications like the campaigning of *Cathy's Book* does on the respective web pages. Much more likely advertisers can substitute any item from a narrative by a specific brand name from a sponsor's offer. Whereas TV and cinema productions are mandatorily advised to mark product placement of any kind (e.g. in the credits), novels are currently unrestricted by juridical control. With this lack of external limitation novels become an attractive equivalent to advertainment movies or other filmic features.

These movies (like moving editorials) are longer than regular advertising spots from TV or even from cinema. They can last up to five or ten minutes and contain a complex narrative that is suited to best showcase the advertiser's product or product range. While print novels can tell an advertainment story in a classic literary fashion, e-books may even show a structural similarity to an advertainment movie. In this case all kinds of media from an advertainment campaign might be integrated into the digital text, even existing advertainment can be added to the content of an e-book.

Hypertextual distribution of brand names and product placement

To carry out the names of their literary brands as well as to promote the sponsor's product range, "advertising novels" make use of the hypertextual possibilities that are provided on the internet. The online representation of novels may contain various multimedia features, which can possibly go far beyond the possibilities of the print versions. Furthermore, online publications provide much easier access to previously unknown texts and topics than their respective print versions. Even language barriers can be bridged, up to a certain level, by placing more visual than textual content (Ludes 2001: 60 ff.).

For example, *Procter&Gamble's* advertising publication *Cathy's Book* is complemented by a huge variety of media on the novel's online presence. Each novel of the trilogy holds a proper domain with individual multimedia offers for readers and fans.

The first part of Cathy's Book mainly reintroduces the key characters of the novel (Cathy's Book 2015). The webpage presents numerous sketches and drawings of all relevant characters as well as imagery of key elements of the narrative. These drawn features frame the centre of the start page, where the *Cathy's Book* app is prominently featured. This app was released after the publication date of the initial novel, which means there is no relation or link to the featured product found in the print version.

The first sequel of the series, *Cathy's Key,* also holds a proper webpage with a variety of additional features (Cathy's Key 2015). This site contains references to social media platforms such as *Facebook* and *YouTube*. These references on one hand clearly advertise further media platforms, but neither the main webpage nor the linked social media market or sell any products that do not belong to the *Cathy's Key* complex. The hyperlinks lead to other formats, but always keep the focus on the main brand name. As the advertised "brand", the novel's heroine Cathy Vickers is a fictional character and not concretely available for sale, there are no further traces of external sponsoring. The multi-mediatisation of the brand *Cathy's Book* (including the sequel) is a perfect example of self-marketing or self-branding. One could argue whether or not the references to the social media platforms *Facebook*, *YouTube* or *MySpace* can be seen as advertisements for these names, which are brands themselves. Especially *YouTube* can be a proper commercial source as popular accounts can serve as pay-per-click advertising platforms.

Cathy's Ring concludes the series with a digital media offer consisting of various social media references (Cathy's Ring 2015). Here, the advertising aspect of the book's webpage becomes more obvious. Buttons on the start page address the visitor concretely and suggest buying the print and audio versions of the whole trilogy. One click further concrete advertisers come into play: the audio books as well as the *Cathy's Book theme song* are available for download on *iTunes*. The printed novels are on sale at various online bookstores such as *Amazon*, *Powells* or *Books-A-Million*. The references of these book-stores can on one hand be reflected in the same manner as the social media platforms from the last example *Cathy's Key*. On the other hand – and more importantly – these virtual book-stores do not sell print, audio or e-books from the trilogy exclusively, but also a multitude of other products. The offer on these web pages might change daily, so the references do not even lead to a specific product or product range, but lead the reader (or online follower) to a more or less undefined commercial space. Sponsoring can in this case only be an attractive option for bigger conglomerates such as *Procter&Gamble*, because smaller brands or companies usually do not hold product ranges with a similar fast-changing variety.

The fictional character Cathy Vickers can further be found (and *friended*) on *Facebook* and *MySpace*. The complex also holds a proper account on *YouTube*, where among others a series of trailers or tutorials for other features – such as the *Cathy's Book* app – are on offer. Jannis Androutsopoulos comments on the large amount of clustered media as well as the high level of involvement on the reader's side as follows:

> What we see on any YouTube page is neither just audio-visual content nor just a thread of comments, neither just image nor just language, but rather a complex configuration of semiotic components. YouTube was the first digital environment that introduced a tripartite order of content that may seem rather common today, but revolutionized the structure of multimodal web platforms in its early days. Its centre part is a (usually short) video clip that is publicly available for users to watch, save, share and discuss. This central piece of content is complemented by audience responses, which are likewise publicly available and open to counter-responses by other users. Finally there is the hosting space, i.e. the individual webpage on which each video is framed by additional information, such as viewing statistics, recommendations of similar content, navigation bars and other elements (Androutsopoulos and Tereick 2016: 356).

The children's novel series *Mackenzie Blue* is featured online on the webpage of the publishing house *HarperCollins*. The respective subpage introduces comic versions of all relevant characters from the series (HarperCollins Chilfren's 2015). Furthermore, additional information on the work complex of *Mackenzie Blue*, which is not necessarily mentioned in the book series, can be seen online.

The category *Blue Extras* invites readers to send e-cards to friends and share (positive) comments on the novel series. By sending these e-card the reader actively participates in the distribution of the brand *Mackenzie Blue* among his/her peer group and with this contributes to the overall marketing of not only the novel series but also all inherent product placement.

As opposed to the self-selling-strategy of the *Cathy's-Book*-complex the webpage of *Mackenzie Blue* leads to a hyperlink with the same title. This website does indeed contain a smaller section with drawings from the novel, but mainly features external advertising content (Mackenzie Blue 2015).

Around one quarter of all web pages for children contain an average amount of five advertisements (e.g. in form of sponsored posts or banners). In more than 50% of the cases these advertisements or even whole advertainments are not marked as commercial sources (Dreyer, Lampert, and Schulze 2014: 36). While paperbacks of course keep exactly the same format and status they were bought in, the additional online platforms can constantly be updated. Especially in the case of children's literature, current press coverage mentions the parent's serious concern with this fast-changing and therefore almost uncontrollable media-conglomeration.

Conclusion and outlook

Contemporary literacy in general follows the same intentions as traditionally delivered ever since the development of the art of writing: the author's central focus is set on telling an independently created narrative for academic or entertaining reasons. Nevertheless, the growing amount of sponsorship deals, which is constantly present in the feuilleton, marks the beginning and establishment of a literary sub-genre. As is notable with every upcoming trend, the development of an "advertising novel" by positioning brand names in novels in exchange for sponsorship deals depends on the reader's choice. If "branded books" fail to impress, the production of such publications might be discontinued in the near future.

Another component for the success of sponsored literature is the technical development. As web designers take responsibility not only for the entire setup and visual appearance, but also for the technical features of web pages, they automatically participate in the creation of a possible digital genre (Giltrow 2013: 717 ff.). Flexible online advertising is also reported to be one of the most challenging formats of contemporary product presentation (Ertel and Laborenz 2015: 412). The necessity of skilful technical construction changes the requirements for authors and might open a bigger market for publicists like Stewart, Weisman and Briggs, whose career background must not mandatorily be literary.

Last but not least the future development of literature-based advertainment depends on upcoming changes in the respective jurisdiction. Currently, there are now strict laws to prohibit advertising in books or e-books, but if juridical changes are brought up in the near future, these might bring certain regulations to the literary advertainment industry. Possible measures might include the duty to mark a commercial product in the same manner as seen in TV productions. In an extreme case literary product placement might even be fully prohibited, especially in the case of literature for children.

References

Androutsopoulos, J. and J. Tereick. 2016. "YouTube: language and discourse practices in participatory culture". In *The Routledge Handbook of Language and Digital Communication,* edited by Alexandra Georgakopoulo, and Teresa Spilioti, 354-370. New York: Routledge.

Angermann, F. 2005. *Special Ads – je mehr desto besser? Eine experimentelle Untersuchung zur Wirkung von Sonderwerbeformen im*

Fernsehen. Marburg: Tectum.

Baumgarten, D. 2013a. "Product-Placement in der (digitalen) Gegenwartsliteratur: Ein Commercial Turn?" *Zeitschrift für Literaturwissenschaft und Linguistik* 172: 128-131.

—. 2013b. *Ästhetische Transfers zwischen Literatur und Werbung.* Marburg: Tectum.

Bomnüter, U., and Patricia Scheller. 2014. *Filmfinanzierung. Strategien im Ländervergleich: Deutschland, Frankreich, Großbritannien und USA.* Second Edition. Baden-Baden: Nomos.

Cathy's Book. 2015. Accessed December 26, 2015. http://www.cathysbook.com/

Cathy's Key. 2015. Accessed December 26, 2015. http://www.cathyskey.com/

Cathy's Ring. 2015. Accessed December 26, 2015. http://www.cathysring.com/

Dreyer, S., Claudia Lampert, and Anne Schulze. 2014. *Kinder und Online-Werbung. Erscheinungsformen von Werbung im Internet, ihre Wahrnehmung durch Kinder und ihr regulatorischer Kontext.* Leipzig: VISTAS.

Ertel, A., and K. Laborenz. 2015. *Responsive Webdesign. Anpassungsfähige Websites programmieren und gestalten.* Second edition. Bonn: Galileo Press.

Ess, C. M. 2016. "Choose now! Media, literacies, identities, politics". In *The Routledge Handbook of Language and Digital Communication,* edited by Alexandra Georgakopoulo & Teresa Spilioti, p. 412-416. New York: Routledge.

Fiske, J. 2011. *Introduction to Communication Studies.* Third Edition. London: Routledge.

Giltrow, J. 2013. "Genre and computer-mediated communication". In *Pragmatics of computer-mediated communication*, edited by Susan C. Herring, Dieter Stein, and Tuija Virtanen, 717-737. Berlin: De Gruyter.

Hanson, R. E. 2014. *Mass Communication. Living in a Media World.* Fourth edition. Thousand Oaks: SAGE Publications, Inc.

HarperCollins Children's. 2015. Accessed December 26, 2015. http://www.harpercollinschildrens.com/kids/gamesandcontests/features/mackenzieblue/

Jessica, G. 2008. "Young Adult Novels Plumb New Depths Of Product Placement." Jezebel. February 20. http://jezebel.com/358651/young-adult-novels-plumb-new-depths-of-product-placement

Klein, E. 2014. "Multiple Mona Lisa. Art as a tool of advertising". In *Advertising and Design. Interdisciplinary Perspectives on a Cultural*

Field, edited by Beathe Flath and Eva Klein, 61-77, Bielefeld: transcript.

Ludes, P. 2001. *Multimedia und Multi-Moderne: Schlüsselbilder. Fernsehnachrichten und World Wide Web – Medienzivilisierung in der Europäischen Währungsunion.* Wiesbaden: Westdeutscher Verlag.

Mackenzie Blue. 2015. Accessed December 26, 2015. http://www.mackenzieblue.com/website/

Potter, W. J. 2005. *Media Literacy.* Third edition. Thousand Oaks: SAGE.

—. 2009. *Arguing for a general framework for mass media scholarship.* Thousand Oaks: SAGE.

Sachau, M. 2011. *Linksaufsteher*. Berlin: Ullstein.

The Guardian. 2001. "Jewellers sponsor Fay Weldon's latest literary gem." Accessed December 26, 2015. http://www.theguardian.com/uk/2001/sep/04/pressandpublishing.fiction

The Guardian. 2014. "The car's the star: William Boyd gets into Land Rover tie-in deal." Accessed December 26, 2015. http://www.theguardian.com/books/2014/nov/13/william-boyd-land-rover-product-placement

Weyand, B. 2013. *Poetik der Marke. Konsumkultur und literarische Verfahren 1900-2000*. Berlin: De Gruyter.

A CITY CALLED *OTTO*: HOW A MARKETING CAMPAIGN BECAME AN (UN)WANTED SUCCESS

ANGELIKA BERGIEN

Abstract

This paper examines linguistic and socio-economic strategies as they are used in city branding. The City of Magdeburg, capital of Saxony-Anhalt, serves as an example of how different media and different interactive techniques can be coordinated to increase the promotional effect. Since 2010 Magdeburg uses the slogan "Ottostadt Magdeburg", and therewith refers to its history, which is connected to two great men who were both called *Otto*: Otto the Great, who made the city his capital and from there ruled the Holy Roman Empire, and Otto von Guericke, who revolutionised the sciences in the 17th century by establishing the physics of vacuums. The campaign itself aims at raising the identification of Magdeburg's residents with their city as well as to raise national and international awareness in order to attract investors, tourists and students.

The aim of the study is twofold: firstly, to find out what makes city branding successful, and secondly, to find out what happens when the residents themselves use the campaign for their own purposes, e.g. by modifying, destructing or reinterpreting slogans. Is it true, as agencies do not tire to maintain, that a campaign is successful as soon as people start joking about it?

Introduction

Cities throughout the world are increasingly importing the concept and techniques of product branding for use within place marketing. As Kavaratzis and Ashworth (2005: 506) point out:

> Places, especially cities, have long felt a need to differentiate themselves from each other, to assert their individuality in pursuit of various economic, political or socio-psychological objectives.

This trend raises the question how useful city marketing is as a method to attract residents, tourists and firms. City marketers frequently treat places as if they were consumer products. The usual result of this "commodification" (Hospers 2010: 183) is a marketing campaign with associated logos, slogans, adverts, brochures, exhibitions, displays, web sites, events and attractions. Slogans like *Scotland with Style* (Glasgow), *A Taste of Life* (Randers), *There is Nothing beyond Groningen* or *I Amsterdam* illustrate this development. Today, most German cities bear slogans, but not all of them are successful. For example, a survey among Berlin's inhabitants revealed that 60 per cent of all informants disliked the campaign *Be Berlin*, because they felt it had been dictated from above. Many inhabitants do in fact prefer Berlin's unofficial slogan *Arm, aber sexy*, "poor, but sexy" (See Lange 2014).

Since the mid-nineteenth century, cities have directed their marketing efforts not only at tourists but also at households and businesses. City marketing was used, for instance, to attract settlers to the American West and to entice families and firms to post-war towns and suburbs across Europe. Since the mid-1980s, however, local authorities started to use city marketing as part of their urban development policies. In particular, large cities use marketing in the hope to differentiate themselves from one another in order to compete, and to attract new investments, new companies or new residents. According to Lombarts (quoted in Hospers 2010: 184):

> City marketing is a long-term process and/or policy instrument including all those different, related activities that are aimed at attracting and retaining specific target groups for a particular city.

Against this background, city branding is only one of the elements of city marketing, paying special attention to the analysis of a place's identity, image, brand values and the development of marketing communication strategies. In short, city brands are made of "promotional tactics and identity claims", they shape a sense of place and "are better thought of as narratives or 'place stories' ", as Ashworth et al. (2015: 5) observe. This includes a collective and interactive construction of the meaning of a particular city. The latter aspect was, for example, used in the Expo marketing campaign for Milan in 2015 (De Carlo et al. 2009), where, among others, personalization techniques were applied to ascribe human personality traits to the city. Participants were asked to imagine Milan as a person and to describe them, their gender, behaviour, clothes, characteristics, and lifestyle. According to De Carlo et al. (2009: 18), there was a high degree of consensus over Milan's personality. In many of these personality profiles Milan is described as a "she", a beautiful and successful middle aged businesswoman with a face-lift, intimately entwined with fashion, design and culture, and sometimes with a drug-addiction.

It is clear, of course, that city marketing is more complex than product marketing. One difference is "place fuzziness" (Hospers 2010: 185), that means, unlike products, the boundaries of places are often vague and overlapping. Another difference is that city marketing cannot control all consumer experience; in other words, we as consumers decide for ourselves what aspects of the place to consume. A third, especially important difference is the fact that places affect people more than products. Over time, most people develop emotional and socio-economic ties with a place. This is not always the case with products.

Instruments of city branding

In the course of the last 20 years or more, place management authorities have developed a tool-box of local planning instruments that are widely familiar. According to Ashworth (2009: 11), there are three techniques that are used, namely "signature or flagship structures", "event hallmarking" and "personality association", which may be combined in a campaign.

In signature or flagship structures the visual qualities of buildings and urban design are important to local planners. The process of using a flagship building to stimulate wider cultural and economic development is sometimes known as "Guggenheiming" after the tendency of this museum to house itself in distinctive and challenging modern buildings. (See Ashworth 2009: 15.)

With regard to event hallmarking, places organise and sponsor temporary events in order to obtain a wider recognition that they exist but also to establish specific brand associations.

The focus of this present paper will be on the third technique: personality association.

Personality Association

When they search for a unique identity, places associate themselves with a named individual in the hope that the unique qualities of the individual are transferred by association to the place. As Ashworth (2009: 11) puts it:

> This technique could be called the "Gaudi gambit" in recognition of the successful personality branding of Barcelona in the 1980s with an extremely distinctive architect and designer of some 60 years earlier, such that the image of the city is now inseparable from the creative work of the artist. This was, however, neither the first nor the final occasion when this technique has been used. Indeed, the early and evident successes of this technique have prompted an almost universal application of it in the belief that it is a sure and relatively easy route to successful branding.

However, as will be seen in this paper, personality association is not always an easy route to successful branding. Some personalities prove more suitable than others. Visual artists are easier to treat in this way than those producing non-visual products. The more distinctive the creative work or the more memorable the person and life, the easier such branding will become. There is, for example, a Gaudi in Barcelona, a Mackintosh in Glasgow, a Dali in Figueres, a Hundertwasser in Vienna or a Raphael in Urbino. Musicians as diverse as Mozart (Salzburg), Presley (Memphis), Wagner (Bayreuth), or writers like Jane Austin and Bath, the Bronte's Yorkshire, Goethe and Schiller's Weimar are also fairly commonplace and are not merely reflecting senses of place but contributing towards shaping them.

The mythological existence of a personality is no disqualification but does make competing claims easier, not least because of the large tourism revenues involved. King Arthur's "Camelot" is currently claimed by Winchester in Hampshire, Tintagel in Cornwall and Cadbury Castel in Somerset (Ashworth 2009: 12-13).

It must also be mentioned that some personality associations can be inappropriate or completely undesirable: Al Capone's criminal activities took, for example, place in Chicago. The Hitler family came from Braunau in Austria, and Weimar, the place of Goethe and Schiller, is also associated with Hitler's concentration camp Buchenwald.

The market valuation of the association may also change over time. Place-personality associations may long outlive their usefulness. For example, the 16th century moralist churchman John Knox who conveyed useful values such as probity, diligence and sobriety to an Edinburgh in the industrial age, but becomes "a somewhat doubtful asset to a city transforming itself into a culture, entertainment and tourism centre" (Ashworth 2009: 2012).

The converse situation where the renown of the personality fades before its usefulness to the place is also possible. This difficulty of change powered by fashion is even more evident when the names of celebrities are used. This idea implies some living person usually from sport or entertainment enjoying a media induced fame, in the hope that the fame of the celebrity will transfer to the place. The unstable reputation of many celebrities today may be one reason why it is hardly possible to find an example for city branding with living celebrities. If at all, we find them in city nicknames, like *Schumacher Kempten* for the birth place of Ex Formula 1 driver Michael Schumacher.

There are other problems which show that the technique of personality association may be far from being a straightforward and an almost inevitably successful exercise. This will be illustrated with the new official name of the city of Magdeburg.

The Otto campaign in Magdeburg

Magdeburg is the capital city of the state or Bundesland of Saxony-Anhalt in Germany. It is situated on the Elbe River and was one of the most important medieval cities of Europe. Today it has 230,000 inhabitants, and, like many East German cities and towns, it is a place that copes with brain drain, an ageing community and population decline.

Emperor Otto I, the first Holy Roman Emperor, who lived from 912 to 973, was the founder of the archbishopric of Magdeburg and is buried in the city's cathedral. In mediaeval ages, Magdeburg was one of the largest German cities and a notable member of the Hanseatic League. Magdeburg was destroyed twice in its history: in the 30 Years' War (1618–1648) and towards the end of World War II. Apart from the cathedral there is not much that reminds us of mediaeval Magdeburg. From 1949 up to 1990, Magdeburg formed part of the former German Democratic Republic. After German reunification huge parts of the city and its centre were rebuilt in a modern style.

Nowadays Magdeburg is a traffic junction as well as an industrial and trading centre with only few architectural attractions. Like other East German cities or towns, it is faced with difficult demographic developments, since especially young people move away in search for work. And like many other cities in the world the city has to tackle great financial problems.

Since 2010 Magdeburg bears the slogan "Ottostadt Magdeburg", and with it refers to its history which is connected to two great men who were both called *Otto*: One is Otto the Great, who made the city his capital in the 10th century and from there ruled the Holy Roman Empire, and the other is Otto von Guericke, who revolutionised the sciences in the 17th century by establishing the physics of vacuums in 1650. He became especially famous for his experiment with eight horses that were not able to pull apart two hemispheres of metal because of the vacuum inside them.

There is, in fact, a third and more modern Otto in Magdeburg: a branch office of the worldwide operating multichannel retail business with the name *Otto*. Although many inhabitants first think of this retail business when they hear the name *Otto*, it is officially not considered in the campaign.

The campaign itself aims to raise the identification of Magdeburg's residents with their city as well as to raise national and international awareness in order to attract investors, tourists and students. The residents should be reminded of the rich and powerful past of their city and look to the future with great confidence, whereas tourists, students and investors shall become curious about Magdeburg. (See *Die Ottostadt Magdeburg*.)

The *Ottostadt* marketing tools consist mainly of posters that show more or less well-known persons that are somehow connected to Magdeburg and holding up signs referring to their own background or talents and transfer them directly to Otto (Figure 1).

Fig. 1. Persons that are somehow connected to Magdeburg and the slogans "Otto is Olympic", "Otto makes history", "Otto holds together", "Otto sings", "Otto conducts research". (Source: Landeshauptstadt Magdeburg / Dezernat Wirtschaft).

– posters created by Magdeburg's residents and companies, who use the campaign for their own purposes, for example, *Otto eats sushi*, *Otto loves animals*, *Otto protects the climate*, *Otto kalypse now*. The idea is identification through participation (Figure 2 and Figure 3).

Fig. 2. Advertising poster from a young theatre group in Magdeburg using the Otto corporate design to advertise their theatre project "Otto kalypse now". (Source: Landeshauptstadt Magdeburg/Dezernat Wirtschaft).

Fig. 3. A distillery promoting a product with the logo "Otto drinks absinthe" (Source: Landeshauptstadt Magdeburg / Dezernat Wirtschaft).

– the re-naming of shops, businesses, institutions, objects so that they include the name *Otto*. Examples are *Ottomat* for a cash machine in a bank, *Otto Bäckerei* (a bakery), *Otto-fit,* the name of a company selling hearing aids*, and Otto Baskets*, Magdeburg's basketball team.

Fig. 4. The logo of Magdeburg's basketball team *Otto Baskets*, including Otto von Guericke's two hemispheres. (Source: Wersoma GmbH Magdeburg).

All these Ottos in Magdeburg and the events and activities related to them can be called "Ottoscape"—a notion adapted from Giovanardi's example "Raphaelscape", in which he refers to "urban designscapes as the network of activities and artefacts that produce place-identity within cities" (2011: 55).

In 2015, i.e., five years after the campaign had started, the organisers came to the conclusion that the campaign did not fully live up to expectations. Although it was better known in Magdeburg, it has not helped to make Magdeburg better known in Germany.

In order to find out how familiar young people are with the campaign, a spontaneous survey with 50 students of English at Magdeburg University was conducted in 2015. It revealed that although 98 per cent of all participants had heard about Otto, only half of them (54 per cent) really knew who the two historical Ottos were. And even fewer knew the logos or when the campaign had started (see Figure 5).

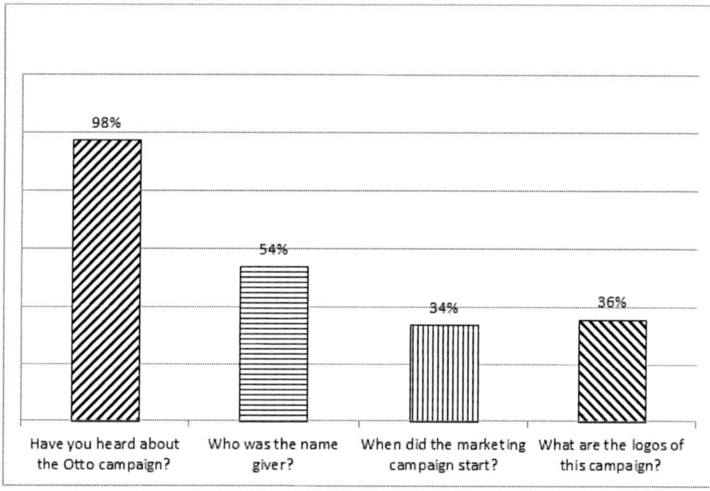

Fig. 5. Participants' familiarity with the Otto campaign (positive answers).

In the same survey personalization techniques were used to find out whether the content of the official campaign reflected ideas of Magdeburg's inhabitants about their city. Participants were asked to describe Magdeburg as a person. The results of this survey show a rather heterogeneous picture. A marketing campaign can, of course, not address all individual ideas about Magdeburg, since it is aimed at different groups with different interests and therefore characterised by simplification. However, answers like "wants to answer everyone's expectations" or "does not always know what she really wants" may be reflected in the city's marketing strategy with two very different historical personalities who share the same name (see Extracts 1 and 2):

Extract 1

> Magdeburg is a concerned person who wants to answer everyone's expectations. Since this isn't possible there are people who really love Magdeburg and people who don't. Magdeburg is a pliable person. He is in his late 20s and seems to act young and old at the same time. Magdeburg gives as much as it can to others, but doesn't get as much back. To love this person, you have to understand the complexity of it.

Extract 2

> Magdeburg is a middle-aged woman who, at first sight, is no beauty and who does not always know what she really wants. It is possible to hate her ignorance and narrow-mindedness, but you can also love her for her caring nature and affection.

Since its launch in 2010, the Otto campaign has been caught in the crossfire of criticism, but, as pointed out in Lutz (2012), managers of the marketing agency in charge are still optimistic:

> Those existing reinterpretations of the campaign indicate that the residents are involved in it and actually deal with it. It would only be alarming if people fully neglected the campaign. Our agency knows that a campaign was successful as soon as people start joking about it and – at its best – is taken up by the satire magazine *Titanic*.

What makes the Otto campaign more successful than its predecessors is that residents modify or reinterpret slogans for their own purposes. This is perhaps not always a wanted success, especially if opponents of the city's or government's policy use Otto slogans such as *Otto shuts down University departments*, *Otto cuts trees* or *Otto gets on people's nerves* for their critical statements.

Attributes leading to a successful personality campaign

A major problem of the Magdeburg campaign is the vagueness of the name *Otto*. At the beginning of the campaign city planners placed emphasis on the emperor of the 10th century. A number of events and exhibitions were devoted to him. But our knowledge about the person Otto is meagre. He was buried in Magdeburg, he initiated the building of the first cathedral, and it is said that his favourite palace was in this city, but we do not know anything about the person Otto. How should identification with such an old personality about whom we do not know very much work? By including the second Otto in the campaign, the mayor and inventor Otto von Guericke, the organisers sought to play with the potential ambiguity of the name.

The name *Otto* was originally intended to stand metonymically for success, strength, courage and open-mindedness, like the emperor, to make the city unique as a brand. In the course of five years, however, the name *Otto* accumulated thousands of associations and developed into a kind of self-runner. Today many people no longer recall the once intended unique selling proposition in connection with the name *Otto*. In the course of time, the emperor and the inventor have become what in German is called "Otto Normalverbraucher", an idiom with the name *Otto* meaning "ordinary citizen" or "average consumer". Indeed, with every new slogan, the name *Otto* loses more and more of its concrete referential objects, namely the emperor, the inventor and the city.

As a consequence, city planners and advertising agencies now increasingly focus on one name bearer only: the inventor Otto von Guericke from the 17th century to promote Magdeburg by public live performances of Guericke's Hemisphere experiment from 1657 in several German cities. The logo for these activities, however, still includes emperor Otto the Great on horseback, as can be seen in Figure 6.

Fig. 6. Otto von Guericke and the logo "Otto is an inventor". (Source: Landeshauptstadt Magdeburg / Dezernat Wirtschaft).

The central question is whether it would be worthwhile associating what remains a modern city to the unspecific attributes of a 10th century emperor or a 17th century inventor. A similar problem is described by Ashworth (2009: 13) in connection with the promotion of Rotterdam as "city of Erasmus" at the beginning of the 21st century. Desiderius Erasmus (1466/9-1536) was probably born there but lived longer and produced more work in Cambridge, Venice, Freiburg im Breisgau and Paris, all of which could, if they wished, lodge a more convincing claim. So the man is not firmly attached to this particular city, and the inhabitants of Rotterdam are largely unaware of the life or work of Erasmus. Ashworth's main argument is that philosophy is difficult to present in a visual way and it is uncertain how 16th century humanism can be expressed.

According to Ashworth and Kavaratzis (2015: 125–126) there is a check list of attributes leading to success or at least avoiding failure:

1. The personality should be widely known or at least capable of being popularly promoted in the targeted markets and the link between person and place should be feasible and credible,
2. The association should be sustainable over time,
3. The personal attributes transferred to the place should enhance or reinforce the desired brand. It should convey associations that have a contemporary value to the brand being created. Notoriety is not enough.

In the light of these criteria it is obvious that the two Ottos are not so widely known; it was wishful thinking by the city planners. The personal attributes were created by the marketing agency and by the city. Apart from the few facts about their lives and in particular about von Guericke's invention we do not know enough about the persons in order to develop associations. Their attributes are all very general with positive connotations (e.g. strength, courage, open-mindedness) and equally applicable to other historical figures. It is, in other words, simply not clear what attributes are being transferred.

In addition, there are other dangers. If, for instance, the place is successfully associated with a historical personality, the resulting anxiety is that the diversity (and depth) of local cultures is lost. Salzburg becomes monopolistically synonymous with Mozart, Liverpool with the Beatles and Nottingham with Robin Hood. Thus, places may become imprisoned in single episodes of their long history and particular expressions of their diverse local culture at the expense of all the rest. According to Ashworth and Kavaratzis (2015: 131), "we need to be aware that culture is very commonly oversimplified in place branding". Magdeburg, for example, organises regular Otto festivals in old costumes or events based on the place's mediaeval past, which is not to everybody's liking. This is due to the fact that brand communication favours the spectacular and the immediate to capture attention and then simplicity and brevity to convey the message simultaneously to different markets: potential investors, entrepreneurs, tourists or residents. In other words, brand communication requires the reduction of content to its simplest in which all complexities or distractions of meaning have been filtered out, leaving a rest, which may be no more meaningful than *I Amsterdam*, *Be Berlin*, *totally London* or *Wir sind Otto* ("we are Otto") in the case of Magdeburg.

Concluding remarks

City marketing is often seen as a simple promotion trick. It involves, however, much more. It is a long-term process aimed at satisfying the needs of a city's different target groups (Hospers 2010: 189-190). Brand recognition alone, regardless of the attributes acquired, can be worse than useless; it may become counterproductive, as Ashworth (2009: 20) points out. Giovanardi (2011: 54), who analysed campaigns in Urbino, the painter Raphael's birthplace, warns of the homogenization of cultural richness, the reductionist and controversial selection of "what to show" and "what to hide" as form of social control. In this context, names function like frames (cf. Vigsø 2010) which affect the interpretation of the nature of the city. Which of the frames will become the successful one, depends to a large extent on the logic of media communication.

One thing, however, is for sure: whether or not residents or tourists know the name *Otto,* they will continue to live in or travel to Magdeburg.

References

Ashworth, G. J. 2009. "The Instruments of Place Branding: How is it done?" *European Spatial Research and Policy* Vol. 16 No. 1: 9–22.

Ashworth, G. J. and M. Kavaratzis. 2015. "Rethinking the Roles of Culture in Place Branding". In *Rethinking Place Branding,* ed. by M. Kavaratzis, G. Warnaby, and G. J. Ashworth, 119-134, Springer International.

Ashworth, G. J., M. Kavaratzis, and G. Warnaby. 2015. "The Need to Rethink Place Branding." In *Rethinking Place Branding*, ed. by M. Karavatzis, G. Warnaby, and G. J. Ashworth, 1-11. Springer International.

De Carlo, M., S. Canali, A. Pritchard, and N. Morgan. 2009. "Moving Milan towards Expo 2015: Designing culture into a city brand". *Journal of Place Management and Development* Vol. 2 No. 1: 8–22.

Die Ottostadt Magdeburg. http://www.magdeburg.de/Start/B%C3%BCrger-Stadt/Stadt/Ottostadt (accessed April 30, 2015).

Giovanardi, M. 2011. "Producing and consuming the painter Raphael's birthplace". *Journal of Place Management and Development* Vol. 4 No.1: 53–66.

Hospers, G.-J. 2010. "Making sense of place: from cold to warm city marketing". *Journal of Place Management and Development* Vol. 3 No. 3: 182–193.

Kavaratzis, M. and G. J. Ashworth. 2005. "City Branding: An Effective Assertion of Identity or a Transitory Marketing Trick?" *Tijdschrift voor Economische en Sociale Geografie* Vol 96, No. 5: 506-514.

Lange, A. 2014. Städte schmücken sich mit Slogans. http://www.mittelbayerische.de/panorama-nachrichten/staedte-schmuecken-sich-mit-slogans-21934-art1002238.html (accessed December 3, 2015).

Lutz, H. 2012. " 'otto kalypse now'—A city marketing campaign becomes an (un)wanted self-runner". *Geobrand*, posted on 25/06/2012. http://blog.inpolis.com/2012/06/25/otto-kalypse-now-a-city-marketing-campaign-becomes-an-unwanted-self-runner/ (accessed November 20, 2015).

Vigsø, O. 2010. "Naming is Framing: Swine Flu, New Flu, and A(H1N1)". *Observatorio (OBS*) Journal* 4 (3): 229–241.

From Siberia - with a smile: Naming of Dental Clinics in the Region of Siberia[1]

Oxana Issers

Abstract

The significance of a successful name continues to grow in an increasingly competitive business environment. Today, unlike the Soviet period when dentistry was under the purview of the state, the number of private dental clinics is rapidly growing in Russia. This makes a dental clinic's name relevant in medical business and a clinic has an interest in developing a successful brand name to promote its service.

In research more than 300 names of dental clinics in Omsk and the Siberian region have been analyzed; they are classified according to semantic, pragmatic, structural and etymological criteria. This analysis uncovered that most of the names are generated according to several productive models. Thus, a significant number of names have been derived from the Latin root dent- for "tooth", which allows the name to signify the company's exact profile. Semantically, the same aim of corporate identification is performed by choosing names directly related to or associated with the theme of "Teeth" (Smile, Shine, etc.]). In addition, there is a variety of names that emphasize the semantics of quality. A large group of names contain a very common metaphor for dentistry - "healthy teeth signify beauty, aesthetics, elitism", but the numerous combinations of names constructed with roots "elite-" and "estet-" make these names unoriginal. Frequently names are formed on the basis of conventional associations with an external and "personal" display of dental health, among which a beautiful white smile ranks the highest.

Often, the positioning of a dental clinic is performed through the image of a doctor. Specialists in naming select vocabulary with explicitly positive meanings, including the names of previously renowned doctors. In most cases, they also focus attention on the painless treatment of their patients or emphasize the results of treatment.

This study demonstrates main marketing strategies found in the commercial branding of Russian dental services. Moreover, it provides a basis for drawing conclusions on the formation of city speech environments in a particular Russian region - in Siberia.

Introduction: A Short excursion into Russian naming history

The Formation of naming as a discipline refers to the second half of the 20th century, while the marketing practice of creating effective names has a longer history. In the USA and European countries marketing together with naming has been developing rapidly for over 100 years. James Walter Thompson, an American founder of the advertising agency "J. Walter Thompson Company" (JWT), one of the most outstanding first generation representatives of the advertising business, was one of the first to understand the philosophy of the advertising business, and naming, in particular. His "Thompson Red Book on Advertising" (1889) considered the concept of branding and the importance of naming for promotion campaigns.

There was no naming as a marketing tool in Russia before the 1990s as there was no need for that. This was determined by peculiarities of Soviet economics and production. Advertising was not an instrument of business struggle as there was no competition during socialism in the Soviet Union, but it aimed at promoting different values. Naming was not popular as a service and a great number of trade and consumer service companies did not have individual names. For example, even in Moscow in 1985 there were no ateliers or laundries with their own names (Sokolova 2012). Changes in the sphere of politics, economics and forms of property were an important cause of advertising development and a kind of "naming boom", in particular. Liberating advertising from ideological supervision was a further reason. Today, naming in Russia is developing, but it lags far behind the USA and other Western countries.

Naming as an advertising service in post-Soviet Russia was born with the appearance of translated literature (Charmasson 2000, Frencel 2006, etc.), of specialists and relevant research that took into account not only foreign experience, but also Russian peculiarities (Alistanova 2011, Domnin 2002, Elistratov, Pimenov 2012, Kryukova 2004, Mamleeva, Pertsiya 2005). Initially, naming in Russian style appeared as naming with an eye to foreign companies and an attempt to draw level with a number of them. In addition, several design studios and branding agencies began to announce their naming service at once.

The first agency in Russia specializing in naming was the company Naming.ru (www.naming.ru) founded in 2000. The next to enter the market was a specialized naming agency called LEXICA (www.lexica.ru) in 2003. However, fully-fledged naming agencies have only recently become cost-efficient. Profitability depends not only on the market demand for a "successful name", but mostly on the willingness of customers to buy it. "Self-made naming" is very popular in Russia in our time. in 2004-2005 a few more naming agencies came onto the market: *Mynames* (www.mynames.ru), *Goodname* (www.goodname.ru), etc. It's worthwhile noting the emergence of specialized resources for naming: *Encyclopaedia of Naming* (http://www.encnaming.ru) and blogs on naming, for example (http://www.blog.brandaid.ru).

Today naming is a dynamically developing industry of branding in Russia. Theoretical knowledge of naming practice is considered by marketing and linguistics. Thus, there are a lot of manuals and guidelines on marketing aspects of naming, principles and methods of generations of names in this field are developed intensively, while the study of the linguistic aspects of modern naming in Russia has just started. Linguistic research focuses on the analysis of lexical, semantic, morphemic, word formative peculiarities of commercial names, on cognitive categories of these specific onomastic systems (Emeljanova 2007, Golomidova 1998, 2012, Ivanova 2013, Kazakova 2008, Nakhimova 2011, Shimkevich 2002, Shmeleva 2007, 2014, Trifonova 2006) Linguistic issues on names from the point of view of law are popular as well (Rossinskaya, Galyashina and Zinin 2009, Sokolova 2014, etc).

The significance of a successful name continues to grow in an increasingly competitive business environment of all economic spheres (Names in the Economy 2013). Legislative permission and expansion of medical practice in Russia conditioned an increasing demand for a successful brand name.

Dental care: changes in naming strategy

Today, unlike the Soviet period when dentistry was under the purview of the state and clinics were named by formal entity name - «Стоматология», «Стоматологическая поликлиника» (Stomatologiya – Dentistry, Stomatologicheskaya Poliklinika - Dental Clinic), the number of private dental clinics is rapidly increasing in Russia. This makes a dental clinic's name relevant and a clinic has an interest in developing a successful brand name to promote its service. Of course, this is true not only of Russia.

For example, in 2012 participants of *Internet Marketing Forum* posted a request - call for help (1):

hey guys!!
my friend is coming up with a dental office and she needs help with a name. She will be doing cleaning, fillings, crowns and bridges. At the moment her ideas are : The smile clinic, floss and gloss, brighter smile,

pearly whites, miles for smiles, happy teeth, all smiles, tooth fairy, and perfect smile. All suggestions are welcome. She is in desperate need of one. Thanks!!!

http://www.warriorforum.com/main-internet-marketing-discussion-forum/ (01.05.2012)

Several dozens of people responded to this request and began to offer own versions (2-7).

(1) Ya know...I can't tell you why, but I really like Floss & Gloss. That's the most original dentist's office name I've ever heard!
(2) Combine the words No and Pain and you will get: Nopain Dental Office.
Many people don't go to a dentist because they are afraid of it.
(3) How about "The Tooth Fairy", "Caps & Crowns" ?
(4) Bah! It seems I'm not the first person to think of "Going The Extra Smile".
Similarly, "Nothing But The Tooth" is also taken. So, I settled on "The Tooth Booth". Which is also taken.
Edit: The Fountain of Tooth?
(5) How about Painless Dental, Floss And Smile, The Smiling Dentist?
(6) I don't think it necessarily has to be a "catchy" name.
She could go with something that is a bit generic but would have a good chance of getting ranked, like "Henderson Dental Group." "[city Dental Clinic]".
If she is going to be filing a formal entity, like an LLC, be sure to check that name too. Although she could always file a dba to do business using a name that differs from the formal entity name.

It is interesting to keep an eye on the search for an effective name, but it's useful to emphasize on the next opinion:

(7) While "floss and gloss" is cute and catchy, it might put off some people because it doesn't sound very professional, IMO. She really needs to keep that in mind when choosing a name for her dental practice. ***There's a place for fun, catchy names, but when it comes to anything related to healthcare, you need to use caution.***
I do like "Beautiful You Dental" (which was mentioned above). Just my opinion, but it has a classy, appealing ring to it and sounds more professional.

This discussion revealed some interesting peculiarities of naming in dental services.

They can be summarized in a few words.

1. There are many standard names that "don't catch" in dentistry.
2. There are limitations associated with the specific service.

This was one of the motives for choosing this object of study. To find out peculiarities of naming of dental clinics in Russia and, in particular, in Siberia is the key issue of our research.

Methodology and research materials

During our research, we analyzed more than 350 names of dental clinics in Omsk, the Omsk and Siberian regions (Novosibirsk, Rrasnoyarsk, Irkutsk). We used regional issues of telephone directories "Жёлтые страницы" ["Zheltye stranitsy"] (Yellow pages) to extract the names. Some examples of city signboards were added to the material.

In the cases in which names are presented containing their original spelling in Cyrillic, their transliteration and translation is given in brackets, e.g. *Новая улыбка [Novaya ulybka - New smile].* If transliteration and translation have the same spelling, they are given in one word. Other names are given in the form they are used in, for example, *Smile, Denta, Atribeute.*

Examination of naming uses several linguistics methods: semantic and structural analysis, analysis of word formation and etymology. All names were classified according to structural, semantic, pragmatic and etymological criteria. This analysis uncovered that most of the names are generated according to several productive models. Foremost we can distinguish among them the ones that directly or associatively identify the category of services - dentistry. This can be done both through the structure and semantics of a name. Often these two methods are combined. Let us consider the basic techniques of naming in this area.

Structural identifiers

Firstly, we will start with descriptive names which definitely signify the company's exact profile: *Стоматология [Stomatologiya - Dentistry], Лечение зубов [Lechenie zubov - Teeth treatment], Стоматологическая клиника [Stomatologicheskaya klinika Dental clinic].* This is not to say that these names prevail on the market (only 6% of our material), as the owners have an interest in the effective positioning of a dental clinic. They understand that a recognizable logo of the dental company is not just an external attribute, but a powerful argument to compete for customers.

A significant number of names have been derived from the Latin root *dens (dentis)* for “tooth”, which allows the name to signify the company’s exact profile. The structure of such names is formed in different ways: most of them are constructed with the identifying morpheme *-dent-* at the beginning or end of an abbreviation, a compound word or word combination.

Structural identifiers 1. Dent- at the beginning

Thus, the model with the root *dent-* at the beginning of the word is found in such names as: *Дента-Люкс [Denta-Lyuks - Denta-Lux], Дента Плюс [Denta-Plus - Denta Plus], Дента Рос [Denta Ros], Дента Классик [Dental Klassic – Denta Classic], Дентика [Dentika – Dentica], Дентис [Dentis], Дентфарм [Dentfarm – Dentpharm], Дентолог [Dentolog], Dentstudio, Dent Master,* etc. The final morpheme in such derivatives as a rule expresses ideas of quality, professionalism, prestige: - *lux, - classic, -master, -log*. Among the original names it should be noted *Дентасмак [Dentasmak – Dentsavour],* where the final part of the compound word -*smak* belongs to in Russian colloquial vocabulary and it means “taste, pleasure” (*smak* – in Eng. *savour* -пикантность, вкус, привкус).

Structural identifiers 2. Dent- as final constituent

More often the morpheme *-dent-* is used as a final constituent: *Профидент [Profident], Артдент [Artdent], Витадент [Vitadent], Астрадент [Astradent], Евродент [Eurodent], Омдент [Omdent],* etc. Initial morphemes have common semantics – they are directly or indirectly related or associated with the theme of professionalism, quality, and health: *profi*-(professional), *art- (art), uni-* (uniqueness), *-vita* (life), and so on. These combinations lack originality; most initial morphemes have an international root and are clear without translation. A large group of names contain usual or occasional lexeme with identifier dent- / dant-: *Dentist, Dentika, Dentis,* etc.).

Structural identifiers 3: root -med

Moreover, names constructed with the root *–med* perform the task of identifying the clinic due to structural elements: *Евромед [Euromed], Спарта-Мед [Sparta-Med], Радуга-Мед [Raduga-Med – Rainbow-Med], Виктория-Мед [Viktoria-Med – Victoty-Med], Metromed*. This constituent of a word allows the use of a brand name for an expanded category of medical services.

The advantage of the models mentioned above is an easy identification of a clinic via the dental services offered. However, a significant drawback is obvious. Despite the apparent diversity of names formed on the basis of these models, they do not differ greatly from each other, and the consumer can hardly remember the title of the clinic, except the constituent - dent-. Giving such a name to a clinic means enlarging the list of badly identifiable names of almost identical sound.

Marketer J. Harris called this method of creating a name the "club sandwich" principle and was sceptical about its effectiveness.

> When forced to come up with a great name, many young dentists simply take part of an adjective and attach it to a noun, pretty much "sandwiching" the two words together to create a new word. The results are practice names that have a strange feel to them, and that look and sound weird. A high-end cosmetic practice becomes *CosmetiTeeth.* A classy dental spa becomes *DentaSpa.* It's like mixing maple syrup with mustard. There's nothing wrong with either ingredient, but they just don't go together (Harris 2008).

Semantic identifiers: first associations

Semantically, the aim of marketing identification is performed by choosing names directly related to or associated with the theme of "Teeth". The most popular names of dental clinics in Russia are those which refer to predictable subject areas. Frequently names are formed on the basis of conventional associations with an external and "personal" display of dental health, among which a beautiful white smile ranks the highest: *Улыбка [Ulybka - Smile], Мастерская улыбки [Masterskaya ulybki - Smile repair shop], Новая улыбка [Novaya ulybka - New smile]* or *Smile* (in English spelling). The same mechanism of name formation is true of the following names: Блеск [Blesk - Shine], 32 зуба [32 zuba - 32 teeth], Здоровье [Zdorovye - Health], Норма [Norma - Norm], Коронка [Koronka - Crown]. It is worth noting that the word "коронка" *[crown]* in the Russian language is polysemantic and has a colloquial meaning apart from the terminological meaning relevant to dental services: something "coronal" (derived from the word *корона [crown],* premium quality). Therefore, we deal with polysemy based on the combination of terminological and colloquial meanings in a name.

Names formed on the basis of associations with “personal” display of dental health are the following: *Гармония [Garmoniya - Harmony], Успех [Uspekh - Success], Харизма [Kharisma - Charisma], etc.*

“Classics and modernity”

Having healthy and beautiful teeth is closely connected with ideal appearance and style of beauty that are accepted in European culture. It is reflected in nominations containing semantic components of the highest estimation: *Люксдент [Luxdent], Идеал-Д [Ideal-D], Denta Люкс [Denta Lux]* and so on.

In addition, there is a variety of names that emphasize the semantics of quality (*Superdent [Superdent], Vyshaya kategoriya [The highest category]*). This way can be great if they are not overly used to the point of being boring, - consider J. Harris.

> For example, since many businesses think of themselves as the best in their industry, the world is full of names like *Superior, Pinnacle, Preferred* and so on. While there's nothing inherently wrong with these names, they're overworked. Instead, look for combinations of positive words and metaphors, and you'll be much better served (Harris 2008).

A large group of names contain a very common metaphor for dentistry - “healthy teeth signify beauty, aesthetics, elitism” (so called cliché names in this sphere). The numerous combinations of names constructed with roots *elite*- and *estet*- make these names unoriginal: *Элита [Elita - Elite], Элита Плюс [Elita Pljus - Elite Plus], Эстетическая стоматология [Esteticheskaya Stomatologiya - Aesthetic Dentistry], Эстет [Estet - Aesthet]*. Over 30 clinics in Siberia have this kind of name. In addition, one of the most popular models is formed by the identifier *–dent* and a semantic component with the meaning of “aesthetics”: *Эстет-Дент [Estet-Dent - Aesthet-Dent], Арт-Дент [Art-Dent].*

On the one hand, dentistry belongs to the category of services with the typical classical standard of having healthy and beautiful teeth. Therefore, the desire to emphasize the classical quality of dentistry in names arises: Дентал-Классик *[Dental-klassik - Dental-classic], Класс-дент [Klass-Dent - Class-Dent].*

On the other hand, dentistry is a rapidly developing branch of aesthetic medicine that is reflected in the names with a focus on fashion, style and innovation. Today, in an intensely competitive environment marketers have to seek new ways of positioning. In order to improve the status of a clinic they use “categorical reframing” in names: medical services area changes to the sphere of science: *Институт новых медицинских технологий [Institut Novych Meditsinskich Technologii - Institute of New Medical Technologies]*, or to the sphere of art (studio) – *Арт- Дент [Art-Dent], Дент Студия [Dent studia - Dent studio], Стил-Дент [Stil dent - Dent Style],* etc.

Professionalism in the field of aesthetic dentistry is emphasized by inclusion of the clinic to the category of specialized institutions: *Мастерская улыбки[Masterskaya ulybki - Smile repair shop].*

In general, all names considered come second in quantity (after structural identifiers with the constituent dent-). Names are formed on the basis of common motivations for dental services, namely, explication of quality. This can be effective only if it is presented in an unusual way. The numerous combinations of names constructed with roots *elite-* and *estet-* make these names unoriginal and therefore "not-functional".

Semantic identifiers: secondary associations

Secondary associations are based on the mental connections of the process of dental treatment with components of its situation frame (doctor, painless process, etc.) and metaphors.

At first, the positioning of a dental clinic as well as other medical services is often performed through the image of a doctor. Therefore, to describe them a marketer selects vocabulary with explicitly positive meanings: *Веселый доктор [Veseliy Doktor - Dr. Jolly], Хороший доктор [Khoroshiy Doktor - Good Doctor], Хороший стоматолог [Khoroshiy stomatolog - Good dentist], Ваш стоматолог [Vash stomatolog - Your dentist], Дент Мастер [Dent Master - Dent master], Целитель [Tselitel - Healer].* Often, the positioning of a dental clinic is performed through the well-known precedent names of doctors: *Авиценна [Avitsenna - Avicenna], Эскулап [Eskulap - Aesculapian] (the God of medicine in ancient Roman mythology*) or fictitious names, so-called "speaking names": *Доктор Денталь [Doktor Dental –Doctor Dental].*

Since the owner of a clinic, as a rule, is involved in the process of naming, the Russian practice of naming traditionally uses names of the founders: *Доктор Захаров [Doctor Zakharov], Клиника Феоктистовой [Klinika Feoktistovoy - Clinic of Feoktistova],* etc. The Russian marketers love to use feminine names in naming very much; this could be the name of an owner's wife or daughter: *Светлана [Svetlana], Ольга [Olga],* etc.

Marketer J. Harris calls this method of naming "mistake #1".

> For decades, when a dentist opened a practice it was simply tradition to use their own name as the name of the practice (there has long been a tradition) Robert Smith DDS for example. Later on, dentists got a little more creative and added descriptions such as "Family Dentistry" or "Comprehensive Dental Care" to their own names, which was a step in the right direction but still not up to par with other businesses and corporations. Imagine if you will, Microsoft being called "Bill Gates Software Company". Or, how about Wal-Mart being named "Sam Walton Mercantile". I think you get the point (Harris 2008).

The other problem with using your own name, as J. Harris thinks, is the problem it creates when it's time to sell your practice or bring in an associate and your name becomes a hindrance in the process. Face it, a new practice owner will be much more motivated to buy a practice that will not need a name change. As far as Russian practice is concerned, the professional experience of a doctor and therefore his academic degree is often reflected in the name of a dental clinic: *Стоматологический центр профессора Бокой [Stomatologicheskiy Tsentr Professora Bokoy - Professor Bokoy Dental Center].*

Sometimes the name of a dental clinic presents a "unifying" sema of joint actions of the doctor and the patient: *Стоматолог и Я [Stomatolog i Ya - Dentist and I], Семейная стоматология [Semeinaya stomatologiya - Family Dentistry].*

Metaphors are the productive base for name generation in general. The names of dental clinics in Siberia as well as in Russia often contain metaphors associated with whiteness of teeth: *Жемчуг [Zhemchoug - Pearl], Жемчужина [Zhemchouzhina – Pearl], Жемчужина стоматологии [Zhemchouzhina Stomatologii - Pearl of Dentistry].* The metaphorical meaning of "jewel" is found in the name *Карат [Karat - Carat]* – probably, it relates to the brilliant shine of healthy teeth. The name *Ювелирная работа [Juvelirnaja rabota - Jeweler's work]* is also formed on the basis of secondary associations with the quality of treatment.

Quality of dental service is the base for "prestige appeals" in dentistry naming. Such names as *Кремлевская [Kremlevskaja -Kremlin dentistry] and Империя [Imperija – Empire]* appeal to prestige (however, the outside appearance of the clinic is sometimes in dissonance with the name).

Original names formed on the basis of unusual associations occur rarely in the Siberian region: for example, *Щелкунчик [Shchelkunchik - Nutcracker].* Furthermore, we can meet single non-standard names-metaphors: *Стоматологическая студия «Скульптор» [Stomatologicheskaja studija "Skulptor" -Dental studio "Sculptor"]*. Some names constructed on the basis of fairy tales, myths and legends occur more rarely: *Зубная фея [Zubnaja feja -Tooth fairy]*. Lastly, we can meet some humorous names that are difficult to translate: *Зубастик [Zubastik - Sharp-toothed]*.

Pragmatics of names of dental services

In this regard, the choice of a name is motivated by the understanding of motives and consumer needs. The very fact that a person is afraid of feeling pain and wants to avoid any pain is very significant. Some names explicate or implicate this idea as in *Стоматологическая клиника положительных эмоций* [Stomatologicheskaja klinika pologzitelnyh emocij - *Dentist clinic of positive emotions]*.

Today, the names explicate economy class services and communicate the price such as Первая социальная стоматология Pervaja Sotsialnaja stomatologija ["First social dental clinic"] where affordability is implied by the lexeme "social".

From a grammatical standpoint, these constructions are substantives in names. We can also, however, meet predicative constructions, which can also be called "communicatives": they do not use the nominative, but rather communication units: Будь здоров! *Bud zdorov! [Be treated], Без боли Bez boli [Pain-free], До и после Do i Posle [Before and After], Улыбнись! Ulybnis! [Smile!]*. In most cases, they focus the attention on painless treatment (of their patients) or emphasize the results of treatment.

Language games, puns are not often found in names of dental practices. However, we met a few of them. Thus, the name *Atribeaute* (in Latin spelling) is based on the paronym's attraction with the words *attribute* (*atribut* in Russian pronunciation) and *beauty*.

In our view, this is due to the specifics of the service. Branding in medicine as a whole is based on consumer needs in treatment. Therefore, there is no need for the "long way" from drawing attention to the decision, which is usually presented in the name formed on the basis of complex, multistep associations. Let's remember the opinion of one of the participants of discussion on choice of a name for the US clinics (ex. 8): "There's a place for fun, catchy names, but when it comes to anything related to healthcare, you need to use caution".

That explains the occurrence of single names here constructed through language game – polysemantic, homophony, puns.

Etymology

From an etymological standpoint, apart from roots-identifies *dent-* and *med-* Latin and Greek roots are also popular and found in the following names: *Альбус [Albus – Albous], Альфа [Alfa – Alpha], Оптима [Optima], Омега-Дент [Omega-Dent], Vita Prima,*etc. However, motivation for their choice is not always obvious to the consumer.

Latin spelling in naming is not so popular in Siberian naming practice as in Moscow and St. Petersburg. The greatest part of our materials (about 96%) analyzed here is spelled in Cyrillic.

The names of dental clinics in Siberia sometimes contain toponymic references - although not as often as in the naming of other commercial companies: *Сибирская стоматология [Sibirskaja stomatologija - Siberian dentistry], Стоматология на Заозерной [Stomatologija na Zaozernoj - Dentistry on Zaozernaya Street], Сибирский стоматолог [Sibirskij stomatolog - Dentist of Siberia, Омдент [Omdent]* (Om - shortening of Omsk). However, marketers consider that there are some limitations for names with toponymic reference: if a business is expanded, sold or moves to another place, a new owner has to work on rebranding.

> Taking the street name or local landmark approach to name your practice. In the excitement to open a new practice, many dentists choose to use their city, street name or state flower as part of their practice name. While this may seem like an OK idea at first, it often becomes a problem when the practice grows. One dentist came to me with the fear that he was serving more of the market than his name implied. He had decided to name his practice Fourth Street Dental since his practice had originally opened on Fourth Street in his community. Now that he wanted to open two new practices in adjoining towns he was forced to rethink his entire naming strategy (Harris 2008).

Finally, we cannot but mention several strange and inexplicable names: *Aria, Kavo, Enge* and others. The problem of their semantic motivation is the worst way to find target consumers as J. Harris suppose.

> Making your practice name so obscure, consumers will never know what it means. It's great for a name to have a special meaning or significance – it tells a story that can be used as a conversation creator. However, if the name is obscure or hard to spell or pronounce, the "unique" name you choose may backfire on you and have a negative effect.
>
> Resist the urge to name your company after a mythical Asian dragon or the Latin phrase for "Same Day Crowns". It's not that invented or fabricated names cannot work–sometimes they can. Take, for example,

eBay or Snapple. However, because names like these have no real-world meaning they rely heavily on advertising to convey their meaning, which can cost millions (Harris 2008).

Conclusions

This study demonstrates the main marketing and naming strategies found in the commercial branding of Russian dental services.

1. Most of the names are constructed with direct identification of the services offered. It is performed through the Latin root *dent- / dant-* as a constituent of a word or word combination, and the associated primary nominations as well (*Smile, Shine* and others).
2. The most productive are metaphorical models based on associations with healthy teeth with pearl and indicators of physical beauty and charm: *Гармония [Garmonija - Harmony, Успех [Uspekh – Success], Харизма [Kharizma – Charisma].*
3. Due to the nature of these services in large cities (the patient chooses a doctor, rather than the location of the clinic) anthroponomy is more frequent in the names of dental clinics than toponymy.
4. Medical services (including dental) fall within an area which must be treated seriously. Thus, using a language game in naming in this field occurs rarely.

The study of the naming of dental services in Russia could be useful for analyses of branding and naming peculiarities in medicine, on the one hand, and on the other hand, it provides a basis for drawing conclusions on the formation of city environments in a particular region - in Siberia (for example).

References

Alistanova, F.F. 2011. *Ergonymes of Modern Russian as microsystem*. PhD thesis. Makhachcala.

Charmasson, G. 2000. *Trade Mark: How Create Name which Gives Millions.* St. Peterburg: Piter.

Domnin, V.N. 2002. *Branding: new technologies in Russia*. St. Petersburg: Piter.

Elistratov, V.S., Pimenov, P.A. 2012. *Naming. The Art of nomination.* Moscow: Omega-L.

Emeljanova A.M. 2007. *Ergonymes in linguistic landscape of polyethnic city (business, commercial, cultural and sport objects names as an example).* PhD thesis. Ufa.

Frenkel, A. 2006. *Naming: How Game with Words Became Business.* Moscow: Ozon.

Golomidova, M.V. 1998. *Artificial naming in onomastics*: PhD thesis. Yekaterinburg.

Golomidova, M.V. 2012. "Name creation in ergonomy: traditions vs. actual trends." In *Linguistics of creativity-2: multi-authored monograph.* Editor in chief T.A. Gridina. Yekaterinburg: 63-72.

Harris, Joel. 2008. *The 7 Mistakes of Naming a Dental Practice.* http://www.thedentistsnetwork.net/newsletters/print/harris/printHarris36.html.

Ivanova, E.N. 2013. "The ways of creative nomination (with names of book shop as an example)." In *Ural Philology Bulletin. Language. System. Personality. Linguisticofcreation* 3: 27-31.

Kazakova, S.L. 2008. *Urbanonymes in Lexical System.* http://www.pglu.ru/lib/publications/University_Reading/2008/V/uch_2008_V_00034.

Krukova, I.V. 2004. *An advertising name: from creating to precedency.* Volgograd: Peremena.

Mamleeva, L., Pertsija, V. 2005. *The Anatomy of Brend.* St. Peterburg: Piter.

Nakhimova, E.A. 2011. *Theory and methodic of cognitive and discourse analysis of precedent onyms in the contemporary Russian communication.* Yekaterinburg.

Names in the Economy: Cultural Prospects. 2013. Edited by Paula Sjoblom, Terhi Ainiala, Ulla Hakala. Newcastle: Cambridge Scholars Publishing.

Rossinskaya, E.R., Galyashina E.I., Zinin, A.M. 2009. *Theory of forensic examination.* Moscow: Norma.

Shimkevich, N.V. 2002. *Russian Commercial Ergonomy: Pragmatic and Lingvocutural Aspects.* PhD thesis. Ekaterinburg.

Shmeleva, T.V. 2007. "Great Novgorod onomastic landscape." In *Novgorodica-2006: materials of the International scientific conference* (Sept. 20-22, 2006). Part 1. Great Novgorod:132-140.

Shmeleva, T.V. 2014. *Onomasticon of Russian city.* Saarbruken: LAP Lambert Academic Publishing.

Sokolova T.P. 2014. "Naming examination: genesis, problems, prospects." In *Bulletin of Kutafin Moscow State Law University (MSAL)* 3:142-150.

Sokolova T.P. 2012. "Examination of Trade Marks, Company Names and

Trade Names as the Means of individualization in Russia: Theoretical and Methodological Approaches to the Problem." *Onoma* 47: 263-279.

Trifonova, E.A. 2006. *Naming of business objects: Semantics, Pragmatics, Poetics: On Russian and English Ergonymes materials.* PhDthesis. Volgograd.

References (Russian)

Алистанова Ф.Ф. *Эргонимы современного русского языка как микросистема*: Дис. … канд. фил. наук: 10.02.01 / Ф.Ф. Алистанова. – Махачкала, 2011. – 179 с.

Голомидова М.В. Имятворчество в эргонимии: традиции vs. актуальные тренды // *Лингвистика креатива-2* / Под общей ред. Т.А. Гридиной. – Екатеринбург, 2012. – С. 63-72.

Голомидова М.В. *Искусственная номинация в ономастике*: дис. … д-ра филол. наук. Екатеринбург, 1998. 215 с.

Домнин В.Н. *Брендинг: новые технологии в России*. – СПб: Питер, 2002. – 352 с.

Елистратов В.С., Пименов П.А. *Нейминг. Искусство называть.* Учебно-практическое пособие. – М.: Омега-Л, 2012. – 304 с.

Емельянова А.М. *Эргонимы в лингвистическом ландшафте полиэтнического города (на примере названий деловых, коммерческих, культурных, спортивных объектов г. Уфы):* Дис. … канд. фил. наук: 10.02.01 / БГУ. – Уфа, 2007.

Иванова Е.Н. Приемы креативной номинации (на примере названий книжных магазинов Екатеринбурга) // *Уральский филологический вестник: Язык, система, личность. Лингвистика креатива.* 2013. – №3. – С. 27-31.

Казакова С.Л. *Урбанонимы в составе лексической системы языка* [Электронный ресурс] / Режим доступа: http://www.pglu.ru/lib/publications/University_Reading/2008/V/uch_2008_V_00034.

Крюкова И. В. *Рекламное имя: от изобретения до прецедентности.* Волгоград: Перемена, 2004. 286 с.

Мамлеева Л., Перция В. *Анатомия бренда*. СПб.:Питер, 2005. 190 с.

Нахимова Е.А. *Теория и методика когнитивно-дискурсивного исследования прецедентных онимов в современной российской коммуникации*. Автореф. дис. … д-ра филол. наук. Екатеринбург, 2011. 45 с.

Россинская Е.Р., Галяшина Е.И., Зинин А.М. Теория судебной экспертизы. М.: Норма, 2009.

Трифонова Е.А. *Названия деловых объектов: семантика, прагматика, поэтика: На материале русских и английских эргонимов:* дисс. ... канд. филол. наук. – Волгоград, 2006. – 247 с.

Фрэнкель А. *Нейминг: Как игра в слова становится бизнесом.* М., 2006. 320 с.

Чармэссон Г. *Торговая марка: как создать имя, которое принесет миллионы.* СПб.: Питер, 2000.

Шимкевич Н.В. *Русская коммерческая эргонимия: прагматический и лингвокультурологический аспекты :* автореф. дис. … канд. филол. наук : 10.02.01 – Екатеринбург, 2002. – 23 с.

Шмелёва, Т. В. Ономастикон российского города. – Саарбрюккен: LAPLambertAcademicPublishing, 2014. – 130с.

Transliteration

Alistanova F.F. Ergonimy sovremennogo russkogo yazyka kak mikrosistema: Dis. … kand. fil. nauk: 10.02.01 / F.F. Alistanova. – Makhachkala, 2011. – 179 s.

Golomidova M.V. Imyatvorchestvo v ergonimii: traditsii vs. aktualnye trendy // Lingvistika kreativa-2 / Pod obshchej red. T.A. Gridinoj. – Ekaterinburg, 2012. – S. 63-72.

Golomidova M.V. Iskusstvennaya nominatsiya v onomastike: dis. … d-ra filol. nauk. Ekaterinburg, 1998. 215 s.

Domnin V.N. Brending: novye tekhnologii v Rossii. – SPb: Piter, 2002. – 352 s.

Elistratov V.S., Pimenov P.A. Neiming. Iskusstvo nazyvat. Uchebno-prakticheskoe posobie. – M.: Omega-L, 2012. – 304 s.

Emeljanova A.M. Ergonimy v lingvisticheskom landshafte polietnicheskogo goroda (na primere nazvaniĭ delovyh, kommercheskih, kulturnyh, sportivnyh objektov g. Ufy): Dis. … kand. fil. nauk: 10.02.01 / BGU. – Ufa, 2007.

Ivanova E.N. Priemy kreativnoj nominatsii (na primere nazvanij knizhnyh magazinov Ekaterinburga) // Uralskij filologicheskij vestnik: Yazyk, sistema, lichnost'. Lingvistika kreativa. 2013. – №3. – S. 27-31.

Kazakova S.L. Urbanonimy v sostave leksicheskoj sistemy yazyka [Elektronnyj resurs] / Rezhim dostupa: http://www.pglu.ru/lib/publications/University_Reading/2008/V/uch_2008_V_00034.

Kryukova I. V. Reklamnoe imya: ot izobreteniya do pretsedentnosti. Volgograd: Peremena, 2004. 286 s.

Mamleeva L., Perciya V. Anatomiya brenda. SPb.: Piter, 2005. 190 s.

Nahimova E.A. Teoriya i metodika kognitivno-diskursivnogo issledovaniya pretsedentnyh onimov v sovremennoj rossijskoj kommunikatsii. Avtoref. dis. … d-ra filol. nauk. Ekaterinburg, 2011. 45 s.

Trifonova E.A. Nazvaniya delovyh objektov: semantika, pragmatika, poehtika: Na materiale russkih i anglijskih ehrgonimov: diss. ... kand. filol. nauk. – Volgograd, 2006. – 247 s.

Frehnkel' A. Nejming: Kak igra v slova stanovitsya biznesom. M., 2006. 320 s.

Charmehsson G. Torgovaya marka: kak sozdat imya, kotoroe prineset milliony. SPb.: Piter, 2000.

Shimkevich N.V. Russkaya kommercheskaya ehrgonimiya: pragmaticheskii i lingvokulturologicheskii aspekty : avtoref. dis. … kand. filol. nauk : 10.02.01 – Ekaterinburg, 2002. – 23 s.

Shmelyova, T. V. Onomastikon rossijskogo goroda. – Saarbryukken: LAP Lambert Academic Publishing, 2014. – 130s.

Sokolova T.P. 2012. Examination of Trade Marks, Company Names and Trade Names as the Means of individualization in Russia: Theoretical and Methodological Approaches to the Problem. Onoma 47: 263-279.

Notes

[1] The research is supported by Russian Humanitarian Science Foundation (grant № 14-04-00487).

Internet Name Contests as a New Means of Advertising Name Invention in Russia

Irina Kryukova and Anton Kryukov

Abstract

By the general term "advertising name" we mean the name of any object that happens to be advertised. Internet name contests can show the native speakers' attitude to such names. We consider these contests to be complex communicative events made possible by means of contemporary online communication. Large amount of data determined the usage of classification and primary statistical processing methods. The discourse analysis of name contests enables the researcher to decompose the complicated process of name invention into successive stages.

Introduction

In this report we are going to present a minor part of a bigger survey on the linguistic portrait of a naming person in modern Russia. Owing to the data analyzed previously, we can determine 5 conventional types of naming persons, and each of these has its own peculiarities: 1) a person equipped with the right to give a name to an object; 2) such a person's friends and relatives; 3) a collective of people united by a set of common activities, connected to the named object; 4) naming agencies; 5) contributors of internet name contests (Крюкова 2011). The last type of naming persons is new in modern Russia; this phenomenon has not been thoroughly studied yet.

The aim of this research is to detect a common concept of "what is the right way to make up an advertising name" by studying internet name contest cases.

The generic term advertising name is used here to mean the name of any advertised object (names of goods, services, commercial ventures etc.) (Крюкова 2004). There are some other special terms traditionally used in Russian onomastic papers. For example, ergonym (orig. from Greek ἔργον for deed and ὄνομα for name) stands for a proper name referring to a group of people organized according to some business interests, such as a union, a society, an enterprise or a section. The pragmatonym (orig. from Greek πράγμα for thing or commodity, and ὄνομα for name) stands for a proper name denoting a trademark (Подольская 1988: 178, 113). In spite of the variability of semantic structure and different denotative references, we may regard advertising names as a single body of onomastic lexis. They all have much in common: all of them belong to one conceptual field and denote the objects subjected to advertisement; they are alike in their pragmatic orientation and the probable impact on the addressee is taken into account at the stage of invention; they denote the symbol of an individual object, which comprises verbal as well as non-verbal components (Kryukova 2008: 397).

Internet name contests demonstrate public attitude towards these names, developed by the members of big groups of people who are united at the same time by the same nominative task.

We have intentionally taken a variety of contests as the data for study. They differ as to the number of participants, and they all were aimed at naming different groups of advertising names.

Two of them were held to name cars (pragmatonyms). Both took place in 2010. The first one resulted in naming a new AvtoVAZ model (IC-1). The other was intended to find a name for a perspective city car. It has never been put into serial manufacturing, but several years ago, the Russian media widely discussed the business idea of the project and the features of the car. (IC-2). Among the contests we have analyzed, those two are the biggest as to the number of competing names (over 14000 for both) and territorial coverage. People from all distant Russian regions took part, from Kaliningrad in the west to Vladivostok in the east. It allows us to draw some conclusions on the wide scale of Russian language and culture.

Unlike the previously mentioned contests, the third contest that was selected for analysis was mostly local. It was held in 2012 in Saint Petersburg and its goal was to find a name for a chain store company (ergonym) (IC-3). The contestants submitted 1212 variants. Having analyzed this event from the communicative standpoint, we can judge on the nominative tastes of the metropolis's inhabitants.

The fourth event was aimed at giving a name to a housing complex (urbanonym). The contest took place at the city Web portal of Votkinsk, a small town in Udmurtia (IC-4). The jury collected 127 names. In spite of the fact that this number is relatively small, it still contributes to our research as a vivid display of nominative tastes in small Russian towns.

In our analysis we did not limit ourselves to the winning entries only, instead we examined the whole corpus of competing names. This principle enabled us to analyze more than 15000 entries. Having studied that array of data we have made suggestions on contemporary linguistic tastes of Russians. We also employed text abstracts, such as authors' metalinguistic commentaries on winning names, forum users' opinions, and the final decisions of the juries or contest organizers.

That approach determined the usage of a complex methodology, which included:

- Discourse analysis of the contests as communicatively significant activities;
- Onomasiological analysis of competing names, combined with classification techniques and quantitative estimation.

Discourse analysis of internet name contests

Discourse analysis was introduced by Zellig Harris in 1952 (Harris 1952). It gradually acquired an interdisciplinary character, and now this term is frequently used by linguists, sociologists, and anthropologists. Scholars slightly differ in its definition, but mostly they explain it as the means to examine human communication in various cases. There are several well-developed procedures of discourse analysis (Fairclough 2003: 191 – 194; van Dijk 2007: 18 – 20; Leontovich 2011: 104 – 118). It helps when researching into the forms, functions, contextual and social dependences of the communication process. Depending on the goals of an analysis, the volume of data may vary from a single brief text to a large corpus of texts, referring to a certain communicative event. Accordingly, discourse analysis can be structured chronologically, as the communication expands. This methodology helps to reconstruct communicative events over time, and that is why we decided to use it.

Here we regard these contests as complex communicative events, which are effective owing to the usage of contemporary computer technology as the means. The structure of such an event is characterized by the following consecutive stages:

1. Posting an announcement on a web-site, together with the terms and conditions of the contest. Circumstances vary, but one can easily determine at least three common rules for every competition of this kind.

A competing name must be unique, so it can not be easily confused with some other name, no previously registered domain names or trademarks; this can lead to disqualification (IC-2),

A competing name should be original and recognizable (IC-4).

Every name must be checked so that it cannot be similar to or the same as names previously sent to the contest (IC-3).

The choice of names can be limited by special requirements of the organizers. For instance, the name of a new LADA car should meet the manufacturer's standards: it should have the word LADA as the first part, and it must be written in Latin characters (IC-1). And, vice versa, the name of the housing complex should be Russian and regionally determined (e.g., it can be connected with local sights or bear the name of a famous native, Pyotr Tchaikovsky, for example) (IC-4).

The demand for brevity. It is the demand for the name to be relatively short and easy to pronounce (2-3 words at most, maximum 7 letters or 7 syllables in each etc.).

The submitted car name must be 4-7 characters long (IC-1).

The Contest Committee accepts variants of names (each one must not include more than 3 words, but the more laconic – the better) (IC-3).

The name of the housing complex must not exceed two words (IC-4).

The demand for morality. The author is firmly requested to use only pleasant images and associations, as well as moral ones. In the commercial realm any negativity is out of the question.

The Contest Committee has the right to reject a name, if it is against the moral code or contradicts Russian legislation. We also do not accept evidently absurd variants (IC-1).

The Committee has the right to issue a warning to an author who uses inappropriate, indecent or provocative expressions towards the Contest, the jury or other authors, and which can trigger conflicts (IC-3).

Words, names, objects which arouse negative reactions of the audience are prohibited (IC-4).

This is how the general form and content of an advertising name is determined.

2. Collecting competing names and name legends. Here we observe a clear dependency between the peculiarities of suggested name variants, the named object and the characteristics of participants as a group.

We once came across a contest looking for a name for a housing complex in a small and provincial town of Votkinsk, in which patriotic patterns prevailed. The dominant seme was "place" («Провинция» – Province, «Зеленая роща» – Green grove, «Родные берега» – Native shore). The names suggested for a Saint-Petersburg grocery chain contained the seme "taste" («Вкусный» – Tasty, «Поэзия вкуса» – Poetry of Taste, «Русский вкус» – Russian taste). There were also plenty of English lexis and puns («Властелин вкуса» – King of taste, «Food-тут» – «тут» means "here", «Питер-food»).

When it comes to a car brand, the seme "technical performance" comes forward. It is noteworthy: the competitors of car branding contests generally extend the typical features of web trolling to name contest boards, and suggest provocative and generally inappropriate variants, just for fun (Lada Finita, Lada Dokole, Lada Zanuda, Lada Kapez) (IC-1a).

Sometimes authors submit some remarks, so-called name legends, if the rules of the contest contain such a demand.

Authors of name legends often demonstrate their linguistic tastes, for example, through commentaries based on metaphors.

> *Here is my name for the car: QUANT, QUANTUM.*
> *SUBSTANTIATION AND the NAME'S POTENTIAL USAGE:*
> *Quantum is an undivisible unit, which can be punned in advertisement. It is semantically connected with such topics as SPACE and STARS. If QUANT/QUANTUM is selected for the name of the car, people would feel its relation to physics. It is certain to inspire trust, and is likely to result in people's support. QUANT is similar to QUATRO, which might also be important. QUANT is logically connected with "quantization", which can be understood as a model range: QUANT – 1, QUANT – 2, QUANT – 3* (IC-2a).

Sometimes participants undertake a thorough linguistically adequate semantic analysis of the name.

> *Welcome Guest Grocery Store Chain*
> *GUEST is the basic word here. V. Dal. Explanatory Dictionary of the Living Great Russian Language: ГОСТЬ (GUEST) – a foreign merchant, who does not belong to the area where his trade is located. T. F. Efremova. Explanatory Dictionary of the Russian Language. Here a wider definition is used: ГОСТЬ (GUEST) – a merchant. The second word is ЗВАНЫЙ (WELCOME). In Efremova's dictionary this adjective refers to "a person who received an invitation". Contextually it corresponds to WELCOME. This can be referred to a seller (a welcome merchant is the one, whom everyone likes to deal with), as well as a customer (every client is welcome at the store).*

Therefore, the name WELCOME GUEST triggers the following associations:

- image-wise this chain is customer-friendly; it has a credit of trust, and customers treat it as a welcome guest;

- as for the customers of these stores, the company sees them as welcome guests and expresses this attitude towards hem.

This attitude to WELCOME GUESTS is reflected in Russian idioms and proverbs (IC-3a).

The analysis of name legends displays the general creative approach of the participants to the contest. But what is more, it shows their ability to work with words very carefully.

3. Juries—organizers of the contest and naming specialists—select a short-list. It is noteworthy, that in most cases, the jury members remain anonymous throughout the whole of the contest procedures; only the event's ordering company officials know their names. At this stage the names are checked on their correspondence to patent legislation. As a rule, the officials pick the variants with clear inner forms and/or national-cultural connotations.

For example, here is the top ten contesting names of the chain store: «Званый гость» – Welcome Guest, «Невский привоз» – Nevsky Market, «Торговые причалы» – Shopping Quays, «Марка.spb» – Marka.spb, «Рецепты вкуса» – Recipes of Taste, «Питерский привоз» – St. Pete's Market, «Соседушка» – Stable Companion, «На вкус» (На вкус и цвет) – Own Taste (Everyone to His Own Taste), «Круглый стол» – Round Table, «Скатерть» – Tablecloth (IC-3). And this is how the best names for the housing complex were rated: «Комфорт» – Comfort, «Первая линия» – First Row, «Симфония» – Symphony, «Чебаки» – Tchebaks (dialectal for Votkinsk residents), «Богатеевка» – Bogateyevka (this word was invented by the author specifically for this contest; cp. Rublyovka, a famous place of living for rich Muscovites, originates from *рубль* – "rouble", while Bogateyevka from богатый – "rich"), «Ландыши» – Lilies of the Valley, «Славный» – Glorious, «Солнечный проезд» – Sunny Driveway (IC-4a). The organizers of the best car name contest selected five best names: «Аванс» – Advance, «Аз» – Az (the first letter of ancient Slavic alphabet), «Колесница» – Chariot, 27, 777 (IC-2b). The jury of the LADA contest decided not to announce the top ten, for the best names were to be used for the manufacturer's perspective models (IC-1a).

In spite of the difference between the nominated objects and the different scales of contest data, not all the juries were inclined to include the names appealing to their sense of humour in the shortlists. Names for stores and housing complexes are characterized by their clear inner form. All of them were Russian in language. And as for the urban vehicle contest, some numeric variants were selected as the best ones.

So, in the above-mentioned cases, the winning names were Солнечный проезд housing complex – Sunny Driveway, Званый гость grocery stores – Welcome Guest. A new LADA car got a laconic name in Roman script, as it had been assigned by the contest organizers: LADA GRANTA. As for the contest for the best name for a city car, the jury declined to choose the winner.

4. The fourth and final stage represents an open on-line voting contest and the announcement of the results. It is when naming persons and addressees often change their communicative roles. Former participants act as judges, often showing disagreement with the official jury. It was most vividly displayed in the discussion over the results of the LADA contest, where LADA GRANTA was finally picked out as the winner.

> *What a dumb name. It is unusual. It has no message. Again, "granta" sounds close to граната – "grenade". Lada Friday is the best* (IC-1b).
>
> *The contest was bought and paid for! The real winner is Mikhail Boyarsky, a popular actor and singer. His variant was LADA KANALYA*. It got 99% according to people's vote* (IC-1b) *(* — canaille was one of his famous character's signature word).*

The final word rests with the jury, but the experts' viewpoint is rarely shared by the public. The audience values the creative skills of the authors above all. People want entertainment, they do not really care about commercial effectiveness.

Onomasiological analysis of name contests' corpus

However, for the purposes of this study it is more relevant to perform an onomasiological analysis of the entire corpus of name contests.

Onomasiological analysis traditionally starts with a given concept and investigates the words that are used to name that particular concept. It can help us find out which mechanisms are used to introduce different words for the same concept. The main purpose of onomasiological analysis is to discover patterns in a group of conceptually related words (*Cognitive Exploration of Language and Linguistics* 2004: 36). In this case, it helps us to trace an advertising name from the general picture of its form and content to the realization of this picture in certain language units. This approach allows us to make up groups of names with common structural semantic features.

Let us illustrate this with the help of the most explanatory case – the best commercial name contest "My own name for an urban vehicle". It was held by Yarovit Motors Company in the summer of 2010. They also presented a brand new concept of a city car, but it never reached the production line. The contest itself also failed. As mentioned above, the jury decided not to announce the winner. Eventually the final name — Yo-Mobile — was suggested by the project's chief designer Vladimir Tsesler. Nevertheless, applicants submitted about 2000 variants; organizers received 11365 bids (IC-2). We regard all of them as unique linguistic data, for it reflects the peculiarities of contemporary Russian linguistic consciousness.

By the term "linguistic consciousness" we mean a set of cognitive structures which have been formed with the assistance of social knowledge, connected with language signs – lexemes, idioms, word collocations, texts, associative thesauruses. As N. Ufimtseva notes, linguistic consciousness cannot serve as the object of analysis if the process of its realization is in process. It should be regarded only as the result of something, which has already happened (Уфимцева 2011: 204).

The onomasiological analysis of car name variants enables us to divide them into several groups, based on their authors' reasoning. Here they are, in order of frequency:

1) Artificial names (33.5%), totally unmotivated from the addressee's point of view (like Атель, Иллирия, Айрос, Прива) or partially motivated – they symbolically indicate, that it is a car for the use in town, that it is Russian, and that it is made by Yarovit Motors Company. There were three elements most frequently used by the competitors:

- гор (городской, urban): Автогор, Горфренд, Горус, Горбиль;
- рус (русский, Russian): Эльрус, Ерус, Аврус, Рускат;
- and яр («Яровит»): Яроград, Ярэкс, Yarson, YarON.

The average modern Russian native-speaker is surrounded by unmotivated global brands and, so, got used to this.

2) International names (22%), mostly English, in original spelling (Dream, Empire, Wind Road); words of other languages are also possible: for instance, Italian (Uno, Fuori) or even Sanskrit (Veda – knowledge, Авега – knowing the way). For the majority of Russian natives such names are non-motivated, but their authors always imply a certain sense – we can judge by looking through the comments on their contest entries. Sometimes they indicate a connection with existing brands (Априори –

cp. Lada Priora), or demonstrate the deconstruction of a foreign word. For example, INCARNATION – IN'CAR'NATION (INCARNA, INCAR). These names indicate post-modernist aesthetics applied to nominative practice. They conform to the basic semantic principle of post-modernism, which is synonymous with deconstruction. Deconstruction is connected with the procedure of stratification, dismantlement, decomposition of linguistic, logocentric and phonocentric structures (Derrida 2000: 55), as well as pluralistic alignment of various views on the same issue.

3) Names for a car derived from anthroponyms (17.5%). It is a kind of a long lasting trend in industry, particularly in the Western world. As we know, one of the first automobiles in the world was once called Mercedes. This category also comprises acronyms, if they formally correspond to a personal name: ALENA – ALternative ENergy Automobile. However, most entries of this group have been formed from the name of the project's main investor, Russian billionaire Mikhail Prokhorov, via transonymization (Прохор, Прошка, Мишка, Мишук) and various morphological means (Миха-мобиль, Прохорово, ПРО-град). It is noteworthy that many contributors associatively appealed to existing luxury car brands. For example, one suggested the name Прош (PROSCHE), which ironically alluded to PORSCHE. Evidently, popular marketing means, like puns, affected the authors' nominative preferences.

What is more, the words from this group clearly indicate how the nominative intentions of the contributors and the organizers mismatched each other. The contest holders regarded the competition as a serious matter, as the means to solve a marketing problem. The applicants took it for a chance to show off their comic skills. Many entries evidently were not intended to win. However, they also enable us to trace some linguistic trends. A significant number of variants concerning Russian state leaders were supplied with sarcastic comments: Путобиль (for the uniformed), Медобиль (for United Russia Party members, a bear, медведь, is at its logo), Медвепут (no fear of traffic jams). This is how critical thinking—through irony—is reflected in modern nominative practice.

4) Metaphoric names, which are symbolically connected with certain characteristics of the new car (16%). First, zoomorphic onyms sharing the seme "small size". The Yo-Mobile was a compact town car, and its size was one of the positive features the marketing wished to stress. Examples include: Чижик (small bird), Блоха (flea), Ласка (vair), Хорь (fitchew), Мопс (pug-dog) – cp. Volkswagen Beetle).

Second, the names containing the seme "moving". They are mostly derived from Russian and foreign nouns (Карета (carriage), Колесница (chariot), Telega (horse cart), Маршрут (route), Курс (track), Trasser).

We think that the words with strong national cultural connotations also belong to this group. These names were formed on the basis of ancient Slavic anthroponyms and theonyms: Лучезар, Светозар, Пересвет, Ратмир, Перун, Свагор. This is very likely connected with the name of the car producing company – Yarovit (Велояр, Ярогор), and maybe with an existing Russian car brand Svyatogor, which is, frankly speaking, not very popular. These words also correspond to the growing fashion for everything which seems and looks ethnically Russian.

5) Names with positive semes in their meaning structure, which have no primary connection with the automobile industry (8.5%). In Russia many of them are often used as brands. Some of them are onymized words of the natural language (Простор, Парус, Лидер, Гений, Спутник), and not only nouns (Аз, Ура!). Other variants were made up due to transonymization from astronyms (Сириус, Алькор, Аврора, Зодиак), personal names (Дарья, Матрена, Гавриил), names of fictional characters (Колобок, Ассоль, Дульсинея), and toponyms (Байкал, Юрга, Валдай, Карелия, Алтай).

Among the others (2.5%), it is worth noting numeric names. There were not many such entries, but the jury included some of them in the short list: 777 (seven is a lucky number, it is sure to bring triple luck) or 27 (the 27th article of the Russian constitution states the right to free travel). It is quite clear that these words cannot be included in any of the enlisted groups without a proper metalinguistic commentary.

Conclusion

In conclusion we must admit that the discourse analysis of internet best advertising name contests enables the researcher to decompose the complicated process of name invention to successive stages. It displays the nominative preferences of large groups of people, united contemporaneously by a single nominative task.

Further onomasiological analysis of the results of the contests proves that Russian speakers' mass consciousness operates the following steady associative links:

- with existing naming trends, Russian as well as worldwide;
- with popular advertising techniques (puns, no visible motivation for the mass audience);
- with post-modernistic aesthetics, oriented towards decomposing existing forms;

– with peculiar features of internet communication (irony, critical thinking, competing in wit).

This analysis offers the challenge for further investigation on the linguistic portrait of a collective naming person and mass addressee.

References

Cognitive Exploration of Language and Linguistics. 2004. / ed. By Rene Dirven and Marjolin Verspoor. 2nd rev. ed. Amsterdam: John Benjamins Publishing Company.

Fairclough, N. 2003. *Analysing Discourse.* New York: Routledge.

Harris, Z.S. 1952. *Discource Analysis.* Language. 28:1:1.

Kryukova, I. 2008. "Russian Advertising Names as a Matter of Linguistic Fashion." *Onoma. Journal of International Council of Onomastic Sciences* 43: 397-410.

Van Dijk, T.A. 2007. "The Study of discourse: An Introduction." In Discourse Studies/ Ed. T.A. van Dijk. Vol. 2. London: Sage, xix–xli.

Деррида, Ж. 2000. *Письмоиразличие.* М.: Академ. Проект [Derrida, J. 2000. Writing and Difference. Moscow: AcademicProject].

Крюкова, И.В. 2004. *Рекламное имя: от изобретения до прецедентности.* Волгоград: «Перемена» [Kryukova, I.V. 2004. Advertising Name: from Invention to Precedency]

Крюкова, И.В. 2011. *Речевой портрет субъекта искусственной ономастической номинации* // Человек в коммуникации: мотивы, стратегии и тактики: кол. монография. – Волгоград: «Перемена», 2011. С. 155-166. [Kryukova, I.V. 2011. Speech Portrait of an Artificial Onomasic Nomination Subject. In Person in Communication: Motives, Strategies, Tactics: Multi-Author Monograph].

Леонтович, О.А. 2011. *Методы коммуникативных исследований.* – Гнозис. [Leontovich, O.A. 2011. Methodology of Communication Studies. – Gnosis].

Подольская, Н.В. 1988. *Словарь русской ономастической терминологии.* – М: Наука. [Podolskaya, N.V. 1988. Dictionary of Russian Onomastic Terminology. – Moscow: Nauka].

Уфимцева, Н.В. 2011. *Языковое сознание: динамика и вариативность.* М.: Институт языкознания РАН, 2011. [Ufimtseva, N.V. 2011. Linguistic Consciousness: Dynamics and Variation. Moscow: Institute of Linguistics, Russian Academy of Sciences, 2011].

Sources

IC-1 — http://www.lada.ru/konkurs/ (accessed May 23, 2015).

IC-1a — http://www.drive2.ru/b/4062246863888387495/ (accessed May 28, 2015).

IC-1b — http://www.forum.mista.ru/topic.php?id=498080 (accessed May 28, 2015).

IC-2 — http://www.yarovit.com/news/184.htmlhttp://www.onexim.ru/ru/media/pressreleases/245/ (accessed May 27, 2015).

IC-2a — http://md-prokhorov.livejournal.com/61137.html?page=1#comments (accessedMay 27, 2015).

IC-2b — http://www.km.ru/avto/content/opublikovany-pyat-luchshikh-nazvanii-dlya-avtomobilya-prokhorova (accessed May 27, 2015).

IC-3. —http://www.litsovet.ru/index.php/konkurs.view?konkurs_id=424

IC-3a — http://www.litsovet.ru/index.php/konkurs.comments?konkurs_id=424&&&&&&&&comments_page=1 (accessed May 25, 2015).

IC-4 — http://votkinsk.net/node/64643 (accessed May 23, 2015).

IC-4a — http://votkinsk.net/node/64701 (accessed May 24, 2015).

THE INTEGRATION OF THE BRAND NAME IN THE ADVERTISING TEXT

ANTJE LOBIN

Abstract

In market communication that aims at establishing a dialogue with the customer, brand names do not occur in isolation. Rather, they are integrated in the advertising text by means of morphological, syntactic and lexical patterns. This study is based on a corpus of French, Spanish and Italian newsletters of the brand NIVEA dating from the years 2010 to 2013. It is supposed to reveal similarities and differences with regard to linguistic patterns in newsletters of different countries.

Introduction

In market communication brand names do not occur in isolation but are embedded in textual contexts in multiple ways. In this regard, the present contribution focuses on the question of the morphological, syntactic and lexical environments in which brand names occur. The study is based on a corpus of French, Spanish and Italian newsletters from the years 2010 to 2013.

Periodic newsletters are commonly used in external corporate communications as an appropriate measure to establish and maintain a dialogue with customers and to strengthen customer loyalty. This is of relevance in times of globalisation and growing competitive pressure in which intensive maintenance of the customer base becomes more and more important and the relation between customer and brand is of increasing significance.

My case study focuses on NIVEA e-mail newsletters. NIVEA is a protected trademark that was established by the Beiersdorf AG in 1911. What started as the original NIVEA cream has become a large brand family with more than 500 different products. The corpus comprises 50 French, 22 Spanish and 17 Italian newsletters. While the Spanish and Italian newsletters are published monthly, there is no clear pattern in the frequency of publication of the French newsletter (which often has less text than the other two). Due to the significantly higher number, only 50 out of 100 newsletters that were published during the investigation period have been considered in this case study. These 50 French newsletters were published between February 2012 and September 2013. The aim of this study is to identify and classify linguistic forms and patterns which occur and to find possible dominant patterns in the individual languages.

The brand name as part of nominal phrases and coordination

The brand name NIVEA serves as a determiner in nominal phrases. Significant differences in productivity can be observed between the subcorpora. While in the Germanic determination order the determiner precedes the determined element, the determined element precedes the determiner in romance languages. Both types occur in the Italian newsletter collection: In the example NIVEA *shop* [21.09.12] the brand name precedes the determined element, which is an Anglicism, in line with the Germanic determination order rules. In contrast, the noun phrases *newsletter* NIVEA and *community* NIVEA [22.12.11], which also include Anglicism, follow the Romanic determination order rules. Other instances following the Romanic determination order that have been created on the basis of Italian nouns are (in alphabetical order): *innovazione* NIVEA [21.09.12], *novità* NIVEA, *prodotti* NIVEA[1] [06.12.11], *sito* NIVEA [01.12.10], *solare* NIVEA [27.06.12]. Concerning the noun phrase *novità* NIVEA, in 12 of 17 occurrences in the Italian subcorpus, it appears in the following context: Personalized address *Ciao Antje* followed by the imperative *Scopri le ultime novità* NIVEA*!* [e.g. 20.06.13], meaning *Discover the latest* NIVEA *innovations.*

The Spanish subcorpus contains only two noun phrases created from the brand name NIVEA, one displaying a borrowed syntactical pattern and following the Germanic word order, the other following the Romanic determination order rules. In the example NIVEA *Haus* [22.12.10], which has been created by means of a Germanism, the modifier NIVEA is situated in anteposition. In contrast, in *productos* NIVEA [20.09.12] the brand name stands in postposition.

The French language appears to be most productive in terms of creating noun phrases from the brand name NIVEA. The French subcorpus comprises 13 different types, all of which can be attributed to the Romanic determination order model. From a semantic perspective, the occurrences can be grouped into the following categories: “community”, “products” and “brand communication”.

Semantic category	**Examples**
community	*membres* NIVEA [23.05.12] *famille* NIVEA [27.06.13] *conseillères* NIVEA [02.02.12]
products	*produit(s)* NIVEA [20.12.12] *innovation* NIVEA [29.10.12] *déo* NIVEA [06.06.13] *hydratation* NIVEA [28.09.12] *serviette de plage* NIVEA [27.06.13]
brand communication	*concours* NIVEA [29.01.13] *logo* NIVEA [03.07.12] *mag'* NIVEA [29.04.13] *websérie* NIVEA [18.10.12]

Table 1. Semantic categories of French noun phrases from the brand name NIVEA.

Strictly speaking, the examples *déo* NIVEA and *mag'* NIVEA are rather blendings of the brand name and the clipped nouns *déodorant* and *magazine.*

It is striking that the French noun phrases created from a noun and the brand name NIVEA are frequently preceded by a second person possessive. These syntagmatic structures can be divided into the categories "products" and "brand communication". Examples of the category "products" are: *votre anti-rides* NIVEA (*anti-wrinkle*) [20.12.12], *vos soins* NIVEA (*care*) [18.07.13], *vos soins anti-rides* NIVEA (*anti-wrinkle care*) [25.04.12], *vos produits corps* NIVEA Q10+ (*body products*) [06.02.13], *votre vanity* NIVEA [14.03.12]. The category "brand communication" includes examples such as: *votre websérie* NIVEA [03.07.12]. Following Hernández Toribio (2006: 85), the use of the possessive pronoun in advertising texts conveys the availability of the advertised products to the recipient: "El empleo del posesivo es interesante puesto que contribuye a transmitir al destinatario la impresión de accesibilidad de lo ofertado." According to Calabrese (1989: 168f.) possessives establish a close and affective relationship between the producer and the customer. He states: "[l'aggettivo] possessivo […] lega il produttore al consumatore in una sfera affettiva, o unisce di amore eterno il prodotto e il suo acquirente." In the three subcorpora there is only one syntagma that is formed by including the 1st person possessive adjective, namely the French structure *nos experts* NIVEA (*our experts*) [12.06.12; 01.05.12].

The French newsletter collection contains 4 types of syndetic structures in which the brand name NIVEA is linked to a second constituent by the conjunction "and" represented by the ampersand. This second constituent can be a brand name as in NIVEA *&/et* REEBOK [22.11.12] or in SMARTBOX *&* NIVEA [20.11.12]. It can be a personal pronoun, as can be seen in the name of the customer loyalty platform NIVEA *&* MOI[2] [18.10.12]. Or the brand name is linked to a personal name as in the case of artist Rihanna: Rihanna & NIVEA [29.07.12]. In these syndetic structures, the brand name appears in the first or second position.

The grammatical functions of the brand name and its syntactic context

Syntactically, we differentiate between the use of the brand name in object or in subject position. In all three subcorpora the brand name NIVEA functions as a direct object of the verb "to follow". It appears in the requests: *Segui* NIVEA (it.), *Sigue* NIVEA (span.), *Suivez aussi* NIVEA *sur* [*Icons*: Twitter, Facebook, You Tube] (fr.).

In the Italian subcorpus, there is one example of the use of the brand name in connection with an expression of emotion, namely: *Se anche tu ami* NIVEA *vota subito***.** (*If you too love* NIVEA *vote immediately.*) [13.10.11]. Furthermore the verb, on which NIVEA as a direct object depends, can express the process of buying, as we can see in *Comprare* NIVEA *conviene ancora di più!* (*Buying* NIVEA *is even more advantageous!*) [29.04.13].

In Spanish, also the imperative form is used: *Vive* NIVEA*!* (*Experience* NIVEA*!*) [08.03.11]. Concerning the use of the imperative in advertising Myers (1994: 47) states: „Note that advertisers use commands, not because telling you to do something really makes you do what they say, but because it will create a personal effect, a sense of one person talking to another." As has already been mentioned, this is of major importance in the context of strengthening customer loyalty.

In the majority of cases, the brand name NIVEA takes the grammatical function of the subject. In this context, SVO constructions expressing transmission, in which the brand name NIVEA occurs in the subject position, and the second-person personal pronoun occurs in the object position, deserve special attention. Hernández Toribio (2006: 81) explains the advantage of using this structure: Not only does it allow to personalise the text and to refer to the consumer by means of the second person pronoun, it also serves to highlight the product. In this regard, Hernández Toribio (2006: 81) distinguishes between "verbs of material transmission"[3] and "verbs of communicative transmission"[4]. Verbs conveying material transmission are *regalare* (it. *to offer*), *regalar* (sp. *to offer*), *enviar* (sp. *to send*), *ayudar* (sp. *to help*), *offrir* (fr. *to offer*), *rembourser* (fr. *to refund*).

Material transmission	**Examples**
Italian subcorpus	NIVEA *ti regala un anno di spesa!* (NIVEA *offers you one year of free shopping!*) [21.09.12]
Spanish subcorpus	NIVEA *quiere ayudarte a financiar tu boda.* (NIVEA *would like to help you finance your wedding.*) [07.05.13]
French subcorpus	NIVEA *vous rembourse 50% sur votre après-soleil.* (NIVEA *refunds you 50 % of your after-sun.*) [22.07.13]

Table 2. The brand name NIVEA in the context of material transmission.

In the category "communicative transmission" we find the verb "to wish" in all three subcorpora. Further verbs are *ringraziare* (it. *to thank*), *suggerire* (it. *to propose*), *invitar* (sp. *to invite*), *informar* (sp. *to inform*), *agradecer* (sp. *to thank*), *proposer* (fr. *to propose*), *inviter* (fr. *to invite*).

Communicative transmission	**Examples**
Italian subcorpus	NIVEA *ti augura un magico Natale!* (NIVEA *wishes you a magic Christmas time!*) [22.12.11]
Spanish subcorpus	NIVEA *te desea Feliz Navidad.* (NIVEA *wishes you merry Christmas.*) [23.12.11]
French subcorpus	NIVEA *vous souhaite une année de douceur et de plaisir!* (NIVEA *wishes you a year full of comfort and pleasure!*) [29.01.13]

Table 3. The brand name NIVEA in the context of communicative transmission.

It is striking that, whenever the consumer is addressed by means of the second person pronoun, this is done in an informal way in Italian and Spanish, whereas in the French newsletters the consumer is addressed formally. The brand name NIVEA also occurs in subject position outside the above mentioned structures, as different examples show. The corpus material shows that, especially in Italian, one group of verbs is important, which, from a semantic perspective, expresses emotional care. Examples of sentences expressing emotional care are in Italian: NIVEA *ti protegge anche in vacanza!* (NIVEA *protects you even on holiday*) [27.06.12] and in French: *Ce mois-ci* NIVEA *vous chérit.* (*This month* NIVEA *cherishes you.*) [10.02.12]. A further Italian example is *coccolare* "to cuddle".

A third, quite heterogeneous category of occurrences in which NIVEA takes the grammatical function of the subject comprises a structure in which reference is made to the consumer by the possessive adjective of the direct object. This can be seen in the *Italian* statement NIVEA *ama la tua pelle da*

100 anni. (NIVEA *has loved your skin for a 100 years.*) [13.10.11]. In the French corpus we found the example *Alors que l'été s'installe,* NIVEA *prépare vos vacances.* (*While summer is coming up,* NIVEA *prepares your holiday.*) [18.07.13]. Sentences with this structure are statements, except for the following French intonation question: NIVEA *fait partie de votre famille depuis toujours?* (*Has* NIVEA *always been part of your family?*) [14.02.13].

Considering verb semantics in the cases in which the brand name appears as subject, we see the creative aspect in the examples of all three subcorpora. The Italian corpus contains the syntagma *unirsi per creare* (*to unite in order to create*): *Ecco perché* NIVEA *e l'esperta di fitness Sarah Maxwell si sono unite per creare un programma semplice e su misura per te!* (*This is why* NIVEA *and the fitness expert Sarah Maxwell have united in order to create a simple and customized program for you!*) [27.06.12], the Spanish one the verbs *diseñar* (*to design*): NIVEA *ha diseñado gracias a Rihanna una experiencia única donde podrás sentirte una estrella [...]* (*Thanks to Rihanna* NIVEA *has designed a unique experience where you will feel like a star* [...]. [10.08.11]) and *preparar* (*to prepare*). The French material contains the verbs *créer* (*to create*): NIVEA *a créé le Démaquillant Yeux Double Action* (NIVEA *has created the Double Effect Eye Make-Up Remover.* [18.12.12]) and also *préparer* (*to prepare*). Furthermore, the aspect of community building can be observed in the Italian and the French examples. In Italian, it is expressed by means of the verb *coinvolgere* (*to involve*): NIVEA *ha coinvolto più di 7.000 donne nel processo di ricerca e sviluppo di un nuovo prodotto anti-age [...].* (NIVEA *has involved more than 7.000 women in the research & development process of a new anti-age product.*) [27.05.13]. In French, we have the syntagma *faire partie de* which has already been mentioned above. The verbs also serve to express emotion as can be seen in the French example: NIVEA *met les familles à l'honneur!* (NIVEA *honours the families!*) [29.04.13].

The brand name in conjunction with prepositions

The brand name NIVEA also occurs in conjunction with various prepositions expressing a multitude of relations. The introductions *en* (in Spanish) and *chez* (in French) in conjunction with the brand name are used to express a sense of locality: *En* NIVEA *somos especialistas en cuidar tu piel.* (*At* NIVEA *we are specialists taking care of your skin.*) [20.09.12]; *Chez* NIVEA *nous avons inventé un déo efficace.* (*At* NIVEA *we have developed an effective deodorant.*) [06.06.13].

The origin "from" is expressed by the use of the following prepositions: *da* in Italian, *de* in Spanish and the prepositional phrase *de la part de* in French. This is often, but not always, used in the instruction to unsubscribe the newsletter, as can be seen in the French and Spanish examples: *Para no recibir más información por e-mail de* NIVEA; *Si vous ne souhaitez plus recevoir d'emails de la part de* NIVEA, *cliquer ici*. In the Italian example NIVEA is the sender of season's greetings: *Tantissimi Auguri di Buone Feste da* NIVEA*!* [23.12.10].

In Spanish, the name of the originator is expressed by the preposition *por*: *Un espacio innovador creado, diseñado y pensado por* NIVEA *especialmente para ti.* (*An innovative space created by* NIVEA *especially for you.*) [05.05.11]. The Italian subcorpus comprises an example which includes the Anglicism *by*: *Vinci una delle 60* VESPA *Special Series by* NIVEA*!* (*Win one of the 60* VESPA *Special Series by* NIVEA*!*) [21.09.11].

Indication of for whom something is intended or done is expressed by the prepositions *per* (in Italian) and *para* (in Spanish). No examples of usage could be found in the French subcorpus. In the Italian corpus we found *Condividi la tua passione per* NIVEA. (*Share your passion for* NIVEA). [22.12.11]. A further example is: *È stato un anno importante per* NIVEA. (*It has been an important year for* NIVEA.) [22.12.11], which could be detected in a similar way in the Spanish corpus: *2011 ha sido un año muy especial para* NIVEA. [23.12.11].

In Italian, a topic is usually introduced by using the function word *su: Quanto ne sai su* NIVEA*?* (*How much do you know about* NIVEA*?*) [31.01.13]. This pattern can be observed in neither French nor Spanish. In Italian, affiliation and participation are expressed by the preposition *di*, in Spanish by *de* and in French by *de*. The following table contains the instances in the different languages:

Affiliation / participation	**Examples**
Italian subcorpus	*la forza di* NIVEA (*the strength of* NIVEA) [06.12.11] *sul palco di* NIVEA*!* (*on the stage of* NIVEA*!*) [06.12.11] *altri fan del brand* NIVEA (*other fans of the brand* NIVEA) [01.12.10.]
Spanish subcorpus	*¡Hazte fan de* NIVEA*!* (*Get a fan of* NIVEA*!*) [17.11.11] *la página de* NIVEA (*the website of* NIVEA) [17.11.11] *la nueva linea de* NIVEA (*the new line of* NIVEA) [09.02.12] *los productos de* NIVEA (*the products of* NIVEA) [29.09.11] INVISIBLE FOR BLACK & WHITE *de* NIVEA [18.04.12]
French subcorpus	*le lait corps sous la douche de* NIVEA (*the In-Shower Body Moisturiser of* NIVEA) [29.10.12]

Table 4. Affiliation and participation.

In connection with the brand name NIVEA, the Italian preposition *con* can have various meanings. It may have an instrumental function as in: *Con* NIVEA *resti in forma senza stress!* (*Using* NIVEA *you keep in shape without stress!*) [27.06.12], *Con* NIVEA *più stile per il tuo look, più cura per i tuoi capelli!* (*By using* NIVEA *more style for your look, more care for your hair.*) [30.11.12], *Leggi con* NIVEA. (*Read by means of* NIVEA.) [27.05.13], *Con* NIVEA *vinci PHILIPS.* (*By means of* NIVEA *win PHILIPS.*) [30.11.12]. It can also serve to express combination, accompaniment or presence: *Vinci un week end con* NIVEA. (*Win a week-end with* NIVEA.) [26.04.12]. Or it expresses the manner: *La tua estate inizia con* NIVEA. (*Your summer starts with* NIVEA.) [27.05.13]. The French subcorpus comprises only one example of the preposition *avec* expressing accompaniment or manner: *Après les vacances, continuez à prendre soin de vous avec* NIVEA. (*After the holidays, go on caring for yourself with* NIVEA.) [02.10.12]. In the last example cited here, the French preposition *entre* indicates the close relation between brand and consumer, combining the brand name and the second-person personal pronoun: *Entre* NIVEA *Crème et vous c'est une longue histoire...* (*Between you and* NIVEA *Crème it's been a long story...*) [06.06.12].

Summary

We have seen various patterns by means of which the brand name can be integrated into an advertising text that aims at establishing a dialogue with the customer. The brand name NIVEA serves as a determiner in nominal phrases. In this regard, significant differences in production can be observed between the subcorpora. The Italian and Spanish newsletter collection comprise examples of noun phrases following the Germanic and the Romanic determination order rules. Both include Anglicism, which do not occur in the French material. This might arise from the severe language policy in France. The French language appears to be by far most productive with regard to creating noun phrases and possessive syntagmas from the brand name NIVEA. From a semantic perspective, the occurrences can be grouped into the following categories: "community", "products" and "brand communication".

Concerning syntactic aspects, all three subcorpora comprise examples of the brand name NIVEA as a direct object of the verb "to follow". Moreover, there are three different categories in which the brand name occurs as subject: 1) Ditransitive verbs expressing communicative and material transmission, 2) Transitive verbs which express emotional care, 3) A third, quite heterogeneous, category comprising Italian and French sentences in which the second person is not the object, but reference is made to the consumer by the possessive adjective of the object.

Finally, the brand name NIVEA occurs in conjunction with various prepositions phrasing a multitude of relations. The introductions *en* (in Spanish) and *chez* (in French) in conjunction with the brand name are used to convey a sense of locality. All three subcorpora comprise examples of prepositions or prepositional phrases expressing the origin. The variable usage of the Italian preposition *con* is striking, expressing an instrumental function, accompaniment and manner. The French preposition *entre* indicates the close relation between brand and consumer, combining the brand name and the second-person personal pronoun.

In conclusion, I would like to answer the question of the dominant patterns in the individual languages. How is the brand name NIVEA used in Italian, French and Spanish texts to strengthen customer loyalty? In French, the availability and close relationship between the brand and the consumer are expressed by syndetic constructions, as for example NIVEA *& me*, and by means of syntagmas which include a second person possessive adjective. The originator is not implied in the French subcorpus, neither is the expression of something being intended for NIVEA. Thus, the integration of the brand name in the text focuses on the recipient. In Italian, the relationship between brand and consumer is expressed by means of affective lexical elements such as verbs of emotional care. The latter are used in both the following ways, NIVEA as the agent or the object of an action. With regard to the three-agent-constructions used to express transmission, the verbs of material transmission easily dominate the Italian subcorpus. In Spanish, a strong mark of affiliation and participation can be observed by using the preposition (*de*) which precedes the sender NIVEA. With regard to verbs expressing communicative and material transmission, in the Spanish material the verbs of communicative transmission dominate. Furthermore, the following neologisms could be detected, in which brand and customer are brought as close together as possible: *Diviértete, mímate, relájate, sorpréndete...* NIVÉATE*!* [05.05.11] *Nivéate* is a reflexive imperative form of the verb *nivearse*, which is a deonomastic derivation of the brand name.

This study was supposed to reveal similarities and differences with regard to newsletters in different countries. The synchronic analysis of the integration of the brand name in the advertising text to serve the relation between brand and customer should also include the consumers' perspective. In this regard, an impact analysis could give information about the extent to which consumers feel addressed by the brand. A second question which might be more difficult to answer consists in giving an explanation about the reasons for choosing specific patterns rather than others in the different speech communities.

References

Calabrese, Omar. 1989. "Il marinismo in serie. Una lingua tra neo-arcaismo e paleo-neologismo". In *Una lingua in vendita. L'italiano della pubblicità*, edited by Angela Chiantera, 159-78. Roma: La Nuova Italia Scientifica.

Hernández Toribio, Isabel. 2006. *El poder de la palabra en la publicidad de radio*. Barcelona: Ediciones Octaedro.

Myers, Greg. 1994. *Words in Ads*. London: Hodder Arnold.

Notes

[1] Variant: *Acquista almeno 2 prodotti a scelta NIVEA […]*! [26.04.12].

[2] There are 38 examples in which the free first-person singular subject pronoun is used to refer to the customer loyalty platform.

[3] He lists the following Spanish verbs: *dar, ofrecer, proporcionar, regalar, devolver, hacer, enviar, abonar, facilitar, garantizar, mandar.*

[4] He lists the following Spanish verbs: *proponer, decir, recomendar, desear, comunicar, anunciar, enseñar, recordar, explicar, aconsejar, pedir, contar, brindar, hablar.*

PART II:

NAMES AS MARKERS OF NATIONAL/CULTURAL/REGIONAL IDENTITY

THE RHETORIC OF PSEUDONYMS IN VIRTUAL LANGUAGE

DAIANA FELECAN

Abstract

This paper will analyse users' pseudonyms in electronic space (leaving out name forms that convey users' real identity). The approach will try to establish, with the help of psycho-, socio- and pragmalinguistic methodology, the cognitive mechanism that is essential in locutors' decision to stray from their official identity through a self-built, fictitious yet relevant (motivated) identity.

1. Introduction

1.1. Participants in virtual interlocutionary acts make up a community that is individualised especially on the level of their manifested nominal identity. This is a result of the expansion that communication in virtual space has gained in the past years—along with the decline of other types of communication (such as unmediated, face-to-face communication)—and of the impact that it has on the preservation and consolidation of (socio-economic and affective) interpersonal relationships.

This paper analyses false user names (*virtual pseudonyms*, *VPs*) of certain communicators in electronic space. With the help of *psycho-*, *socio-* and *pragmalinguistic methodology*, the present approach aims at establishing the main cognitive mechanism that underlies locutors' decision to deviate from their official identity by virtue of adopting a self-built, fictitious yet relevant (motivated) identity. From this perspective, the study sets to prove that the use of false user names can be accounted for either by the denotata's clear desire to ensure their anonymity in a virtual community, or by their lack of courage to take responsibility for what they assert through a posted message.

1.2. Going undercover in virtual space is on a par with an individual's assuming a role in which s/he does not feel in any way restricted within the scope of the newly created existential surrogate. The most relevant reason for this substitution lies in the way in which name bearers understand that they can exert their freedom of expression. Thus, by abandoning their actual name (*nomen verum*), real persons are protected by the anonymity conferred by their new identity (*nomen falsum*)[1]. User names are former real names or nonce lexical creations that have been turned into false names.

Among the psychological motivations that determine individuals to reject their real identity by virtue of another, an invented one, the following can be mentioned:

- The aesthetic dissatisfaction as regards one's real name;
- The lack of courage to take responsibility for the truth of asserted speech acts;
- The lack of self-confidence;
- The wish to reduce social distance between oneself and other locutors with a real or fictitious identity;
- The state of anonymity creates the illusion of the collapse of all sociolinguistic barriers, allowing for the lack of (self-)censorship and violation of the (cooperative and politeness[2]) principles of civil dialogue, without any consequences on the deontological level of conversational exchanges;
- The wish to duplicate (to become another *self* than the contingent one).

1.3. VPs are users' favourite mottos, their gate of access to discourse. They activate various functions upon receipt, such as informative, affective and persuasive ones, sometimes even going as far as conveying a threat. At all events, VPs challenge readers to an engaging, reconstructive interpretation.

Based on their degree of codification, VPs operate a selection of the target audience. There are different categories of VPs depending on receivers' possibility to adjust their reading competency to a given communication situation. For instance, there are *opaque* VPs (which imply the activation of readers' preceding knowledge) vs *transitive* VPs (which are lexically and grammatically simple and semantically transparent).

The *corpus* consists of 300 VPs gathered from various online social networks (especially Facebook), from discussions about the political-economic situation in present-day Romania: see, for example, the disagreements between the employees/supporters/opposers of different Romanian mass media trusts over the latter's ability to persuade consumers (i.e., to communicate political beliefs and draw capital from publicity). Rivalry between the aforementioned parties is mirrored, among other verbal means (particularly ones that express conflict), by the unofficial nominal phrases (VPs) that locutors use when conversing on electronic forums that explore this sociolinguistic variable.

2. Proper names: role and function

The role of a proper name is to establish an existence in the civilian space (on the macrosocial level) to which one belongs, by recording it in an official nomenclature. However, a proper name may also define an existence in a diaphasically marked environment, on the microsocial level (in one's family, among peers and friends, and so on), in which locutors practice the removal of real names from common use and their substitution with unofficial ones (nicknames, bynames, hypocoristics, user names or pseudonyms).

One cannot talk about constancy as regards the function of proper names. Its variability vacillates depending on the verbal means that facilitate the achievement of interaction.

In the case of direct communication (face-to-face dialogue), a proper name can take the form of a preface to interventions in the main text (the lines of a dialogue). At the same time, a proper name may play the role of an optional index (an indexical sign), as its evocation is not a *sine qua non* condition in the constitution of the interlocutionary situation. Speakers' position in each another's vicinity spares them the explicit expression (literal naming/name-calling)/metalinguistic expression of identity, apart from the case in which they aim at actualising the naming function (invoking/calling the targeted allocutor by his/her name, when there is a situation of anthroponymic homonymy: several locutors that bear the same (first) name). Thus, the conative function of a name is doubled by the function of ostensive super-identification: the referent is actualised by means of a gesture and the identifying role of his/her name is increased through a deictic value (***This one*** *(of the two bearers of the name Michael)*). Nevertheless, in other instances, a name is employed for phatic reasons. It is meant to check/attract interlocutors' attention during an act of communication, by transgressing a morphological category: a name (proper noun) may also be used as an interjection – *Michael!* as an equivalent for *Hey!/Watch out!*. Once it acquires the new status, the proper name leaves the *genus proximus* that established it (of proper names in general, without lexical meaning). Put differently, it becomes a part of the category of words with "absolute motivation" (see above the status of interjection), as it develops semantic relevance ("internal form") when read pragmatically.

In the case of indirect communication, the occurrence of a referent's name (*those in the third category – les troisièmes*, in the terminology coined by Nølke *et alii* 2004) is mandatory. A grammatical instrument, *recte* a third person pronoun, does not have the "semantic" capacity to clearly replace the denotatum.

The two aforementioned means of interaction in real communication may also be found in communication mediated by electronic devices. The latter constitutes the framework of the present paper, starting from the premise that, in the past twenty years, computers have steadily and permanently seized us, those in *realia*, from one another, to the detriment (or to the benefit?) of our dislocation to *virtualia*.

3. The geometry of communication with duplicate senders

3.1. The owner of a virtual pseudonym is semantically embedded in the *rigid designator* (the sign used for the identification of an existence). The latter is a derivative from a base-sign or a new sign altogether. Thus, the risks that result from a substitution of this kind endanger the harmony of social relationships and have repercussions on the efficiency of interindividual communication.

By violating the principle of individual relevance (real selfhood), the speech acts performed by a false locutor may be considered counterfactual. A "fictitiously" *original self* is likely to produce utterances whose referent can only be identified on the level of the history that defines it: an untrue, "unserious" history. An opposite interpretation is also possible: a false identity shelters an individual from any consequences that s/he might have to face as a result of expressing an opinion to which one is committed. However, no action of this kind could restore conventional communication, in which certain pragmatic parameters (linguistic maxims) must be observed to achieve its success (the correct decoding of the communicative intention).

The sender is an undetermined self, whose ideology (in fact, the only personal parameter that can be identified) is salient in the position adopted in relation to a topic of a specific nature (the debate topic announced in a certain post).

The receiver that adheres to a fabricated identity is either plural ("public opinion") or targeted (usually when the sender's discourse contains "traces" of the targeted audience, the narratee). As the sender is not indicated, therefore not forced to reveal his/her identity, s/he can resort to a fake signature. Cyberspace is an "identity workshop" (Parks and

Floyd 1996), the medium in which two or more fabricated identities communicate with one another. From this perspective, the diegesis written in electronic space replicates the pattern specific to fictional narrative space, with the difference that in CMC the context can almost always be identified in factual reality (comments about present-day events in politics, society, high life, and so on).

Sharing a common (linguistic) code is the ideal communicative situation (knowing and following the norm). Nevertheless, in virtual space, it is habitual to break all the rules of verbal conduct, as long as any trace of formality is abolished and familiarity overrides the appropriateness normally required in a communication situation in the name of absolute freedom of expression.

Virtual code is defined, first and foremost, by the absence of consistency as regards a single contact language, which is acknowledged as the interlocutors' natural idiom. The "flagellation" of linguistic purism (lexical insertions from other languages besides the mother tongue in the host language – see Romglish, for instance) is the most widespread attitude among users of socialising networks. One of the conditions in the precise recovery of a message is for two agents of an act of communication to share a code, as otherwise comprehension is deviated. The person who introduces the message assumes the risk of its not being perceived or of its only being approximated, as the receiver is unknown.

The channel of communication is extremely flexible and does not display any constraints regarding the observance of the principle of appropriateness (*tò prépon*). On the contrary, this channel is created by virtue of the suspension of every orthographic, stylistic, pragmatic or any other kind of barrier. (The most significant censorship that a message can be subjected to consists of removing the entire phonetic body or only a part of it and filling in the omission with suspension dots.) Therefore, false identity is encouraged/underpinned by the specific nature of the channel of communication.

3.2. Digital dialogue is socially instituted as a form of written communication. Thus, on the level of a sender's concern for writing rigour, messages in the online and offline environment should be close to the written variant of the language used in real communication (which is more thorough with respect to the compliance with writing guidelines). Nonetheless, electronic messages reproduce, with increasing faithfulness, the "model" of oral communication. The oral channel of communication has effects on the configuration of texts (opting for certain forms of expression).

Virtual dialogue is a communication arch-genre, as it combines several "media" that contribute to the generation of a message. In this respect, a virtual message may be conveyed like real oral messages, by means of *verbal* elements, *paraverbal* ones (the complete inventory of possibilities of technical enrichment of a message, which are provided by programme or computer settings) and *nonverbal* ones (various emotional states, expressed by means of emoticons). All of the above make up the *mixed syntax* of *instantaneous language* that is characteristic of virtual communication.

Although participants in a dialogue are in a situation of mediated interaction, the rules of prototypical (face-to-face) verbal interaction seem to be altered to a very little extent. Mutual visual observation may be achieved by accessing a highly complex inventory of para- and nonverbal elements, which allows interlocutors to have a seemingly real communication, despite their "meeting" being filtered by parameters that are specific to the virtual environment of communication[3].

The concomitance of thinking and "oral" writing/typing leads to a certain fragmentation of the message (which affects the organisation of the macrotext, the discursive system). This is materialised in word truncations, ellipses, breaks, repetitions, rephrasing, anacolutha, interruptions, syntactic simplification (short and coordinated sentences), and others. Locutors' concern for adapting to the interlocutors—in the sense of the former's permanent care for keeping alive the latter's interest (the use of the vocative case and interjections as means of checking one's attention is replaced by (paraverbal, iconic) means that are typical of electronic communication: for instance, buzzing)—is significantly reduced. It is assumed that receivers are focused on the message, whose content is not threatened by paraverbal "intruders" that may affect the quality of face-to-face dialogue[4].

3.3. As was already mentioned, a major difference between the two means of communication, i.e., the real and the virtual ones, consists of how the statement of nominal identity functions. While in real-life interaction the actualisation of a name is negotiable, in electronic communication the materialisation of a name is not optional, as the occurrence of a user name is a prerequisite of the programme accessed. The space that is meant for the user name is part of the technical configuration; it is a presetting, an intrinsic segment of a given website (see Stommel 2007: 149). As an integral part of the communication technology, completing the field that is intended for user names is compulsory both in the case of direct communication (i.e., simultaneous interaction, in which users are connected to the network at the same time) and in stand-by communication (in which users are connected to the network at different, successive times). In order to gain access to online programmes, a user has got the freedom to log in with his/her official name or its (unofficial) substitute. This paper will only take into consideration examples of false user names, obtained either through the lack of total superposition over the phonetic body of the initial name, or through the latter's complete removal (cancellation).

Thus, by means of the phrase *virtual pseudonyms* one understands those nominal surrogates with identifying function, whose form/formula only partially reveals users' real names or categorically deviate from them. In other words, a virtual pseudonym is the user name that replicates an official name to a certain extent or digresses from it entirely.

4. Virtual pseudonyms: linguistic and social signs

4.1. Pseudonyms have a twofold nature: they are *language signs* (consisting of language material) with a *social* aim (they identify existents in virtual public space with more precision than real names)[5]. A name giver may opt for the material part of a pseudonym to be exclusively letter-based (comprising letters from various alphabets) or composite (containing alphanumerical characters)[6]. Regardless of the compositional choice (transparent or opaque), the correct decoding of a virtual pseudonym depends on the context in which it appears (see Stommel 2007: 159), the sharing of encyclopaedic knowledge and the history of the exchange of messages between interlocutors. A virtual pseudonym implies linguistic, rhetorical and pragmastylistic mechanisms of decoding, in various shapes and combinations, realised with specific intentions.

Thus, as regards pseudonyms, one can refer to a *material*, *iconic*, *denotative* dimension, which is the "informative" component of the nonlinguistic background of a post, the technical, instructive part of a name. It provides information about the *connotative iconic* dimension (the totality of potential interpretations associated with a certain pseudonym).

As previously stated, the signification of a virtual pseudonym—a linguistic sign that fully satisfies the functioning conditions of a *rigid designator*—is contextually limited and it expresses a projection ("it would seem to be") rather than a description, *via nomen*, corresponding to the reality (see Stommel 2007: 158). Once "embedded" in a pseudonym, the agent of a name commits "self-incrimination" by disconnecting oneself from actuality, from one's "finite" status in real life, and connecting to the (more) relaxed status in the virtual world. The "ritual death" in the civilian society is followed by a rebirth under the same or different gender. Thus, the determination of the gender appurtenance of a pseudonym's owner is impossible, just as one cannot retrieve his/her official biography. From this viewpoint, VPs are names that describe an asexual identity, an undetermined and undeterminable gender (see Stommel 2007: 146).

4.2. The lexical-semantic architecture of a virtual pseudonym is built either from transparent material, which allows for the identification of a name giver's locutionary intention, or from opaque material, which obscures the illocutionary force of the message. More often than not, the actual text[7] (i.e., a comment posted in virtual space by the bearer of a certain name), a user's introduction to discourse, is achieved through his/her taking a stand in relation to an interlocutor's message. For instance, in the case of a pseudonym like *Pulică Badea chiar el* ("the genuine Dickie Badea"), in the construction of the name the nominator uses sexual symbols that are nullified by the diminutive form of the word (the noun denoting the male reproduction organ *pulă* "dick" > *pulică* "dickie"). At the same time, the name giver employs the mechanism of quotation: the hypotext (the original text) *Mircea Badea chiar el* ("the genuine Mircea Badea") is partially replicated and modified in the direction aimed by the new bearer. In this example, it is salient that the secondary user's intention is to adopt the real identity (the "illustrious name") of the initial owner and highlight, by means of the hypotext, his negative (verbal) behavioural traits. At the same time, one cannot disregard the pattern of the pseudonym adopted by Mircea Badea, the bearer to whom the unofficial name belongs *de iure*: *Mircea Badea chiar el* is made up of a noun phrase + adverb + third-person personal pronoun, singular form. Semantically, the second part of the phrase—which is equivalent to an emphatic pronoun: *M. B. însuși* ("M. B. himself")—has the role of confirming, guaranteeing the authenticity of the individual behind the nickname; put differently, it achieves the full superposition of the name (as *rigid designator*) and name bearer. There may be several real or fake persons that bear or borrow the official name *Mircea Badea*, but the explanatory complement *chiar el* (a recent utterance that was coined by the public figure and established in the mass media by means of recursive usage) eliminates, as the real owner wishes to make sure, any shadow of a doubt that one may have as regards his identity. The intention to specify, to remove doubt is doubled by the wish to "incriminate" himself: if in visual public space (Mircea Badea is the producer and host of a pamphlet television show and one of the most publicised Romanian figures) a certain (self-)censorship of one's verbal behaviour is required (due to the formal particularity of the channel that airs this show), social networks (especially Facebook) annul any kind of constraints against offensive and defamatory language. In this respect, *Mircea Badea chiar el* needs to be read in the sense of the separation of the said public figure's conscience into *Mircea Badea—the producer of television shows* vs *Mircea Badea—the character in virtual space*, without inhibitions, the authentic (*chiar el* "actually him"), uncensored one. Through this indexical mention, the locutor delineates his virtual territory, which is defined by the principle of freedom of expression, and distinguishes himself from other users with whom he might intersect as a result of anthroponymic homonymy or identity theft (people who use a famous name as a personal name). For the latter users, the faithful or fragmentary preservation of the initial bearer's name—by adopting it as a personal name—may create, one the one hand, the illusion of identifying (temporarily, until discovered) with the borrowed personality of their idol or, on the contrary, a person whose beliefs they do not share. On the other hand, it may give the impression of seizing that important figure's "social face". The fact that a person's nominal identity is used as another's own identity and, implicitly, the set of positive or negative values—with the "prolonged release" of the nominal palimpsest of reference—that are associated with the former reveal the need of users with false names to turn into someone else than who they truly are.

5. Form and interpretation of virtual pseudonyms

Virtual pseudonyms develop specific patterns of construction. Their correct decoding depends on the discovery of the (argumentative, (un)clarifying, intertextual) discursive conventions that underlie them.

Starting from a predominantly rhetorical interpretation, the present study aims at delimiting certain types of pseudonyms in Romanian virtual space, with the following as the main directions of interest:

a) Pseudonym *architecture* (*morphology*):

- One-word pseudonyms: *Catindat* (Romanian *candidat* "candidate"), *Freestyle*, *Gigi*, *Guru*, *Intelectual* (Romanian, "intellectual"), *Jack*, *Justițiarul* (Romanian, "the vigilante"), *Lucid* (Romanian, "lucid"), *Lulutz* (Romanian hypocoristic), *Miștocaru'* (Romanian, "the joker"), *Pensionar* (Romanian, "pensioner"), *Sfinx* (Romanian, "sphinx"), *Titirez* (Romanian, "spinning top"), *Vânătorul* (Romanian, "the hunter");

- Phrasal pseudonyms: *Abba Cabba*, *Acid Photo*, *Aiurea de tot* (Romanian, "totally messed up"), *Breaking News*, *Ciuco Giumbixx*, *Comunist serios* (Romanian, "serious communist"), *Cretzy Cretzy* (Romanian *creț* "curly"), *Dark Moon*, *Depeste Pulpe* (Romanian, "above the calves"), *Dumnezeu Tatăl* (Romanian, "God the Father"), *Egal cu zero* (Romanian, "equal to naught"), *El Grande Comandante*, *El Pubius Unum* (mock Latin phrase), *Exhaustivul băsist* (Romanian, "the exhaustive Băsescu follower"), *Justițiar politic* (Romanian, "political vigilante"), *Lancea dreptății* (Romanian, "the spear of justice"), *Lingăul de hemoroizi chiar el* (Romanian, "the genuine haemorrhoid licker"), *Litigii Judiciare* (Romanian, "legal issues"), *Mucea LABA'dea chiar el* (Romanian, "the genuine Wannabe Wanker-giver"), *Necunoscut Nimeni* (Romanian, "unknown nobody"), *non stop*, *Omu' paiangăn* (Romanian, "the spider man"), *Robo Man*, *Senioritaa Fify* (Spanish *señorita* "miss" + *Fify*), *sincaistu vesel* (Romanian, "the happy graduate from "Gheorghe Șincai" College"), *Tic Tac*;

- Sentence pseudonyms: *Afară cu PSD* (Romanian, "out with the (members of the) Social Democrat Party"), *Basescu, ia-ti securistii inapoi* (Romanian, "Băsescu, take back your *Securitate* officers"), *Băsesculabalamuc* (Romanian, "Băsescu to the mad house"), *BăseCuristu'* (Romanian, "Băsescu the *Securitate* officer" or "Băsescu the ass-kisser"), *FutProști* (Romanian, "(I) fuck stupid"), *Ghici Cine* (Romanian, "guess who?"), *Hulk Tedomină* (Romanian, "Hulk dominates you"), *Hulk tefutengura* (Romanian, "Hulk fucks you in the mouth"), *Miss'erupe* (Romanian, "I don't give a damn"), *Ponta e TziganMincinos* (Romanian, "Ponta is a lying gypsy"), *Provoacă la sparring pe Badea* (Romanian, "challenge Badea to sparring"), *Romania Te Iubeste* (Romanian, "Romania loves you"), *Văru' te rezolvă* (Romanian, "cousin will fix you up");

b) *Lexical-semantic dimension*:

- Appellatives: *Canadezul* (Romanian, "the Canadian"), *Guardian*, *Huliganul* (Romanian, "the hooligan"), *Justițiarul* (Romanian, "the vigilante"), *The Anonymous*, *The băimărean* (Romanian *băimărean* "an inhabitant of the town of Baia Mare"), *Votant PSD* (Romanian, "voter for the Social Democrat Party");

- Anthroponyms: *BăsElena Udrea* (*Băsescu* < *Băsescu* + *Elena*), *Bengiamin Calmantu Femeilor Unicatu* (Romanian, "Benjamin, the one and only women's soother"), *Cato Cenzorul* (Romanian, "Cato the Censor"), *Ioan*, *George George George*, *Gimmy Ciu*, *Mercur Sivenus*, *Napoleonbăsescu* (< *Napoleon* + *Băsescu*);

c) *Stylistic resources*:

c_1) *Argumentative devices*:

- *Referential anchorage*[8]: designating the initial referent by means of name "abuse":

Cato Cenzorul ("Cato the Censor") – cultural reference to the Latin Antiquity: Marcus Porcius Cato (bynamed *Cato the Elder* or *Cato the Censor*), writer and politician, known for his wisdom, scrupulousness and fight against corruption; by taking over his name, the locutor wishes to pass for a person that wants to correct the vices of the society;

Dumnezeu Tatăl ("God the Father") – biblical reference to the Creator; the locutor claims he holds the absolute Truth and is the preacher of the Right Path;

- *Expressive-decorative description*[9]:

Comunist serios ("serious communist") – by means of this pseudonym, the locutor refers to the people who are nostalgic about the former totalitarian regime (they associate the idea of communism with seriousness: the cult of work and social equality); nevertheless, the locutor might also wish to remove certain misconceptions of the system's opposers, who commonly associated communists with lack of sobriety.

c_2) *Devices of (deliberate) obscurity*: the ability of a virtual pseudonym to allow for alternative readings, with the interlocutor becoming an accomplice in the making of the text. Most of the structures investigated follow construction patterns based on tropes that exaggerate the formal values of words. More often than not, the pattern of pseudonyms exploits puns[10]:

- *Homonymy* and *paronymy*:

BăseCuristu' – syntactic homophony; two possible readings:

I. The apocope *Băse* (*Băsescu*) + an agentive nominal derivative, unarticulated form, from the Romanian appellative *cur* ("ass", slang equivalent of the noun *fund* "bottom"): *Curistu'* "the person who kisses someone's ass, who has got no dignity"; this interpretation tallies with Hämäläinen (2013: 222), who claims that "The function of the capital letter may be to highlight the borderline between lexemes";

II. The interjection *Bă* ("hey") + an appellative consisting of the reading together of an apocope form of the proper name *Băsescu*, -

se-, and the agentive appellative *curistu*, which make up an appellative with a marked pejorative meaning, with historical reference to a period that triggered numerous emotions in the Romanians' collective mentality: the era of sad remembrance (communism);

Depeste Pulpe – paronymy <= homonymy of two words (*depeste*): possible readings:

I. Simple preposition *de* "of" + simple preposition *peste* "above";

II. Simple preposition *de* "of" + appellative *pește* "fish" (written as *peste*, as the system of writing user names does not allow the use of diacritics);

Doareu ("just me") – homophonous homonyms: the locutor announces the exclusivity of his opinion, considered the only valid stand;

emy grant – syntactic homophony: possible readings:

I. *emy* – hypocoristic (< *Emil/Emily/Emilia*) + potential proper name (*Grant*);

II. As a result of reading the two components together, an appellative is obtained: *emigrant*; the locutor could even be an *Emil* that exploits this ambiguity;

Mercur Sivenus – homophonous homonyms: the two planets, *Mercur* ("Mercury") *și* (conjunction, "and" – *si*, in the body of the virtual pseudonym, due to the impossibility to write it with diacritics) *Venus*;

Miss'erupe – homophonous homonyms: a slang saying, with the meaning of "I don't care", "je m'en fische/fous";

- *Referential ambiguity*: several recurring semantic fields to which the VPs analysed pertain could be noticed:

- VPs with an *unidentifiable real referent*:
    - The semantic field of *genericity*:

Breaking News – the locutor believes s/he is the sole knower of the (shocking) announcement that s/he makes through the comment;

Catindat – the pseudonym refers to the device of anonymisation used by the Romanian playwright I. L. Caragiale in the play *D'ale Carnavalului* ("Of the carnival"), when he "names" one of the characters *Un catindat* ("a candidate"). The character in virtual space pokes fun at the social/political role of *candidate*; the mockery also results from the willingly incorrect spelling (intertextual reference); *Cetateanul Turmentat* (*Cetățeanul Turmentat* "the tipsy citizen") – a pseudonym that refers to another character created by I. L. Caragiale (in the play *O scrisoare*

pierdută "A lost letter"); he is "the average person on the street, whose simple yet commonsensical questions mirror the disillusion and even stupefaction of normal people in relation to the immorality of electoral undertakings in an apparently participative democracy, albeit false and fabricated in reality" (*Wikipedia*, "Cetățeanul turmentat", orig. Romanian, my translation). The greatest mystery for this citizen is the candidate for whom he should vote: "Eu cu cine votez?" ("Who do I vote for?");
Curat ca Lacrima ("squeaky clean") – the pseudonym consisting of an adjectival phrase semantically embeds an immaculate person, whom cannot be reproached for anything. Stylistically, this is a simile that entered the register of fixed phrases and can refer to objects (actualising a denotative reading) and to people (actualising a connotative reading: moral, spiritual impeccability);
Eu missterios ("mysterious I") – reference relativisation. This kind of self-referentiality violates the principle of referent uniqueness salient in the utterance situation on the deictic axis *ego – hic – nunc*. The plurivocal *self* is highlighted by the adjectival determination *misterios* "mysterious" and this *self* can be identified in the person of any potential locutor that says *I*. As the *I* lacks ownership reference, i.e., as it is obscured, vaguely functional yet multifarious (the unlimited proliferation of referents), the semantic saturation of the first-person singular deictic is impossible. It can acquire reference through the image in a photo or, on the contrary, it can increase the ambiguity of the reference;
Guru – designates the role of the visionary, who foresees events and whose word is law to the followers, although this law does not always tally with official laws;
Necunoscut Nimeni ("unknown nobody")/*Un oarecare* ("some person")/*The Anonymous* – generics that mark one's getting lost in anonymity, the lack of an individualising status achieved by means of a semantically saturated nickname. *Necunoscut Nimeni* is a binary pseudonym, with both terms taken from the field of individual anonymity: the former is a derivative obtained by means of negative prefixation (the negative prefix subsumes the word under the sphere of anonymity), while the latter term emphasises the bearer's plunging into insignificance, as the individual deliberately misses any chance to be individualised by means of a name. The structure could be read as a first name + family name or vice versa;

Nedumeritu ("the confused one", masculine form) – a generic name for the people that are not convinced by any political party. It designates the position of not understanding the meaning of a message: confusion stems precisely from the lack of knowledge regarding the context that is called to mind;
Ion/Jack – generic pseudonyms, whose sonority is ethnolinguistically bound. *Ion* is a highly localised first name for the Romanians, as is *Jack* for English speakers;
El Pubius Unum (Latin sounding pseudonym, used in view of giving the impression of elite, but coined without making the appropriate phrasal agreement), *Guardian*, *Huliganul* ("the hooligan"), *Miștocaru'* ("the joker") – pseudonyms that connote neutrality;
Intelectual ("intellectual"), *Pensionar* ("pensioner"), *Vânătorul* ("the hunter") – pseudonyms that designate socio-professional categories (transparent appellatives referring to certain social and moral qualities);
Votant PSD ("voter for the Social Democrat Party") – a potential supporter of the Social Democrat Party, who openly expresses his/her political option;

- The semantic field of *justice/the law*:
Justițiarul ("the vigilante") – a pseudonym that can be replaced by an anthroponym (nickname);
Justițiar politic ("political vigilante": narrows down the field of application of the pseudonym to a single domain, i.e., politics) – the locutor takes on the role of a sort of *vox populi*, who fines the deviations of the figures on the scene of politics from political, social and moral norms, as well as other kinds of rules (the figures in question are political representatives of local administrations and those from central bodies – the presidency, government, ministries, national agencies, and others);
Lancea dreptății ("the spear of justice") – the pseudonym designates the instrument by means of which justice is obtained;
Legis (genitive form of the Latin appellative *lex*, *legis* "law") – the determiner of a phrase with an elliptical head, but which can be recovered in a noun (with the definite article) of the kind *Omul* (*legii*) ("the man (of the law)"). The name giver does not find it important to identify the holder of justice, but considers that it is crucial to delineate the referential sphere under which the holder is subsumed and to which s/he belongs: *Legea* ("the law");

Litigii Judiciare ("legal issues") – the pseudonym consists of the very object of an online conversation: legal issues, whose solution is briefly provided in virtual space;

- *Detoponymics*: suggest locutors' appurtenance
- to a geographical area: *Moldo Alex* (Moldova);
- to a hometown: *The băimărean* ("the inhabitant of the town of Baia Mare") (the adjective is a nominalised hybrid, which designates an inhabitant of the town): the change of the morphological-semantic category (from an oikonym it becomes an anthroponym) is achieved by means of the definite article and derivation with the categorial suffix *-ean*;
- to a country: *Canadezul* (Canada) (detoponymisation by means of suffixation);

- Real names of personalities (established cultural, literary and historical names): *Cato Cenzorul* ("Cato the Censor"), *Urmuz* (a Romanian writer);

- Exotic-sounding compounds: *Anakra Kra*, *Bughy Yo*, *Hotti Heels*, *Kym Kym*;

- Puns: *Cretzy Cretzy*, *Elly EllysZa*, *Luky Luk*, *Karmangieru G-Spock Mystique*, *Master Blaster*, *Kosmotrekker*, *Monad Danom*, *Mikky TK*, *Triodeluxe Anian Foresan Doracil*;

- Sophisticated, highly contextualised phrases: *Bengiamin Calmantu Femeilor Unicatu* ("Benjamin, the one and only women's soother");

- *Ad-hoc* pseudonyms: *Acid Photo*, *Cico Giumbix*, *Ciuco Giumbixx*, *Dany Mereu Dany* ("Dany always Dany");

- "Sandwich words": *Ana Partyzana* – a pseudonym that was formed through the insertion of a word inside another, for euphonic reasons (the new phonetic body recovers, on the aural level, as a result of sound play, the initial name: *Ana Blandiana*, a Romanian poet and opposer of the communist regime);

- Portmanteau words: *Jimi Hendrixrock* – a pseudonym obtained through the contamination of a famous proper name, *Jimi Hendrix*, with the appellative that denotes the music genre which the artist approached (*rock*);

- VPs with an *identifiable real referent*:
  Băsescu, ia-ţi securiştii înapoi ("Băsescu, take back your *Securitate* officers"), *Băsesculabalamuc* ("Băsescu to the madhouse") – the opposers of Băsescu's regime reproach the former president for having had connections with the *Securitate* (the Romanian secret police) and the group that formed around him would implicitly pertain to the same oppressive system. The two pseudonyms are directive speech acts, with the latter being an imprecation in which the predicate in the imperative mood is absent (*Du-te la balamuc!* "go to the madhouse"). The madhouse, an institution for the mentally ill, becomes a synonym for prison;
  Mucea LABA'dea chiar el – the graphic play is an artifice by means of which the name is abused. Ambiguity is preserved thanks to the alternation capital letters – small letters, aimed at emphasising the word segment targeted: *LABA'dea* = simple preposition *la* "at" + the proper name *Badea* vs common noun *laba* (*labă*, *labe* "foot, feet", "the part of a leg below the ankle in quadruped animals and human beings"), which has got sexual connotations in slang language (the noun becomes a synonym for the appellative that designates the male sexual organ).

c_3) *Intertextuality devices*: pastiche and parody (the ludic imitation of another text – hierarchical reorganisation: the source text becomes secondary, while the alternative (simulated) text is brought to the foreground). Intertextual pseudonyms challenge readers' *competencies* (idiomatic, expressive, cultural, and others, implying that the sender and receiver share the same background of encyclopaedic knowledge), their *intuition* and *capacity to make associations*. See, for example, *polyphonous pseudonyms*, which result from the process of lexical-semantic embedding of previous utterances (belonging to other locutors):

- Variations of a single structure: on a certain socialising website (Facebook), the user name of a Romanian television host, Mircea Badea, is *Mircea Badea chiar el* ("the genuine Mircea Badea"). Among the names of the users with whom he converses there are *Carici Badea chiar el* ("the genuine Prick Badea"), *Căcat Badea chiar el* ("the genuine Shit Badea"), *Lingăul Badea chiar el* ("the genuine Ass-kisser Badea"), *O labă Badea chiar el* ("the genuine Wanker Badea") and *Pulică Badea chiar el* ("the genuine Dickie

Badea”), all of which are pseudonyms obtained by means of parody. Their correct decoding demands that receivers be firmly secured to the shared *conversational history* (which predetermines the name givers’ choice for such name forms). Through this mechanism, the initial text—*Mircea Badea chiar el*, the quality certificate that functions as a marker of authority—is deconstructed, subjected to partial transformation and rebuilt under a modified form, but one that can be recognised by other users. The intention of abusing the original name is playful, ironic, deprecatory, satirical and moralistic. The resulting construct must preserve “traces” of the old text, so that the language game could be more than “discourse potentiality”.

6. Conclusion

As a result of the analysis performed, one can notice that on the websites considered pseudonyms with sexual and slang connotations are predominant, based on the fact that virtual space is uncensored, norms of social, moral and verbal conduct are annulled (inhibitions disappear) and no longer govern the conversational pact.

The examples investigated overemphasise their pseudonymic quality and point out a role, a certain type of discourse, especially of a mocking, cutting kind. VPs are strategies of accentuating form; in contemporary electronic communication, these name tags are on a par with the content of the messages they precede.

The following main features of the corpus investigated could be delineated:

- Playful creativity is used with the intention to *dissimulate*: locutors most often employ a false name, in view of publicly undermining their interlocutor (by abusing, twisting their real names);
- The comical-satirical effects of the nominator-locutor’s intention to discredit, denigrate the target public figure are deliberate or accidental (cf. also Zafiu 2001: 38–40);
- There is a link between the bearer of a pseudonym and the subject of a discussion: “[…] the link between a pseudonym and a topic is motivated by the association with a certain fact or aspect that is conditioned culturally, historically, politically, and so on, and can be decoded depending on each reader’s “background”” (Răuțu 2007: 448, orig. Romanian, my translation);

- VPs are heterogeneous linguistic creations (involving different idioms); these designating expressions display varied sizes (from a minimal noun phrase to sentences);
- There exists the use of autochthonous or universal symbols and literary motifs, achieved by means of intertextuality;
- The employment of hypocoristics and diminutives is rare (the meaning effect created by a diminutive is the reduction, the removal of the irregularities that language use can produce). When these devices of lexical dynamic occur, they are applied to words with sexual connotations, in slang register;
- Of the onomastic phenomena that underlie the formation of pseudonyms, one can mention the *detoponymisation* of names of regions, cities, and others, and the *anthroponymisation* (*deappellativisiation*) of semantic categories in the field of socio-professional and political terminology, as well as terms in other domains.

References

Cvasnîi Cătănescu, Maria. 2006. *Retorică publicistică: de la paratext la text* [Journalistic rhetoric: from paratext to text]. Bucharest: Editura Universității din București.

Bidu-Vrănceanu, Angela, Cristina Călăraşu, Liliana Ionescu-Ruxăndoiu, Mihaela Mancaş, and Gabriela Pană Dindelegan. 2005. *Dicţionar de ştiinţe ale limbii* (DSL) [Dictionary of language sciences]. Bucharest: Nemira.

Hämäläinen, Lasse. 2013. "User Names in the Online Gaming Community Playforia". In *Names in the Economy: Cultural Prospects*, edited by Paula Sjöblom, Terhi Ainiala, and Ulla Hakala, 214–29. Newcastle upon Tyne: Cambridge Scholars Publishing.

Kerbrat-Orecchioni, Catherine. 2007. "La "cyberpolitesse": formes de l'adresse, ouverture et clôture dans les courriers électroniques" [Cyber-politeness: forms of address, introduction and closing in electronic letters]. *Quaderns de Filologia. Estudis Lingüístics* XII: 35–56.

Martin, Marcienne. 2013. "La vocation plurielle du pseudonyme sur Internet" [The plural vocation of pseudonyms on the Internet]. In *Numele și numirea. Actele Conferinței Internaționale de Onomastică „Numele și numirea"*, ediția a II-a: Onomastica din spațiul public actual, Baia Mare, 9-11 mai 2013 [Name and Naming. Proceedings of the Second International Conference on Onomastics "Name and Naming": Onomastics in Contemporary Public Space, Baia Mare, May

9-11, 2013], edited by Oliviu Felecan, 785–92. Cluj-Napoca: Editura Mega, Editura Argonaut.

Nølke, Henning, Kjersti Fløttum, and Coco Norén. 2004. ScaPoLine. *La théorie scandinave de la polyphonie linguistique* [ScaPoLine. The Scandinavian theory of linguistic polyphony]. Paris: Éditions Kimé.

Parks, Malcolm R., and Kory Floyd. 1996. "Making Friends in Cyberspace". *Journal of Computer-Mediated Communication* 1 (4). Available online: http://onlinelibrary.wiley.com/doi/10.1111/j.1083-6101.1996.tb00176.x/full (accessed April 10, 2015).

Răuțu, Daniela. 2007. "Despre funcția ludică a "pseudonimelor" din presa actuală" [On the ludic function of "pseudonyms" in contemporary mass media]. In Limba română – stadiul actual al cercetării, *Actele celui de-al 6-lea colocviu al catedrei de limba română (29-30 noiembrie 2006)* [The Romanian language – the current state of research. Proceedings of the sixth Colloquium of the Romanian Language Department (29-30 November 2006)], edited by Gabriela Pană Dindelegan, 447–52. Bucharest: Editura Universității din București.

Stommel, Wyke. 2007. "Mein Nick bin ich! Nicknames in a German Forum on Eating Disorders". *Journal of Computer-Mediated Communication* 13 (1): 141–162. Available online: http://onlinelibrary.wiley.com/doi/10.1111/j.1083-6101.2007.00390.x/epdf (accessed April 10, 2015).

Wikipedia. "Cetățeanul turmentat" [The tipsy citizen]. Available online: http://ro.wikipedia.org/wiki/Cetățeanul_turmentat (accessed April 10, 2015).

Zafiu, Rodica. 2001. "Pseudonime" [Pseudonyms]. In *Diversitate stilistică în româna actuală* [Stylistic diversity in contemporary Romanian], 38–40. Bucharest: Editura Universității din București.

Notes

[1] "[…] *nomen falsum* is the name by which an Internet user is known by his/her peers in a given virtual community; it is also defined by significant creative richness. However, all these virtual identities coexist with the one corresponding to the *nomen verum*, the official name established by law. While a proper name institutes a link that connects an individual to one's "self" and the civilian society, a *nomen falsum* marks the relationship between a netizen and the virtual society of the Internet" (Martin 2013: 786, orig. French, my translation).

[2] "Thus, politeness is not absent from the interaction between humans and computers, but it is especially present to a significant extent in the communication between computer operators. Internet users' need for politeness has even allowed

for the establishment of the *netiquette*, a neologism (a portmanteau word resulting from the blending of two English words, "net" and "etiquette") that designates a kind of code of good manners, which the "citizens of the Internet" (the netizens) are supposed to observe if they wish for the communication between them to develop in the most harmonious and effective way possible" (Kerbrat-Orecchioni 2007: 35–36, orig. French, my translation).

[3] "[...] the ability to communicate on the Internet mainly observes the same basic principles as those underlying the ability to communicate by means of traditional written exchanges or in face-to-face oral interaction [...]" (Kerbrat-Orecchioni 2007: 36, orig. French, my translation).

[4] "[...] netiquette also includes rules that are specific to this particular type of communication: recommendations related to the technical constraints of a network (one needs to observe certain norms regarding coding and decoding), warnings against anonymity and its effects of cancelling responsibility ("Do not fabricate your identity") or rules that highlight the fundamentally *hybrid* character of electronic communication. The situation is well known: this type of communication is achieved in written form (it is a kind of decontextualised, distance communication, which develops exclusively via the visual channel and exploits semiotic material that is exclusively graphical); however, the speed of the exchanges creates, to a certain extent, the illusion of face-to-face communication, which obviously serves as a model for the various forms of electronic communication" (Kerbrat-Orecchioni 2007: 37, orig. French, my translation).

[5] "Used in groups that detach themselves from the society or are even in conflict with it, anthroponyms of this kind display two characteristics; on the one hand, they are used to conceal official identity and, on the other, they have the status of autonyms. The Internet underpins the redefinition of a user's identity, which is recorded in a pseudonym that will become his/her digital identity. The onomastics of pseudonyms in virtual society is defined by their creativity, but these autonyms may also fulfil another function besides designation" (Martin 2013: 785–786, orig. French, my translation).

[6] On dealing with user names in an online gaming community, Hämäläinen (2013: 216–217) considers that these onymic forms consist of two parts: an *identifying* one ("the name's lingual part") and a *supplementary* one (which distinguishes a "name's user from other users with the same identifying part").

[7] The discursive intervention that "completes" a certain pseudonym does not have the role of a mere accessory that accompanies the basic utterance (the virtual pseudonym). It clarifies, informs, (un)complicates, stirs receivers' interest and even manipulates them. The rhetorical-linguistic artifice stimulates the perlocutionary component of the speech act in the sense of resorting to inferential processes and the actualisation of an interlocutor's cultural competency.

[8] Anchorage is the "operation of signalling a referent by means of a common/proper noun or a noun phrase" (Cvasnîi Cătănescu 2006: 208, orig. Romanian, my translation).

[9] An expressive-decorative description "is a combination of subjectivised presentation and idealised presentation, formally underpinned by the selective use

of (praising) adjectives and nouns (denoting precious metals); moreover, this type of description facilitates the proliferation of eulogistic figurative language, with a symptomatic predilection for hyperbole, simile, epithet and metaphor" (Cvasnîi Cătănescu 2006: 211, orig. Romanian, my translation).

[10] Paronomasia is "a figure of speech, a wordplay based on the ambiguity that results from the association/substitution of two words that are similar on the sound level (homophonous), but have different meanings, in view of obtaining a comic effect". Paronomasia "is achieved by means of deliberate exploitation of several linguistic phenomena" (homonymy, polysemy, paronymy and antonomasia) (DSL 2005: 90, orig. Romanian, my translation).

WHAT IS "EUROPE" AND "EUROPEAN"?

MARJA KALSKE

Abstract

In 1994 the words 'Europe' and 'European' often indicated something that was 'advanced', 'cultural' or 'fine'. These words usually did not have economic connotations, even though the EU is an economic organisation. The media tried to "sell" the EU to the Finns by using as "fine" connotations as possible. Nowadays the situation has changed. For instance, when current newspaper texts speak about Europe, they refer to the "western world", no matter whether the countries are members of the EU or not.

Background

Obvious things are not always obvious to everyone. This is the *motto* of this text.

In September 1994, when Finland was preparing the referendum on European Union (EU) membership, the words "Europe" and "European" were often seen in newspapers. It is apparent, however, that the words were used—purposefully or unconsciously—to refer to a variety of different concepts. There were differences not only in the connotation of each word but also in the referents. The media discussions about this topic at the time were very animated and emotional, but when reading them, it seems obvious that the authors are referring to entities that are either partly or completely different from each other.

A typical example of such discussions resembled the following[1]:

- We must go to Europe.
- Where (to)? We are in Europe!

Questions

The referendum on European Union membership in 1994 was an important point in history. As a linguist, I was concerned when I noticed that those who took part in this debate were referring to different concepts when using the same words. Therefore, I began to analyse the different meanings and contents of these important words.[2]

The questions I asked during that period were different from the matters that I will analyse in this article, because back then, in 1994, people did not see the economic and political difficulties that arose in the EU later on. For instance, the socio-economic crisis of Greece had not yet happened, and there was not such a large asylum crisis as the current one. The questions I consider are: "What different meanings do the texts refer to when using the terms Europe and European in 1994 as opposed to the year 2015?" and "What does this variety in meaning tell us about the writers' values?"

Methods and materials

The first step in this research was to analyse the contents[3] and meanings[4] of the words in question. When analysing names such as "Europe", it is necessary to discuss the content, not the semantics, of the words.

First, I analysed the Finnish dictionary definitions of these words; as a result, the terms used in this paper are the Finnish equivalents (Eurooppa and eurooppalainen).

The dictionaries used are the following:

A) Nykysuomen sanakirja, 1973
B) Suomen kielen perussanakirja, 1990
C) Kielitoimiston sanakirja, 2006

The contents and meanings of the words 'Europe' and 'European' were also analysed in different contexts in the widely respected Finnish newspaper *Helsingin Sanomat*. I compared the two ways these words were used on two separate occasions: (1) In September 1994, when Finland was preparing the referendum on joining the EU; and (2) in 2015, when the EU encountered various political and economic difficulties, which may have significantly affected the evolution of the words' connotations.

Results

The definitions of the words "Europe" (Finnish: "Eurooppa") and "European" (Finnish:"eurooppalainen") in the Finish dictionaries are as follows:

Dictionary A:
1. European civilization
2. Appreciated: continental, to get to the European level

Dictionary B:
1. European civilization
2. Europeans and Americans

Dictionary C:
1. European civilization
2. Europeans and Americans

It is not clear how these definitions should be interpreted. First of all, it is important to note that the term "European civilization" can have neutral, positive or negative connotations.[5] Also, it is evident that these dictionaries assume Europe is a cultural unity; however, it is still unclear as to whether they are referring to the entire geographical area of Europe, or to a larger area, if we take into account the fact that European civilization has spread to other continents.

In 1973, the dictionary admitted that "European" can also have strong positive connotations, such as in the following phrase: "to get to the European level". Nevertheless, later on this meaning eventually went out of use. It is not clear which area is referred to by this phrase either. On the one hand, it could refer to Europe minus the Nordic countries. On the other hand, it could refer to Western Europe (so not to the Soviet Union), or to the whole continental area from The Urals to the Atlantic Ocean. In political texts of that time, western democratic Europe and eastern, socialist countries were often seen as polar opposites.[6]

In 1990 and 2006, the dictionary definitions refer to European civilization in nearly the same way as in 1973, except they also define the word by using its opposite, American civilization. Since Europe and America are used simply as geographical labels, this definition can be neutral—neither positive nor negative—but the interpretation depends on the cultural and political opinions of the writer and the reader. In Europe, many people think the positive connotation of "European level" in 1973 has now disappeared. Since Europe and America both belong to the same western world, it is remarkable that they are compared to each other instead of being compared to areas with drastically different cultures, such as Asia or Africa.

The words *Europe*, *Eurooppa*, *European* and *eurooppalainen* are used in *Helsingin Sanomat* as follows.

Examples: September 1994.

"Fog is spreading in Europe."

"The European contest for the championship will take place in Prague."

These sentences can easily be understood as references to Europe as a geographical unit, without involving politics or prestige issues.

"The Centre for Social Welfare [in Finland] is already in Europe."

This statement means that the Centre for Social Welfare is similar to the corresponding organizations in the EU, even though Finland was not yet a member of the union. It is also clear in this sentence that to be "in Europe" has a positive connotation.

"The EU referendum is a matter of Finland's place in Europe."

"Will we like to belong to the A-class team of 13–16 countries 8= EU] or to the B-team?"

These statements suggest that the real or better side of Europe is located inside the EU.

"European schooling began in Helsinki, during the autumn of 2008."

"During the first two school years, schools will admit children of the European chemical agency personnel and the school personnel."

In this case, "European" refers to the EU in a neutral way.

Examples: March 2015.

"Professor Bengt Holmström (Massachusetts Institute of Technology) criticized the European universities."

Most likely, this statement refers to Europe geographically, not only to the EU. However, "European universities" could include the Russian universities as well, or else only the universities in Western Europe.

"The political map of Europe is spreading."

"Peculiar political friendships have appeared in Europe."

In these examples, "Europe" refers to the EU in particular. They were written in a time of financial crisis in Greece, during which the members of the EU had opposing opinions concerning a plan for dealing with the problem.

Examples December 2015:

"In the European asylum seeker crisis, a ship patrol of Finnish marine solders participated in the EU crises control operation."

Again, Europe refers to the EU but the statement is neutral, not positive as it was in 1994.

"The results of the conflicts are also seen in Europe – bombs in Paris and asylum seekers in Tornio [Finland].

The European refugee crisis has reached a new level."

In these examples, "Europe" refers to the western part of geographical Europe. In fact, they do not refer to the EU alone, but rather to the entire western part of the continent. The connotations here are rather neutral.

Conclusions

In 1973, the dictionary's definition of "European" put Europe in a very positive, even superior, light. However, it remains unclear which part of Europe it referred to geographically. Consequently, this definition could be viewed as a reference to either Western Europe or Eastern Europe—including the Soviet Union—or both.

In 1994 "Europe" and "European" often meant something "advanced" or "fine". However, during that period, these words were associated not with geographical Europe, but with the EU. The authors of these texts tried to sell the EU to the Finns by using positive connotations. Today, in 2015, however, there is nothing similar to be found: the Europe-euphoria has disappeared. Currently, the name "Europe" can refer to the entire geographical area of Europe, to the western part of the continent alone or to the EU. Furthermore, the name "EU" no longer has any specific positive connotations, but it is used in a neutral way. Due to various recent crises that occurred within the EU and throughout the entire continent of Europe, EU euphoria has disappeared—and perhaps the European cultural arrogance along with it.

References

Bertills, Yvonne 2003. *Beyond identification: proper names in children's literature*. Åbo.'

Helsingin Sanomat. 1994, 2015. Helsinki.

Jungar, Sune. 1986. *Neuvostoliitto—supervalta. Venäjän ja Neuvostoliiton historia*. Heikki Kirkinen et al. Helsinki.

Kalske, Marja. 2005. *Suomessa syntyneiden hevosten nimistö*. Turku.

—. 2008. "Eurooppa ja eurooppalaisuus". *Specimena Fennica*. Tomus XIV, Savariae: 101–111.

Karlsson, Fred 1976. *Johdatusta yleiseen kielitieteeseen*. Helsinki.

—. 2003. *Yleinen kielitiede*. Uudistettu laitos. Helsinki.

Kielitoimiston sanakirja 1. 2006. Ed. Eija-Riitta Grönros et al. Jyväskylä.

Kiviniemi, Eero, and Pitkänen, Riitta, and Zilliacus, Kurt. 1974. *Nimistöntutkimuksen terminologia. Terminologin inom namnforskningen*. Helsinki.

Lyons, John 1977. *Semantics*. Cambridge.

Maliniemi, Aarno 1933. *Henkilönnimet esihistoriallisena ja katolisena aikana*. (46-57). Etunimikirja. 1947 Red. Hannes Teppo and Kustaa Vilkun. Helsinki.

Mill, John Stuart 1906. *A System of Logic: ratiocinative and inclusive: beeing a connected view of the principles of evidence and the methods of scientific investigation*. London, New York and Bombay.

Nykysuomen sanakirja1. 1973. Ed. Matti Sadeniemi et al. Porvoo.

Ogden, C[harles] K[ay] – Richards, I[vor] A[rmstrong] 1966. *The Meaning of Meaning. A Study of the Science of Symbolism* by C. K. Ogden and I. A. Richards with Supplementary Essays by B. Malinowski and F. G. Crookshank. 10. Edition. London..

Notes

[1] Kalske 2015.

[2] Kalske 2008.

[3] Mill 1906, 20-21; Maliniemi 1933, 535; Kiviniemi-Pitkänen-Zilliacus 1974, 29,52; 45, 50-51; Karlsson 1976, 229-230; Lyons 1977, 219-221; Kalske 2005, 40.

[4] Ogden-Richards 1966, 9-13; Lyons 1977, 219, Karlsson 2003, 205; Kalske 2005, 40-41.

[5] Bertils 2003, 31-32; Kalske 2005, 40 – 41.

[6] Jungar 1986, 445-448, 462-464.

"FOLLOWING IN THE FOOTSTEPS OF NAMES": COMMERCIAL ERGONYMIA IN LINGUISTIC LANDSCAPE OF THE BALTIC COUNTRIES

SOLVITA POŠEIKO

Abstract

The institutions' and companies' names, or ergonyms, that create the commercial ergonymia of public space in the linguistic landscape of 9 cities of the Baltic countries are explored in the article. Therefore, it is a significant part of an onomastic landscape (in a narrow sense), linguistic landscape, and urban landscape (in a broader sense). The author focuses on the use of language in the name signs, opinion of the local population regarding the language situation in ergonymia and the linguistic landscape in general. To better understand the functionality of the name signs and the information provided by them, the perception and interpretation of the particular ergonyms are analysed.

Introduction

The title of the article is based on a reference to James Anderson's TV series "Murder, she wrote", i.e., from a free translation of this title into the Latvian language—"Following the footsteps of crime". Each episode of the TV show begins with a depiction of a mysterious crime; then the main protagonist—a teacher and a writer Jessica Fletcher absolutely accidentally encounters some aspect of the crime, and gets involved in the investigation and, usually, is the one who solves the case. Often, at the end of an episode, it turns out that the crime is typically committed by a person or group of people, though, in fact, the episode is made up of a sum of various routines and situations, and the result of investigation may surprise even the most attentive spectator.

Why is this research linked to the TV series, and how can the study of commercial names, or ergonyms, be compared with detective stories? There are two main reasons for such a comparison. First of all, it is a wish to put on the hat of a detective and figure out what the names of companies of the Baltic countries reveal about the language situation. Name signs in a city is one of the types of the linguistic landscape language signs; there are relatively more name signs rather than posters or advertisements in the city (see further in the text), and they are located in different places and are presented in different formats. They have a significant role in formation of information space and language situation. On the one hand, they reveal linguistic practices and the trends in the commercial nominations; on the other hand, they impact the written language tradition and the cultural processes. Thus, raising the issue is closely related both with the linguistic and cultural aspects of the commercial names, and an economic perspective of ergonyms and languages used. Secondly, it is of no less importance how the name signs are perceived and interpreted by the sociolinguistic participants: business owners and employees, passers-by and respondents to the associated experiment who have no social experience of the name displayed, of the name that is unknown. The informative potential of each commercial name with its concentration of ideas, language tools, and symbols should be highlighted; so the reader could decode it like a detective story, which is created in the postmodern tradition, by applying the theoretical principles of post-structuralism (i.e., playing with meanings of individual elements and words, parts of text, and themes in various contexts and believing that, in this way, it is possible to construct a conceptual meaning), (Lyotard 1984, Iļjin [Ильин] 1996, Bart [Барт] 2001, Kolmane 2013). The idea encoded in the text of the name by its author may significantly differ from the reader's interpretation that is influenced by language skills, socio-cultural knowledge, and experience.

Exploration of these two issues (ergonymia as the result of a particular language policy and management, and perception and interpretation of the name signs) comprises the research part of the article providing a sociolinguistic review of the pool of commercial names, or ergonymia as a significant element of the onomastic landscape (in a narrow sense) and the linguistic landscape (in a broader sense) in the Baltic countries.

Methodological and theoretical framework

Latvia, Lithuania and Estonia are multilingual and multicultural countries that are located in an adjoining geographical space in the Baltic Sea region. All three share a similar history during the last century and relatively similar ethno-demographic situations (especially Latvia and Estonia), which have also determined different manifestations of language contacts. Immediately after the restoration of independence of the Baltic countries at the end of the 20th century, a number of sociolinguistic developments of vital importance occurred: a shift in language hierarchies (with titular languages taking the place of Russian) supported by state language laws and various types of regulatory documents, and the gradual introduction into linguistic practice in various areas of life (e.g., administration, education, culture), the re-evaluation of Russian-speaking linguistic self-sufficiency and linguistic attitudes towards Baltic titular languages, and language market expansion to a free, Western-oriented economy.

Linguistic landscape research was carried out during a period from 2008 through 2014, and developed in the doctoral thesis "Language and its functionality in the urban public sphere: Linguistic landscape of the Baltic States". Nine cities are important Baltic regional centres, but capital cities, were not selected as objects of research: Daugavpils, Valmiera, Ventspils (Latvia); Alytus, Druskininkai, Visaginas (Lithuania); Narva, Pärnu, Viljandi (Estonia). The nations' capitals were deliberately not chosen because they have the capital status as a country's international calling card—oriented more towards tourists and international communication—which does not accurately reflect the true situation in the country at large (Gorter 2006). In turn, language use in the public space of regional cities more precisely reveals local context. The following criteria were considered when selecting the cities: (1) Ethnic, cultural and linguistic uniformity (Valmiera, Viljandi and Alytus); (2) Russians and the Russian-speaking population as a local majority (Daugavpils, Narva and Visaginas); (3) Long-standing and stable traditions of tourism (Ventspils, Pärnu and Druskininkai).

The research uses the linguistic landscape approach (Gorter 2006, Backhaus 2007, Gorter, Shohamy 2009, Hélot, Barni, Jansens, Bagna 2012, Gorter, Marten, Van Mensel 2012) for data acquisition, analysis and interpretation, which combines quantitative (photography of public information) and qualitative data collection techniques (semi-structured interviews with company/institution directors or employees, random passers-by) with data analysis and interpretation, which is also synthesized with other theories (e.g., multilingualism, language economy, gender studies, etc.). Language sign analysis according to sociolinguistic criteria defined in linguistic landscape research (e.g., place, authorship, text genre, language use, hierarchy, translation method) and subsequent correlation investigation is carried out using the statistical programs *Microsoft Office Excel* and *SPSS*. In turn, an associative experiment has been carried out, in order to reveal the most common models of ergonym interpretation, and the semantic components of individual words or symbols (Kiss, Armstrong, Milroy, Piper 1973).

Sources for the research consisted of 7,347 language signs–written messages in public spaces, demonstrating completeness of text, features of a defined text genre, objectives and functions, which potentially can be read by anyone and from which information can be used for any purpose. Additionally, 95 partly structured interviews with employees of tourist information centres (TIC), various establishments and companies, and random pedestrians; 44 email correspondences with TIC, employees of state establishments and private companies; and 38 tables were acquired as a result of an associated experiment about perception and interpretation of ergonyms for data analysis and interpretation.

The term *ergonym* is formed by a combination of the Greek word meaning 'work, trade' and the word meaning 'name, title'. In Latvian linguistics, the term is defined as a "proper noun that designates a union of people that is created for a specific purpose: an organization, company, institution, etc." (Skujiņa 2007: 109). In Russian linguistics, where a notable and stable tradition of ergonyms has been established, the term *ergonym* is defined in a similar way, as a "proper noun that designates different unions of people: institutions, organizations, associations, corporations, societies that are united by a specific direction of activity and certain type of activities" (Podolskaya [Подольская] 1988: 151). Even nowadays, Russian linguists define ergonyms as names that indicate the functional sphere of an institution or company (shop, firm, market, sports centre, cinema etc.) and a union of people formed for the purpose of certain action" (Kryukova [Крюкова] 2004, Yemelyanova [Емельянова] 2007, Turayeva [Тураева] 2012, Lozovoy, Nazvanova [Лозовой, Названова] 2013). In German scientific literature, the term is used to refer not only to industrial units, companies and institutions (governmental, cultural, educational) or unions of individuals, but also to names of goods and services (e.g., groceries, clothes and cars), names of art pieces, TV and radio shows, press publications, best-sellers, children toys, and the names of military objects (Bauer 1985, Eckkrammer, Thaler 2013). However, scientific publications in English most often pay attention to separate types of companies, showing word combinations, for example, in the names of cafés, shops, hair salons etc.—generally, the general term is more rarely used. In single discussions about commercial ergonyms, the term *business name* is used instead.

When evaluating ergonym research and extraction methods and approaches as well as research issues, a number of theoretical and methodological trends can be observed: 1. Research material is excerpted from the official registry of state institutions and companies, phonebooks, and electronic databases. Linguistic landscape approach as a data acquisition method is used comparatively rarely—it only has been directly declared in a small number of studies in the past few years (Dimova 2007, Edelman 2009, Tan 2011, Sjöblom 2013, Bergien 2013, Hasanova 2014). 2. Studies are dominated by the synchronic approach; only a few studies provide characterization of changes in ergonyms under the influence of culturohistorical and political conditions (Voroshilova [Ворошилова] 2007, Amirova [Амирова] 2011, Pošeiko 2015a, b). 3. The associative experiment is often used together in conjunction with ergonym content analysis, component analysis and analysis of structural semiotics, in order to elucidate particularities of ergonym perception and types of associations. Application of the psycholinguistic approach is quite common, with the purpose of characterizing the intentions (motivation, ideas and purpose) of the sender (nominator), intention (understanding and interpretation) between the ergonym and the addressee (recipient), strategies of psychological manipulation, as well as socio-pragmatic role (Samsonova, Shchitova [Самсонова, Щитова] 2012, Shcherbakova [Щербакова] 2009). 4. Ergonyms are mainly analyzed in the creation and semantic aspects of structural grammatical models, particularly focusing on the orthographical, morphological and lexical levels, and forming lexical semantic groups and conceptual models. The semiotic aspect of the signboard analysis is also important, focusing on verbal and non-verbal text attitudes, and in geosemiotics—as well as correlations between space, the sign, and the information contained therein (e.g., Lou 2007). In the context of their formation, issues such as figurative language (metaphors and metonymies, occasionalisms), linguistic creativity and wordplay are often studied, providing characterization of separate and conspicuous graphic elements, original language and paralinguistic tool utilization (e.g., Butakova [Бутакова] 2013, Frey 2008, Sadykova [Садыкова] 2012, Shebalov [Шебалов] 2004, Norman [Норман] 2006, Pietarinen 2000). 5. Issues of identity and gender are also brought to attention in different studies (Fernández 2009, Prokudina 2011, Pošeiko 2014a, b), focusing on the linguocultural aspect of ergonyms (e.g., the colour of the thematic group in the lexicon of ergonyms of Perm (Russia)—Bogacheva 2011) and regional aspects (e.g., view of businesses in opposition international local in correlation with their names–Bergien 2013). Sociolinguistic issues are also discussed, emphasizing application characteristics of a foreign language element (often one language—for example Italian or English) and frequency in ergonyms (e.g., Friedrich 2002, Schlick 2002, Khosravizadeh, Sanjareh 2011). 7. The role of the commercial discourse in the development of onomastic studies is demonstrated by the special issue of the onomastics journal *Onoma* (Vol. 43, 2008), dedicated to commercial ergonyms, that contains interdisciplinary articles on innovations, trends and tendencies in strategies of ergonym formation (Bergien, Kremer, Zilg 2008: 7–23), plagiarism (Leblanc 2008: 73–90), usage of pseudo-languages (Rieger 2008: 149–175) and multimodality (unification of linguistic, acoustic, and visual elements; name geometry, colours–Sjöblom 2008: 351–380), formation characteristics of catering company and grocery product names (Ronneberger-Sibold 2008: 221–250) publicity in the context of advertisement and economic profit. The twofold nature (linguistic and economic) of ergonyms is also emphasized in other individual studies that analyze cooperation between linguistic and marketing tools in ergonyms (Cotticelli Kurras, Trovato, Vigolo 2012, Sadykova [Садыкова] 2012).

Ergonymia of the Baltic countries: general data analysis

In the Baltic countries, ergonyms comprise a significant part of the written public information; as independent textual units, in total, 2242 name signs, or 30.5% of all language signs, are found. It is the largest group of the language signs in the linguistic landscape of the Baltic countries. To have a general picture, it can be compared with other language signs. 23% of the language signs are texts providing information about the institution's or company's work organization and news, for example, the outdoor signs displaying business hours and the notices informing about discounts or new arrivals; 4% of the units are street signboards. The highest percentage of the name signs is fixed in Alytus (37%), the least—in Pärnu (11%).

In Druskininkai, 64 outdoor advertising informative texts provided by hotels have been detected; 30 of them are hotel name signs; this means that tourism is one of the main business activities and economic development directions in the town. In the interviews, the same was confirmed by the staff of the hotels and by the employees of the Tourism Information Centre (TIC); they emphasise that the visitors from the neighbouring countries (Latvia, Estonia, Russia, Poland, and Belarus) often come to rest and to have a medical treatment in the hotels, health resorts, and water amusement parks. On the other hand, in Daugavpils, more than in other selected cities, the signs of educational institutions were identified, that is, 17 language signs, including 9 name signs, revealing that the city offers a wide range of educational opportunities of different levels and interests, which allows us to recognize the city as an important educational centre.

Above all, commercial ergonyms comprise 91% of all names. This shows that the commercial sector has an important role in shaping the language environment and that the linguistic appearance of ergonyms, although regulated by the State Language Law, is relatively less restrictive due to the permitted exceptions.

It is important to consider whether the institution/company is independent or belongs to a regional, national or international business network. This may affect the linguistic environment of the city, which reflects the relationship between the language policy at the microscopic level to the particular institution/company only, or to a number of organizations on a narrower or broader scale. It may also shed light on another issue: namely, if and how the international companies adapt the outdoor advertising information to the local language environment.

Likewise, the independence of the institutions and companies or their belonging to an international group reveal the market trends and provides information regarding two questions: how well developed the local business is and how interesting each city seems to the international corporations in order to expand the operational area of their business.

In the cities selected for the study, the names of local institutions/companies dominate—altogether 39% of the excerpted ergonyms. They are unique in the local environment, pointing to the uniqueness of these individual institutions and local companies in the context of the Baltic countries. For example, in Viljandi, 65% units of the excerpted 246 name signs are ergonyms of the local institutions and businesses, in Visaginas—55% of 130 name signs, in Daugavpils—52% of 546 name signs. Fewer (22 %) are state-level chain company ergonyms (e.g., the chain store *LaTS* 'abbreviation–**La**tvian **T**rade **S**ociety' in Latvia, *Lietuvos spauda* 'Lithuanian Press', *Säästuoptika* 'Discount Optics' in Estonia, etc.). Ergonyms of international chains and institutions are noted in only 16% of cases (e.g., branches of the bank *Swedbank* 'Bank of Sweden', gas station *Statoil*, sporting goods shop *Sportland*, etc.). Larger percentages of international companies' ergonyms are observed in Narva and Valmiera, i.e., 19% of the registered name signs, the least in Alytus—11% of the cases. It shows that the impact of external economics on the local language environment is insignificant. It also must be noted that international companies comparatively often respect the language environment of the branch location; in the Baltic countries, titular language use can be observed in a total of 48% of the name signs of international companies (often in Lithuania—63%, more rarely in Estonia—33%).

Taking into account the socio-linguistic functions of language and the database of the Baltic linguistic landscape, the ergonyms are classified into 19 groups according to the institution's and the companies' operational area (See: Table 1). It should be emphasized that only commercial names without considering the public institutions' ergonyms, unless these institutions provide the services for a charge, are explored in the article.

Sociolinguistic domains	**Establishments**
Education	General school, interest education centre, driving school
Culture	Culture centre, museum, cinema, theater, art gallery
Religion	Church
Tourism	TIC, tourism travel agency
Catering	Café, restaurant, pizzeria, confectionery
Accommodation	Hotel, hostel, guest house
Entertainment	Club, bar, casino, bowling
Beauty	Hairdresser, solarium, beauty salon
Sports	Fitness centre, sports hall, stadium, skating rink
Healthcare	Medical practice, dental clinic, pharmacy, optics, hospital
Manufacturing	Bakery, brewery, building material factory
Communication	Television, radio, press, mobile networks, post
Traffic	Bus station, train station, taxi office
Government, administration	City council, board of education, development planning unit
Finance	Bank, credit institution, pawn shop
Security	Security, fire-fighting and rescue service, police station, insurance company
Law	Law firm, notary, court
Trade	Various shops, kiosk, supermarket, wholesaler
Household services	Cobbler, locksmith, electronics repair shop, dry cleaning, sewing workshop

Table 1. Ergonyms groups of sociolinguistic domains.

The suggested classification of groups is developed, bearing in mind that the ergonyms of particular groups (e.g., health (pharmacy), beauty care (hairdressing), communications (post office)) are also applicable to the trade as denotations named by those which are related to the supply and sales of goods. Also, several store types are related to the ergonyms of the other groups, like a cosmetics store—with beauty care, a book store—with culture and education, a honey shop—with health care, and so on. The trade sector as a specific group is separated for two reasons. The first, because the scheme of the language signs analysis requires identification of individual sub-groups of stores (e.g., electronics, flower shop, furniture, and other stores), which allows a differentiated view on the creation and usage trends of various kinds of ergonyms in a trading area. The second reason is a dual function of other groups of institutions/enterprises; trade is only one of their activities. For example, the basic function of a pawnshop is to offer pledged loans, but it is also possible to purchase items that are not redeemed in the contracted time (trading function).

Name signs of commercial enterprises (44 %) are dominant in the research area that indicates the importance of commerce in the Baltic countries. Most of these commercial enterprise names consist of individual shop ergonyms (860, including clothes (26%), groceries (8%), households (8%), electricals (6%), cosmetics (4%), jewellery and costume jewellery (4%) stores) followed by catering company names, beauty parlor, health care and finance company ergonyms, and lastly, names of state/municipal and administration institutions. Finally, the name signs of educational, cultural, and religious institutions comprise only 5% of all language signs, which could be explained by the fact that only a few educational institutions (especially pre-school and general secondary education institutions) are located in the city centre. There is mostly just one culture house, a couple of museums and exhibition halls in the city in contrast to the location frequency of banking institutions or coffee shops. Also, it has to be noted that the socio-economic aspect is different in each city, so, for example, in Daugavpils, there are 11 name signs of hairdressing salons, but there is only one such ergonym in Viljandi. However, in Viljandi, there are the most pharmacy' ergonyms (13), in comparison to only 2 in Visaginas.

Typically, linguistic methods of ergonym creation in the Baltic States are: (1) institution and business type and the use of nomenclature words indicating products or services in the proper noun function, separately or together with symbolic names (that is, direct and mixed name establishment — "Audumi" 'Textile fabrics' in Ventspils, "Kompiuterių taisykla" 'Computer repair' in Alytus, "SPA Day Beaty Salon Mona Liza" in Pärnu); (2) transnominization (ergonyms based mostly on place names and anthroponyms—hotel “Druskininkai”, night club “Holivuda” ‘Hollywood’ in Ventspils, dress shop “Dorina” in Narva, men hairdresser “Kristaps” Valmiera). Names that are out of the ordinary are symbolic ergonyms, based on connotative precedent sources—cultural history, literature, and mythology (e.g., hotel “Senasis Paštas” ‘The old Post’ and “Dainava” ‘Name of Lithuanian cultural and historical region’ in Druskininkai, kafé, bar “Amrita” ‘Drink of Good immortality (from Sanskrit)’ in Viljandi). Particular symbolic names are found only in 266 signboards (e.g., optics “Pelėda” ‘Owl’ in Druskininkai, shop “Liepa” ‘Linden’ in Alytus, bar “Play in” in Pärnu, restaurant “Pasaules brīnumi” ‘World wonders’ in Daugavpils); (3) the tolerance of spelling, punctuation and style errors (e.g., stylistically inaccurate compound word creation, failure to separate equal parts of a sentence with a comma); (4) the use of diminutives and reference to the target audience (e.g., shop and kafé “Pie Anniņas” ‘To little Anna’ in Daugavpils, sewing-shop “Modīte” ‘Small Fashion’, gift shop „Kurzemīte” ‘Small Kurzeme (one of the Latvian region)’ in Ventspils, striptease bar “Gentelmen’s club’ in Viljandi, shop “Rotaļlietas bērniem” ‘Toys for kids’ in Valmiera). There are three children goods store ergonyms “ELEFANTiK” ‘little elephant’ identified in Narva depicting Russian language morpheme (likewise as *кот—котик* ‘cat—kitten’).

Especially typical of name sign visual design techniques are the capitalized initial letters throughout the text, stylization of certain letters or words and direct image use in the verbal information.

To perform sociolinguistic analysis of ergonyms, the content analysis of the laws and regulations was conducted to clarify the procedures for the official written language usage in the name signs in public spaces (as it should be, prescriptive norm), and then it was compared with the real situation in the linguistic landscape of the Baltic countries (as it is, descriptive analysis).

Ergonym formation in regulative normative documents in the Baltic countries

In Article 18 of the State Language Law of Latvia adopted in 1999, it is stipulated that “The names of institutions, public organisations, undertakings (companies) founded in the Republic of Latvia shall be created and use thereof shall be in the official language.” In turn, Article 21 stipulates that “If a foreign language is used concurrently with the official language, the text in the official language shall be placed in primary position, and it may not, in its form or contents, be smaller or narrower than the text in the foreign language" (http://likumi.lv//doc.php ?id=14740, 19.12.2015.). Articles 9 and 10 of the Cabinet Regulations No. 294 "Regulations on the creation and use of names of institutions, public organizations, enterprises (or commercial entities) and name of events" provide an amendment to the State Language Law indicating that "in symbolic names, newly created words that fit into the system of sounds and forms of Latvian language, as well as the words or proverbs of the classical languages that have traditionally been used in many cultures, also can be used." In turn, Article 11 of the Regulations provides that "in writing of names of private organizations and enterprises (commercial entities), [...] only letters of Latvian or Latin alphabet can be used. Words and expressions offending public morals cannot be used in names." (http://likumi.lv/doc.php?id=10130, 20.12.2015.).

Paragraph 16 of Article 7 ("Names") of the State Language Law adopted in Lithuania in 1995, says that "Names of all enterprises, establishments and organizations, functioning in the Republic of Lithuania shall be formed adhering to the norms of the Lithuanian language and the resolutions of the State Commission of the Lithuanian Language." In Paragraph 18: "Names of organizations of ethnic communities, their informational signs may be rendered in other languages along with the state language. The format of signs in other languages cannot be larger than that of signs in the state language." (http://www3.lrs.lt/pls/inter/ www_tv.show?id=91765,6953, 30, 21.12.2015.).

In Estonia, several sections of the State Language Law adopted in 1995 are related to the linguistic depiction of ergonyms. In the context of linguistic landscape, the most important is Paragraph 16 of Article 4 "Language of information" providing that (1) Signs, signposts, business type names and outdoor advertisements, including outdoor advertising, installed in a public place with the purpose of political campaigning, and the notices of a legal person shall be in Estonian. (2) The translation of the text into a foreign language may be added to public signs, signposts, business type name and outdoor advertisements; thereby the text in Estonian shall be in the forefront and shall not be less observable than the text in a foreign language. (3) Upon using a brand as a sign of the place of business of a person or in outdoor advertising the part of a brand in a foreign language that includes essential information about the place of business and goods or service offered shall be presented also in Estonian, without damaging the distinctiveness of the brand. In turn, Paragraph 20 stipulates that "The international form of the Estonian business names [...] in the Latin alphabet shall be identical to the form used in Estonia. Names written in a language that uses another alphabet the transcription rules established on the basis of the Names Act shall be applied" (https://www.riigiteataja.ee/en/eli/ee/Riigikogu/act/506112013016/consolide, 21.12.2015.).

Generally, after evaluating state language laws, as well as commercial laws, it has been observed that normative documents regulating language use in the Baltic States stipulate national language and Latin alphabet use, and if companies are used, information in the national language must be placed in a central location, and must not be noticeably less prominent due to smaller letters or a different font. In the private sphere neologisms are allowed to be created according to the sounds and system of the state language, but no insults or hate speech are allowed.

The language situation in ergonymia of the Baltic countries

In name signs in the Baltic countries, 14 different languages have been detected in all. Apart from the titular languages (i.e., Latvian, Lithuanian, Estonian), English and Russian languages (see further), as well as Latin (1.4%), Italian (0.8%), German (0.8%), French (0.5%), and Swedish (0.4%) language have been detected. However, the frequency of use of these individual languages in commercial signboards should be considered rather as an exception, not a trend. It is interesting that the use of the Latin language is primarily found in the signboards of pharmacies and law firms which suggests that the graduates of medical and legal science education programs as well as the practitioners in the field have a basic knowledge of Latin, and so it can be used in the company's name. As an example from another socio-linguistic area, the translation bureau *Exlibris* 'Bookplate' in Alytus could be mentioned.

Perhaps the language policy and text minimalism characterising name signs lead to monolingual name signs dominating in Baltic countries, 81% of the cases altogether. When comparing ergonymia at the country level, it is evident that situations in Latvia and Lithuania are similar regarding the number of monolingual name signs (in both countries—86%), less frequently in Estonia—70% of the cases. After analysing monolingual ergonyms at the city level, it can be observed that monolingual ergonyms are most often used in Valmiera (92% of all name signs registered), in Alytus and Visaginas (in both cities—90%), the least frequent in Narva (60%) and Druskininkai (70%) (See: Table 2).

City	1 language	2 languages	3 or more languages
Daugavpils	85	14	0.9
Valmiera	92	8	-
Ventspils	83	16	0.5
Pärnu	84	16	-
Narva	60	34	3.4
Viljandi	87	12	0.4
Alytus	90	9	0.4
Druskininkai	70	26	4
Visaginas	90	9	-

Table 2. Percentage of ergonyms (%) according to number of languages used.

However, quite often ergonyms are written in two languages—17% of the cases altogether. A particular example is Narva, where bilingual name signs comprise more than 1/3 of all ergonyms registered there. In Narva, typical language combinations observed in the bilingual name signs are: Estonian and Russian (32%); English and Estonian (19%); Estonian and English (12%); Russian and Estonian (8%); German and Estonian (6%); Latin and English (3%). As shown by statistics, in 33% of the bilingual name signs, titular language is used in the second position, mainly after text in English.

In other cities, in general, there is a tendency to locate bilingual ergonyms more frequently in the cities where tourism has a significant role in the city's economic development, especially in Druskininkai and in Pärnu, where tourism has established traditions, as well as in Ventspils (See also: Marten, Lazdiņa, Pošeiko, Murinska 2012: 199–308), hence there is an increased need for information in additional languages, including in ergonyms, indicating, for example, category of institutions and companies.

More than two languages are found in about 2% of cases; most often the multilingual name signs are found in Druskininkai (4%) and Narva (3.4%). As an example, a signboard in Druskininkai can be mentioned, where the name of the company and the offered service—shoe repair—is provided in 4 languages: Lithuanian, Polish, English, and Russian. In Viljandi, a trilingual signboard of the antiquity shop was found providing information in Estonian, English, and Russian. In Narva, the sequence of languages in a trilingual signboard of the currency exchange office is as follows: Estonian, Russian, and English, which indicates a different language hierarchy, adapted to the local environment and its socio-linguistic situation.

Analysis of the information division in the name signs, where more than one language is used, shows that bilingual and multilingual ergonyms with the same amount of information in all the languages are observed in the linguistic landscape as often as ergonyms with differing amounts of information in each language (in both cases—50%). It is important to highlight the fact that the translation into another language (or languages) is not offered in more than half of the cases, i.e., 54% of the name signs. Information contained in the name sign and provided in other languages is translated literally (directly) in 17% of ergonyms, but partial translation into other languages is used in 14% of the name signs. It shows that the information of the name signs is separated into two or more languages in a way, on the one hand, trying to expand the audience and attract a larger number of customers, as well as showing respect to different groups of language users, on the other hand, not encouraging a language learning and use, especially in the cities where the country's basic ethnos is a minority (Estonians in Narva and Latvians in Daugavpils).

Evaluation of language signs regarding sociolinguistic functions shows the following tendencies: (1) translation of nomenclature units in the signs regarding financial services is given in the language of the title nation (e.g., *Hansabanka* in Latvia, *Hansapank* in Estonia, *Hansabankas* in Lithuania); (2) signs from health and sports sectors often feature terms in foreign languages; (3) beauty parlor signs show a wide application of visual images and Romance languages (French, Spanish, Latin and Italian), phrases in English and a change in language code at the textual, sentence-, and verbal level; (4) a wide application of the English language is observed in the information of the entertainment sector (gambling halls, casino and night club language signs), English is used in name signs and signs displaying opening hours, as well as in advertisements, presenting what the specific company offers for purchase (e.g., drinks, erotic shows) or to win (grand prizes).

Ergonyms in Russian are mainly used in Narva, in 13% of all cases, indicating their informative function for the Russian-speaking population (e.g., "Одежды" 'Clothes', "Ремонт обуви" 'Cobbler', "Магазин" 'Store'). Name signs in Russian are also characterized by simplicity of visual design (without visual images and variations in formation), which is not highlighted in the linguistic landscape. Evaluating the usage of other foreign languages indicates the following: (1) the German language is more common in signs of individual shops and construction companies in

Narva (44 % of all language signs where German is used); (2) the Latin language is more common in name signs of shops (clothes, household articles, construction goods), pharmacies and insurance companies in Narva, Viljandi and Daugavpils; (3) the Italian language is most frequently featured in ergonyms of clothing and shoe stores, children and gift shops, cafes and hair salons in Daugavpils and Narva; (4) the French language is more frequently used in name signs of cosmetics and bath stores as well as beauty parlors in Ventspils and Narva; (5) the Polish language is most common to the Druskininkai public space, mainly in language signs of hotels and catering companies, but also in shoe store language signs, church messages, posters and hair saloon language signs; (6) the Spanish language is mainly used in language signs of shoe and clothing stores; (7) the Swedish language is most common in "SEB" bank signs in Valmiera, Daugavpils and Narva, where it is featured as the full name of the abbreviation. In short, linguistic diversity can be observed in name signs and product or service advertisements from international companies (demonstrative sign use) to local businesses.

Finally, the question of the combination of letters and transliteration, which makes it difficult to determine the language, shall be explored. Examples include the supermarket chain "Rimi" and insurance company "Aviva" in Alytus, where choice of the language is not clear, though the sign contains the use of the Latin alphabet. In names of the store "Romaška" 'Chamomile' (Daugavpils), the beauty salon "Metšta" 'Dream', and the bar "Priboi baar" 'Coast waves bar' in Narva Russian words depicted with Latin alphabet letters are used. These examples raise the question of what is the primary way to identify the language—the content or the form?

Respondents' "testimonies" about language usage

In interviews with the employees of commercial companies, the question that was most frequently asked was about the name of the company and the language of choice for the name of the company. The most frequent response to the first question was: "I do not know why the company has this name", additionally explaining that the respondent is just an employee and that has been the owner's choice. For example, the excerpt of the interview with the employee of the store *Laretta* in Rezekne in 2007 (I—interviewer, R—respondent):

> I: "Do you know why the store has the name *Laretta*, what does it mean?"
> R: "I cannot answer this question, it belongs to the owner, and I don't know."

> I: "But what associations do you have? Perhaps that is a girl's name, because it is not *Loreta*, but *Laretta*? And with two *t's*?"
> R: "Mhm, sounds good, attractive. Don't know, girl's."

In this case, it is evident that the employee distances herself from the responsibility to build and maintain the company's public image, her pragmatic goal (to work in the company) is stronger than her feeling of affiliation to the company. Hence, there is no desire to go into (to find out and pass on information about the company, including written information about the outdoor visual design).

Overall in the cities of the Baltic countries, there are four issues that are raised regarding the use of languages in the commercial name signs: (1) compulsory use of the state language; (2) the symbolic meaning of the state language and the function of providing cultural and historical information; (3) the need for the English language; (4) other languages.

The most popular belief is that each ergonym should be in the state language, as it is provided by the state language law; a desire to highlight the important cultural, historical, or geographical facts or concepts, and the company's property rights in this way is subordinated to the law. For example, the employee of the restaurant "Rātes Vārti" 'The Town Hall Gates' (Valmiera) in 2013 explained that

> the name is selected in the way the inhabitants of the city do not forget history, but other visitors learn new information about the city, raise their interest [...] I believe there was no doubt about the choice of language, because Valmiera is a Latvian city.

To the additional question about the names in other languages, for instance, Italian, French, or Spanish, the same employee replied that

> it is not nice if all the shops in Latvia would be named, for example, in French. What would that suggest about us, Latvians, having our own language? [...] Therefore it is important to have laws that restrict this kind of names.

This comment, firstly, reveals the main conditions for ergonym creation: culture and history as a motivating source of the ergonym, a clear goal, and an idea about what messages contained in the name to the reader, and the choice of language which is determined by the location. Secondly, a strong affiliation to the Latvian language can be felt in the interview; thirdly, the state language is clearly an instrument to express the ethnic identity in the public space as well. Finally, laws and regulations are clearly required to regulate use of the state language (to limit arbitrariness).

The role of the company's location (the city and, in this case, the street) in the choice of language is also recognized by the employee of Druskininkai Hotel "Laisves" 'Freedom', confirming that she does not know why the name is not in another language, for instance, in English. In her opinion, it is more common to have the signs in English or another foreign language in the large cities, but this is a small town, so the hotel's name is in its own language. In this comment, it is necessary to point out two important issues: firstly, a small town syndrome, because Druskininkai is opposed to the big cities, where the traditions of the language use are different; secondly, an indirect proclamation of linguistic identity, because instead of the term "state language", the words "own language" are used. However, it should be emphasised that the selection of a name is related not only to the same name of the street, but also to the idea of national self-confidence, thus the choice of the state language is reasonable.

In Visaginas, the salesperson at the local grocery store "Monika" said that

> the name is based on the owner's daughter's name, which is in Lithuanian.

In reply to the question whether there was no desire to write something in English or another foreign language in the sign, the answer was strictly negative, because

> there is no need for that; there are not many tourists in the city.

So, in this case, the conceptual side (content) was primary in creating an ergonym, a form (language) had a secondary importance. Foreign language usage is evaluated from a pragmatic point of view—if there are no specific language readers, there is no need for it; the function of a symbolic importance of foreign language is not mentioned at all.

Mandatory compliance with the State Language Law was particularly pointed out by the commercial companies' employees and passers-by that were interviewed in Narva and Daugavpils. Perhaps that may be explained by the ethnic situation and the relatively low level of the state language proficiency in oral and written communication, which embarrass local inhabitants in situations when someone is interested in the use of languages in the city's public space. As an example, an opinion of the photo shop owner in Narva on the choice of language used in the name signs and in the linguistic landscape in general could be mentioned:

> Similarly as in Latvia, it should rather be Latvian language in the first place, likewise here we need, first of all, in the state language, and then in another language, that is, in Russian. Therefore it is written in two languages. The first should be the Estonian language, the second—any other language. The fact that they write in English, in my opinion, is because of the "big mind." People both in Estonia and in Latvia, firstly, have to write in their own language, so all could understand. I am personally very annoyed when it is written in English, but, of course, many do that. In my opinion, that is not right. Of course, they think that it will attract tourists, but they come in any case, if they need that service or product. It will not help if the information is in English.

The comment, in particular, highlights the need for the use of the state language in each country: it does not deny the possibility of using other languages, though not their priority usage in written messages. Furthermore, in the interview, an implicit justification of Russian language usage can be noted by pointing out that, in the public texts, the information in the national language could be followed by a different language. Finally, the respondent rather straightforwardly demonstrates a negative attitude towards the use of English in the linguistic landscape, questioning its socio-pragmatic importance in the' attraction of tourists.

Language choice is largely based on the affiliation to the state; national motivation (belonging to the country and the language of the titular nation) as a language choice criterion has been proposed as one of the most essential conditions in the creation of a written text. Hence, the state language has to link an addresser with the main target audience (writer with readers—the country's indigenous peoples), it has to be felt as an important symbolic value (according to language choice criteria by Karan (2011) and Spolsky (2009)).

The employees of international companies try mainly to avoid commenting on the company's name explaining that as a choice of the foreign owners and a lack of awareness about the grounds for this choice. Moreover, quite often it is clarified that the company's name is based on the specific international company's products, therefore the language is the same as in the company's ergonym (e.g., cosmetics store and the manufacturing company "Golden Rose" (English) in Daugavpils; children clothing store and the manufacturing company "pippi" (Swedish) in Valmiera).

The English language is mainly characterized as neutral language that is not linked to any local ethnic or social group (a respondent in Daugavpils: "English is English. It does not signify anything itself, and does not take a position. Tourists, Latvians and Russians alike understand it—whoever wants to and whoever needs to"), a tool for the expansion of the market (a respondent in Visaginas: "English is not common in this city, because there are only small stores here. If there were larger stores, you would also see English and other foreign languages"), a foreign, unnecessary element in the linguistic landscape (according to a worker at the Ivolita Hotel in Druskininkai, "everything in English is a little bit foreign, and to be honest, the number of tourists is not dependent on the language of the hotel name. It is dependent on whether the hotel is good for the tourist, and whether he'll come back is dependent on that. He does not care what the name is").

The use of other foreign languages is perceived as a language symbol, in order to make the selected lexeme sound euphonic or interesting, or to directly characterize the company (e.g., characters in Daugavpils as an identification sign for Chinese restaurants, word combinations in French language to identify a cosmetics brand, etc.).

Quoted excerpts of the interviews with the employees of the companies and the interviews in general reveal that the use of the state language is perceived as a mandatory condition for the creation of the company's sign; in some cases, the use of other languages is permitted, though after considering the sociolinguistic situation of the company's location. The local city population is perceived to be the readers and the target audience of the name signs. Also, the interviews with the companies' employees lead to the conclusion that, in the creation of a symbolic ergonym, the creators consider both euphony and ease of use, as well as the indication of the company's property rights, and local culture and history. This practice is clearly demonstrated by a large number of anthroponyms revealing the significance of exposing the personal identity and expressing the affiliation in a public space, and a number of symbolic ergonyms are linked to the business location.

Perception and interpretation of ergonyms

The students of the Rezekne Academy of Technologies—24 local students in the study year 2012/2013 and 14 *Erasmus+* exchange students in the study year 2014/2015—were asked to evaluate the companies' name signs—30 name signs in total, that is, 10 name signs from each country. The ergonyms were selected randomly and were demonstrated in a *PowerPoint* presentation in four student groups; in the results, 38 completed tables were collected. In the questionnaires, the respondents were asked to describe the content of each ergonym (if it is readable and understandable, what is written and in what language, primary associations about the name or the signboard), possible location (respectively, country) and type of company (e.g., store, coffee shop, tailor shop).The summary of the results obtained demonstrates that the students were able to determine both the type of business and its location only in one-third of the cases on average. According to the respondents, identification of the location was facilitated by the use of a state language (language as a sign of recognition), unless there were words without visible phonetic differences (for example, "Galerija" 'Gallery' and "MŪZA" 'Muse'—both in Latvian and Lithuanian); while difficulties were presented by the foreign language use, unless reflected a specific local feature. Identification of the language has not caused any problems to most of the students, even if the lexical meaning of the names was not written (understood). The students (including foreign students) admitted that phonetic differences have helped in identification of the titular language.

The summary of the results acquired during the experiment shows that there are certain tendencies in the interpretation of name signs:

1. Ergonyms with personal names mainly refer to hair salons, clothing stores or beauty parlors, but ergonyms with flower names refer to flower shops and in two cases—hair salons. For example, the English-language ergonym of the women's clothing store *Design by Inna* was believed to be a clothing store (8), beauty salon (7), hairdresser (4), tailor (3), or a design studio (2).

2. The whole ergonym or individual parts of it are likened to the Latvian language lexicon by phonetic and semantic resemblance, thus the name interpretation is based on onomatopoetic association, that is, search and discovery of phonetic resemblance; less frequently students have tried to base their judgements on interpretation of etymologizing semantics, attempting to explain the etymology of the respective words. For example, the café name "SKRYDIS" 'Flying' in Alytus was associated with the Latvian word *skroderis* 'tailor' and the associated business. Similarly , the second part of the local newspaper's name "Dainavos žodis" 'Dainavo's word'—*žodis* was associated with the Latvian language word *zobs* 'tooth' perceiving an ergonym as a name sign of a dental clinic. At this point, not only should linguistic competence be noted but knowledge of the respective culture (in this case, knowledge of the cultural and historical regions of Lithuania and the press) is essential as well. In both cases, the students have sought to build their understanding on etymologising semantic interpretation, by trying to explain the etymology of the name.

3. The ergonym is most often perceived in its direct meaning. For example, the name of a bar in Valmiera, "tinte" 'ink', is most commonly

guessed to be a stationery shop or bookstore, also a drycleaner (as in ink stain). The name of Visaginas' shopping centre "Domino" is associated with gambling halls, Pärnu's coffee shop "Kadri" 'female name in Estonia'– mostly with photo shops, but also with camera stores and photo museums. In these cases language association is dominant, using literal translations for lexemes featured in company names and attributing them to the company type.

4. Personal experience is taken into account in interpretation of the name, illustrating the demonstration of ontological associations; previously acquired knowledge and life experience are primary in the explanation of names. An example is the Daugavpils pizzeria "DIĀNA", the signboard for which was associated with a confectionery because of its use of purple and yellow. Children goods store "ЧEBURASHKA" 'Topple' is associated with the childhood's "ponchiki" 'doughnuts', the popular cartoon, teddy bear and the emblem of the Olympics. Oddly, the name of the beauty supply store "Glamour" is associated both with something extravagant and stylish, but also with something tasteless, of less quality seeking to be shown as valuable. These examples, in turn, reflect a demonstration of the ontological associations; background knowledge and life experience provide primary explanation of these names.

5. The language used in the name sign is mostly recognized, though the lexical meaning of the word of word combination is not always understood. There were only a few errors in language identification observed, for example the misattribution of the wine bar name "SENFORTIS" (a contraction of the Lithuanian words *senasis* 'the ancient' and *fortas* 'fort') to English.

The results of the experiment illustrate that symbolic names do not provide sufficient information by themselves to accurately characterize their sociopragmatic functionality; the information essential to do so is instead obtainable from additional information and non-verbal tools: various artefacts (e.g., the shape of the signboard, the shape of the building), colours, symbols and images (e.g., pictures of flowers—flower shop, a man or woman in profile with a highlighted, voluminous hairdo—hairdresser). Perhaps, a number of direct names in the linguistic landscape of the Baltic countries and a small total number of metaphorically symbolic names are some of the reasons why the respondents are not able to adequately perceive and interpret the symbolic ergonyms in socio-pragmatic context without additional linguistic and non-verbal information about the specifics of a particular business. In the explanation, both ontological and onomatopoeic, as well as language associations that are related with the etymologising and addressative semantics are considered.

Conclusion

The largest role in the formation and maintenance of the linguistic landscape (language environment) and public information is played by business owners and employees in commercial and private spheres (especially local businesses-stores, cafés, hairdressers and repair shops) and also local inhabitants. The most frequently found language signs are name signs (ergonyms), other signs of businesses or establishments (e.g., entrance signs, opening hour signs), advertisements and posters. Their knowledge of the state language laws or guesses as to its content—as well as their understanding of the interaction between economics and language, language competencies of and attitudes toward state, regional, minority, and foreign languages form the basis of the language situation in the Baltic linguistic landscape. In general, the ergonymy and linguistic landscape reflects the observance of normative documents regarding language and public texts due to political and language power motivation, but also the influence of sociopragmatic and social identity on language choice.

In evaluating expressed opinions, it can be concluded that in general, positive or neutral opinions are expressed about the aforementioned languages in the linguistic landscape, that interviewees strongly support the mandatory use of the state language in all public information, which is justified by the use of English or another chosen language in public texts (out of consideration for economics or the international functionality of language), and that Russian language, on one hand, is considered as a supported language with regards to the ethnodemographic makeup of the cities and its functionality in different spheres of life, but on the other hand, is seen as a restricted language, only to be used in specific places, sociolinguistic functions, and language signs. In public discourse, the language choice is determined by linguistic norms (as it must be) and language functionality at the local (city) and international (European, post-Soviet) levels.

References

Backhaus, Peter. 2007. *Linguistic Landscapes: A Comparative Study of Urban Multilingualism in Tokyo*. Clevedon: Multilingual Matters.

Bart, Rolan [Барт, Ролан]. 2001. *S/Z. Moskva: Editorial URSS* [Москва: Эдиториал УРСС].

Bauer, Gerhard. 1985. *Namenkunde des Deutschen*. Peter Lang.

Bergien, Angelika, Kremer, Lunger, Zilg, Antje. 2008. "Commercial Names as Indicators of Innovation and Change New Reflections and Challenges." *Onoma. Commercial Names*. Vol. 43. 7–23.

Bergien, Angelika. 2013. "From Solar Valley to Shadow Mountain: Identity Construction in Location-based Company Names." In *Onomastics in Contemporary Public Space* edited by Felecan, O., Bugheşiu A. 106–119. Cambridge Scholars Publishing.

Dimova, Slobodanka. 2007. "English shop signs in Macedonia." English Today. Vol. 23. Issue 3: 18–24.

Eckkrammer, Eva Martha, Thaler, Verena eds. 2013. *Kontrastive Ergonymie Romanistische Studien zu Produkt- und Warennamen*. Berlin: Frank & Timme.

Edelman, Lou. 2009. "What's in a name? Classification of proper names by language." In *Linguistic Landscape: Expanding the Scenery*, edited by Shohamy, E., Gorter, D. 141–154. New York: Routledge.

Frey, Julia. 2008. *Shop names & Word Games*. France Today. No. 21: 43–45.

Friedrich, Patricia. 2002. "English in advertising and brand naming: sociolinguistic considerations and the case of Brazil." *English Today*. Nr. 18: 21–28.

Gorter, Durk, ed. 2006. *Linguistic Landscape: A New Approach to Multilingualism*. Clevedon: Multilingual Matters.

Gorter, Durk, Marten, Heiko, Van Mensel, Lou, eds. 2012. *Minority languages in the Linguistic Landscape*. Palgrave Macmillan.

Hasanova, Dilbarhon. 2014. "English as a trademark of modernity and elitism." *English Today*. Vol. 26 Issue 1: 3–8.

Iljin, Ilja Petrovic [Ильин Илья Петрович]. 1996. *Poststructuralism. Deconstructivism. Postmodernism.* [Постструктурализм. Деконструктивизм. Постмодернизм.] Moska: Intrada [Москва: Интрада].

Karan, Mark. 2011. "Understanding und forecasting ethnolinguistic vitality." *Journal of Multilingualism and Multicultural Development*. Vol. 32. No. 2: 137–149.

Khosravizadeh, Parvaneh, Sanjareh, Bagheri. 2011. "English Shop Signs and Brand Names." *Brand. Broad Research in Accounting, Negotiation, and Distribution*. Volume 2, Issue 2: 32–40.

Kiss, George R., Armstrong, Christine, Milroy, Robert, Piper, James. 1973. "An associative thesaurus of English and its computer analysis." In *The Computer and Literary Studies* edited by Aitken, A. J., Bailey, R.W. 153–165. Edinburgh: University Press.

Kolmane, Ināra. 2013. "Poststrukturālisms." In *Mūsdienu literatūras teorijas*, edited by Ieva Kalniņa. 93–110. Rīga: LU Literatūras, folkloras un mākslas institūts.

Lyotard, Jean-Francois. 1984. *The postmodern condition*. Theory and history of literature. Volume 10. Minneapolis: University of Minnesota Press.

Lou, Jackie. 2007. "Revitalizing Chinatown Into a Heterotopia. A Geosemiotic Analysis of Shop Signs in Washington, D.C.'s Chinatown." *Space and Culture*. Vol. 10. No. 2.: 170–194.

Marten, Heiko, Lazdiņa, Sanita, Pošeiko, Solvita, Murinska, Sandra. 2012. "Between Old and New Killer Languages? Linguistic Transformation, Lingua Francas and Languages of Tourism in the Baltic States. Linguistic Landscapes". In *Multilingualism and Social Change* edited by Hélot, Christine, Barni, Monica, Janssens, Rudi and Bagna, Carla. 289–309. Peter Lang.

Pošeiko, Solvita. 2014a. "Ergonyms of education and culture spheres in the two cities of Baltic States." *Journal of Education, Culture and Society* 1: 299–311.

—. 2014b. "Linguistic and semiotic creation of the main signoboards of the local companies in the Baltic states." *Linguistic and cultural diversity in space and time*. Program & Book of abstracts. 3rd Linee+ conference: 38.

—. 2015a. "Kreatīvie publisko zīmju izveides līdzekļi Baltijas valstu pilsētvidē." *Via Latgalica* VI: 91–110.

—. 2015b. "Прагматизм и лингвистическая креативность в эргонимике Латвии и Эстонии." Ежегодник финно-угорских исследований / Yearbook of Finno-Ugric Studies.

Rieger, Maria Antoinette. 2008. "Alles PICCO BELLI oder was? Form und Funktion pseudo-italienischer Produktnamen im deutschen Lebensmittelmarkt." *Onoma. Commercial Names*. Vol. 43: 149–175.

Schlick, Maria. 2003. "The English of shop signs in Europe." *English Today*. Vol. 18. Issue 2: 3–17.

Shohamy, Elana, Gorter, Durk, eds. 2009. *Linguistic Landscape: Expanding the Scenery*. New York, NY & London: Routledge.

Sjöblom, P. 2013. "Commercial Names in Finnish Public Space." In *Onomastics in Contemporary Public Space* edited by Felecan, O., Bugheşiu A. 161–171. Cambridge Scholars Publishing.

Sjöblom, Paula. 2008. "Multimodality of Company Names." *Onoma. Commercial Names*. Vol. 43: 351–380.

Skujiņa, Valentīna, ed. 2007. *Valodniecības pamatterminu skaidrojošā vārdnīca*. Rīga: LU Latviešu valodas institūts.

Spolsky, Bernard. 2009. *Language Management*. Cambridge: University Press.

Tan, Peter, 2011. “Mixed Signals. Names in the Linguistic Landscape Provided by Different Agencies in Singapore.” *Onoma*. Vol. 46: 227–250.

Амирова, Роза Мунировна. 2011. Татарская эргонимия города Казани. Казань: Казанский университет.

Богачева, Мария Владимировна. 2011. “Лексика тематической группы “цвет” в народной фразеологии пермского края и эргонимах г. Перми (лингвокультурологический аспект).” Вестник Пермского университета. Российская и зарубежная филология. № 4: 18–26.

Бутакова, Екатерина Сергеевна. 2013. “Лингвистическая креативность в Томской эргонимии.” Вестник ТГПУ (TSPU Bulletin). No. 3 (131): 146–152.

Ворошилова, Екатерина Викторовнаю 2007. Ономастикон города Канска как отражение истории и культуры народа. Тюмень: Тюменский университет.

Емельянова, Аксана Михайловна. 2007. Эргонимы в лингвистическом ландшафте полиэтнического города (на примере названий деловых, коммерческих, культурных, спортивных объектов г. Уфы). Уфа: Уфа университет.

Крюкова, Ирина Васильевна. 2004. Рекламное имя: от изобретения до прецедентности. Волгоград: Волгоградский государственный педагогический университет.

Лозовой, Алексей Юрьевич, Названова, Ирина Александровна. 2013. “К проблеме номинации. Особенности современной эргонимии.” Раздел I. Проблемы филологии. http://izv-tn.tti.sfedu.ru/wp-content/uploads/2013/10/4.pdf, 23.05.2015.

Подольская, Наталья Владимировна. 1988. *Slovar ruskoj onomasticeskij terminologi*. Словарь русской ономастической терминологии. Москва: Наука.

Садыкова, Наиля Альбертовна. 2012. “Эргоним в дискурсе саморекламы.” Вестник ВЭГУ. № 3 (59): 164.–168.

Самсонова, Екатерина Сергеевна, Щитова, Ольга Григорьевна. 2012. “Информационный потенциал иноязычных эргонимов.” Вестник. Выпуск № 1.: 175.–181.

Тураева, Айна Рашидовна. 2012. Социолингвистический и структурно-семантический аспекты эргонимических комплексов на юге Великобритании и России. Пятигорск: Пятигорск университет.

ADVERTISING AFRICAN COFFEE: BRANDING STRATEGIES BETWEEN PITY AND COLONIAL FANTASIES

MARIE ANTOINETTE RIEGER

Abstract

The country-of-origin effect is a marketing strategy which is also used to promote African coffee. However, unlike other cases, when it comes to Africa, product quality is rarely the central selling point. More often the promotion is based on colonialist images of Africa as in the fair trade market with its patriarchal attitude, resembling all too much the colonial ideology of the White man's civilizing mission or in the mass market where "Africa" remains the projection screen for White wishes and dreams as it has been for centuries. The present article focuses on the names under which African coffees are sold and it will be shown that the naming strategies used by different market segments are good indicators of the way Africa and African people are presented in the relative advertising copies.

Introduction

The German search term *Kolonialwaren* leads to astonishing results. On the one hand, there are links to a number of dictionaries. According to the authoritative *Duden Dictionary* this by now obsolete and rarely used term once stood for "foodstuffs and luxury goods [from overseas]"[1] such as sugar, coffee, tea, cocoa, rice, spices and tobacco. The seemingly innocent allusion to the goods' vague origin "from overseas" is, on the other hand, perfectly in line with a number of links to websites of shops whose names contain the element *Kolonialwaren*. These results are once more proof of the Germans' widespread amnesia regarding their own colonial history.[2]

The short-lived German colonial empire was anything but a success story and least of all in economic terms.[3] Interestingly though, colonial commodities constituted a driving force for the development of marketing strategies such as branding:

> Prominent among the first brand-name products to appear in Germany in the 1880s were luxury consumables–particularly the so-called *Kolonialwaren*, goods such as chocolate (Sarotti), cocoa (Stollwerck), margarine (Palmin), or tobacco, particularly cigarettes (such as Manoli). (Ciarlo 2011: 127; emphasis in original)

This is the more surprising since, even during the German colonial heyday around 1900, the only consumer products from its own colonies were coffee and cocoa. Nevertheless, around "the turn of the twentieth century a new advertising motif began to appear [...] the figure of the African 'native'" (ibid.: 55). Although the emergence of this motif is due to "a great many forces and influences" (ibid.: 157), its effectiveness seems to be related to the fact that Africa and African figures were ideal projection screens for the dual fantasies of power and exotism:

> Images of Africans, like images of women, were embedded in hierarchies that were claimed to be natural, but unlike domestic gender ideologies, colonialist framings brooked no possibility for firsthand interaction (in the metropole) that might counter or undermine said ideology. As an imaginative device, African figures were thereby all the more useful for their remoteness. Second, Africa as a region was a relative newcomer to the German cultural sphere, which allowed it to be more easily mapped and remapped with new commercial motifs. China was just as "exotic" and distant; but 300 years of imported decorated porcelain [...] presented an imposing corpus of Chinese illustration that left less space, visually, for Germans to draw their own fantasies. (ibid.: 212)

Not least, the brutal wars in East (1905-1907) and Southwest Africa (1904-1908) lead to an increasingly racist, infantilizing representation of Africans as the only way to preserve this highly effective motif. In his detailed study *Advertising Empire. Race and Visual Culture in Imperial Germany*, David Ciarlo comes to the conclusion that the once

> allegorical figures gelled into types, types serialized into stereotypes, and stereotypes hammered into racial icons. The emergence of a hegemonic vision of racial uniformity in Germany–of black difference and white supremacy–lay as much in the origins of mass consumer society as in the colonial project itself. The imaginary of colonial power lay close to the heart of modern consumer society. (2011: 304)[4]

On the basis of these considerations I originally intended to investigate how "foodstuff and luxury goods" from Africa are promoted in present-day Germany. A preliminary search, however, resulted in the realization that the only commodity with a considerable country-of-origin factor is coffee. This insight can be seen as the study's first result: the only former *Kolonialware* for which its African origin has become a selling point is coffee.

The object of investigation is therefore inevitably limited to coffee, which is, furthermore, promoted as African coffee. The study focuses primarily on the names under which these coffees are sold. In the next chapter I will present the selection criteria and composition of my corpus which will then be analysed both from a linguistic and a functional point of view. Building on this, I will discuss in detail the underlying naming strategies and will show that the analysed names are good indicators of the way Africa and African people are presented in the relative advertising copies. The paper will conclude with a brief summary.

Corpus

The corpus has been sampled by searching the Internet between March and May 2015. To begin with, the websites of the most popular German coffee brands were examined [5] with the result that only four out of thirteen offer coffee with the selling point of African origin. Search entries such as "Coffee from Africa" and "African coffee" led to eight more suppliers.

These 12 umbrella brands belong to three market segments. The first segment is represented by the major coffee brands *Dallmayr, Melitta, Tchibo*, and the Austrian *Meinl*, with all in all 15 different sub-brands. From now on this segment of the market will be labelled "major brands". The second segment serves the fair trade market and is represented by *Eine Welt e.V. Leipzig, El Puente, Gepa*, and *Kaffee Pura*, also with 15 sub-brands. This segment will be labelled "fair trade". The last segment is made up of the four local suppliers *Bortfeld, Caligo, Kafrika*, and *Zurheide* which offer in all 27 sub-brands. This segment will be labelled "niche market".[6] Thus, it was possible to put together a sample of 57 names, which will be analysed in the next chapter.

Each of the 57 names denotes a certain type of coffee (beans) which is part of a range of similar products. Since the retailers' market significance and the names' legal status, i. e. whether they are registered trademarks or not, are irrelevant with regard to the objectives of this study, all names will be called "product name(s)", hereinafter PN.

PN Analysis

The PN analysis will be carried out in two steps: step one will focus on the formal and semantic characteristics of the single elements of which the

PN are composed. Building on this, step two will look at the relationship between naming element and product.

Linguistic Analysis

The corpus comprises 21 PN which consist of just one element[7], whilst 21 more PN are made up of two, 12 PN of three, and 3 PN of four elements, for a total amount of 111 tokens. Against all expectations, the near totality of elements, i. e. 104 tokens, is drawn from natural languages comprising 60 onomastic and 44 lexical items.[8]

There are 75 types[9], in particular 36 onymic, 32 lexical, and 5 unclassifiable types as well as 2 concept forms (*Konzeptformen*)[10]. The group of 36 onymic types consists mostly of toponyms: 18 choronyms (*Afrika*, 12 African countries[11], 3 regional land units[12]), 2 oronyms (*Elgon, Kilimanjaro*), 1 hydronym (*Abaya*), and 11 oikonyms (1 city[13], 8 small settlements[14], 2 coffee farms[15]). In addition there are 3 names of farmer cooperatives[16], the ethnonym *Masai* as well as *Sidamo* and *Yirgacheffe*, which are both used as choronyms and ergonyms.

Regarding choronyms with different spellings in German and in English, the German form appears for *Afrika, Ruanda*, *Sambia* and *Simbabwe* whereas both forms can be found in the cases of *Ethiopia*/*Äthiopien, Kenya*/*Kenia*, and *Tanzania*/*Tansania*.

Approximately two-thirds of the 32 lexical types come from foreign languages: along with 11 words drawn from the German lexicon, i. e. *Bio* ("organic"), *Bohnen* ("beans"), *der* (definite article: masculine, singular), *Gorilla, Kaffee* ("coffee"), *Kooperative*, *Leipziger* ("inhabitant of Leipzig")[17], *Mischung* ("blend"), *Mocca*, *Perlbohne* ("peaberry"), and *pur* ("pure") there are 13 types from English (*African, black, blend, blue, crown, estate, Ethiopian, fancy, mount, mountain*, *peaberry, plantation, reserve*), 2 from Romance languages (*café, liberté*)[18], 3 from Swahili (*harambee* "heave ho!", *kahawa* "coffee", *nyanda* "plains, plateaus"), and 1 from Chichewa[19] (*pamwamba* "on top/top"[20]), whilst the remaining 2 (*AA, AAA plus*) are drawn from the East African coffee grading system[21]. From a morphological point of view these lexical elements comprise 20 nouns, 7 adjectives, 1 definite article, 1 interjection. 2 out of 7 adjectives are deonymic derivations (*African* and *Ethiopian*), and 5 out of 20 nouns have the function of *generic proper names*[22].

Both concept forms are created by back-clipping an existing source form: *Cappu* < cappuccino; *Tansan* < Tanzania[23], whilst the linguistic status of 5 items remains uncertain: *Keta* may derive from the name of the Ethiopian town *Keta Wayu*[24], *Forrest* may be an alienated form of "forest", and *Yambo* an alienated form of the informal Swahili greeting *jambo* ("hello, hi")[25]. With regard to *Ajadi* and *Rocko*, no explanations, not even hypothetical ones, could be found.

Functional analysis

It has been shown in the previous chapter that the PN analysed consist almost exclusively of elements drawn from the onomasticon and the lexicon of natural languages. Furthermore, most onymic and lexical components are closely linked to the product itself. This basic result suggests that the primary function of most elements is to inform about actual product properties. There is however a small number of elements which do not provide factual information about the product since they are expressive rather than descriptive of what makes their primary function the–more or less targeted–elicitation of connotations and associations.[26]

The 68[27] functional types can therefore be divided into a first main group comprising 49 *descriptive* elements and a second much smaller group comprising 19 *expressive* elements. With regard to the first group, 34 elements indicate the products' (actual) origin and 15 refer to other product properties. The origin-related elements, however, do not have the same promotional value. Elements referring to Africa as a whole, as well as to African countries and regional land units, are rather *general* indications of origin. In contrast, references at the micro-level, such as villages, farms and cooperatives, are perceived as *valuable* indications of "small scale single-origin".

The same distinction between "general" and "valuable" is true with regard to the remaining descriptive elements. There are 8 quality labels which are specific to African coffee, i.e. A-grades, *Perlbohne/peaberry*[28] or particular types of coffee (*Sidamo, Yirgacheffe, Rocko Mountain, Pamwamba*[29]). The remaining 7 elements relate to (much) more generic properties (*Kaffee, Mocca, blend/Mischung*), and are not product-specific (*bio, reserve*) or are generic, such as the element *pur*, which is used to mark coffee from a single country[30]. Even so, the last two elements are not recognised quality references but are classified as descriptive elements, since they are transparent in meaning and function.

For their part, the 19 expressive elements can be divided into two subgroups. A first subgroup comprises 14 elements whose relationship with the product ranges from transparent, semi-transparent and indeterminate to opaque: a couple of elements aim at valorising the product, i. e. the high-value word *crown* (awarded to an Ethiopian coffee because it "is characterised by the unique and unmistakable character of

[top] qualities"[31]) and the element *nyanda* (‚plateaus'). The latter may be motivated by the quality feature "highland coffee," since the coffee "made from *Tanzania Nyanda Beans*"[32] originates from the Kilimanjaro region. Even without notions of Swahili, the element's intended meaning of "special coffee variety" is transparent through the co-text (but so far it seems to be an utterly fictitious variety).

The elements *Café, Cappu* and *Tansan* are considered expressive rather than descriptive because of their alienated forms. Similarly *kahawa* and *Abaya* are classified as expressive elements even though the former is the Swahili word for coffee and the latter the name of an Ethiopian lake[33], but neither notion can be regarded as common knowledge. Furthermore, the region around Lake Abaya seems not to be linked to coffee growing, processing or trade.

The following three elements have in common that their relationship to the product becomes more and more indeterminate. The element *black* in the PN *Black African Blend* may–innocently–be understood as a kind of high-value word since "black" in advertising is a signifier of elegance, high-value, and luxury[34]. But in this particular case it may also be associated to–far less innocent–fantasies about the so called "*Black* Continent"[35]. The element *fancy*–perhaps borrowed from the grading system of Hawaiian Kona coffee[36]–may upgrade an otherwise undistinguished Kenyan coffee. The element *blue* may derive from the dark blue–and once more elegantly looking–packaging of a coffee named *African Blue*. Whilst the element-product relationship of the last three elements is indeterminate but still perceptible, the relationship between the seemingly meaningless elements *Ajadi, Forrest, Keta* and *Yambo* and the product remains opaque.

The last 5 components are in a class of their own insofar as they clearly point *beyond* the product. This means also that additional information is needed in order to comprehend their significance: the element *Leipziger* literally refers to the location of the German retailer but is also the name of—and synonymous with—a fair-trade oriented joint initiative of various associations based in Leipzig.[37] The component *Liberté* refers to coffee-growing as a means of liberation from poor living conditions.[38] The name *Gorilla Mountain*, instead, is meant as a tribute to a gorilla population in Uganda.[39] The official motto of postcolonial Kenya, *Harambee,* wants to be reminiscent of the fruitful cooperation between "members of the catholic church and the plantation workers,"[40] whilst the element *Masai* is intended as a tribute to "One of the most heart-rending examples of love for Kenyan coffee", i. e. "the story of Karen Blixen"[41]. These five components in particular are not only expressive–as opposed to informative–but aim at a high emotional involvement of the target group which is typical of experience-oriented marketing strategies.[42]

To sum up, the elements differ clearly with regard to their main function. Most elements are informative with regard to actual product origin and properties. Among these there are, however, rather generic elements along with much more specific ones which not only inform about the product but also aim at its valorisation. The former are classified as elements providing "generic origin-related information" (GenOrigE) and "generic property-related information" (GenPropE), the latter as elements providing "valorising origin-related information" (ValOrigE) and as "valorising property-related information" (ValPropE).

The smaller group of expressive elements seeks instead to evoke positive connotations, fanciful associations and emotional involvement. They are uniformly classified as "expressive" (ExpE).

Naming strategy and conceptions of Africa

At first glance the 57 PN appear to be quite similar. In fact, 41 PN contain at least one origin-related element, whereas 18 consist exclusively of origin-related components. 25 of the remaining 39 PN with mixed components contain at least one general or valorising descriptive element. This reiterates the essential result that the main function of most PN is to inform about the product with a clear focus on origin. A closer look, however, reveals that the differences are in the details. Furthermore, it will be shown in what follows that these differences are of decisive importance with regard to the image of Africa and African people conveyed by the PN.

The 27 PN of the niche market segment consist of 52 components, and with an average of 1.9 components per PN they are slightly longer than the PN of the other two segments. The niche market PN are characterised by two key features: a. all but 4 elements are *descriptive*; b. all but 4 PN contain at least one *valorising* element (with a total of 27). Indeed, 13 of the total of 14 ValOrigE pertain to this group, and 15 elements are of the ValPropE type.

The typical one-part name in this segment consists of a ValOrigE, e. g. *Butegana, Muramba,* or a ValPropE, e. g. *Pamwamba, Sidamo*. The typical multi-part name comprises the country of origin, i. e. a GenOrigE, which is however specified either by a ValOrigE, e. g. *Äthiopien Amaro Gayo, Uganda Bukonzo Kooperative,* or by a ValPropE, e. g. *Malawi AA, Kenia Perlbohne*. In some cases the country of origin is specified by both valorising types, e. g. *Äthiopien Shakisso Plantation Sidamo, Tanzania Utengule Estate Peaberry.*

The analysis of the components and the relative examples show clearly that the niche market PN focus on the product by promoting its high quality properties. This is confirmed by the fact that the products are generally described in detail with regard to their origin, taste, and best methods of preparation (of the beverage). Fair trade and environmental certificates are common but not used as special selling points. Significantly different from the other two market segments is the attitude toward the African producers who are recognised as competent, self-acting stakeholders.[43]

The outliers in this group are not mere coincidences. Three of the four expressive elements (*Gorilla Mountain, Keta, Forrest*) are found in two PN promoted by the same retailer. In fact, this retailer is a local delicatessen chain whose stalls are located in supermarkets[44] and therefore aim at a more general target group than the three other niche providers who are coffee specialists. Later on it will be shown that this kind of PN is typical of the major brand segment.

The PN from the fair trade segment[45] also show a quite uniform picture but the naming-strategies are completely different. The 15 PN consist of 24 elements, and with an average of 1.6 components per PN they are slightly shorter than the PN of the other two segments. Unspecific elements are characteristic: there are 9 GenOrigE and 4 GenPropE which are generally not specified by valorising elements. Even the 8 ExpE are mostly rather plain and unimaginative: *café* (4), *cappu, Yambo, Leipzig, Liberté*. Typical one-part PN consist of a GenOrigE, e. g. *Bamenda, Oromia*, *Mount Elgon*; multi-part PN are typically a combination of GenOrigE + GenPropE (*Afrika Kaffe, Ruanda Kaffee*) or ExpE + ExpE (*Cappu Café*, *Café Liberté*).

From the analysis of the components and the relative examples, it should be clear that the marketing focus is decidedly not on the product itself. Instead the company and its social commitment are central.[46] In this respect, the PN *Der Leipziger*–which focuses exclusively on the German organisation behind this "partnership coffee"–is emblematic. The general perspective is from us to them, the company seeing itself as a "'bridge' between north and south" which aims at "supporting"[47] its project partners. These are not seen as autonomous and serious business partners but as "friends" for whom the company's friendship is "a great asset"[48]. The foundations of this fruitful friendship were seemingly laid by the colonial power, which insisted on the necessity of "growing more and more cash crops"[49] in order to give the Africans of today the possibility to buy "covers for their huts"[50]. Not quality but pity for the deprived of this world is the central selling point.[51]

The slightly colonial undertone emerging from the general patriarchal attitude and some expressions found in the fair trade segment become even more evident in the major brands segment. Its 15 PN consist of 26 elements, and with an average of 1,7 components per PN they are only slightly longer than the fair trade PN. There are three striking features: a. 10 of the 19 expressive elements are concentrated in this segment; b. there are only 3 valorising elements; c. the typical PN is a combination between GenOrigE + ExpE, e. g. *African Blue, Ethiopian Crown, Ethiopia Abaya, Kenya Harambee, Kenya Fancy, Kenya Kahawa, Tansania Nyanda Bohnen.* The impression of prefab stereotypes is reinforced by the fact that 10 PN out of 15 have a first component which refers to Ethiopia, Kenya, or Tanzania.

As the examples show, the focus in this segment is again not on the product: the selling point is the experience-oriented creation of imaginative worlds. In particular, Kenya, Tanzania, and Kilimanjaro (*Kilimanjaro, Tanzania Kilimanjaro*) are places filled with fantasies which are constantly fuelled by light fiction and films set in (East-)Africa.[52] These images are so uniform that the landscapes are interchangeable: "The image of the Serengeti landscape (or any other African park) in these films is entirely wild and natural, without history or social context" (Shetler 2007: 2)[53].

The elicitation of fantasies about untamed nature and exotic adventures in deserted landscapes may be seen as an innocuous pastime but there are also a couple of openly colonial references. As already mentioned, the PN *Harambee* seeks to emphasize the trouble-free cooperation between "members of the catholic church and the plantation workers"[54]. However, the advertising copy omits the fact that the plantation in question, the Nyeri Hill Farm, was founded in 1890 by White[55] catholic missionaries and is still owned by the catholic church[56]. The PN *Masai* aims to create a similarly colonial-minded reference to a "heart-rending example of love for Kenyan coffee," omitting, however, that Karen Blixen wrongfully took possession of African land to realize a White woman's dream. But the colonial view is not confined to the past. The coffee *African Blue* was promoted by a commercial[57] in which a White (German) woman is the owner of the coffee plantation where African workers grow coffee for a White company. Besides this particular constellation of White master and African workers, it is a commonplace that the controlling and evaluating experts are Whites.[58]

Summary

The starting point of this study was the observation that the term *Kolonialwaren* is still used as part of business names such as *Schwarzenbach Kolonialwaren*[59], *Kolonialwaren Lambert*[60] or *Holtorf Feinkost & Kolonialwaren*[61], to name just a few. Hence, the research question whether African products are promoted with a similar lack of critical distance toward their own colonial past. From the beginning it became apparent that the only product with a sensible country-of-origin effect is African coffee.

The detailed analysis of 57 PN given to African coffees promoted on German websites could show that, of the eight requirements for brand names listed by Ronneberger-Sibold, the most important seems to be requirement c): "a brand name should highlight the qualities of the product, i. e. be motivated to a certain degree" (2015: 2193). Despite the resulting relatively high degree of uniform and rather plain building blocks, it was demonstrated that the analysed PN are market-segment specific. Furthermore, it was also shown that the segment-typical PN is indicative of the image of Africa and African people promoted through the advertising copy[62]: *Niche market* PN focus on the products' high quality. As a logical consequence the African partners are presented as competent stakeholders at eye level. *Fair trade* PN, on the other hand, simply state that the product is "coffee from some African country". The relative websites prioritise the companies' social commitment, assigning second place to the product's quality. The clear selling point is not a unique taste experience but a good conscience. However, it has to be critically stated that the attitude towards their African partners is clearly patriarchal and therefore reminiscent of colonialist ways of thinking. *Major brand* PN differ from the previous PN by a high number of expressive components aimed at the elicitation of connotations and associations. This, combined with the advertising copies and images, means that "Africa" has definitely been reduced to the function of a projection screen for White wish fulfilment.

Part of this projection screen is also made up of predetermined roles for Whites and for Africans: whilst the numerous images show White people as experts, supervisors and owners "[t]he African is there to do the work so that you (the viewer) can consume." It should be noted that this comment, made by David Ciarlo (2011: 210), concerns a coffee advertisement of 1909.

Appendix

	PN	Company
1.	Äthiopien Amaro Gayo	Bortfeld
2.	Ethiopia Sidamo Shakisso Plantation	Bortfeld
3.	Kenia AA Mukure	Bortfeld
4.	Malawi AAA Plus Pamwamba	Bortfeld
5.	Ruanda Musasa Dukunde Kawa Kooperative	Bortfeld
6.	Tanzania Peaberry Utengule Estate	Bortfeld
7.	Uganda Bukonzo Kooperative	Bortfeld
8.	Sidamo	Caligo
9.	Black African Blend	Caligo
10.	Kavugangoma Burundi	Caligo
11.	Ethiopia	Dallmayr
12.	Ethiopian Crown	Dallmayr
13.	Kilimanjaro	Dallmayr
14.	Masai	Dallmayr
15.	Yirgacheffe	Dallmayr
16.	Der Leipziger	Eine Welt e.V. Leipzig
17.	Afrika Kaffee	El Puente
18.	Bamenda	El Puente
19.	Café Liberté	El Puente
20.	Cappu Café	El Puente
21.	Oromia	El Puente
22.	Ruanda Kaffee	El Puente
23.	Ruanda Kopakama	El Puente
24.	Yambo	El Puente
25.	Bio Café Kagera	Gepa
26.	Café Ruanda Pur	Gepa
27.	Kilimanjaro	Gepa
28.	Mount Elgon	Gepa
29.	Sidamo	Kaffee Pura
30.	Yirgacheffe	Kaffee Pura
31.	Butegana	Kafrika
32.	Karumandi	Kafrika
33.	Muramba	Kafrika
34.	Mushonyi	Kafrika
35.	Pamwamba	Kafrika

36.	Rocko Mountain Reserve	Kafrika
37.	Sidamo	Kafrika
38.	Suke Quto	Kafrika
39.	Yirgacheffe	Kafrika
40.	Ethiopia Mocca Sidamo	Meinl
41.	Kenya Fancy	Meinl
42.	Sidamo	Meinl
43.	Tanzania Kilimanjaro	Meinl
44.	Tansania Nyanda Bohnen	Melitta
45.	African Blue	Tchibo
46.	Ethiopia Abaya	Tchibo
47.	Kenya Harambee	Tchibo
48.	Kenya Kahawa	Tchibo
49.	Tansan Ajadi	Tchibo
50.	Äthiopien Mocca Sidamo	Zurheide
51.	Äthiopien Keta Forrest	Zurheide
52.	Kenia AA	Zurheide
53.	Kenia Perlbohne	Zurheide
54.	Malawi AA	Zurheide
55.	Sambia AA	Zurheide
56.	Simbabwe	Zurheide
57.	Gorilla Mountain Mischung	Zurheide

References

Aßner Manuel et al., eds. 2012. *AfrikaBilder im Wandel? Quellen, Kontinuitäten, Wirkungen und Brüche*. Frankfurt a. M. et al.: Peter Lang.

Baer, Martin. 2006. "Von Heinz Rühmann bis zum Traumschiff. Bilder von Afrika im deutschen Film." In *AfrikaBilder. Studien zu Rassismus in Deutschland*, edited by Susan Arndt, 151-161. Münster: Unrast.

Ciarlo, David. 2011. *Advertising Empire. Race and Visual Culture in Imperial Germany*. Cambridge, Massachusetts, and London, England: Harvard University Press.

Conrad, Sebastian. 2012. *Deutsche Kolonialgeschichte*. München: C. H. Beck.

Cotticelli Kurras, Paola. 2013. "Italian Commercial Names: Brand and Product Names on the Globalised Market." In *Onomastics in Contempory Public Space*, edited by Oliviu Felecan, and Alina Bugheşiu, 257-276. Newcastle upon Tyne: Cambridge Scholars Publishing.

Esch, Franz-Rudolf. 2005. "Markenpositionierung als Grundlage der Markenführung." In *Moderne Markenführung. Grundlagen – Innovative Ansätze – Praktische Umsetzungen*, edited by Franz-Rudolf Esch, 131-163. Wiesbaden: Gabler.

Fleischer, Wolfgang, and Irmhild Barz. 2012. *Wortbildung der deutschen Gegenwartssprache.* 4. Auflage; völlig neu bearbeitet von Irmhild Barz unter Mitarbeit von Marianne Schröder. Berlin and Boston: de Gruyter.

Fuhrmann, Wolfgang. 2013. "Der Urwald." In *Kein Platz an der Sonne. Erinnerungsorte der deutschen Kolonialgeschichte*, edited by Jürgen Zimmerer, 56-67. Frankfurt a. M., and New York: Campus.

Gißibl, Bernhard, and Johannes Paulmann. 2013. " 'Serengeti darf nicht sterben'." In *Kein Platz an der Sonne. Erinnerungsorte der deutschen Kolonialgeschichte*, edited by Jürgen Zimmerer, 96-108. Frankfurt a. M., and New York: Campus.

Gutjahr, Ortrud, and Stefan Hermes, eds. 2011. *Maskeraden des (Post-) Kolonialismus. Verschattete Repräsentationen ‚der Anderen' in der deutschsprachigen Literatur und im Film.* Würzburg & Neumann.

Hamann, Christof, and Alexander Honold. 2011. *Kilimandscharo. Die deutsche Geschichte eines afrikanischen Berges.* Berlin: Klaus Wagenbach.

Hamann, Christof, and Alexander Honold. 2013. "Der Kilimandscharo." In *Kein Platz an der Sonne. Erinnerungsorte der deutschen Kolonialgeschichte*, edited by Jürgen Zimmerer, 81-95. Frankfurt a. M. and New York: Campus.

Machnik, Katharine. 2009. "Schwarzafrika". In *Afrika und die deutsche Sprache. Ein kritisches Nachschlagewerk*, edited by Susan Arndt, and Antje Hornscheidt, 204-206. Münster: Unrast.

—. 2009. "Schwarzer Kontinent". In *Afrika und die deutsche Sprache. Ein kritisches Nachschlagewerk*, edited by Susan Arndt, and Antje Hornscheidt, 207-208. Münster: Unrast.

Martin, Peter. 2001. *Schwarze Teufel, edle Mohren. Afrikaner im Bewußtsein der Deutschen.* Hamburg: Hamburger Edition.

Mohammed, M. A. 2008. *Modern Swahili Grammar.* Nairobi, Kampala, Dar es Salaam: East African Educational Publishers.

Mükke, Lutz. 2009. *‚Journalisten der Finsterni'. Akteure, Strukturen und Potenziale deutscher Afrika-Berichterstattung.* Köln: Herbert von Halem.

Nübling, Damaris, Fabian Fahlbusch, and Rita Heuser. 2012. *Namen. Eine Einführung in die Onomastik.* Tübingen: Narr.

Platen, Christoph. 1997. *"Ökonymie". Zur Produktnamen-Linguistik im Europäischen Binnenmarkt.* Tübingen: Max Niemeyer.

Quaas, Ruben. 2015. *Fair Trade. Eine global-lokale Geschichte am Beispiel des Kaffees*. Köln, Weimar and Wien: Böhlau.

Rieger, Marie A. (2015): "I nomi degli altri nella letteratura coloniale per ragazzi sull'Africa orientale (1890-1945)." *Il Nome nel testo. Rivista internazionale di onomastica letteraria*, vol. XVII, ~~pp.~~ 107-119.

Ronneberger-Sibold. 2015. "Word-formation and brand names." In *Word-Formation. An International Handbook of the Languages of Europe*, vol. 3, edited by Peter O. Müller, Ingeborg Ohnheiser, Susan Olsen, and Franz Rainer, 2192-2210. Berlin and Boston: De Gruyter Mouton.

Schmiedel, Roland. 2014. *Schreiben über Afrika: Koloniale Konstruktionen. Eine kritische Untersuchung ausgewählter zeitgenössischer Afrikaliteratur*. Frankfurt a. M. et al.: Peter Lang.

Sturmer, Martin. 2013. *Afrika! Plädoyer für eine differenzierte Berichterstattung*. Konstanz and München: UVK.

Schweiger, Günter, and Gertraud Schrattenecker. 2005. *Werbung. Eine Einführung*. Stuttgart: Lucius & Lucius.

Shetler, Jan Bender. 2007. *Imagining Serengeti. A history of Landscape Memory in Tanzania from Earliest Times to the Present*. Athens, Ohio: Ohio University Press.

Speitkamp, Winfried. 2006. *Deutsche Kolonialgeschichte*. Stuttgart: Reclam.

Wolter, Stefanie. 2005. *Die Vermarktung des Fremden. Exotismus und die Anfänge des Massenkonsums*. Frankfurt, New York: Campus.

Zeller, Joachim. 2008. *Bilderschule der Herrenmenschen. Koloniale Reklamesammelbilder*. Berlin: Ch. Links.

Websites consulted

Coffee companies

http://shop.meinl.com/euro_de/
http://www.bortfeld-kaffee.de/index.php?id=97
http://www.caligo-coffee.de/
http://www.dallmayr.com/
http://www.der-leipziger.de/
http://www.el-puente.de/
http://www.gepa.de/home.html
https://www.kaffeepura.de/
http://www.kafrika.de/
http://www.melitta.de/
http://www.tchibo.de/

http://www.zurheide-kaffee.de/

Other websites

http://definitions.uslegal.com
http://de.statista.com
http://ethiopianfinecoffees.com/
http://geoview.info/
https://law.resource.org/pub/eac/ibr/eas.130.1999.html
http://misozicoffee.com/
http://translate.chichewadictionary.org/
http://www.bremen.de/holtorf-feinkost--kolonialwaren-seit-1874-39961714
http://www.citipedia.info/
http://www.coffeereview.com/
http://www.duden.de/
http://www.empower-yourself-with-color-psychology.com/
http://www.kolonialwaren-lambert.de/
http://www.konacoffeebeans.org/
http://www.stjohnthebaptistkenya.org/
http://www.schwarzenbach.ch/

Notes

[1] „Lebens- und Genussmittel [aus Übersee]“. (http://www.duden.de/rechtschreibung/Kolonialwaren, bracket in original [last visit: 20.12.15]).

[2] On the reasons cf. Rieger 2015.

[3] “[D]er wirtschaftliche Nutzen blieb für Deutschland gering” [the economic success was modest for Germany] (Conrad 2012: 54). On this regard cf. also Speitkamp 2006: 84-90.

[4] On the relation between colonialism and the beginnings of mass consumption cf. also Wolter 2005; on the development of commercial visual representation of Africa and Africans cf. in particular Zeller 2008; on the historical evolution of the (German) image of Africa and Africans cf. Martin 2001; on current developments cf. Aßner et al. 2012.

[5] The selection was based on a survey of the most popular coffee brands in 2013 and 2014 (http://de.statista.com/statistik/daten/studie/171525/umfrage/konsum-roestkaffee--und-bohnenkaffemarken-im-letzten-monat/ [last visit: 03.06.15]).

[6] The URL of these brands are listed in the *Reference Section*, the list of the analysed product names is located in the appendix.

[7] The term “element” corresponds to “single word” in all but four cases: The 2-part proper names *Amaro Gayo* (Ethiopian coffee farm), *Dukunde Kawa* and *Suke Quto* (names of coffee farmer associations from Rwanda and Ethiopia), as well as the coffee grade *AAA Plus*, are counted as one item.

[8] “A brand is a name and/or a symbol that uniquely identifies a seller's goods or services in the market” (http://definitions.uslegal.com/b/brands-and-brand-names/ [last visit: 20.12.15]). This legal requirement of „uniqueness“ and the marketing requirement of „distinctiveness“ usually result in a high number of extragrammatical word creations and pure fantasy names. On this topic cf. also Cotticelli Kurras 2013: 258-259, Nübling, Fahlbusch and Heuser 2012: 267-268, and, in particular, Ronneberger-Sibold 2015: 2192-2194.

[9] Tokens drawn from different languages referring to the same extra-linguistic object are counted separately.

[10] On “the currently most influential overall morphological typology of brand names […] the one by Platen” (Ronneberger-Sibold 2015: 2194) cf. Platen 1997: 38-45 and its concise description in Ronneberger-Sibold 2015: 2194.

[11] Burundi, Ethiopia (7), Kenya (6), Malawi (2), Ruanda (4), Sambia, Simbabwe, Tanzania (3), and Uganda.

[12] Bukonzo (county in Uganda), Kagera (region in northwest Tanzania), and Oromia (regional state of Ethiopia).

[13] Bamenda, capital of the North West Region in Cameroon.

[14] Butegana (Burundi), Karumandi (Kenya), Kavugangoma (Burundi), Mukure (Kenya), Muramba (Rwanda), Musasa (Rwanda), Mushonyi (Rwanda), Shakisso (Ethiopia).

[15] Amaro Gayo (Ethiopia), Utengule (Tanzania).

[16] Dukunde Kawa (Rwanda), Kopakama (Rwanda), and Suke Quto (Ethiopia). Information about settlements, wet mills, washing stations, coffee farms and farmer associations found on product websites has been counterchecked by means of other sources, e. g. location websites such as www.citipedia.info and, when available, producer websites such as http://ethiopianfinecoffees.com/ and http://misozicoffee.com/ [last visits: 20.12.15]).

[17] Cf. Fleischer and Barz 2012: 204-205.

[18] The appellative *café* is used four times. Only as part of the PN *Café Liberté* can it be classified as French, whereas the remaining three occurrences can be drawn from French, Spanish or Portuguese alike.

[19] Official language in Malawi.

[20] Cf. http://translate.chichewadictionary.org/ [last visit: 20.12.15]).

[21] Cf. *East African Standard Green coffee beans – Specification* (https://law.resource.org/pub/eac/ibr/eas.130.1999.html [last visit: 20.12.15]).

[22] The 5 items are *estate, mount, mountain* (2), *plantation* and the German *Kooperative* (2). On the status of generic proper names (*Gattungseigennamen*) cf. Nübling/Fahlbusch/Heuser 2012: 44f.

[23] For a concise description of word-creation in brand names cf. Ronneberger-Sibold 2015: 2197-2202.

[24] *Keta Wayu* is a populated place located in the Ethiopian region of Oromia, which is a centre of the Ethiopian coffee industry
(cf. http://et.geoview.info/keta_wayu,333157 [last visit: 20.12.15]).
[25] The Swahili implosive stop consonant *j-* [/ʃ/] in "jambo" and the approximant *y-* [/j/] in *Yambo* are both postalveolar and palatal and may sound very similar for non-native speakers of Swahili.
[26] Cf. Platen 1997: 53.
[27] The difference between 75 form-based and 68 functional types is due to the fact that GPN, *Bohnen* "beans" and the definite article are not counted separately.
[28] „Throughout the world, the coffee fruit occasionally produces a single, rather than a double, bean. […] these beans are often separated from normal-shaped beans and sold as a separate grade of the same coffee. According to coffee folklore, peaberry grades are considered superior to normal grades from the same crop […]."
(http://www.coffeereview.com/coffee-reference/coffee-categories/anomalies/peaberry-caracol/ [last visit: 20.12.15]).
[29] Despite intensive internet research it was not possible to determine beyond doubt whether the names *Pamwamba* and *Rocko Mountain* refer to the coffees' provenance or whether they have to be considered ergonyms. In any case they are known coffee varieties from Malawi (Pamwamba) and Ethiopia (Rocko Mountain).
[30]http://www.gepa-shop.de/essen-und-geniessen/kaffee-espresso/kaffee/ursprungskaffees.html [last visit: 20.12.15].
[31] Cf. http://www.dallmayr.com/coffee/our-brands/coffee-selection/ethiopian-crown/ [last visit: 20.12.15].
[32]http://www.melitta.de/de/BellaCrema-Selection-des-Jahres-2015-780,233157.html [last visit: 20.12.15].
[33] The word *abaya* could also refer to the whole-body garment worn by Muslim women but since the packaging of the coffee *Ethiopia Abaya* displays an imaginative Ethiopian warrior with bare neckline and arms this interpretation seems to be somewhat unlikely.
[34] Cf. for example
http://www.empower-yourself-with-color-psychology.com/color-and-marketing.html [last visit: 20.12.15]).
[35] The concepts of *Schwarzafrika* ("Black Africa") and *Schwarzer Kontinent* (‚Black Continent') for Africa are still colonial-laden. On this subject cf. Machnik 2004: 204-208.
[36] On the grading system of Hawaiian Kona coffee cf.
http://www.konacoffeebeans.org/ [last visit: 20.12.15]. The element *fancy* may be borrowed from the Kona grading system since the retailer has on offer both *Kenya Fancy* and Kona coffee. In either case, however, no explanation of the term is granted; cf. http://shop.meinl.com/euro_en/coffee.html [last visit: 20.12.15].
[37] Cf. http://www.der-leipziger.de/index.html [last visit: 20.12.15]).

[38] Cf. http://www.el-puente.de/fairtrade/fr/,,shop,artikel_anzeigen,277,co1-13-223/World-Prayers-Day-France/Food/Caf%C3%A9-Libert%C3%A9.html [last visit: 20.12.15]).

[39] Cf. http://www.zurheide-kaffee.de/kaffee-mischungen/ [last visit: 20.12.15].

[40] Cf. http://www.tchibo.de/neu-grand-classe-kenya-harambee-10-kapseln-p400067576.html [last visit: 20.06.15]).

[41] Cf. http://www.dallmayr.com/coffee/our-brands/grand-cru-cafe/masai/ [last visit: 20.12.15]).

[42] Cf. Esch 2005: 138-141. On this subject cf. also Schweiger and Schrattenecker 2005: 32-34 and 196-198.

[43] A good example of this relationship at eye level are the advertising copies at http://www.bortfeld-kaffee.de/index.php?id=63 [last visit: 20.12.15].

[44] Cf. the retailer's homepage (http://www.zurheide-kaffee.de/premium-sortiment.html [last visit: 20.12.15].

[45] A detailed overview of the German Fair-trade market is Quaas 2015.

[46] Further confirmation of this thesis is the fact that the company logos are generally very prominent on the packaging. Cf. for example the (coffee) packaging on https://www.el-puente.de and www.gepa.de [last visit: 20.12.15].

[47] For both citations cf. http://www.el-puente.de/index.php?key=be41cfdea4a7fdff26c7b14563a5c25f&language=gb [last visit: 20.12.15].

[48] Cf. http://www.gepa-shop.de/essen-und-geniessen/kaffee-espresso/cafe-raritaeten/bio-cafe-kilimanjaro.html [last visit: 20.12.15].

[49] https://www.el-puente.de/fairtrade/de/9,be41cfdea4a7fdff26c7b14563a5c25f,info,html_pp,Afrika,ta,143,,,,,1/index.html?suchbegriff=ta0%20Kagera%20Coop.%20Union [last visit: 20.12.15]. This remark about the allegedly far-sighted intervention of the colonial masters is accompanied by a photo showing a shabbily dressed African in a seated position, eyes down and one bare foot with just a handful of coffee beans in front of him. The stereotype of Africans in trousers but with bare feet was already used in ads around 1900 as a visual shorthand "hinting that Africans would never completely escape their primitive nature. This juxtaposition of dress against undress could be argued to be both referencing the progress of the civilizing mission and at the same time marking its ultimate limits" (Ciarlo 2011: 191). What is more, the advertising copy conceals the fact that the cash crop economy began to be successful where "heimische Gesellschaften die neuen Möglichkeiten […] in eigener Initiative nutzten" [native societies used the new possibilities on their own initiative] Speitkamp 2006: 84-85).

[50] http://www.el-puente.de/fairtrade/de/9,be41cfdea4a7fdff26c7b14563a5c25f,info,html_pp,,,250/Unsere-Partner/Projektuebersicht/Afrika/Demokratische-Republik-Kongo/SOPACDI.html [last visit: 20.12.15].

[51] In this respect it is essential to present Africa as crisis-ridden, poverty-stricken continent where people depend on external support. This presentation format is

perfectly in line with the image of Africa depicted in the media. On this topic cf. Mükke 2009 and Sturmer 2013.

[52] On the role of Africa in contemporary German literature and films cf. Gutjahr and Hermes 2011as well as Schmiedel 2014; on what he calls "the lasting Africa-Boom" in the entertainment media cf. in particular Schmiedel 2014: 22-24; on the past and present relationship between Germany and the "mythical" Kilimanjaro cf. Hamann and Honold 2011.

[53] On the imaginary worlds of the *Urwald* ("primeval forest") cf. Fuhrmann 2013 and *Serengeti* cf. Shetler 2007 and Gißibl and Paulmann 2013.

[54] Cf. http://www.tchibo.de/neu-grand-classe-kenya-harambee-10-kapseln-p400067576.html [last visit: 20.06.15]).

[55] The capitalization serves to point out that "Black" and "White" are not natural or self-evident categories, but social constructions with political consequences and meanings.

[56] The farm's colonial history is described in detail in a 10-page leaflet which can be downloaded from the *St. John the Baptist Catholic Church* official website (http://www.stjohnthebaptistkenya.org/ArchdioceseFarms.htm [last visit: 20.12.15]).

[57] Cf. http://www.tchibo.de/privat-kaffee-nachhaltiger-anbau-c400000886.html [last visit: 20.06.15]). It seems that the commercial is no longer available. However a couple of screenshots and the transcript of the dialogue were archived by the author.

[58] Cf. http://www.melitta.de/de/BellaCrema-Selection-des-Jahres-2015-780,233157.html and http://www.dallmayr.com/coffee/our-brands/coffee-selection/ethiopian-crown/ [last visit: 20.12.15]).

[59] Cf. http://www.schwarzenbach.ch/ [last visit: 20.12.15].

[60] Astonishingly, this shop is specialised in raw milk cheese [sic!] (cf. http://www.kolonialwaren-lambert.de/ [last visit: 20.12.15]).

[61] Cf. http://www.bremen.de/holtorf-feinkost--kolonialwaren-seit-1874-39961714 [last visit: 20.12.15].

[62] The authors media-supported presentation at the International Conference *Names in the Economy V(erona)*, June 24-27, 2016, could show that packaging and advertising images heavily support the idea of Africa emanating from the relative advertising. A detailed presentation of this aspect is however beyond the possibilities of this article.

NON-TRIVIAL URBANONYMS IN MOSCOW COMMERCIAL SPACE[1]

TATIANA SOKOLOVA

Abstract

The purpose of this contribution is to investigate non-trivial urbanonyms as elements of Moscow commercial space. Attention has been paid to misleading foreign-sounding names, legal and socio-linguistic causes of such names. Particular attention is devoted to different linguocreative techniques of non-trivial urbanonym invention: semantic and spelling puns, quasionymisation, transonymization, phonetic and graphic play. The process is illustrated with examples of commercially successful and unsuccessful, offending and scandalous names.

The material is studied from both the linguistic and the legal perspective, and the author recommends thorough naming examination to rule out the risk of making an unfortunate, ethically questionable or incorrect onomastic choice.

Introduction

This chapter presents the results of the linguocreative activity on coining Moscow urbanonyms in the aspect of naming examination—a new type of the linguistic examination, which is only taking shape at the interface between onomastics, linguistics and jurisprudence (Sokolova 2016.) Urbanonyms as elements of a commercial space can attach legal status—trademarks or service marks, company names and trade names. Naming examination is the analysis of a name as a unit of language and conversational speech (at all levels: lexical, semantic, morphemic, word-formative, phonetic, grammatical), as a part of a specific onomastic system (subsystem), and at the same time as a means of identification of an object in the legal aspect (Sokolova 2013: 374–376).

This study deals with non-trivial urbanonyms, i.e. the names of shops, cafes, restaurants, travel agencies, living complexes as found in Moscow commercial space and attempts to investigate the causes and factors that brought these creative names to life. This involves studying the linguistic mechanisms of creating new Russian urbanonyms on the base of the morphosyntactic and semiotic analysis of names, as well as method of complex description: verbal and visual elements, special cultural, ethical, aesthetic and social features.

Moscow urbanonyms have been borrowed from street signs as well as from different websites, including those of the Moscow Administration, of Rospatent (Federal Institute for Industrial Property), the Federal Tax Service of Russia and forums of consumers of goods and services.

The representation of the material analyzed in the chapter is as follows: Russian names contain their original spelling in Cyrillic, their transliteration and translation given in brackets, e.g. *Кадушка* (*Kadushka*– "small tub, usually for pickling vegetables and mushrooms"). English and other foreign names are given in their original form as they appear on the signboard, e.g. *SALAMANDER, Carlo Pazolini, Le Bouchon, ZENDEN*. Some of the names have two forms of spelling and are used both in the foreign language and in Russian, in such cases, both options are given as equal, e.g. *Басконu / Basconi*; *Донатто / Donatto*.

Foreign and foreign-sounding Moscow urbanonyms

Moscow commercial space is mainly foreign. Muscovites perceive such foreign and foreign-sounding urban names as strange, exotic and therefore attractive. So, borrowings are of paramount importance in urban naming, though it is not the case that the potential of the Russian language has been used up. The usage of foreign lexical units (appellatives, toponyms, anthroponyms) is based on pragmatic approach. The study of modern urban onomastic space makes it possible to observe the process of borrowing and to find out the motivating qualities underlying the proper names under analysis. The use of the collected data has allowed researchers to investigate urban names not only from the point of view of sociolinguistics and creative linguistics (Remchukova et al. 2015) but also from the aspect of naming examination (Sokolova 2015: 22).

The sway of foreign and foreign-sounding names upon Russian posters, signs and billboards has been a matter of ongoing debate in mass media, since many foreign urbanonyms look and sound weird and alien to the Russian eye and ear. Such discussion is not new. Even the famous Russian writer F.M. Dostoyevsky in 1863 wrote: "Lord, are we true Russians? Why does Europe have such a powerful, magical calling influence upon us?" In the 20th century another world-renowned Russian writer A.I. Solzhenitsyn warned of the danger of an "international English word wave" (Solzhenitsyn 1990).

And now this influence has become stronger. This issue is discussed not only by linguists, but also sociologists, economists and statesmen, including the country's top leadership. Even the President of the Russian Federation V. Putin has argued against superfluous foreign words in Russian signs and billboards in various cities and towns (tass.ru/ obschestvo).

Moscow is Russia's most Romanized city and Moscow authorities struggle with the dominance of foreign words on urban signs. To do so, the Moscow Administration has taken steps to limit the use of the Latin alphabet in local urbanonyms, yet the problem is still far from being resolved. For example, of the 12 signs in a house on Prospect Mira 6 use Latin alphabet: *ECCO, THOMAS MUNZ, SALAMANDER, City, PIZZA*, etc. Is it possible to replace those signs with Russian equivalents? To what extent is a Russification urban requirement to be considered as justified?

From a legal perspective, the status of commercial urbanonyms may vary within wide limits:

(1) trademarks and service marks are to be submitted to a name-giving examination and be registered with the Federal Service for Industrial Property (FIPS);
(2) company names are subject to registration with the Federal Tax Service of Russia, but no examination is required;
(3) trade names (in Russian legal terminology *kommercheskoye oboznacheniye* "trade designation") are not normally subject to registration and do not pass any examination.

So the owners of trademarks, service marks and company names have the legal right to use foreign and foreign-sounding names in advertisements and on signs, in accordance with established legal procedure. It is perfectly normal for foreign languages to be used as an attention-grabbing device, meant to attract the potential customer with an exotic-sounding name. Thus, signs *ECCO, THOMAS MUNZ, SALAMANDER* are legitimate and cannot be removed or replaced by Russian ones.

It should be noted that such legal and registered names seen on posters and signs are few in the Moscow commercial space. Most of what one is likely to see or hear are trade names (commercial designations), which means that their owners are not allowed to use foreign names on their signs, not even if transliterated into Russian. This rule is, however, all too frequently violated.

The greatest number of names written in foreign languages regards clothing, footwear, furniture, jewellery and household appliances shops (see Sokolova 2014a: 362–365). Among the most popular, attractive non-Russian names on Moscow signs appear to be those in Italian; with their typical and easily recognizable morphemic and phonetic indicators *-o* (*-io*), *-i* (*-etti, -ani, -ini, -li*): *Giorgio Armani, FRANCESCO DONNI, Roberto Cavalli, Sergio Bellini, Cappelletti,* and others. Since Italian goods hold a powerful attraction for the Russian consumer some Russian-based companies go so far as to pass themselves off as Italian brands: a ruse, which enables them to fix higher prices for their commodities and stimulates customer interest. To illustrate, no footwear designer *Carlo Pazolini* has ever existed, but in 1992 Russian engineer Ilya Reznik started manufacturing shoes and invented the trademark *Carlo Pazolini*, which is now a chain of shoe shops in Russia, posing as an Italian import. *Donatto* clothing shops attract consumers with advertising slogans like: "Feel yourself Italian in a Donatto suit!" But the labels reveal that *Donatto* garments are made in Russia. Limited Liability Company "Апрель XXI век" ("APRIL XXI Century") in 2010 officially registered the *Donatto / Донатто* trademark as an artificial word unrelated to the Italian language and Italian style.

The Russian origin of the trademark *Basconi* was noticeable before rebranding (with two Russian words included in the name–*обувь* (obuv'–"shoes") and *аксессуары* (aksessuary–"accessories"); but after rebranding the name appears to be truly Italian *Basconi*. The businessman Ifraimov Talhum Haevich registered the trademark *Basconi / Баскони* in 2011 as a fictional word with no dictionary meaning.

Why is it possible in Russia to register foreign-sounding Trademarks?

Naming as the process of creating a unique name for the company, product or service, and the analysis of how this name will affect the potential customers is a fairly recent Russian phenomenon. If in Europe and America, the process of naming developed at a rapid pace, in Russia in the sphere of urban names it hardly existed—there was no need due to the peculiarities of the economy and production (See Sokolova 2012: 264-266). The situation began to change with the appearance of appropriate specialists, the large amount of translated literature and our own research on the topic of naming that took into account, above all, foreign experience. Russian developers of new names focused primarily on the experience of the American naming agencies (e.g. Naming.ru became one of the first agencies in Russia to deal with naming). Therefore, many terms and concepts in the naming field were borrowed from the US practice.

American jurisprudence distinguishes five categories of trademarks, ranked by degree of inherent distinctiveness:

(1) Generic names identify an entire class of products or services; they are the weakest type of names and cannot be granted trademark protection (*Cigarettes*, *Milk*, *Dog Food*).
(2) Descriptive names immediately convey an idea of the ingredients, qualities or features of the goods or services and are not eligible for trademark protection (*Three-Day Blinds*, which sells window blinds that are ready to pick up three days after you place your order).
(3) Suggestive names "evoke a characteristic of the underlying good" (*Greyhound Lines*). Suggestive names draw on the power of metaphor and analogy to create positive associations in customers' minds.
(4) Arbitrary names are "real" (dictionary) words used out of context (*Shell* for an oil company, *Apple* for a technology company).
(5) Fanciful names are coined (invented) and have no inherent meaning other than the one assigned (*Kodak*, *Xerox*).

Suggestive, arbitrary and fanciful trademarks are the easiest to protect, descriptive marks offer protection under certain circumstances and generic marks never offer protection (www.uspto.gov).

We emphasize that *fanciful trademark* is a fictional trademark (artificially created word), and the dictionary gives the same definition (http://www.multitran.ru/). However, Russian name-givers translated the word *fanciful* as *фантазийный(fantazijnyj–"fantasy")*.

Dictionaries of the modern Russian language have not recorded a new, special meaning of the adjective *фантазийный* ("fantasy") and give a traditional definition:

фантазийный ("fancy"): adj. 1. relevant to a noun fantasy, associated with it; 2. created by fantasy of a designer (usually about the smell of perfume); 3. differs by originality, complexity, extravagance (usually about clothes). (http://dic.academic.ru).

The Russian National Corpus recorded the appearance of a new word in the legal discourse in one linguistic usage:

X5 Retail Group patents drinks with the names "Twitter" and "Facebook" // RBC Daily, 2010.11.29: "the claimed designation is a word, wearing a fantasy character" (http://ruscorpora.ru).

An analysis of FIPS trademark databases (http://www1.fips.ru/) shows that in applications for registration of trademarks (service marks), as well as in the expert studies of means of individualization, the word *фантазийный* ("fantasy") is used as a linguistic calque of the English word combination (*fanciful brand name*). However, this term was artificially taken out of the above system (the American classification of trademarks by degree of distinctive character and the degree of legal protection).

Consequently, as applied to the Russian means of individualization, the scope of the concept *fanciful* enlarged so that the word incorporated three trademark categories: arbitrary (e.g. *Уважай СЕБЯ / Respect YOURSELF* (leather goods, shoes, advertising), *Ладушка* (*Ladushka*–an old Russian female name *Лада* (*Lada*) with the diminutive suffix) (household cleaning products), fanciful–*Беконово* (*Bekonovo*), *Мясье* (*Mjasje*), *Молокоша* (*Molokosha*) and suggestive *Лапушка-Малышка* (*Lapushka-Malyshka*– "honeybunch"–"baby") for children's furniture, *Кадушка* (*Kadushka*– "small tub, usually for pickling vegetables and mushrooms") for restaurant.

And a formula such as "this verbal designation has fantasy tonality for a list of goods and services" is used in order to overcome problems with Russian Law since, according to the Civil Code of the Russian Federation, official registration of misleading and confusing trademarks is not allowed (Article 1483 of the Civil Code).

Therefore in legal practice the adjective verb *фантазийный fantazijnyj* ("fanciful") has a functional meaning "irreal", not related to a factual name, toponym, anthroponym, factual product or service.

For instance, consider the urbanonym (trademark) *Мосье Башмаков* (*Monsieur Bashmakov*). Knowing the Russian word for "shoe" *башмак* (*bashmak*) and seeing a man with red gunboats on a sign, you understand that the signboard is connected with shoe selling or repairing: *Bashmakov* ← *Bashmak* ("shoe"). But in the trade mark application this name is declared as fanciful, i.e. the name-giver emphasizes that the trademark has no relation either to shoes or to a person named *Bashmakov*, although the name was fixed in the dictionary (Unbegaun 1972: 155). Naming examination reveals the actualization of the inner form of the surname *Bashmakov* from the pre-Christian name *Bashmak* ("shoe"; Veselovsky 1974: 30), which is of playful ironic politeness - Monsieur (BTS 2000: 558). The semantics of both words is updated by a nonverbal component of the combined trade mark: the image of a man in a green tuxedo, top hat and huge red boots.

Returning to the above foreign-sounding trademarks (*Carlo Pazolini, Донатто / Donatto, FRANCESCO DONNI, BASCONI* etc.). I want to emphasize that they have been officially registered by Rospatent as being fanciful. In order to put an end to the appearance of such misleading consumer trademarks naming examination is necessary.

The question of similarity of trademarks to the extent of mixing

In analyzing foreign-sounding trademarks, I should add that some companies intentionally simulate a well-known brand to attract more consumers. Thus, the brand name and company name *Zarina* resulted from the rebranding of St. Petersburg-based manufactory *Первомайская Заря* (*Pervomayskaya Zarya*). *Zarina* (Fig. 1), which happens to sound like the diminutive of *Заря* (*Zarya*–"daybreak"), which provides for a certain continuity of tradition, yet has a foreign phonetic component to it and one can see similarity with the well-known brand *Zara* on phonetic and graphic levels (Fig. 2).

Figure 1.

Figure 2.

Sometimes the owners of well-known brands appeal to the judiciary to protect their legal rights. Thus, Giorgio Armani appealed to the Intellectual Property Rights Court of the Russian Federation to declare invalid the decision of the Chamber of Patent Disputes, which had denied the Armani request to invalidate the registration of verbal trademark *ARMAN*. The Italian company (GIORGIO ARMANI S.P.A. Milan, Swiss Branch Mendrisio; Via Penate 4, 6850 Mendrizio) stated that the trademark *ARMAN* (ООО "ГРИН ЛАНД", проспект Вернадского, д. 94, корп. 5, Москва, 119571–LLC "GREEN LAND", Vernadsky Prospekt, h. 94, bld. 5, Moscow, 119571) is confusingly similar to the brand *ARMANI*, because the name is completely included in the trade mark of the applicant and differs only in one letter (www.rapsinews.ru).

While a marked phonetic similarity between two words *ARMANI* and *ARMAN* may be noted, their logos are completely different (Fig. 3, Fig. 4). Thus, the Court dismissed the applicant's claim and noted in its decision the following reasons: lack of semantic similarity of signs because the word *Armani* has Italian origin, while *ARMAN* is Armenian or Afghan (Pushtu) and means "dream, hope"; lack of phonetic and visual similarities—there is a stylised depiction of an umbrella—and finally, lack of data establishing any trademark confusion amongst consumers.

Figures 3 and 4.

In rejecting the Giorgio Armani claim, the Court held that the naming examination reveals an inextricable link between verbal and nonverbal components in a creolized trademark.

Linguocreative techniques of non-trivial urbanonyms

Wilfully or instinctively a name-giver creates a new designation using linguocreative techniques. An analysis of the urban-names data shows that a name's originality is achieved through creative naming units based on diverse types of language games.

Lexical and phonetic play on the typical structural-semantic models in naming occurs frequently, e.g. instead of the normative collocation *парад войск* (*parad voysk*–"ceremonial parade") cafe *Парад котлет* (*Parad kotlet*–"cutlet parade") appears; instead of the regulatory *Дедушка Мороз* (*Dedushka Moroz*–"Grandfather Frost") café *Бабушка Мороз* (*Babushka Moroz*–"Grandmother Frost"). The nominator often deliberately violates the rules of collocation, thus creating a comic effect, e.g. the name of the grocery store *Мясной комфорт* (*M'asnoj comfort*–"meat comfort").

Semantic derivation is often chosen on the basis of paronimic attraction, e.g. the grocery store *Мясье*: Мясье ← мясо+ месье (Mjasje ← mjaso ("meat") + mesje ("monsieur")'.

Incorporation is one of the most common ways to create a new urban name: home goods store *UJUTERRA*: *уютерра* ← *уют* (*ujut*–"cosiness") + *терра* ("terra"); a restaurant *Пастарианец* (*Pastarianets*–"pastarian" (a mix of two words *pasta* and *vegetarian*).

Graphic play is also a very popular way of inventing a non-typical urban name and attracting the attention of potential consumers of goods and services, e.g. cafe *ДереWня* (*DereWnya–derevnya* means "village" and instead of Cyrillic letter *В* (*дереВня*) Latin *W* is written.

The housing estate *Випушки* (*Vipushki*) appeared in Moscow; name-giving explains this name as a living complex for VIPs, but the suffix -*ушк*- (-*ushk*-) adds a derogative shade of meaning.

Analysis of linguocreative activities in the field of urban nomination has revealed quasionymisation as a productive model of nomination. Quasionymisation means giving a proper-name form to an ordinary appellative (Vasilyeva 2005: 187). As the result of such naming quasianthroponyms appear: dairy products' shop *Молокофф* (*Molokoff*) from *молоко* (*moloko*–"milk"), meat products' shop *Мясновъ* (*Mjasnov*) from *мясо* (*mjaso*–"meat"), *Букетофф* (*Buketoff*) from *букет* (*buket*–"bouquet of flowers"), cargo firms *Грузовичкоф* (*Gruzovichkoff*), *Грузовичков* (*Gruzovichkov*) from the diminutive of *грузовик* ("autotruck"), furniture company *Мебелефф* (*Mebeleff*) from *мебель* (mebel–"furniture"). Such quasianthroponyms are formed by using a Russian patronymic suffix -ov (-ev). The use of its foreign-language equivalent *-off* in urbanonyms reflects the nominators' desire to give the names an unusual appearance: *Едофф* (*Edoff*) is a network of recognizable, conveniently-located grocery stores. *Едофф* (*Edoff*) is the result of quasionymisation from *еда* (*jeda*–"food") and a semiotic ally meaningful nonverbal component (Fig. 5). S. Goryaev and O. Olshvang define this phenomenon as surname imitation (Goryaev and Olshvang 2013: 148–156).

Figure 5.

Quasitoponyms are the second productive model of quasionymisation: A company producing windows *Окошкино* (*Okoshkino*) from *окошко* (*okoshko*–"little window"), shops *Коляскино* (*Kolyaskino*) from *коляска* (*kolyaska*–"baby carriage"), Беконово (*Bekonovo*) from *бекон* (*bekon*–"bacon").

Transonymization is another widely-accepted method in naming. Numerous examples in housing estates' naming have been presented (Sokolova 2014b). There are residential complexes in Moscow named *Wales*, *Kent* and *Berkshire*. But why these very names? The choice is determined by the naming experts'—not always accurate—knowledge, their personal taste, as well as the degree of fame of these "beautiful names". Naming agencies do not work for ordinary people, focusing instead on well-off buyers, so the extension of foreign place names is expanding. New names of districts appear: *Chelsea*, *Greenwich*, *La de FANS*. Thus, toponyms become brands.

But simple transonymization is insufficient for truly creative naming. In fact transonymization is accompanied by suffixation and semantic and spelling puns. The name of a travel agency *Мальдивиана* (*Maldiviana*) is coined from toponym *Maldives* (Islands) by the formant *-ana* (cf. Latin Parisiana, Baconiana). The name of the housing estate *МОНАКОВО* (*MONAKOVO*) is formed from toponym *Monaco* using the typical Russian toponymic formant *-во* (*-vo*), which is a homonym of the exclamatory particle *ВО!* (*VO!*) that means "high quality" (BTS 2000: 138). This word is accompanied with a nonverbal component—a princely crown.

Urbanonyms with the name *Мадагаскар* (*Madagascar*) have become commonplace, but the baby products shop *Модагаскарррр* (*Modagaskarrrr*) becomes unconventional by substituting letter *O* for *A*. As a result the first part can be read as *Мода* (*moda*–"fashion") while the reduplication *rrr* is an imitation of roaring; thus the allusion to the popular animated film becomes semiotically meaningful.

A further example: a few years ago I presented the name of the housing estate *Шоколад* (*Shokolad*–"chocolate") as a creative one (Sokolova 2014). Nowadays it has become trite: many urban objects have adopted the name. And to appear *au courant* a name-giver uses a pun: not *Шоколад* (*Shokolad*), but *Шиколад* (*Shykolad*–from the French *chic*); Or the travel agency *Все в ШИКоладе* (*Vsjo v SHYKolade*–"everything is Chicolate") promising *chic* rest.

The word ДОМ (*dom*–"house") is a mundane component of shop names, but can be used creatively in such names as *Крышкин дом* (*Kryshkin dom*, china shop) from *крышка* (*kryshka*–"a cover for a saucepan"), *Крошкин дом* (*Kroshkin dom*) from *крошка* (*kroshka*–"baby"), which are associated with the well-known fairy tale Кошкин дом ("Cat's house") by the famous Russian poet S. Marshak.

The grocery store *ряДом* (*rjaDom*) is another example of creative naming (Fig. 6). This name can also be read both as the adverb *рядом* (*rjadom*–"nearby"), and as *ряд* (*rjad*–"row of shopping stalls"), and graphical accentuation of the letter *Д* (*D*) in the middle of the word emphasizes the connection with the word *дом* (*dom*–"house").

Figure 6.

A final creative naming model is the use of popular phraseological units in unusual context or graphics: *Селяви* (*Selavi*–фр. c'est la vie–"That's life!") for a strip club; *Дай пять!* (*Daj pjat*–"give me five!") for a manicure salon; *Без нервов!* (*Bez nervov!*–"No nerves!") for a travel agency; *Руки вверх!* (*Ruki vverch!* –"Hands up!") for a brasserie.

The name-givers often explain their reasons for linguocreativity:

> Insolent retro cafe Sorry, Babushka is for those who remember that in the 80s youths said "Sorry, Babushka" to a person who was not in the know and was quite conservative … (www.nightparty.ru).

Babushka means "grandmother" or "elderly woman" (Fig. 7).

Figure 7.

The phrase *ТоДаСе* (*ToDaSjo*) in Russian means "this and that", but likewise it is an imitation of Japanese phonetics. It is the name of a sushi bar, and pronouns *To* (this) and *Ce* (that) on the sign are represented as two living participants in a dialogue having meals (Fig. 8).

Figure 8.

A phrase can be created artificially for imitation, e.g. *Пара ногас* (*Para nogas* from Russian *пара* (para–"pair") and *нога* (noga–"foot") by the pseudo Spanish formant *-as*) (shoe shop favorite Spanish shoes).

A phrase can be precedent, e.g. the sushi bar *Kill Bill*. This bloody name refers to the famous film and colour scheme (yellow, black and red) foregrounds the semantics of the word *to kill*. The interior of the nightclub *ZONA*–slang argotic "prison" (BTS 2000: 370) re-creates a prison atmosphere. The name of the shop *Бухни* (*Bukhni*) expresses the argotic appeal for drinking "Let's drink!" (BTS 2000: 106). Scandalous names such as these create a negative response in the majority of citizens and have become the subject of controversy in the Federal Antimonopoly Service and in the media. Naming examination can help with an objective consideration of controversial urbanonyms.

The farther from the city centre, the less common the presence of the Latin alphabet is. More domestic names appear on the billboards: The barber shop *ЭКОНОМ-ЧИК* (*EKONOM-CHIK*): the first part of the word refers to those who are not well-off, the second is a diminutive suffix, but at the same time *ЧИК* (*chik*) in Russian mimics the sound of hair-cutting. This word is accompanied with a nonverbal component—a pair of scissors (Fig. 9).

Figure 9.

The pet shop *ЛапУсик* (*LapUsik*): the word *Лапусик* is diminutive and means "a pet", the graphic play shows the pet's feet and whiskers.

Concluding remarks

This chapter provided an illustration and discussion of Moscow commercial space from a linguistic and juridical viewpoint. According to the Civil Code of the Russian Federation, a city sign must contain information specifying the profile of the facility it represents, alongside its name (Article 54). We have identified a large number of misleading foreign-sounding names. What is more, we consider fanciful and pseudo-fanciful names as the result of creative speech activity, which requires further linguistic, sociolinguistic and juridical investigation.

Database analysis showed that nominators used different linguocreative techniques to invent non-trivial urbanonyms, in particular semantic and spelling puns, quasionymisation (often with graphic play). It should be noted that quasianthroponyms are more common than quasitoponyms.

But often the results of linguistic creative activity violate the rules of law and language. A naming examination of creative urbanonyms finds commercially successful and unsuccessful, offending and scandalous names, as well as foreign-sounding names, which mislead the consumer. It is necessary, therefore, to work out a juridical-linguistic analytical procedure to deal with the conflicting results in creative naming. Not only the pragmatic but also the aesthetic and ethical aspects should be taken into account.

In order to regulate Moscow's commercial space, naming examinations should be carried out on a regular basis. This would, on the one hand, help to avoid unacceptable, incorrect, offending names, and, on the other, help to place unusual, attractive to goods and services consumers names on signs.

References

Civil Code of the Russian Federation (Part IV) issued on December, 18, 2006. № 230. FZ (as amended on December, 31, 2014). http://www.consultant.ru/ (accessed November 15, 2015).

Efremova, T. ed. *Современный толковый словарь русского языка под редакцией Т.Ф. Ефремовой* [Modern explanatory dictionary of the Russian Language]. http://dic.academic.ru/contents.nsf/efremova/ (accessed May 10, 2015).

Federal Tax Service of Russia [Федеральная налоговая служба]. https://www.nalog.ru/eng/1.html (accessed May, 2015).

FIPS. Information resources. Open registers [ФИПС. Информационные ресурсы. Открытые реестры]. www1.fips.ru/wps/wcm/connect/content_ru/ru/inform_resources/ (accessed May, 2015).

Goryaev, Sergey and Olshvang, Olga. 2013. "Anthroponyms in commercial name models: Surname imitation". In *Name and Naming: proceedings of the Second International Conference on Onomastics: Onomastics in contemporary public space: Baia Mare, May 9–11, 2013*, edited by Oliviu Felecan, 148–156. Cluj-Napoca: Mega: Argonaut.

Kuznetsov, S.A., ed. 2000. *Большой толковый словарь русского языка* (BTS). [Big explanatory dictionary of Russian]. St. Petersburg: Norint Publ.

Официальный портал Мэра и Правительства Москвы [The official portal of the Mayor and Government of Moscow]. https://www.mos.ru/ (accessed May16, 2015).

Remchukova, E.N., Sokolova, T.P. and Makhiyanova, L.R. 2015. "Проблемы нейминга: новые русские урбанонимы в лингвокреативном аспекте" [Naming Problems: New Russian Urbanonyms in a Linguocreative Aspect]. *Gumanitarnye, sotsial'no-ekonomicheskie i obshchestvennye nauki* 9: 328–333.

Russian Agency for Legal and Judicial Information. http://www.rapsinews.ru. (accessed May16, 2015).

Russian National Corpus [Национальный корпус русского языка]. http://ruscorpora.ru/ (accessed May 10, 2015).

Sokolova, Tatiana. 2012. "Examination of Trade Marks, Company Names and Trade Names as the Means of Individualization in Russia: Theoretical and Methodological Approaches to the Problem." *Onoma* 47: 264—266.

—. 2013. "Naming expertise of Moscow urbanonyms." In *Name and Naming: proceedings of the Second International Conference on Onomastics: Onomastics in contemporary public space: Baia Mare, May 9–11, 2013*, edited by Oliviu Felecan, 369 – 378. Cluj-Napoca: Mega: Argonaut.

—. 2014a. "Unconventional anthroponyms in Moscow urban names." In *Unconventional Anthroponyms: Formation Patterns and Discursive Function*, edited by O. Felecan and D. Felecan, 354–369. Cambridge Scholars Publishing.

—. 2014b. "Proper Names of Housing Estates in Contextualized Analysis (From Appearance to Usage by the Members of a Community)." In *Proceedings of the XXIV ICOS International Congress of Onomastic Sciences* [Els noms en la vida quotidiana: Actes del XXIV Congrés Internacional d'ICOS sobre Ciències Onomàstiques]. *Names in daily life*, edited by Joan Tort i Donada and Montserrat Montagut i Montagut. Barcelona: Generalitat de Catalunya.

Sokolova, T.P. 2015. "Нейминговая экспертиза в гражданском судопроизводстве: организационные и методические проблемы" [Naming examination in civil procedure: organizational and methodical problems]. *Zakony Rossii: opyt, analiz, praktika* 9: 22–27.

—. 2016. *Нейминговая экспертиза: организация и производство* [Naming examination: organizing and procedure]. Moscow:

Urlitinform Publ.
Solzhenitsyn, A.I. *Русский словарь языкового расширения.* [Russian dictionary of language expansion]. www.solzhenitsyn.ru/.../russkiy_slovar_yazikovogo_rasshireniya. (accessed May 11, 2015).
Superanskaya, A.V., Staltmane, V.E., Podol'skaya, N.V., Sultanov, A.Kh. 2009. *Теория и методика ономастических исследований* [Theory and technique of onomastic researches]. Moscow: Knizhnyi dom "LIBROKOM".
TASS Society. Putin opposed the Romanization. tass.ru/obschestvo/1670170. (accessed May 11, 2015).
Unbegaun, B.O. 1972. *Russian Surnames*. London: Oxford University Press.
USPTO. United States Patentand Trademark Office. www.uspto.gov. (accessed May 11, 2015).
Vasilyeva, N.V. 2005. *Собственное имя в мире текста* [Proper name in the world of the text]. Moscow: Academy of humanitarian research Publ.
Veselovsky, S.B. 1974. *Ономастикон: Древнерусские имена, прозвища, фамилии* [Onomasticon: Old Russian names, nicknames, family names]. Moscow: Nauka.
On the Approval of Administrative Regulations for the Provision of State Services by the Moscow Department of Mass Media and Advertising http://www.dsmir.mos.ru/ (accessed November 15, 2015).
Federal Law of the Russian Federation of 06.01.2005 № 53-ФЗ. Concerning the State Language of the Russian Federation. http://www.google.com/base.consultant.ru/cons/cgi/online.cgi?req (accessed November 24, 2015).
Баскони. RU. https://basconi.su (accessed May 2015).
Едофф. RU. http://www.edoff.ru.
Каталог: от А до Я. Рестораны Москвы. Выбор заведения. www.restoran.ru/msk/catalog/restaurants/all. (accessed May 2015).
Клуб Sorry, Babushka! Москва. geometria.ru/places/sorry-babushka. (accessed May 2015).
Клубы Москвы. http://www.moshol.ru/clubs.html (accessed May 2015)
Лучшие рестораны и кафе Москвы. www.gettable.ru/cafe (accessed May 2015).
Магазины Москвы. zoon.ru/msk/shops. (accessed May 2015).
Моллы.Ru. http://.malls.ru (accessed May 2015).
Необычные кафе и рестораны Москвы. kafe.msk.ru. (accessed May 2015).

Ночные клубы Москвы. www.nightparty.ru. (accessed May 2015).
Рекламные агентства, Москва. Список лучших. www.2do2go.ru/msk/places/uslugi/reklamnye-agentstva (accessed May 2015).
Рекламные агентства Москвы. www.all-agency.ru. (accessed May 2015).
Рестораны Москвы. www.afisha.ru/msk/restaurants. (accessed May 2015).
Рестораны Москвы. kudago.com/msk/restaurants. (accessed May 2015).
Российские бренды, которые притворяются иностранными. http://www.adme.ru/fas/rossijskie-brendy-kotorye-pritvoryayutsya-inostrannymi-66781. (accessed May 2015).
Студия маникюра Дай пять. http://zoon.ru/msk/beauty/studiya_manikyura_daj_pyat_v_tts_universiti. (accessed May 2015).
Торговые центры Москвы. www.localway.ru. (accessed May 2015).
Турфирмы Москвы. Список туроператоров. givetour.ru. (accessed May 2015).
Турфирмы Москвы, туроператоры и турагентства в Москве. www.tursvodka.ru. (accessed May 2015).
Туроператоры, турагентства, туристические компании. www.spr.ru. (accessed May 2015).
Я потребитель. http://yapotrebitel.ru/shops?pa=77&srt=0 (accessed May 2015).
Znakoved. все о товарных знаках. https://www.znakoved.ru/poisk_tovarnyh_znakov. (accessed May 2015).

Notes

[1] This chapter was supported by the Russian Foundation for Humanities, grant 15-04-00282.

LEXIS WITH ETHNOCULTURAL SEMANTIC COMPONENTS IN MOSCOW RESTAURANT NAMING[1]

LYAYSAN ZAMALETDINOVA

Abstract

It is well known that a commercial name often plays a dramatic role in attracting new audiences. The article investigates two trends in contemporary Russian naming: a) using lexis with ethnocultural semantic components (exotic vocabulary, precedent phenomena, and national onyms) and b) applying creative linguistic techniques. The sphere of commercial naming is characterized by increased linguistic creativity determined by pragmatism. As a result, commercial names are considered as forms of *widespread linguistic creativity*.

Introduction

It is commonly known that a commercial name often plays a critical strategic role in business development and communication building. An ideal restaurant name attracts potential customers' attention, differentiates the place from other competitors, informs a customer about the cuisine, and forms its unique image (Miller and Muir 2004). This is especially true for a megalopolis visited by many tourists such as Moscow.

According to the statistics, the catering industry in Moscow was in constant growth till 2014. Even though the situation has now changed due to a number of social, economic and political reasons, the Russian capital is still a wealthy city with huge tourist traffic. As a result, a highly developed catering industry offers locals and foreigners a multitude of restaurants serving traditional dishes from diverse cultures (Russian, Eastern, Chinese, Japanese, Georgian, Italian, French, American, Mexican, etc.).

This study shows that the problem of attracting both locals and foreigners is often solved by finding a balance between national (i.e., related to a given culture) and universal (international) semantic components of a word used in naming. According to the analysis, one of the most efficient ways that restaurants may inform customers and at the same time differentiate themselves from competitors is by using **lexis with ethnocultural semantic components**.

Ethnocultural components can be actualized in naming in different ways, which arise from a nominator's communicative goals. Our study highlights the following groups of commercial names exploiting this lexis: a) names actualizing an ethnocultural component; b) names actualizing an international / universal component.

Actualizing ethnocultural semantic components in naming

The research reveals several most actively used groups of lexis which actualize ethnocultural semantic components. They are a) toponyms; b) exotic vocabulary; c) national onyms.

First of all, it should be pointed out that using **toponyms** is the most obvious way to identify a place specialization: Russian cafe *Камчатка* [Kamchatka], Italian restaurant *Тоскана* [Tuscany], Georgian cafe *Батуми* [Batumi], American steakhouse *Chicago Prime*. These names do not often actualize connotative semantic meanings but only create a certain "national aura". Despite this, cultural and historical components of a proper name can be displayed in the interior design, in the menu or in the advertising texts.

On the other hand, there is the phenomenon of the so-called "false toponymic naming". This means that nominators use words connected to a specific culture but not to the menu. For example, there are Russian cafes with a typical menu (which usually includes a standard set of dishes of different cuisines) called *Авиньон* [Avignon], *Стокгольм* [Stockholm], and *Амстердам* [Amsterdam]. These places are usually located in upscale areas, and a nominator's motivation is determined by his/her desire to find a beautiful and unusual name. In this case, s/he apparently uses the well-known communication strategy of "*status raising*" (Issers 2009: 47).

The other group of words actively used in restaurant naming is **exotic vocabulary**, primarily referring to traditional dishes and drinks names: Georgian restaurants *Харчо* [Kharcho], *Хачапури* [Khachapuri], Russian café *Ватрушка* [Vatrushka], Italian cafe *Pesto*, and so on. Such commercial names are self-evident for a potential customer since decrypting associations and metonymies is unnecessary. This naming strategy is actively used in different countries, which is explained by its communicative effectiveness.

However, there is a trend specific to Russian commercial naming. That is, the exploitation of ***the Soviet-period vocabulary***: *Советская чебуречная*

[The Soviet Cheburechnaya], *Рюмочная* [Rumochnaya], *Столовая №1* [Canteen №1]. Denoting special establishments, which were popular in the USSR, these words are supposed to touch the target audience's sense of nostalgia. It makes this naming method successful in the communicative aspect.

One of the most interesting examples of so-called nostalgic naming is *Страна, которой нет* [The country, which doesn't exist]. Not being a single word but a nominative sentence, this restaurant name is atypical from a structural point of view. The meaning of the phrase attracts the potential customer's attention: "the country, which does not exist" obviously denotes the Soviet Union. The easily decoded association is supported by the restaurant's location (in the historical center), its cuisine (Russian, Georgian, Uzbek) and logo. Therefore, the potential customer perceives the communicated message easily: *this country no longer exists, but we remember and love it; that is why we are reviving it here, at our restaurant.*

Personal names, i.e. the ones traditional for a specific culture, also actualize ethnical semantic components: German pub *Ганс и Марта* [Hans and Martha], Georgian restaurant *У дедушки Вано* [At grandfather Vano's], etc. Using these traditional onyms facilitates the formation of a clear parallel between the urbanonym and the place specialization. Moreover, kinship terms such as *uncle, baba* [grandmother], *grandfather*, etc. are often used in this kind of naming, which helps to create a cozy atmosphere.

The urbanonym *Ivan* - name of a traditional Russian restaurant is based on a given name, which has a number of connotative meanings (Russian Onomastics and The Onomastics of Russia 1998: 78–80) and associations with a Russian man. Nevertheless, the name representing the national culture is Romanized, which seems to be the nominator's attempt to find a balance between national and universal semantic components.

Thus, it is obvious that the commercial names of the first type are based on well-known ethnocultural components, clichés understandable to any customer.

Actualizing universal semantic components in naming

There are, however, urbanonyms actualizing universal connotations with the help of, first and foremost, **precedent phenomena**: Italian restaurant and karaoke bar *Джельсомино* [Gelsomino], French restaurant *Жан-Жак Руссо* [Jean-Jacques Rousseau], Russian restaurant *Пушкин* [Pushkin], etc. The names of this type focus on a cultured audience with deep knowledge of literature, art, and history. On the other hand, a nominator may not want a customer to «recognise» precedence. In this case, cultural components indicate the nominator's high cultural level, while of the precedent names, there remain only some ethnical indicators. For example, *Жан-Жак Руссо* [Jean-Jacques Rousseau] positioning is, *"An inexpensive, entertaining, and noisy bistro with true Parisian atmosphere"*. Obviously, the precedent name is not explained at all. Moreover, customers usually just call the place *Jean-Jacques*.

However, as a rule, cultural components of precedent phenomena play a great role in place positioning. For example, *Denis Davydov* restaurant is named for the Russian poet and hero of the Patriotic War of 1812. Its slogan is, *"A restaurant with Russian character"*; the "Menu" section is subtitled: *"Traditional Russian and gourmet trophy French cuisines"*. The website also contains biographical information about Denis Davydov.

On the other hand, a number of traditional Russian restaurant names actualize phenomena comprehensible only to Russians. For example, one of the biggest fast food chains in Russia is named after a folk tale "*Teremok*", the main idea of which is hospitality. The main dishes on the menu are traditional pancakes and porridges, and staff greet each customer with the old-fashioned: "What would you like, sudar?"[2] In our opinion the communication strategy - from the place name to the design and the communication style - fully corresponds to the restaurant concept and can thus be considered very successful.

Other earlier names from the folklore sphere are quite often used in commercial naming. For example, *Самобранка* [Samobranka, a marvelous cloth, which helps to set a rich table], *Илья Муромец, Добрыня* [Ilya Muromets, Dobrynya - famous warriors, heroes of Russian epic legends]. From the point of positioning and communicating with potential customers, these names are almost always successful, even with foreigners. Despite the fact that the latter may be not be familiar with Russian folklore. In any case, they will appreciate the authenticity of these places thanks to non-verbal means of communication such as interiors, uniforms, etc.

Our study shows that there are some other lexical groups used in commercial naming to identify the restaurant's "nationality". These include various colloquialisms (*Ёлки-палки* [Elki-palki]); precedent phenomena from the sphere of the Soviet cinema (*Жестокий романс* [A Cruel Romance]) or music (*Подмосковные вечера* [Moscow-area evenings]).

It is important to highlight an important trend in contemporary Russian naming, which is especially typical in megalopolises: the use of **creative**

linguistic techniques. The term *linguistic creativity* is defined as a speaker's ability to create linguistic innovations at all language levels and use them in the communication process (Gridina 2002).

Today the sphere of linguistic creativity includes media texts, communication on the Internet, and naming (Linguistics of creativity: multiauthor book 2012); (Remchukova 2010). It should be pointed out that the creative function of the language in these texts is used primarily to reach specific communicative goals. Therefore, we should establish a principal difference between the creativity of literature and *widespread linguistic creativity* (Remchukova 2013).

One of the most actively used linguocreative techniques in naming is that of using Roman letters. It has a few functions.

First of all, Roman letters are often used in naming restaurants that are targeted primarily at foreign visitors (most of these places are located in big hotels or in the central streets of the city): *Siberia Moscow* (a mansion in central Moscow), *Café russe* (Ritz-Carlton hotel), etc. Thus, Roman letters are used as a means of communication with the target audience, and so these examples cannot be considered linguocreative urbanonyms.

Secondly, the technique usually informs potential customers of a place's specialization. For example, the most widespread method of naming Italian restaurants is using real (or pseudo-real) Italian words with positive connotations: *Semplice* [Simply], *Bocconcino* [A Piece], *Casa di famiglia* [Family House]. Moreover, even in cases when a customer can not recognize the language, the commercial name will probably be well perceived thanks to the Roman spelling. Russians often perceive foreign goods to be of good quality, fashionable and attractive. Thus, using Roman letters becomes an argumentation technique (Annenkova 2012).

These extralinguistic aspects have caused an increased "Romanization" of Moscow's onomastic landscape. Unfortunately, there are many examples of the meaningless use of the Roman alphabet as a slavish tribute to fashion. However, there are linguocreative commercial names where Roman components play an important communicative role. Thus, the English definite article in *The Веранда* [The Patio] may indicate the unique character of the place: there are many patios, but this is the one. We can not know if the creative name demonstrates a nominator's linguistic competency. However, the commercial name itself is obviously successful.

Graphic hybridization is a linguistic technique that allows the creative exploitation of the possibilities offered by the language. For example, mixing Roman and Cyrillic letters in *МариVanna* [Marie Vanna] produces an original language game with homophones: *МариVanna* –

Марь Иванна [Mar' Ivanna], the character of popular Russian jokes. This folklore reference should amuse customers and at the same time inform them about the place's cuisine (it is a traditional Russian restaurant). Supposedly, the Roman elements also demonstrate that *МариVanna* is an international network: there are also several *Mari Vanna* restaurants in the UK and the USA. However, the Cyrillic is missing in these names, demonstrating the unique character of graphic hybridization in Russian naming[3].

Graphic hybridization in the Russian onomastic landscape may be viewed from another aspect: the **mixing of old and contemporary Cyrillic letters**. For example, *Пушкинъ* [Pushkin] is written according to the rules of pre-revolutionary Russian spelling, with a final *yer (ъ)* letter. It used to be written in the final position following consonants and lacked its own phonetic value. The letter was eliminated in 1918, and it is used in contemporary naming as a reference to the tradition, and therefore, to high quality.

Thus, ethnocultural semantic components, which are actualized by using adequate lexis (exotic vocabulary, precedent phenomena) and creative linguistic techniques (language games), first of all, inform customers about the specific character of a place, its cuisine and concept. Secondly, they can influence the target audience especially if additional communication means such as graphic hybridization are used. Finally, the lexis actualizes cultural semantic components, which identify the target audience (Russians or foreigners). On the other hand, actualizing cultural context often demonstrates the nominator's cultural competence. In such cases he is not only an entrepreneur who wants to sell his services but also a person engaged in augmenting the cultural space of the city.

References

Annenkova, I. 2012. *World contemporary media world view: linguistic philosophy aspect*: PhD abstract. Moscow.

Gridina, T. 2002. "Language game as a linguocreative activity." In *Language. System. Personality. Language game as a linguocreative activity. A personality forming in ontogenesis*, 26-27. Yekaterinburg.

Issers, O. 2009. *Linguistic manipulation*. Moscow: Flinta: Nauka.

Linguistics of creativity: multiauthor book. 2012. Under the general editorship of T. Gridina. Yekaterinburg: The Ural State Pedagogical University publishing house.

Miller, J.; Muir, D. 2004. *The Business of Brands*. Chichester: John Wiley & Sons Ltd.

Remchukova, E. 2010. *The creative potential of Russian grammar*. Moscow: URSS.

—. 2013. "Widespread linguistic creativity: standards breaking". PFUR Bulletin. Series «Theory of Language. Semiotics. Semantics» 2: 83–90.

Russian Onomastics and The Onomastics of Russia: Dictionary. 1998. Corr. ed. O. Trubachev. Moscow: Shkola-Press.

Notes

[1] Funding acknowledgement: The publication of the paper is supported by the RFH grant 15-04-00282.

[2] *Sudar* and *sudarynya* are pre-revolutionary respectful forms of address which are not used in contemporary Russian.

[3] This trend is common to all commercial establishments. Thus, in *Sweet Lana* (a beauty salon) we can see phonetic segmentation of the Russian name *Svetlana* (which is probably the owner's name) into two parts: *sweet*, a word with positive connotations, clearly familiar to most potential customers, and *Lana*, a pet form of *Svetlana*.

PART III:

LINGUISTIC FEATURES AND STRATEGIES OF NAMES

L'ECONOMIA FILTRATA DAL LINGUAGGIO POLITICO. DAL FUNZIONALISMO ORGANICO DELLA PRIMA REPUBBLICA AL POPULAR CHIC

MASSIMO ARCANGELI

Abstract

In the late seventies and in the beginning of the following decade, Italian political language begins to turn decisively towards sectors such as economics and finance, loosening its ties with the legal and humanistic tradition. With the political involvement of Silvio Berlusconi, the famous businessman (who defined his choice of ingagement with a football metaphor, "discesa in campo"), the process of absorption of the economic and financial vocabulary into the political language reaches its maturity, though not its final stage. This is accomplished by Matteo Renzi, who grew up in the school of Obama. The current prime minister ritualizes and "dematerializes" this vocabulary, adding many ingredients for a new political intent to present itself as a brand, determined to promote its ideals as if they were brand values.

L'insostenibile pesantezza dell'aziendalese politico

17 ottobre 2013. Mario Monti si dimette da presidente di Scelta Civica. Il già defunto Super Mario lascia il partito europeista e liberale, cui aveva dato vita nemmeno un anno prima, per effetto dell'autocombustione di una leadership che molti gli rimproverano di non aver mai avuto. «C'è forse una lezione, in questa parabola», scrive il giorno dopo Valerio Ceccarelli sul quotidiano "la Repubblica": «il potere è una bestiaccia che consuma anche le migliori personalità» (*Il tramonto di SuperMario che doveva salvare il Paese*). Soprattutto quando – andreottianamente – quel potere è venuto di fatto a mancare.

La goccia che fa traboccare il vaso è l'ennesimo attacco sferrato da Monti al governo dopo il varo, il martedì precedente, della Legge di Stabilità, e le insanabili spaccature interne che ha generato. E mentre il premier Letta rientra gongolante in Italia dopo l'incontro alla Casa Bianca con Obama, riponendo come uno scolaretto nel suo zaino la lezione sulla *fiducia* e sull'*ottimismo* ascoltata dal presidente americano, gli italiani sono costretti a mandar giù un beverone indigesto di sigle e di acronimi, di tecnicismi della finanza e dell'economia, di burocratismi e aziendalismi diffusi nei giorni precedenti dai media, e perlopiù attinti al testo della legge che ha preso il posto della vecchia Finanziaria. In molti casi, per giunta, senza nemmeno il conforto di una spiegazione o di un commento.

La *Trise* (TRIbuto SErvizi comunali), divenuta involontariamente *Tirse* in bocca al premier e ribattezzata *Triste* da Giulio Tremonti. La *Tasi* (TAssa Servizi Indivisibili), di cui inquieta la rima con l'oriental-teutonica *Stasi*. La *Tari* (TAssa RIfiuti), destinata a evolvere nella *Tarip* (Tassa RIfiuti Prodotti); sostituirà la *Tia* (Tariffa Igiene Ambientale) e la *Tares* (TAssa Rifiuti E Servizi), che dal 1993 eravamo abituati a chiamare *Tarsu* (TAssa Rifiuti Solidi Urbani). E poi gli *ecobonus* e le *tax expenditures*; le *deduzioni* (totali o parziali) e la loro allegra brigata (*dedurre* e *dedotto*; *deducibile* e *indeducibile*; *deducibilità* e *indeducibilità*); gli *incapienti* e i *salvaguardati*; gli *alleggerimenti* (del *patto di stabilità*) e l'*indicizzazione piena* (delle pensioni); la *rivalutazione all'inflazione* e quella di *cespiti* e *partecipazioni* a carico delle imprese; la *leva fiscale*, la riduzione del *cuneo* (sempre *fiscale*), i moltiplicatori (*fiscali* o *catastali*); i *finanziamenti in deficit* e i *servizi indivisibili*; la *suddivisione degli obblighi tributari* e la *tassazione degli immobili strumentali*; il *prelievo di bollo sui depositi e titoli* e l'*esposizione al debito pubblico*; il *contributo di solidarietà* e la *cassa integrazione in deroga*.

Il viceministro economico Stefano Fassina – si sarebbe dimesso il 4 gennaio 2011, per i contrasti insorti con la linea dettata al PD dal neosegretario Renzi – scrive in un intervento sul suo blog per l'"Huffington Post": «In Italia, i soggetti più forti continuano a interpretare i loro legittimi interessi secondo un paradigma insostenibile». Che è anche il paradigma dell'insostenibilità di un linguaggio – fra neopolitichese, burocratese e aziendalese – che non vuole proprio cambiare; quello stesso di tanti renzismi economici, sia pure controbilanciati da una consistente dose di linguaggio corrente, familiare, confidenziale.

Un americano a Firenze. La riforma del lavoro secondo Renzie

Alle 8.20 del 9 gennaio 2014 l'ex Rottamatore, ormai conquistato alla scuola di Obama e Berlusconi, così cinguetta su Twitter: «Il #jobsact è bozza che sarà definita il 16 *gen* e poi diverrà *doc* tecnico. Gradite idee, critiche, commenti. Email matteo@matteorenzi.it».

Ecco la bozza di cui parla Renzi:

L'obiettivo è creare posti di lavoro, rendendo semplice il sistema, incentivando voglia di investire dei nostri imprenditori, attraendo capitali stranieri (tra il 2008 e il 2012 l'Italia ha attratto 12 miliardi di euro all'anno di investimenti stranieri. Metà della Germania, 25 miliardi un terzo della Francia e della Spagna, 37 miliardi). Per la Banca Mondiale siamo al 73° posto al mondo per facilità di fare impresa (dopo la Romania, prima delle Seychelles). Per il World Economic Forum siamo al 42° posto per competitività (dopo la Polonia, prima della Turchia). Vi sembra possibile? No, ovviamente no. E allora basta ideologia e mettiamoci sotto.

Parte A – Il Sistema

1. Energia. Il dislivello tra aziende italiane e europee è insostenibile e pesa sulla produttività. Il primo segnale è ridurre del 10% il costo per le aziende, soprattutto per le piccole imprese che sono quelle che soffrono di più (Interventi dell'Autorità di Garanzia, riduzione degli incentivi cosiddetti interrompibili).

2. Tasse. Chi produce lavoro paga di meno, chi si muove in ambito finanziario paga di più, consentendo una riduzione del 10% dell'IRAP per le aziende. Segnale di equità oltre che concreto aiuto a chi investe.

3. Revisione della spesa. Vincolo di ogni risparmio di spesa corrente che arriverà dalla revisione della spesa alla corrispettiva riduzione fiscale sul reddito da lavoro.

4. Azioni dell'agenda digitale. Fatturazione elettronica, pagamenti elettronici, investimenti sulla rete.

5. Eliminazione dell'obbligo di iscrizione alle Camere di Commercio. Piccolo risparmio per le aziende, ma segnale contro ogni corporazione. Funzioni delle Camere assegnate a Enti territoriali pubblici.

6. Eliminazione della figura del dirigente a tempo indeterminato nel settore pubblico. Un dipendente pubblico è a tempo indeterminato se vince concorso. Un dirigente no. Stop allo strapotere delle burocrazie ministeriali.

7. Burocrazia. Intervento di semplificazione amministrativa sulla procedura di spesa pubblica sia per i residui ancora aperti (al Ministero dell'Ambiente circa 1 miliardo di euro sarebbe a disposizione immediatamente) sia per le strutture demaniali sul modello che vale oggi per gli interventi militari. I Sindaci decidono destinazioni, parere in 60 giorni di tutti i soggetti interessati, e poi nessuno può interrompere il processo. Obbligo di certezza della tempistica nel procedimento amministrativo, sia in sede di Conferenza dei servizi che di valutazione di impatto ambientale. Eliminazione della sospensiva nel giudizio amministrativo.

8. Adozione dell'obbligo di trasparenza: amministrazioni pubbliche, partiti, sindacati hanno il dovere di pubblicare online ogni entrata e ogni uscita, in modo chiaro, preciso e circostanziato.

Parte B - I nuovi posti di lavoro

Per ognuno di questi sette settori, il JobsAct conterrà un singolo piano industriale con indicazione delle singole azioni operative e concrete necessarie a creare posti di lavoro.
a) Cultura, turismo, agricoltura e cibo.
b) Made in Italy (dalla moda al design, passando per l'artigianato e per i makers).
c) ICT.
d) Green Economy.
e) Nuovo Welfare.
f) Edilizia.
g) Manifattura.

Parte C - Le regole
I. Semplificazione delle norme. Presentazione entro otto mesi di un codice del lavoro che racchiuda e semplifichi tutte le regole attualmente esistenti e sia ben comprensibile anche all'estero.
II. Riduzione delle varie forme contrattuali, oltre 40, che hanno prodotto uno spezzatino insostenibile. Processo verso un contratto di inserimento a tempo indeterminato a tutele crescenti.
III. Assegno universale per chi perde il posto di lavoro, anche per chi oggi non ne avrebbe diritto, con l'obbligo di seguire un corso di formazione professionale e di non rifiutare più di una nuova proposta di lavoro.
IV. Obbligo di rendicontazione online ex post per ogni voce dei denari utilizzati per la formazione professionale finanziata da denaro pubblico. Ma presupposto dell'erogazione deve essere l'effettiva domanda delle imprese. Criteri di valutazione meritocratici delle agenzie di formazione con cancellazione dagli elenchi per chi non rispetta determinati standard di performance.
V. Agenzia Unica Federale che coordini e indirizzi i centri per l'impiego, la formazione e l'erogazione degli ammortizzatori sociali.
VI. Legge sulla rappresentatività sindacale e presenza dei rappresentanti eletti direttamente dai lavoratori nei CDA delle grandi aziende.

Su questi spunti, nei prossimi giorni, ci apriremo alla discussione. Con tutti. Ma con l'idea di fare. Certo ci saranno polemiche, resistenze. Ma pensiamo che un provvedimento del genere arricchito dalle singole azioni concrete e dalla certezza dei tempi della pubblica amministrazione possa dare una spinta agli investitori stranieri. E anche agli italiani. Oggi stimiamo in circa 3.800 miliardi di euro la ricchezza finanziaria delle famiglie italiane. Insomma, ancora qualcuno ha disponibilità di denari. Ma non investe perché ha paura, perché è bloccato, perché non ha certezze.

Noi vogliamo dire che l'Italia può ripartire se abbandoniamo la rendita e scommettiamo sul lavoro. In questa settimana accoglieremo gli stimoli e le riflessioni di addetti ai lavori e cittadini (matteo@matteorenzi.it). Poi redigeremo il vero e proprio Jobs Act.

Le idee, le critiche, i commenti non si fanno attendere. Maurizio Landini dichiara: «Leggerò il documento di Renzi. Meglio parlare italiano, però, perché io l'inglese non lo capisco». Belli anche i *makers*, ma soffermiamoci su *JobsAct*: *piano per il lavoro*, o *piano per la riforma del lavoro*, sarebbero state due buone alternative anche per il *microblogging* di Twitter; forse un po' generiche, ma anche *job(s) act* è tutt'altro che trasparente:

> In inglese la parola act, in particolare se scritta con l'iniziale maiuscola, identifica un atto legislativo approvato dal parlamento e promulgato dal capo dello stato (una legge). È più probabile che Renzi intenda invece una proposta di legge, ma in questo caso in inglese il termine corretto è bill (e comunque in Italia si deve essere parlamentare per presentarne una). [...] L'ispirazione per Jobs Act va probabilmente cercata in un uso improprio della parola Act, l'American Jobs Act, descritto nel sito della Casa Bianca come "il piano del presidente Obama per creare posti di lavoro" e nome informale di una proposta di legge presentata da Obama al Congresso degli Stati Uniti nel 2011 ma non approvata nella formulazione originale per mancanza del numero sufficiente di voti, quindi rimasta allo stadio di bill o proposal (la terminologia usata nel discorso di presentazione). Che sia proprio da imitare? (Corbolante 2014).

Probabilmente Renzi, ignaro del fatto che gli studiosi italiani, a dispetto dell'esiguità dei fondi erogati alla ricerca, continuano a essere i migliori al mondo, era tutto preso dal suo progetto di chiusura della metà dei nostri atenei. Che è anche un modo per cominciare ad affrontare seriamente il problema dell'ingombrante presenza di una lingua italiana che, in molte università (perlopiù da sopprimere, *of course*), osa ancora ostacolare l'avanzata dell'inglese.

Ma del premier, complice proprio il filoamericanismo di un inglese un po' guascone e un'avventurosità lessicale (annuncite) che ha messo in ombra anche i più disinvolti o inventivi fra i comunicatori della Seconda Repubblica, vale la pena stendere un breve ritratto. Lo faccio risultare – e risaltare – dal confronto con i suoi avversari più temibili in due occasioni importanti: le primarie del Partito Democratico del 2012 e dell'anno successivo.

Bersani, Vendola e Renzi. Tre linguaggi per tre candidati

Autunno del 2012. Pierluigi Bersani (16 ottobre), Nichi Vendola (11 ottobre), Matteo Renzi (10 ottobre), tre personalità comunicative molto diverse, vengono videointervistati da Massimo Giannini per "la Repubblica". Sono i tre più autorevoli candidati democratici alle primarie (la quarta è Laura Puppato), e le videointervste, guardate e ascoltate una dietro l'altra, li inchiodano alla profondità delle loro reciproche differenze. Fra i primi due, però, punti di contatto non mancano. L'ultimo, invece, corre già da solo.

Bersani mostra il profilo meno attraente di quella politica strapaesana il cui campione indiscusso è Antonio Di Pietro: il dipietrese, con la sua essenza ruspante, contadina, del pane al pane e del vino al vino, si converte in lui negli automatismi di una provincia che non c'è più o, forse, non c'è mai stata. È la politica che impugna l'accetta: dà un colpo qua e un colpo là, senza andare tanto per il sottile. Il segretario del PD lascia frasi a metà; mozza o tira via parole (tanto da renderle a volte incomprensibili) come autorizzato dalla rinuncia, da buon settentrionale, a qualche vocale finale di troppo; parla un po' a ruota libera, vittima di qualche battuta al limite del nonsense (come quella sul rischio di «buttare via l'acqua sporca e non solo un bambino, due o tre bambini»); s'incammina per strane vie metaforiche («C'è l'Italia, poi c'è la ditta che è il PD, e il suo progetto per l'Italia, e poi ci sono le persone. La classifica è questa qua»); rimane prigioniero, soprattutto, del vuoto pneumatico di una sonnacchiosa noncuranza comunicativa, che gli effetti prodotti dalle rare impennate fanno addirittura rimpiangere («Non si dica questo, eh, p-per favore, perché vittimismi ne ho sentiti fin troppi. Ne ho sentiti fin troppi di vittimismi. Qui, chi ha del filo da tess... tessa, si combatte. Armi pari, chi vince vince e siam tutti lì a sostenere poi il candidato dei progressisti»). Inizia l'intervista così:

> No io non chiedo, ecco, è l'occasione per cercare di capirsi su questo punto. Io li conosco tutti questi di cui si parla, magari mi ci metto dentro anche me tra quelli da rottamare, li conosco tutti. E parlo con loro, no, e non da oggi parlo con loro. E quindi son buon testimone che tutta questa gente non c'era bisogno di Renzi per... perché facessero una riflessione, non c'era bisogno.

La sua lingua operaiola, iniettata da sempre di consistentissime quote di burocratese (si è ancora convinti, se si è culturalmente in basso, che raffini il parlare) taglia e non ricuce. La sua emilianità casual gli nuoce, e qualcuno avrebbe dovuto dirglielo (o ribadirglielo).

Vendola è la politica in punta di forchetta, ma spesa in una notevole capacità di racconto. Con i suoi snodi e le sue articolazioni, fra improvvise accensioni espressive (alla Savonarola) e poi, ogni volta, il rassicurante ritorno a una raziocinante lucidità da Prima Repubblica, la sua narrazione cerca di evitare la tracimazione della retorica e di sottrarsi al sospetto di un ritorno a vecchi modelli di esibizionismo verbale, di un giuramento di fedeltà a un certo tardo-comunismo pignolo ed estetizzante (alla D'Alema, per intenderci). Parte così il suo intervento a "Repubblica TV":

> Ma io credo intanto che la dea della vendetta abbia disvelato la realtà nascosta dall'ideologia leghista, quella che rappresentava il Sud come il luogo metaforico del male, della corruzione, dello spreco, delle mafie, il luogo antropologicamente votato a ogni esercitazione del Maligno, e il Nord come territorio sfruttato da questo Sud parassitario.

È la politica giocata linguisticamente di fioretto e "armata" di specillo. Vendola focalizza e puntualizza con una forbita e *pasionaria* eleganza d'altri tempi, e tuttavia funziona fino a un certo punto. Discute di realtà e di sostanze, ma le condisce (e, anche qui, burocratizza) troppo: la *danza* e il *feticismo* del denaro; la «voragine di immoralità pubblica» e «il grido e la bestemmia purificatrice»; le «fibrillazioni tragicomiche» del passato e i «dilemmi del tempo nostro»; gli scandali del sistema sanitario, «che assomiglia moltissimo a una flottiglia di sommergibili inabissati e che è molto complicato portare a emersione»; la politica con i «piedi piantati nel dolore sociale» e il grillismo, in quanto discorso del leader, come «semina di idee suggestive»; le giovani generazioni «risucchiate dentro una maledizione, dentro un cattivo sortilegio», e il lavoro come «epopea che ha innervato tutti i grandi movimenti sociali»; la paura come «prodotto finito del modello sociale della destra» e la speranza, la stabilità, la tranquillità come «prodotto finito del modello sociale della sinistra»; l'*avvitamento* dell'Europa nelle «politiche monetariste e liberiste» e l'«idea abbastanza disincantante» offerta dalla sinistra ai suoi cittadini; le «politiche sciagurate» che hanno «definanziato il fondo per la non autosufficienza», le «culture politiche» che *si acconciano* a protezione dei rapporti sociali, il PD che «ha scelto di sostenere Monti come una condizione necessitata». Una lingua, la sua, che non avvicina.

Bersani, in giacca e cravatta, i gomiti spesso piantati sul tavolo o le braccia conserte, appare rigido, imbozzolato, compreso di sé anche quando disintreccia le mani e prende a gesticolare a destra e a manca. È in giacca e cravatta anche Vendola; dritto – e ogni tanto quasi saltellante – sulla sedia, tenta di tenere quanto più possibile le braccia accostate al corpo, ma la passione gli prende spesso la mano (e gli agita il braccio). Renzi, scamiciato e senza cravatta, è l'immagine della politica dell'antipolitica, o dell'antipolitica nella politica. Non ha però bisogno di scomporsi o di sbraitare per farlo capire. Gli basta la sua naturale scioltezza, sorniona e accattivante, per sedurre chi guarda. Gli bastano i toni sottili dell'ironia per far arrivare forte e chiaro il suo messaggio: il modo è di un'aerea leggerezza, anche se le parole sono pesanti come macigni. Le dà, il sindaco di Firenze, altroché se le dà. E sono colpi di maglio. Prende la vecchia politica a sciabolate, a badilate, a randellate; la rottama con il corpo contundente dell'evidenza delle cose.

Vince ai punti su Vendola, mette giù Bersani per kappaò alla prima ripresa. A renderlo imbattibile sul piano della comunicazione una fiorentinità radical chic e stradaiola insieme, le argutezze e le spiritosità di rado banali o gratuite, la sfrontatezza monella di chi sa perfettamente il fatto suo. Piace, e sa di piacere. L'animalità mediatica berlusconiana, che l'ha caricaturato nel bambolotto Renzusconi, si sposa in lui all'estro dell'abbraccio avvolgente di un fiorentinaccio. Scandisce bene le parole, parla il linguaggio di una politica che si dichiara nemica delle ideologie. Conversa amichevolmente con l'intervistatore come fosse seduto al bancone di un bar, convincendo sui vari temi affrontati: cittadinanza e immigrazione; trasparenza e libertà; laicismo e laicità; cattolicesimo e testamento biologico; imprenditorialità e lavoro; sviluppo e soft economy; parità di genere e civil partnership; Europa e made in Italy.

Le sue armi migliori sono l'aderenza a una normale quotidianità (perché, si chiede, «sul tema delle infrastrutture continuiamo ad essere affascinati dal modello delle grandi opere e non mandiamo avanti le piccole manutenzioni, non mandiamo avanti le scuole, non diamo ai sindaci i soldi per sistemare le buche?») e l'impressione che stia sempre dalla parte delle persone comuni (invita ad andare a votare alla primarie perché sono un «meccanismo democratico che toglie il potere di decidere ai burocrati di partito e lo restituisce alla gente»). Il colpo da maestro: «Vorrei che dicessimo con forza che un bambino che nasce in Italia è italiano». Poi aggiunge:

> Vado nelle scuole, vado nelle classi, parlo con i bambini e c'è Lucia e Fatima. Lucia e Fatima parlano con lo stesso accento sbracato fiorentino con la c aspirata, amano Firenze allo stesso modo, mangiano il gelato negli stessi posti, iniziano ad avere le prime cotte, sono alle scuole medie, per gli stessi fidanzatini e però una è cittadina italiana, l'altra no. Questo è un principio di maleducazione civica che stiamo dando ai nostri figli.

Dismessi i panni del giamburrasca, Renzi indossa qui quelli di un padre-sindaco premuroso e amorevole verso i figli-cittadini.

8 dicembre 2013. Chi si aspettava tre candidati pronti a darsele di santa ragione è rimasto (fortunatamente) deluso. Perché il confronto nell'arena meneghina di X-Factor – un fianco a fianco più che un faccia a faccia, perché i tre *competitors* alle primarie del PD non si sono guardati quasi mai – è stato pacato, amichevole, a tratti teneramente fraterno. Matteo Renzi, Gianni Cuperlo e Pippo Civati hanno provato a fare squadra, e

questo è un buon segno; si sono più volte citati a vicenda, da buoni compagni, spesso chiamandosi affettuosamente per nome. Finora tra loro, perlopiù, erano stati botta e risposta a distanza, anche a forza di slogan. Dell'escluso Gianni Pittella, il quarto incomodo, il peggiore («Il futuro che vale»), ma gli altri non scherzano: «Le cose cambiano, cambiandole» (Civati); «Bello e democratico» (Cuperlo); «L'Italia cambia verso» (Renzi), tradotto perfino in veneto da un consigliere provinciale: «No star 'ndar drito! Cambiemo direxion!». Tutti brutti e improbabili, da far quasi rimpiangere il bersaniano giaguaro da smacchiare. Gli spin doctor dei tre candidati segretari potevano far di meglio.

Da 30 secondi a un minuto e mezzo il tempo concesso a ciascuno per rispondere alle 15 domande poste da Gianluca Semprini, il moderatore del confronto televisivo su Sky; quattro le possibilità di replica e controreplica, contenute nei 30 secondi, e poi il pantheon ideale di sinistra (due nomi per ciascuno da fare) e l'appello finale. Il podio, trasparente, è all'americana (i candidati sono in piedi, con davanti un leggio e un timer); il popolo di Twitter giudica le risposte più pertinenti, convincenti o credibili; con il *voting* si risponde da casa alla domanda: «Chi ti sta convincendo di più?». Quanto al *fact checking live*, il riscontro sui dati snocciolati dai tre – in materia rigorosamente economica –, garantito da un pool di economisti dell'ateneo di Tor Vergata, ne avremmo fatto volentieri a meno.

Cuperlo parla per primo, Renzi per secondo, Civati per terzo. Il sindaco di Firenze è fedele solo in parte all'effervescenza del personaggio; gioca in difesa o di rimessa, attento a non oltrepassare la soglia delle schermaglie di circostanza e, soprattutto, a non esporsi troppo. Il dalemiano Cuperlo, per toni e sostanza politica, pare recitare un copione mandato a memoria e ben adattato da un manuale di perfetta nomenklatura, ma è spesso a disagio e impacciato: non riesce a rispettare i tempi di risposta imposti dal match e alterna momenti d'immobilismo fisico, dritto come un palo e stretto nelle (strette) spalle, ad altri di agitazione manifesta. La vera sorpresa è Civati, elegantissimo «candidato di sinistra» (indossa la cravatta più chic). Spigliato, simpatico, divertente, ruba la scena al Rottamatore. Se c'è qualcuno bello e democratico, in questa competizione, è proprio lui.

Refrattario al mezzo, Cuperlo è il volto snob dell'intellighenzia democratica che vorrebbe parlare al cuore e alla ragione insieme: cita Berlinguer, Jefferson, Calvino e Rosa Parks, ma il suo linguaggio implode; sulle questioni più delicate non risponde, divaga o cambia direzione; il massimo che si concede, in termini di "abbraccio" al pubblico, è la menzione di una vespa e del suo cane, con la vecchia barzelletta dell'operazione chirurgica riuscita ma il paziente è deceduto. Perfettamente padrone del mezzo, Renzi dà un colpo al cerchio e uno alla botte, mettendo mano a cielo (il tecnicismo spinto, magari con l'aiuto della lingua inglese, per chi sa intendere) e terra: la battuta di spirito; le mamme e i figli; i banconi del supermercato, la bicicletta che gli hanno fregato, le metafore calcistiche (tra capocannonieri, assist, calci di rigore); le marchette, i becchi e bastonati, i cornuti e i mazziati, i papponi e l'inciucio.

Civati è un'icona pop, un po' fricchettone e un po' scavezzacollo: parla delle ereditarie (a proposito del ricambio nel centro-destra), dello Zecchino d'Oro, dei pontefici che chiamano a casa e il suo partito è invece scollato dai suoi elettori; dice di non fidarsi di Alfano, l'uomo delle leggi ad personam che pensa ancora alla *personam*; ironizza su Gaetano Quagliarello e Luciano Violante, da due anni impegnati sospetti a riscrivere la legge elettorale («secondo me c'è del tenero»); sostiene la necessità di una politica diversa, rispettosa dell'identità di genere, puntando fermo il dito contro il machismo (le palle bisognerebbe tenerle dentro, invece di tirarle fuori); plaude ai tedeschi, che hanno recepito la «mozione Civaten» e compreso le cose realmente da fare: mettersi attorno a un tavolo, favorire la partecipazione, promuovere un referendum fra i propri iscritti. Boccia inappellabilmente il governo Letta, attacca a testa bassa la ministra Cancellieri per la vicenda Ligresti, è chiarissimo sulle unioni fra persone dello stesso sesso: sì ai matrimoni ugualitari, sì all'affido e all'adozione di bambini anche per le coppie omosessuali. Sul tema, se Cuperlo svicola, Renzi intorbida maliziosamente le acque.

Non si è limitato a vincere ai punti, l'allora trentottenne ragazzo monzese dallo sguardo diretto e dal piglio arguto, ma ha oscurato i suoi due avversari. Troppo tardi per rimontare, e però intanto una rimonta c'è. Le risposte del pubblico di Sky alla domanda «Chi ti ha convinto di più?», che vedono Cuperlo attestarsi su un misero 14,18%, gratificano Renzi del 49,32% ma Civati si conquista un bel 36,50%. Sappiamo poi com'è andata. Tra falchi e colombe, cigni e aironi (il premier Letta, agli occhi del senatore Calderoli), il futuro premier avrebbe volteggiato con la scanzonata leggerezza, limpida e sonora, di un fringuello. Ma il suo è comunque perlopiù un modello nel quale alto e basso, formale e informale, tecnico e basico s'alternano e si compongono in varie soluzioni e miscele a seconda delle opportunità. È quanto avviene anche sul piano della proposta dei contenuti, sicché la globalizzazione suggerita dai *mercati finanziari* può bellamente convivere con l'iperlocalismo dei *mercati rionali*, come nello sfrontato e irrituale discorso pronunciato in Senato, il 24 febbraio 2014, prima del voto di fiducia al suo governo (cito dal resoconto stenografico della seduta):

> Se in questi anni avessimo prestato ai mercati rionali lo stesso ascolto che abbiamo prestato ai mercati finanziari, ci saremmo accorti che la prima richiesta è la richiesta di semplicità, di pace, di chiarezza (https://www.senato.it).

La polarizzazione fra sovranazionale e nazionale, o fra sovranazionale e locale (o iperlocale, se a supportare la causa è il dialetto fiorentino: quello dello *spompo* 'spompato', per es., indirizzato a Bersani in un fuorionda del 2013), è un altro aspetto di un'offerta linguistica che si muove retoricamente, con esibita nonchalance, fra i due estremi di un italiano *smart* (o *easy*) e di un inglese tecnicamente spinto:

> Noi non siamo per sottrarre responsabilità ai dirigenti: siamo per dargliele tutte; noi vorremmo che la parola *accountability* trovasse una traduzione in italiano, perché vi sono le responsabilità erariali, quelle penali e quelle civili, però non ce n'è una da mancato raggiungimento degli obiettivi, se non a livello teorico (*ibid.*).

> Oggi il numero dei parlamentari è eccessivo rispetto ai Paesi europei e al *benchmark* internazionale di riferimento: lo sapete meglio voi di me (*ibid.*).

Renzi, ai piani bassi della comunicazione politica in un contesto istituzionale, se ha raggiunto esiti difficilmente comparabili con quelli dei suoi predecessori (cfr. Giansante 2014), ha però avuto anche lui i suoi bravi maestri, in particolare Obama e quel leader indiscusso nella comunicazione politica della Seconda Repubblica che è stato il magnate Berlusconi. Non ha caso i suoi soprannomi contano *Renzusconi* e *Renzama*.

Il Cavaliere, ben conscio del potenziale pubblico della sua figura di imprenditore di successo, ha inciso fortemente sulla virata economica del linguaggio politico dell'ultimo ventennio: si sia riconosciuto nel ruolo di un «presidente operaio», o abbia paragonato un primo ministro a una specie di «amministratore delegato dell'azienda Italia» (salvo attribuire l'etichetta di azienda a una città o a un partito); si sia detto sbucato fuori dalla «trincea del lavoro», al fine di poter raddrizzare la politica; si sia mostrato impegnato a firmare in tv un *contratto* con gli italiani; abbia tirato fuori dal cilindro «promotori della libertà» che suggeriscono *promotori* di altro genere (*finanziari* o *d'impresa*), ottundenti e un po' volgari. Ma la conversione economica della comunicazione politica è stata altresì favorita da una serie di fattori congiunturali in grado di attirare su di sé l'attenzione generale, fra i quali un'interminabile crisi economica, l'introduzione della moneta unica, l'aumento del debito pubblico, la privatizzazione galoppante e la speculazione finanziaria, la forbice sempre più larga tra l'opulenza o l'alta disponibilità di risorse dei pochi e l'indigenza o le ristrettezze dei molti.

Già tra la fine degli anni Settanta, con le prime significative certificazioni di morte della tradizionale politica (cfr. Lonzi 1978), e l'inizio degli anni Ottanta, con la formazione di una nuova classe politica assai più adusa al linguaggio economico-finanziario che a quello umanistico-giuridico cui si ancorava quella precedente, si erano manifestate le prime avvisaglie di una profonda trasformazione proseguita nella seconda metà degli anni Ottanta (i vecchi partiti ormai incapaci di riconvertire istituzionalmente esigenze, pressioni, istanze della società civile: Lupo 2013, p. 166) e portata a compimento, anche grazie al Cavaliere, negli anni Novanta. La declinazione economica del linguaggio politico, pure anticipata dagli interscambi fra politica ed economia già accertabili nei primi anni Settanta, segna un sostanziale perseguimento del «dato sicuro e oggettivo» (Dell'Anna e Lala 2004, p. 47):

> I politici mirano a dare consistenza e validità alle proprie affermazioni facendo ricorso ai numeri, poiché cifre e numeri danno l'impressione dell'obiettività e della concretezza; il loro prestigio sembra derivare infatti non più solo da una certa bravura retorica di sapore umanistico, ma dalla capacità di usare abilmente cifre e statistiche e di misurarsi in prima persona con conoscenze e problemi di tipo economico (*ibid.*).

Del filoeconomismo politico, linguistico e retorico, il montante angloamericanismo è una evidentissima spia, anche in quanto lascito dell'evoluzione del confronto politico – da non trascurare al riguardo gli effetti scaturiti dalla strada intrapresa dal sistema elettorale: dal proporzionale al maggioritario – dalle vecchie formule del consociativismo a quelle di una libera competizione giocata a colpi di marketing e ultimamente, con Renzi, di *political viral marketing*. Tra i «maestrini dalla penna rossa» additati da Beppe Grillo in un post, pubblicato il 30 maggio 2013 sul suo blog (http://www.beppegrillo.it/2013/05/i_maestrini_dal.html), c'è proprio lui, impareggiabile nel far convergere l'attenzione su di sé:

> Renzie, lo statista gonfiato, imperversa con le sue ricette e le critiche al M5S su tutti i canali televisivi preda di compiacenti cortigiane come la Gruber [...]; un venditore a tempo pieno di sé stesso. Vende in giro un sindaco mai usato, come nuovo.

In Renzi il valore dell'anglicismo è più rituale e simbolico che tecnico, in linea con una ritualizzazione e una simbolizzazione dell'economia di cui il premier è maestro e impagabile interprete:

> Si nomina migliaia di volte lo *spread*, lo si definisce con una giaculatoria, ma non si spiega come si sia generato, nonostante i superesperti dell'economia assicurassero di avere tutto sotto controllo. Si aspetta la chiusura delle Borse con lo stesso spirito con cui gli antichi ascoltavano l'oracolo di Delfi. Come se non bastasse pagare lo scotto della recessione, milioni di contribuenti/risparmiatori devono accettare il mistero che fa della finanza una materia oscura, inaccessibile; in altre parole devono accollarsi i danni altrui senza far domande (Priulla 2012, p. 71).

Spread, *jobs act* o *spending review*, in bocca a Renzi, sono mantra di cui non occorre dare spiegazioni, elementi di un universo simbolico:

> Renzi è capace di manipolare i simboli come pochi altri. Dall'esibizione del rifiuto di una scorta all'arrivo in Smart, è un abile creatore di immagini capaci di comunicare senza bisogno di parole, solo con gesti o atteggiamenti. Anche nei discorsi in Parlamento conferma questa sua attitudine, ad esempio quando usa il banco del Governo come la scrivania di un ufficio, con iPad, computer, fogli ed evidenziatori. Vuole dire anche a chi guardi distrattamente i tg, "sono uno di voi, al lavoro per voi" (Giansante 2014).

Bibliografia

Antonelli, Giuseppe. 2009. *Sull'italiano dei politici nella Seconda Repubblica*, in Valvolsem *et al.*, vol. I: 211-234.

Corbolante, Licia. 2014. "Get your [Jobs] Act Together!" http://blog.terminologiaetc.it.

Dell'Anna Maria Vittoria, Lala, Pierpaolo. 2004. *Mi consenta un girotondo. Lingua e lessico nella seconda Repubblica*, Galatina (LE), Congedo.

Giansante, Gianluca. 2014. "La comunicazione di Renzi: dieci elementi che emergono dai discorsi in Parlamento". http://gianlucagiansante.com, 13 marzo.

Lonzi, Carla. 1978. "Mito della proposta cultuale" in Lonzi *et al.*: 137-152.

Lonzi, Marta, *et al.* 1978. *La presenza dell'uomo nel femminismo*, Milano: Rivolta Femminile.

Lupo, Salvatore. 2013. *Antipartiti. Il mito della nuova politica nella storia della Repubblica (prima, seconda e terza)*, Roma: Donzelli.

Priulla, Graziella. 2012. *Riprendiamoci le parole. Il linguaggio della politica è un bene pubblico*, Trapani: Di Girolamo.

Vanvolsem, Serge *et al.* (a cura di). 2009. *L'italiano oltre frontiera. V Convegno internazionale (Leuven, 22-25 aprile 1998)*, Leuven-Firenze: Leuven University Press/Cesati, 2 voll.

BANK NAMES AND SUCCESS: A STATISTICAL APPROACH

ILIA BARANOV

Abstract

There are many "in vitro" experiments exploring connections between the customer's perception of goods or services and their name properties, e.g., purchase intention. Nevertheless, there is a lack of papers examining the connection between actual commercial names "in vivo" and the success of the corresponding businesses. Russian bank names are the subject of this investigation. We used two success indexes: bank lifetime and assets. Lifetimes were investigated by survival analysis in the years 1988–2014; assets were studied by general linear regression in the years 2006–2014. It was found that in regions with smaller gross domestic product (GDP), names had a stronger correlation with the bank's success indexes than names in regions with a higher GDP. Bank assets are more sensitive to name differences than bank lifetimes. Name properties that accompany bank success are masculine gender, absence of negative connotations, and presence of typical banking industry morphemes in addition to "*bank*". Those names contain several morphemes with different topics, have "*bank*" descriptors at the end of the name and are longer than the average name in the banking industry.

Purpose

Many laboratory, "in vitro", experiments explore statistically significant correlations between the linguistic features of a brand name (semantics, phonology, word formation) and the indicators predicting the brand success (e.g., brand recall and recognition, willingness to buy, brand attitude). On the contrary, quantitative research in relation to a brand name and its success in reality, "in vivo", is scarce. Most quantitative studies of brand names concern fast moving consumer goods (FMCG); services are less studied and almost nothing is known about bank names.

When they say, "a business has a good name", they usually mean that there is good balance between the two opposite vectors: on the one hand, a name becomes part of a product or service category and corresponds to the industry's traditions; on the other hand, it stands out from the competition and breaks with the traditions. There might be different proportions in compliance and violation of the traditions in each industry. The purpose of this study is to determine whether there are name properties associated with bank success in reality, and if so, how these properties correlate with the bank industry's naming traditions. This paper continues the author's research in connection to brand name properties and business success "in vivo" initiated on the example of clothing stores (Baranov 2011).

Related Literature

Some researchers believe that a name of a service company is important only to raise brand awareness, to identify friend or foe, and cannot relate an interest to the service (Schultz 2009: 111). Others believe that in the long term, the service name contributes to customer loyalty (Davis 2007). Moreover, a brand name generates a non-neutral attitude to a product, which is difficult to change in a later communication (Zinkhan 1987).

The less the consumer is informed, the more he focuses on external factors—design, advertising and name (Maheswaran 1992). Experts believe that the financial literacy of the Russian population is low and that they are more likely to choose banks according to their appearance than as a result of their financial performance (Kashin 2013). This effect is described for the US mutual funds who receive more deposits simply by changing their names to ones that are more attractive (Cooper 2005).

Several studies looked into the name properties in connection with the standard branding factors.

Agreement in the grammatical gender of a product name with that of a brand name increases brand evaluation (Yorkston 2005). The stronger the brand's anthropomorphization, the more important is this agreement (Skroznikova 2005). However, for goods it is suggested that brand gender is more related to the gender of the typical brand user and to the personality of the brand, than to the actual brand name (Ulrich 2011). The Russian word "bank" is of masculine gender; there are only eight women among the leaders of 100 largest Russian banks (Nikolaeva 2009), which may enhance the male connotation in the perception of the industry.

It was shown that brand awareness is higher for the brand names with a clear meaning and for the names which fit into a product category. Moreover, meaningfulness affects brand awareness only when brand names do not fit into a product category (Kanungo 1968). It was confirmed later that brand awareness is much higher for the brand names, which are regular words rather than non-words, artificial words without lexical meaning (Lerman 2002).

For the products with low customer involvement, descriptive names are preferable to non-descriptive ones. For the products with high involvement, no difference is shown between descriptive and non-descriptive names (Zaichkowsky 1993).

It is known that brand memorability has a positive effect on brand preference (Hutchinson 1994). It was found that high imagery names are remembered better than low imagery ones (Robertson 1987). Clothing shops with evocative names survive on the market longer compared to the ones with abstract names (Baranov 2011). Interestingly, words with negative meaning are remembered more often and more accurately than those with neutral meaning (Kensinger 2003). It is also assumed that unusual names of FMCG can be memorized less easily from a single exposure than the names typical for the category but they can be better memorized as a result of multiple exposure, which is more consistent with the reality of advertising (McCracken 1998).

Easily pronounceable names increase brand recognition and brand preference (Bao 2008). In particular, that is why abbreviations are not recommended. According to our data, abbreviations in the names of clothing stores are indistinguishable in survival from the rest of the sample (Baranov 2011). On the other hand, a strengthening of the abbreviation role is indicated by their increasing frequency in the names of German companies (Kremer 2012).

It was noted that brand names of services are longer and consist of several words more often, as compared to product names. Violation of the good name criteria—sonority, brevity and memorability—probably compensates for the lower tangibility of services as compared to goods. On the contrary, a name built in a way which is unusual for the respective service, increases the risk of failure (Turley 1995).

Hypotheses

We hypothesized that higher assets and better survival are associated with bank names that are:

1) More traditional in the industry, i.e. have masculine gender, higher frequency attributes and indicate the scope of activity in addition to the mandatory morpheme *bank*;
2) More tangible: have a clear meaning, evocative and multisegment, and a longer than average length.

Methods

Bank success has been measured by the time of its existence and the size of annual assets.

The relation between the lifespan of a bank and the properties of its name has been studied in survival analysis (StatSoft 2013a). This method enables us to take into account the banks that continue their activities outside the timeframe. The results are presented in Kaplan-Meier graphs where the horizontal axis marks the bank lifespan and the vertical axis marks the probability of living up to that lifespan. The higher the graph, the longer the lifespan in the market. This method was applied if each distinguished group had at least 40 names.

The degree of connection between the size of bank assets and bank name properties has been analyzed in the General Regression Model, or GRM (StatSoft 2013b). The relation between bank assets and bank name was measured in adjusted coefficient of determination R^2_{adj} expressed in percent. $R^2_{adj} = 1\%$ means that the selected model explains one percent in the assets variation.

In both methods, we consider the model reliable if the statistical significance level of the null hypothesis is $p < 0.05$. To calculate p, chi-square criterion was used in GRM and Gehan's generalized Wilcox test was used in survival analysis. All below mentioned differences in indicators are statistically significant unless otherwise mentioned.

Data

We studied the names of Russian banks created between 1988 and 2014, according to the annual *Interfax-100* rankings (Interfax-100), the Central Bank of the Russian Federation database (The Central Bank), and the web sites www.banki.ru and www.bankir.ru. Banks renamed during the study period were considered separately under each name. The beginning of the bank activity was accepted from the issue date of the general license by the Central Bank. We accept the date of the license revocation as the bank closure.

Most of the banks researched were created in a short period between 1990 and 1994, i.e. in similar economic, political, and linguistic conditions (Fig. 1).

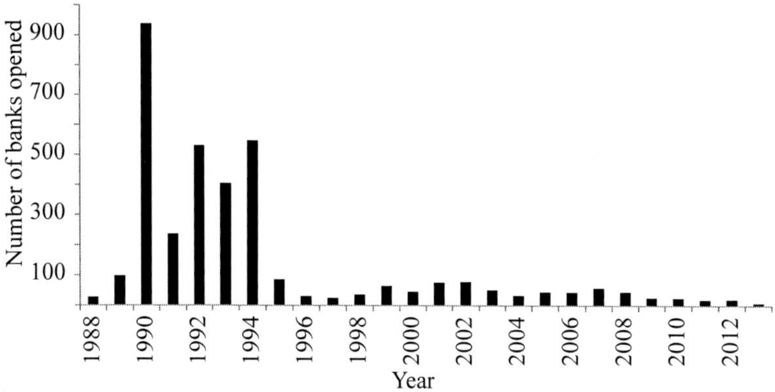

Fig. 1. Bank registration timeline.

Preliminary studies have shown that banks in Moscow have better success rates than banks in other regions, and that the connection of their name with their success is less pronounced. Therefore, they are allocated to a group "Msk" and dealt with separately. Banks in the regions with a large gross domestic product (GDP) are more successful than banks in the regions with smaller GDPs. Therefore, banks in the regions with a GDP which is higher than the average are summed up in a group "High", while other banks are in a group "Midlow". Banks located in Dagestan and banks focusing on agriculture have not been considered for the study. Banks with foreign capital, state banks and banks in banking groups are more successful than others, and have also been excluded from the analysis. State participation in bank capital has been regarded according to data (Vernikov 2009) that cover 98% of state participation in the banking sector. Membership in a banking group is taken into account according to the *Interfax-100* ranking for 2011–2012 (Interfax-100). Foreign participation has been accounted for accordingly (The Central Bank). The size of bank assets has been studied in the timeframe between 2006 and 2014. We calculated natural logarithms of bank assets' share in the total assets of the annual sample (the "Assets"). Each bank has been considered as many times as many years its assets have been known. The sample size for the survival analysis is 2,810 names. The total number of banks in the sample of assets is 5,932.

Results

We studied the following parameters of a bank name.

Gender. 90% of banks names are of masculine gender. Names of neutral and indefinable gender, as well as with mixed gender, are few and have not been considered here. Survival of regional banks with masculine names is higher than that of banks with feminine names (Fig. 2).The gender of names of "Msk" banks is not associated with survival (Fig. 3). The assets of banks with masculine names are bigger that those with feminine names (R^2_{adj} = 1.1%). The largest difference has been shown for the "Midlow" group: R^2_{adj} = 4.3%.

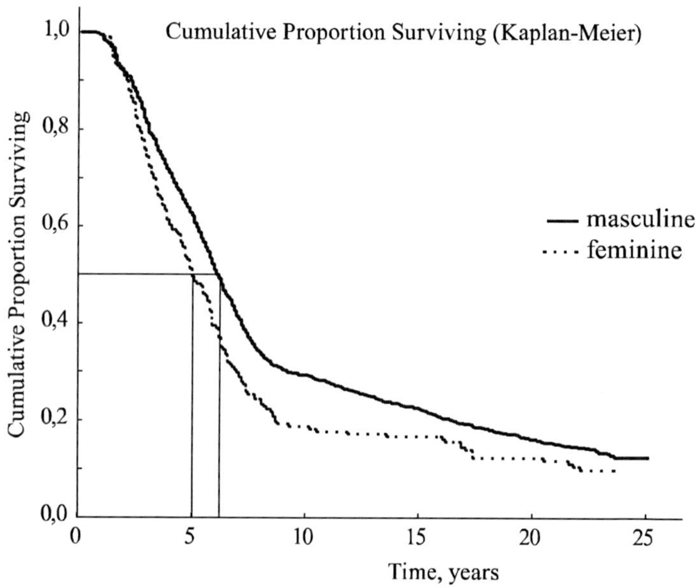

Fig. 2. Bank survival and gender of bank names in regions ("High" and "Midlow" regions together).

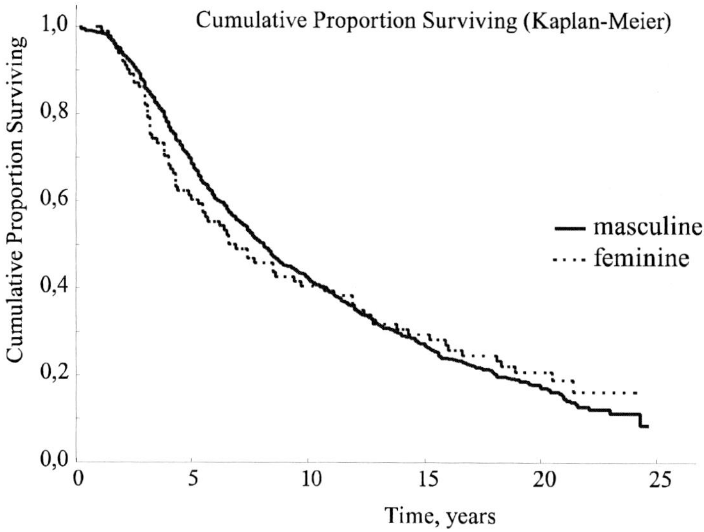

Fig. 3. Bank survival and gender of bank names in Moscow ("Msk").

Several **thematic groups** have been identified in bank names (Table 1).

Topic	**Description**	**Nos.***	**%**	**Examples**
Agnonym	Unclear meaning	480	*17*	*SRB-Bank, Kafkombank, Mirod-Bank*
Smalltopo	Other toponyms	389	*14*	*Balakovo-Bank, Dnovsky, Bank v g. Makaryeve Kostromskoy obl.*
Toponym	Toponyms of Russian administrative regions and other Russian widely-known toponyms	248	*9*	*Murmansk-Bank, Sochiinkombank, Magadan-Kredit*
Regiongeo	Geographical regions, cardinal points	200	*7*	*Povolzhye* "Volga Region", *Zarya Urala* "Dawn of the Urals", *Severo-zapadny* "North-West"
Moscow	Moscow and the Moscow administrative region	49	*2*	*Moskovsky kreditny* "Moscow credit", *Mosnatsbank* "Moscow national"

Branch	Focus on industry, excluding oil and gas	252	*9*	*Promstroybank* "Industry construction", *Kaspryba* "Caspian fish"
Arbitrary	Arbitrary names	175	*6*	*Brizbank* "Breeze", *Logos, Dolina* "Valley"
Size	Big size, power, leadership	154	*6*	*Galaktika* "Galaxy", *Sila* "Force", *Pervy Torgovy* "First in Trade"
Customer	Customer or social	147	*5*	*Narodny Kreditny* "People's credit", *Magnat*
Biz	Business in general, except the word *commerce*	144	*5*	*Management-Bank, Contract*
Foreign	Names with a clearly foreign sound	124	*4*	*Mark Pol bank, Glory Save, Hansacombank*
Finance	Finances, wealth, in addition to word "bank", and if other topics are absent.	100	*4*	*Safire, Capital Credit, Spetsinvestbank* "Special Investment"
Alaruss	Reference to the old Russia, Slavdom, Russianness, Orthodoxy	84	*3*	*Old Kremlin, Moskovia, Kazakbank*
Anthroponym	Anthroponyms, except "Foreign"	39	*1*	*Tatyana, Novahov Capital Bank*
Myth	Mythical characters, astronyms	35	*1*	*Mercury, Sphinx-bank, Kentavr* "Centaurus"
Other	Pointed to the state, Europe, oil and gas	190	*7*	*Regionalno-otraslevoy Spetcializirovanny Avtopromyshlenny bank* = ***Ros**avtobank*
Total		2,810	*100*	

* Here and further below, name shares are given for a survival sample.

Table 1. Distribution of names by topics.

Names with obscure lexical meaning "Agnonym" survive worse than the meaningful names in total. "Agnonym", "Arbitrary" and "Finance" names have lower survival rates than the names referring to "Customer", "Toponym", "Regiongeo" and "Biz" groups. Assets of banks with "Agnonym" names are indistinguishable from the rest. The more common the topic (except "Alaruss" and "Other"), the higher the assets (R^2_{adj}= 43%).

Multisegment names were considered those that can be attributed to several topical groups: *Russky Transportny* "Russian Transport", *Mosstroybank* "Moscow Construction". There are 20% of them in the survival sample. The Survival of multisegment names is higher than the rest only for "Midlow" regions. In the groups "Msk" and "High", survival differences were not found. The assets of banks with multisegment names were higher than others (R^2_{adj} = 1.0%).

Frequent segments. In the survival sample, the 69 most frequent segments of names were isolated that carry meaning (morphemes, their combinations and parts) and occur between 10 and 185 times (Table 2). The mandatory morpheme *bank* was not taken into account. The number of the segment FS has been assumed as a measure of a name being stereotype. Banks with stereotype names (FS = 1 or 2) live on the market longer than ones with FS = 0. Banks with stereotype names also have bigger assets than others (R^2_{adj} = 1.3%). In the group "Midlow", the difference is even more pronounced: R^2_{adj} = 4.0%.

FS	Number	%	Examples*
0	1,604	*57.1*	*Pokrovsky, Leo-bank, Neptun*
1	714	*25.4*	*Novopokrovsky, Zemliane*
2	419	*14.9*	*Gaztransbank, Slaviansky kredit*
3	64	*2.3*	*Neftekhimmashbank, Pervy Dortransbank*
4	8	*0.3*	*Sevzapinvestprombank* "North West Investment Industry bank"
5	1	*0.0*	*Mezhdunarodny kommerchesky bank razvitiya investiciy i tehnologiy* "International Commerce Bank for Development of Investments and Technologies"
Total	2,810	*100*	

* Frequent segments are underlined.

Table 2. Number of frequent segments in bank names.

It should be noted that names with frequent segments are in total fewer than those without them: 1,206 and 1,604, respectively. This happens because of a high proportion of names with two frequent segments.

Relation with the category. With respect to the financial industry (excluding the morpheme *bank*), names were divided into three groups (Table 3). There are twice as many that are unrelated to the category as those related directly or indirectly. In the regions, survival is increasing in this order: "Unrelated" < "Indirect" < "Direct". There is no difference in Moscow. The assets of banks with names unrelated to the banking category are lower than those of the banks with related, directly or indirectly, names. In the regions, this difference (R^2_{adj} = 1.7%) is more noticeable than in Moscow (R^2_{adj} = 0.4%).

Category relation	Description	Number	%	Examples
Direct	At least one segment directly refers to "Finance" (Table 1)	313	*11*	*Master-Capital, Standard Credit*
Indirect	At least one segment is indirectly (by connotation) related to "Finance" (Table 1), or indicates the business sector	623	*22*	*Taler, Platina, Bank mezhotraslevoy promyshlennoy integracii* "Bank for intersectoral industrial integration"
Unrelated	Other names	1,874	*67*	
Total		2,810	*100*	

Table 3. Distribution of names by relation to financial industry.

We consider those names to be **evocative** that appeal to the senses, especially to sight (*Gold-Bank, Bank Prohladny*—"cool" in direct meaning). We excluded toponyms and personal names. There are about 4 times fewer evocative names than abstract ones. Evocative names have lower survival rates than abstract ones. Assets have significant, although weak, positive connections with evocativeness. We assume that names with indistinct, weak evocativeness have bigger assets than both clearly evocative and abstract names. However, dividing the names into groups according to their evocativeness requires a more reliable criterion than the opinion of one author.

We considered **bizarre** names, as opposed to neutral ones, those that stand out against the majority—in meaning, sound or form. Bizarre names were divided into non-negative connotations "Wow" (*Vtoroy* "second"; *Belka* "Squirrel", *Zemliane* "The Terrans") and negative "Boo" (*KHEI* sounds like "cough", *PSA Finans* "DOG's finances", *Bum-bank* "bang", *Pytalovo* "torturing", *Minusa* "losses"). Interestingly, the "Boo" names (7% of the survival sample) are more frequent than "Wow" (2%). Both in survival rates and assets, the "Wow" names do not differ from neutral names; and "Boo" names have lower survival rates and assets than neutral ones, $R^2_{adj} = 0.2\%$.

In terms of the **form,** excluding a detached word *bank*, the most frequent are multi-syllabic acronyms and complex words "AcRo", single nouns "Noun", adjectives "Adj" at *bank*, and acronyms-initialisms "XYZ". Phrases are relatively rare. Numerals and figures are occasionally present (Table 4).

Form	**Numbers**	**%**	**Examples**
AcRo	1,022	*36*	*Promstroybank, Khlebobank*
Noun	785	*28*	*Bank Molniya, Nota Bank*
Adj	466	*17*	*Bank Prohladny, Mezhregionalny investicionno-raschetny bank*
XYZ	267	*10*	*DVSKBank, B.A.M.-Bank, Bi-Si-Di-Bank*
Numerals and figures	22	*1*	*Pokrovsky'92, M2M Prayvet bank, Pervy Russky Nezavisimy Bank* "first Russian independent bank"
Other	248	*8*	*Bank Mestny kredit, Bank Razvitie Stolica, Bank Razvitiya Regiona, Russky Bank Sberezheniy*
Total	2,810	*100*	

Table 4. Distribution of names by form.

Survival rates in Moscow are not associated with the name form; "AcRo" names survive in the regions more than the rest of names. The assets of "AcRo" names are bigger than the rest of the names and the difference is more pronounced in the regions than in Moscow. However, while checking for topic and number of segment, the advantage of "AcRo" disappears. Nouns have fewer assets than other forms without reference to topic and polysemy.

The mandatory **descriptor *bank*** in the names is usually located in one of the four ways (Table 5): a single word at the beginning of a name "b_", a single word at the end of a name "_b", a final of a compound word "zb", a final separated by hyphen "~b".

***Bank* locus**	**Numbers**	**%**	**Examples**
b_	1,292	*46*	*Bank Diamant, Bank Polyarnaya zvezda, Bank Sibnefteekologiya*
zb	854	*30*	*Komisoyuzkoopbank, Bytbank*
_b	322	*11.5*	*Velikie Luki Bank, Beloglinsky bank*
~b	294	*10.5*	*Marks-Bank, Engels-Bank*
Other	48	*2*	*Bankhaus Erbe, Bank-Gerd, Avtomobilny bankirsky dom, Mezhdunarodny kommerchesky bank razvitiya investiciy i tehnologiy*
Total	2,810	*100*	

Table 5. Distribution of names by placing of the morpheme *bank*.

The survival rates and assets of Moscow banks with "_b" locus are significantly higher than the rest ($R^2_{adj} = 0.8\%$). Survival of regional banks changes in that order: ~b = b_ < zb < _b. Their assets change almost in the same order: ~b = b_ < zb = _b ($R^2_{adj} = 1.0\%$).

When checking for the name form, the "AcRo" and "Adj" groups have a pattern: the more frequent is the attachment way of the morpheme *bank*, the higher the assets are for this locus. For the "Noun" and "XYZ" groups, conversely, rarer loci indicate bigger assets. When checking for the *bank* locus, the frequency of name form is not associated with survival rates or assets. In other terms, a modifier at the beginning of the name is better than at the end of the name.

Length. The average length of Russian nouns, adjectives and proper names (mostly toponyms and anthroponyms) is calculated according to the data of the Russian language frequency dictionary (Lyashevskaya 2009). One-word noun bank names are, on average, shorter than nouns in the language. On the contrary, one-word adjective bank names are longer than adjectives in the language (Table 6). Two-word names are found 5.5 times less frequently than one-word names; multi-word names are even rarer.

Average length of words	Proper names N= 2,418	Nouns N= 8,767	Adjectives N=4,234	Average length of one-word names, without "bank"			
				AcRo	Noun	Adj	Sample
Unique words	6.82	7.52	10.15	7.96	6.29	10.74	Survival 1988–2014
Words taking into account frequency	6.28	6.68	8.93	8.07	6.61	10.59	Annual assets 2007–2014

Table 6. Average length of words and bank names.

"Adj" names of a medium length of 10–12 characters have a lower survival rate than longer or shorter ones. For "Noun" or "Agnonym", the relation of survival rates with the length cannot be identified. Longer one-word names with a clear meaning, "Noun" and "Adj", have more assets than shorter names (R^2_{adj} = 1.0% and 3.9%, respectively). In the absence of polysemy, two-word names have more assets than one-word names (R^2_{adj} = 0.5%); there is no effect on survival rates.

Discussion

The banking industry's traditions of naming are only being formed at this point in time and differ from those in the West: in Russia, there are almost no banks named after their founders or that have ordinals in their name. The share of names related to the category, excluding the morpheme "bank", is 35%, which is comparable with the data for the top American brands: 32% (Van den Bergh 1987). In the regions, bank name properties are more often and more noticeably associated with success than in Moscow. This can be explained by a weaker financial literacy of the population outside the capital city as well as their tendency to put greater trust in the typical and the traditional (Magun 2012). Whether this is possible, we would only be able to say after comparing retail banks with investment banks.

Survival graphs suggest that a name has effect in the medium term and its effects are less pronounced at the start and in the long term. Around 1% of variance explained in testing for assets is associated with many extralinguistic factors affecting business success.

Branch traditions and visibility compete with each other, providing a complex pattern of relationships between name properties and the success of the bank (Table 7).

More frequent names are more successful	*Less frequent* names are more successful

<table>
<tr><th colspan="3">Variable</th><th>More frequent names</th><th>Less frequent names</th><th>Survival</th><th>Assets</th></tr>
<tr><td colspan="3">Gender</td><td>Masculine</td><td>Feminine</td><td colspan="2">Feminine < Masculine</td></tr>
<tr><td colspan="3">Meaning</td><td>Meaningful</td><td>Agnonym</td><td>Agnonym < Meaning</td><td>—</td></tr>
<tr><td colspan="3">Topic, without “Agnonym” (see Table 1)</td><td>Finance, Branch, Toponym</td><td>Anthroponym, Myth, Foreign</td><td>—</td><td>Rare < Frequent</td></tr>
<tr><td colspan="3">Multisegmenticity</td><td>No</td><td>Yes</td><td colspan="2">Unisegment < Multisegment</td></tr>
<tr><td colspan="3">Frequent segments quantity</td><td>0</td><td>>0</td><td colspan="2">> 0</td></tr>
<tr><td colspan="3">Category relation</td><td>No</td><td><i>Dir, Indirect</i></td><td>No < <i>Indir</i> < <i>Dir</i></td><td>No <<i>Dir</i> = <i>Indir</i></td></tr>
<tr><td colspan="3">Evocativeness</td><td>No</td><td>Yes</td><td>Yes < No</td><td>No < Yes</td></tr>
<tr><td colspan="3">Bizarre</td><td>Neutral</td><td>Wow, Boo</td><td>Boo < Neutral = Wow</td><td>Boo < Wow = Neutral</td></tr>
<tr><td colspan="3">Form</td><td>Noun, AcRo</td><td>XYZ, Adj</td><td>—</td><td>Noun < other</td></tr>
<tr><td rowspan="6">Bank locus</td><td colspan="2">All</td><td>b_, zb</td><td>_b, ~b</td><td>b_ < (~b) < zb < _b</td><td>~b < b_ < _b</td></tr>
<tr><td colspan="2">Noun</td><td>b_</td><td>_b, ~b</td><td>b_ < ~b < _b</td><td>b_ = _b < ~b</td></tr>
<tr><td rowspan="2">Adj</td><td>Assets</td><td>_b</td><td>b_</td><td rowspan="2">b_ < _b</td><td rowspan="2">b_ < _b</td></tr>
<tr><td>Survival</td><td colspan="2">_b = b_</td></tr>
<tr><td colspan="2">AcRo</td><td>zb</td><td>b_, ~b</td><td colspan="2">~b = b_ < zb</td></tr>
<tr><td colspan="2">XYZ</td><td>b_</td><td>_b, ~b</td><td>—</td><td>b_ < ~b < _b</td></tr>
</table>

Length	uni-segment 1-word	Average	*Short, long*	Adj: Average = worse	*Longer* = better
	Agnonym			—	*Shorter* = better
Number of words		1	*2*	—	1 < *2*
More frequent vs. *less frequent* attributes (number of incomparable attributes is in parentheses)		Total: 17 variables		5 more frequent vs. 5 *less frequent* (7)	5 more frequent vs. 9 *less frequent* (3)

Table 7. Frequency of a name properties and bank success in two methods.

Masculine gender of the name, which is dominant in the industry, as well as use of frequent morphemes in the name, is positively associated with success. Clarity of the name meaning is more common to banks that are more successful. Banks with frequent industry topics in their name show a greater success than the thematically rare ones.

The relation of the name with the banking category is common to successful banks. When such indication is vague (business in general, finances in general), the success of the bank, on the contrary, is lower.

Names that drastically differ thematically or structurally, that are *a priori* rare, have no advantage in success. Names that are negative in the sound or meaning are negatively correlated with success. Multisegmenticity of a name accompanies success. Syllabic acronyms are most typical for the industry. However, this naming method in itself is not superior to others but reflects multisegmenticity more often realized in this structure. The success of longer names also derives from multisegmenticity. Successful loci of the morpheme "bank" are not always the most frequent. We believe that the advantage of the type "_b" names is a result of their greater visibility as compared with the names whose modifier is at the end of the name. A bigger success of the structure "zb" is not independent but reflects the multisegmenticity more often realized in this structure.

Conclusion

Both methods of the study showed consistent results, with the exception of evocativeness. Regression analysis of assets is more sensitive to name properties than survival analysis. This might be due to the fact that the annual accounts indirectly include survival.

In total, the names that are less frequent (but not rare), that is, more visible (*italicized* in Table 7) are more successful. However, visibility is not manifested in the rejection of the bank category traditions but, on the contrary, in an even stronger following. Bizarre names with positive connotations have no advantages over traditional category names. Successful bank names are more concrete, real, and tangible: they are longer than unsuccessful ones, point to the category, cover more than one topic and contain segments frequent in the category. Thus, our hypotheses are partially confirmed.

General expert advice about choosing the name does not directly work for banks. The very fact of a statistically significant association of name and success in the banking sector is surprising and requires further study.

Restrictions and further research

According to our data, the more homogeneous the sample of extralinguistic parameters, the brighter the relations between success and name properties. In order to obtain a sufficient number of cases for these samples, it is necessary to expand the study base. It is recommended to have the same time interval to compare the sensitivity of the methods used. It is appropriate to divide banks according to type of business: investment, corporate, retail, and universal. In addition to assets, one should take into account the profitability ratio and the quality of assets and liabilities, capital adequacy, and the cost of advertising and public relations.

Clarity and evocativeness of the name meaning was evaluated by the author subjectively and could be adjusted by means of a survey of the target audience. The study did not take into account issues of phonetics, in particular, ease of pronunciation. It is to be seen how renaming could affect the state of affairs of a bank. According to our preliminary data, the relation between name and success has been observed by the government, foreign banks and banks within banking groups that were excluded from this study. It is another field for research. Finally, a comparison with other services and products, and banks in other countries could provide a basis for the theoretical interpretation of the results.

Managerial implications

When choosing a bank partner, among the criteria one could include the prognosis of survival, based on the properties of the bank name.

Choosing a name for the business, it is useful to explore the industry in diachrony without relying on general recommendations as to the properties of a good name.

Depending on the development strategy, it is possible to focus on the visibility of the name in the case of advanced strategies, and on the traditional name for a catch-up strategy. For regional banks the name is more important than it is in Moscow. A bank could have a greater chance of success when its name:

- Is masculine;
- Does not sound negative;
- Contains several segments from different thematic fields;
- At least one of those is typical for the banking industry;
- At least one of those is related to finance category, directly or indirectly, in addition to the morpheme *bank*;
- The morpheme *bank* is located at the end of the name with a space;
- Is longer than average length in category.

The services of a naming consultant could also be estimated. In 2006–2014, the difference of average annual assets of banks with feminine and masculine names was 113 million Euros. Taking into account several characteristics of a good name, this gap would increase. The contribution of a name to the annual bank success (R^2_{adj}) is around 1%. If the consultancy fee is specified as one twentieth of this annual profit, it is about 67,000 Euro.

Acknowledgements

I would like to thank Konstantin Babkin, Yeqing Bao, Elena Baranova, Mary Breitman, Vitaly Djuma, Sergey Goryaev, Yulia Shtutina for their help and comments.

References

Bao, Y., A.T. Shao and D. Rivers. 2008. "Creating new brand names: effects of relevance, connotation and pronunciation." *Journal of Advertising Research* 48/1: 148–162.

Baranov, Ilia. 2011. "Store Success and its Brand Name: Survival Analysis." *Marketing and Marketing Research* 92: 122–143. [Баранов, И. 2011. "Успех магазина и его название: статистический анализ." *Маркетинг и маркетинговые исследования* 92: 122–143.]

Cooper, Michael, Hussein Gulen and Raghavendra Rau. 2005. “Changing names with style: Mutual fund name changes and their effects on fund flows.” *Journal of Finance* LX/6: 2825–2858.

Davis, J. Charlene. 2007. “A Conceptual View of Branding For Services.” *Innovative Marketing* 3/1: 7.

Hutchinson, J. Wesley, Kalyan Raman, Murali K. Mantrala. 1994. “Finding Choice Alternatives in Memory: Probability Models of Brand Name Recall.” *Journal of Marketing Research* 31/4: 441.

Interfax-100 Rankings. *Finmarket information agency.* www.finmarket.ru/database/rankings/ [Рэнкинги ИНТЕРФАКС-100. -*Информационное агентство «Финмаркет»*.]

Kanungo, R.N. 1968. “Brand awareness: effects of fittingness, meaningfulness, and product utility.” *Journal of Applied Psychology* 52/4: 290–295.

Kashin, S. et al. 2013. “All by name.” *Sekret Firmy* 11: 79. www.kommersant.ru/doc/2319181 [Кашин, С. и др. 2013 “Все поименно.” *Секрет фирмы* 11: 79]

Kensinger E.A. and S. Corkin. 2003. “Memory enhancement for emotional words: Are emotional words more vividly remembered than neutral words?” *Memory & Cognition* 31/8: 1169–1180.

Kremer, Ludger. 2012. “Von der Vereinsbank in Hamburg zur HVB: Zur Diachronie deutscher Unternehmensnamen.” In *Onomastics goes business. Role and relevance of brand, company and other names in economic contexts,* edited by Holger Wochele, Julia Kuhn and Martin Stegu, 129–140. Berlin: Logos.

Lerman, Dawn and Ellen Garbarino. 2002. “Recall and recognition of brand names: A comparison of word and nonword name types.” *Psychology and Marketing, Special Issue: Psycholinguistics & Marketing* 19/7–8: 621–639.

Lyashevskaya, O.N. and S.A. Sharov. 2009. *Frequency Dictionary of Modern Russian language.* http://dict.ruslang.ru/freq.php [Ляшевская, О. Н. и С. А. Шаров 2009 *Частотный словарь современного русского языка. материалах Национального корпуса русского языка.*]

Magun, V. and M. Rudnev. 2012. “Basic Values of Russians and Other Europeans.” *Problems of Economic Transition* 54/10: 31–64. www.tandfonline.com/doi/abs/10.2753/PET1061-1991541003#.VTXuWUmt_Ns

Maheswaran, Durairaj, Diane M. Mackie and Shelly Chaiken. 1992. “Brand name as a heuristic cue: The effects of task importance and expectancy confirmation on consumer judgments.” *Journal of*

Consumer Psychology 1/4: 317–336.

McCracken, C.J. and M. Carole Macklin. 1998. "The Role of Brand Names and Visual Cues in Enhancing Memory for Consumer Packaged Goods." *Marketing Letters* 9/2: 209–226.

Nikolaeva, E. and A. Fedorov. 2009. "100 leading bankers: resume." *Finans* 20–21: 303–304. www.finansmag.ru/94873 [Николаева, Е. и А. Федоров 2009 "100 крупнейших банкиров: резюме." *Финанс* 20–21: 303–304.]

Robertson, K.R. 1987. "Recall and recognition effects of brand name imagery." *Psychology and Marketing* 4/1: 3–15.

Schultz, Mike and John E. Doerr. 2009. *Professional Services Marketing*. Hoboken: John Wiley & Sons, Inc.

Skroznikova, V.A. 1985. "Rekreatcionno-delovye nazvaniya." *Voprosy geografii*126: 81–89. [Скрозникова, В.А. 1985 "Рекреационно-деловые названия." *Вопросы географии.Географические названия в Москве* 126: 81–89. Москва: Мысль.]

StatSoft, Inc. 2013a. "Survival/FailureTime Analysis." *Electronic Statistics Textbook.* Online: www.statsoft.com/Textbook/Survival-Failure-Time-Analysis

StatSoft, Inc. 2013b. "General Regression Models." *Electronic Statistics Textbook.* Online: www.statsoft.com/Textbook/General-Regression-Models

The Central Bank of the Russian Federation. *Database of credit institutions.* www.cbr.ru/credit/main.asp [Центральный банк Российской Федерации. *Справочник по кредитным организациям*.]

Turley L.W. and Patrick A. Moore. 1995. "Brand name strategies in the service sector." *Journal of Consumer Marketing* 12/4: 42–50.

Ulrich, Isabelle, Elisabeth Tissier-Desbordes and Pierre-Louis Dubois. 2011. "Brand Gender and Its Dimensions." *European Advances in Consumer Research* 9: 140.

Vanden Bergh, Bruce C., K. Adler and L. Oliver. 1987. "Linguistic distinction among top brand names." *Journal of advertising research* 27/4: 39–44.

Vernikov, Andrei. 2009. "Russian banking: The state makes a comeback?" *BOFIT Discussion Papers* 24: 28. www.suomenpankki.fi/bofit_en/tutkimus/tutkimusjulkaisut/dp/Documents/DP2409.pdf

Yorkston, Eric and Gustavo de Mello.2005. "Linguistic Gender Marking and Categorization" Evaluations of Branded Products across Languages." *Journal of Consumer Research* 32/2: 224–234.

Zaichkowsky, Judith Lynne and Padma Vipat. 1993. "Inferences from brand names." *European Advances in Consumer Research* 1: 534–540.

Zinkhan, George M. and Claude R. Martin Jr. 1987. "New brand names and inferential beliefs: Some insights on naming new products." *Journal of Business Research* 15/2: 157–172.

FROM *REAGANOMICS* TO *RENZINOMICS*: THE PUZZLING WORD FORMATIONS OF THE TYPE <PROPER NAME> + -*(ECO)NOMICS* IN GERMAN AND ITALIAN

FIORENZA FISCHER AND HOLGER WOCHELE

Abstract

The paper analyses some examples of naming strategies in the current economical and political press in Italy and in Germany. In particular terms like "Renzinomics" which means and denotes "the financial politic wave by Renzi". From such names a new suffixoid developed, i.e. *–nomics*, which is now building furthers forms, such as *Soccernomics*, *Humanomics* and others.

1. Introduction

The subject of this paper is the creation and usage of a new word formation unit that has been in existence for no longer than 45 years. The unit we are referring to is *-[ec]-o-nomics* and it combines with eponymous elements, based on politicians' anthroponyms, i.e. personal names. The result of said combinations are neologisms and, as mentioned in the title, include *Reaganomics* and *Renzinomics*. We are interested in the development of this new word formation unit, which shares similarities with two other recent word formation units:

1) The English suffixoid/copulative compound unit ***-gate***, in its meaning of "scandal". Based on its first documented use in the word *Watergate* in 1972, it has led to numerous formations of the same type: *Lewinskygate*, *Rubbergate*, *Zippergate*, *Whitewatergate*, *Dirndlgate* etc. (cf. Flach, Kopf, and Stefanowitsch forthcoming).

2) The Italian suffix ***-poli***. This suffix has its origin in Greek *polys*, "city", and has been used in numerous toponyms (*Costantinopoli, Sebastopoli, Napoli, Leopoli* etc.). Since 1992, *-poli* has undergone a

semantic change: in the wake of the successful application such as *tangentopoli* (1992), "city of bribes/city of corruption" referring to Milan in the 1990s, *-poli* has taken on the meaning of "corruption/corruption scandal". Consequently, expressions such as *bancopoli* and *calciopoli* no longer refer to "city of banks" or "city of football", but now mean "corruption in banking" or "corruption in football" (Iacobini 2004: 71).

In contrast, the word formations with *-(o)nomics*, show a higher degree of complexity both with regard to the internal structure of the unit *-(o)nomics* and with regard to the bases of the word formation, their modification, as well as the semantics of these word formations.

In the following discussion we will investigate those aspects in detail. However, it should be noted that, given that we present a preliminary study, not all points can be dealt with exhaustively.

The following should be observed in advance:

1) The suffixoid *-(o)nomics* belongs to the word formation units which Iacobini calls "elementi formativi neoclassici" (2004: 69), the results of which Schweickard (1992: 170) refers to as "gelehrte Bildungen" (Engl. "scholarly formations"). This suffixoid originates in Greek and, via English *[ec-]onomics*, has made its way into Spanish, French, Italian, German, and even Modern Greek.

2) With regard to bases, i.e. personal names, the observation is that after the first documented use in 1969 in *Nixonomics*, referring to US presidential candidate Richard Nixon and his economic policy, the development gained momentum with the emergence of *Reaganomics*. *Reaganomics*, as will be shown, has enjoyed a high degree of adoption and has become an inherent part of the mental lexicon. Additionally, *Reaganomics* became the model for other formations ending in *-onomics*. Moreover, along with *Thatcherism* (alternative formations are available e.g. *Thatcheronomics* and *Thatchernomics*), *Reaganomics*, in connection with the hegemonic spread of neoliberalism, has become the political "Fahnenwort" (i.e. the politically and ideologically charged standard term; cf. Panagl 1998) of the 1980s and 1990s. Eponymous formations on the basis of the family names of US presidents that follow this model are *Carternomics*, *Bushonomics*, *Clintonomics* up until the most recent term *Obamanomics*.

The word formation type <proper name> + *(o)nomics* was initially developed in specialized discourses, more precisely in economic political communication. A paraphrase of its semantics would be "economic policy of X", or more precisely "principles of the economic policy of X", where X stands for a proper name (anthroponym) referring to a politician. The usage of suchlike eponymous formations has spread to semantic areas, which are not necessarily involved in the theory and application of economic policies. Nowadays, we can observe an enormous extension and trivialisation as well as a loss of the previously clearly-cut meaning of these words. Thus, the following formations have been documented:

> *Applenomics*, *E-baynomics*, *Danceonomics*, *Freakonomics* (but also: *Socio-Freak-Onomics* and *Super-Freak-Onomics*), *Frackonomics* (referring to fracking, i.e. oil production), *Gasonomics* (the business aspects of anaesthesiology), *Lobbynomics*, *Soccernomics*, *Waternomics*, *Womanomics*, *Zombinomics*.

Even if the meaning "business in sector X" seems to prevail, there are formations like *Humanomics*, *Euronomics*, *Wikinomics*, and *Neuronomics*, where the first element is neither an appellative nor a proper name. These formations are more difficult to grasp semantically. However, the focus of the article at hand is dedicated to formations with proper names as bases, and more precisely anthroponyms (names for persons). Suchlike eponymous formations shall be contrasted with other competing eponymous formations ending on *-ismo*/*-ismus*/*-ism*, like *Thatcherismus* (German for *Thatcherism*), *Putinismus* (German for *Putinism*), and the Italian *Renzismo*.

2. An Overview of Current Research

Outlining the status quo in the research of word formations ending in *-(o)nomics* is a relatively quick task. The relevant literature on word formation by Fleischer and Barz (2012) for German, and by Grossmann and Rainer (2004) for Italian, ignores this word formation unit. The same is true for Schweickard (1992) for Romance languages (for English, however, see Bauer 2004). Furthermore, dictionaries provide few entries. For example, Wikipedia (https://en.wikipedia.org/wiki/, accessed on June 23rd, 2015) provides definitions only for the following eponymous formations with *-(o)nomics*: *Abenomics*, *Clintonomics*, *Nixonomics*, *Obamanomics*, *Reaganomics*.

As an example, *Abenomics* is defined as follows:

> **Abenomics** [….] refers to the economic policies advocated by Shinzō Abe since the December 2012 general election, which elected Abe to his second term as prime minister of Japan. (https://en.wikipedia.org/wiki/Abenomics, 10.02.2016)

3. Theoretical Foundations

3.1. Terminological Aspects

One basic problem as regards the word formation unit *–(o)nomics* is a terminological one. There is no generally accepted categorisation for forms like *–(o)nomics*. Hitherto, the preliminary term used has been *suffixoid/suffissoide*, coined by Migliorini (1963; see also Serianni 1989: 663), who referred to the bound morphemes derived from the classic languages Latin and Greek. Alternatives provided are the Italian labels "elementi colti", by Dardano/Trifone 1997: 546, or "elementi formativi scientifici", by Serianni (1989: 666). In Italian, and in accordance with Iacobini (2004: 70), the most appropriate term seems to be "elemento formativo neoclassico", i.e. "neoclassical formation element". An even better option for our purposes is "elemento formativo inglese di origine neoclassica", i.e. "English formation element of neoclassical origin".

This decision seems justified, mostly due to the fact that it avoids commitment to whether the word formation element *-(o)nomics* is an affix or a compound element, and whether the involved process is derivation or composition. Thus, the label is neutral, as also Iacobini (2004: 71) stresses:

> Le difficoltà di tipo terminologico dipendono in parte dalla ricerca di un termine unico per un insieme di elementi eterogenei particolarmente difficili da classificare [....] gli elementi formativi non sono un insieme omogeneo né una categoria naturale della lingua. Si tratta di elementi quasi tutti di provenienza allogena, impiegati prevalentemente in registri tecnico-scientifici, il cui motivo d'interesse è dato dalla partecipazione a parole di uso corrente e dall'interazione con le regole di formazione di parola dell'italiano.

In German philology, Fleischer and Barz (2012), referring to borrowing processes, often use the term *Konfix, "*confix*"*, meaning "gebundenes Grundmorphem, das nur in Kombination mit anderen Morphemen vorkommt" (Engl.: "bound root morpheme, that only occurs in combination with other morphemes") (Glück 2010: s.v.; Fleischer and Barz 2012: 63-64). Confixes occur as derivational bases, as compound units, or as both, e.g. {therm-} in *Thermostat*, *thermisch*, *Thermalbad*, *endotherm* (here: "Zweitglied einer kompositionsähnlichen Struktur"; Engl. "secondary unit in a compound-like structure"; Ronneberger-Sibold 2009:142). It is one of the characteristics of confixes (as well as affixoids) that they—in contrast to affixes—carry lexical meaning and are, therefore, autosemantic, while they cannot, in contrast to word stems, form words in their own right (cf. table in Fleischer and Barz 2012: 64).

With regard to word formation in English, Bauer 2005: 104 proposes the term *splinter*:

> By splinter I understand a fragment of a word used repetitively in the formation of new words. Splinters arise through the process of blending […]. Thus *–nomics* in *Thatchernomics* is a splinter, recurring in *Reaganomics*, *Rogernomics*, *Nixonomics*, etc.

3.2. Derivation or Compounding?

As mentioned above, we do not wish to delve into a detailed discussion about whether the investigated formations are derivations or compounds. However, it should be noted that both Schweickard (1992) and Iacobini (2004) refer to this formation type as "gelehrte Bildung" and "composti neoclassici" (Engl.: "neoclassical compound"). Furthermore, both stress that a clear line between derivation and composition cannot always be drawn in these cases. Hence, Schweickard 1992: 170 writes:

> Die klassifikatorische Problematik von Formen mit den Bildungselementen *-mane* und *-logue*, die sich im Zwischenbereich von Zusammensetzung und Suffigierung bewegen, ist bekannt. Die unklare Zugehörigkeit schlägt sich auch in der stark variierenden Terminologie nieder [...].[1]

Iacobini 2004: 72 states;

> I composti neoclassici [poi] non corrispondono pienamente né alla definizione di composto né a quella di derivato della lingua italiana: infatti non sono formati né dalla combinazione di due elementi liberi, così come accade generalmente per i composti dell'italiano (pescecane, capomastro), né dalla combinazione di un elemento libero e uno non libero (un affisso) così come accade per i derivati (barista, rifare).

Additionally, in their chapter on specifics of loanword formation Fleischer and Barz (2012: 101-116) point out that the boundaries between stems, confixes, and affixes with what they call exogenous (in German "exogene") word formation elements are considerably more widespread compared to those with indigenous units. They explain further:

> Die im Deutschen potenziell wortbildungsaktiven exogenen Wortbildungseinheiten […] werden [unter anderem] durch

> Morphematisierung von Segmenten komplexer Fremdwörter (durch Reanalyse) zu aktiven Bildungseinheiten“ (Fleischer and Barz 2012:104)[2]

Fleischer and Barz illustrate the productivity of suchlike elements by means of *tele* in *Teledialog* (German, "phone-based TV voting"), *Telekolleg* ("adult education service" in German speaking areas), *telegen* (German, "telegenic"), etc. and specify:

> Meist handelt es sich bei den exogenen Wortbildungseinheiten um griechische und lateinische Wortstämme, die nicht selten über andere Sprachen ins Deutsche gelangen (ibidem).[3]

If we ignore the aspect of serial formation, or structural group formation, which bring about a semantization process, we could interpret the formations under investigation as "Kontaminationsbildungen" (Engl.: "contamination formations"), portmanteau, blends, or amalgamations (there exists – especially in German scholarship – an abundance of partially synonymous terms, cf. Glück 2000, for *Kontamination*). Thus, we could also categorise these word formations unambiguously as compositions. The second element would be shortened by means of aphaeresis.

Ronneberger-Sibold (2004: 588-589), when looking into brand names of this type, e.g. *Mentholyptus* (from *menthol* + *eucalyptus*), talks about "Konturkreuzung" (German for "contour blend") (cf. below, section 6, for the syllabic-rhythmic overall contour of our eponymous formations based on the accentuated matrix word *economics* and the recognition value important for series formation).

4. Analysis of the Word Formation Type <anthroponym> + *[ec]-(o)-nomics*

If the word formation element at hand were to be analysed from a purely lexical-semantic point of view, we would be dealing with more than a simple suffix. While it is true that ***[ec]-(o)-nomics*** can occur as a free morpheme, it can do that only in its complete variant and only in English language environments. Moreover, the variants shortened by aphaeresis, *-nomics* or *-onomics*, cannot occur as a free element but only in combination with other free elements (appellative, prefixoid or proper name). Nevertheless, it retains its original and autonomous meaning "economic policy", "principles of economics" in similarly formed lexical units. Consequently, it does not behave like an affix occurring as a bound grammatical morpheme.

It is important to mention a second, homonymous lexical morpheme, {nomics²}, which, in contrast to the above, has the meaning "laws of …", e.g. the English appellative *bionomics* ("the laws of life"), which can be used synonymously with *ecology*. Word formations with this second morpheme {nomics²} will not be considered here.

Similar to other classic suffixoids such as *-filia*, *-fobia*, *-logia*, *-mania*, *-metria*, *-trofia* etc., *[ec]-(o)-nomics* is of Greek origin. In its complete variant it consists of *oikoς* "house" and *νόμος* "law". Consequently, the entire meaning would be "principles of housekeeping".

In the English version, whose form was adopted by German and Italian, we find the ending *-ics*, e.g. in *informatics*, *mathematics*, *physics*. The *Lexicographic Description of English* (Benson, Benson, and Ilson 1986: 241) provides the following remarks regarding the ending *-ics*:

> The suffix, reflecting Greek *–ika*, forms nouns that mean "science", "knowledge", "skill", "study", "art". Most of the nouns in our list have one of these meanings and are used with a singular verb. These nouns may agree with either a singular or a plural verb and are marked as sing./pl. or as pl./sing.; the more usual agreement is given first. In general, abstract senses of nouns in *-ics* are associated with singular agreement; concrete senses with plural agreement.

In the work quoted above, the grammatical information "sing./pl." is given for *economics*, i.e. both singular and plural. In the Italian contexts considered here, the new formations occur in feminine singular – quite like the underlying concept *politica economica*, "economic policy". However, in German both singular and plural are in use (cf. section 6).

It has been shown that the first element, i.e. the derivational basis (if we want to speak of word formation in this context) is a proper name. One can also encounter anthroponyms, in which case both first and family names are to be found (*Matteonomics* in the title of the article, and *Renzinomics* in the text[4] – cf. section 6 for the pragmatic aspects of using either first or family names). However, within the scope of this study, eponymous word formations, with a variety of bases, have been found: Toponyms, e.g. *Bhutanomics*, *Turkonomics*, and *Greekonomics*; ergonyms, e.g. *Applenomics*, *Amazonomics*; institutional names like *Fedonomics* (from "FED" = Federal Reserve System, i.e. the central banking system of the US; where the commonly used acronym serves as base from); as well as appellative currency names, e.g. *Dollaronomics* and *Euronomics* (whereby the respective currency policies regarding Dollar and Euro are being referred to).

With regard to morphological structure, it ought to be noted that these eponymous neologisms of the type <proper name> + *-o-nomics* are in contrast to post-determination, which is more commonly used in Italian and in Romance Languages respectively (cf. Baldinger 1968, Wandruszka 1980). The more frequent sequencing in word formations in Romance Languages would be *determinatum* + *determinans*. However, in our research new formations are being made on the basis of the English/Germanic model with the sequence *determinans* + *determinatum*. Due to this inversion in Italian and the Romance Languages respectively, the Anglo-Saxon origins of the word formations under investigation here become rather apparent. In contrast, in German the formation works along the pre-determinational word formation model (approximately with eponymous adjectives as in *Merkelsche Wirtschaftpolitik*, "Merkel's economic policy").

The relatively simple formation rule <proper name> + *(o)nomics* allows neologisms to be formed effortlessly. These neologisms often take over the function of technical terms and expressions in economic texts. Considering the frequency of formations of the same type, one could speak of serial formations, i.e. the formation of a series of words equal in terms of form and content (cf. Glück 1993 for *Reihenbildung*, "serial formation").

Generally, technical terms, which exhibit an onymic component, contribute considerably to the efficiency in technical communication by means of increasing the semantic density in the *signifié* – the content part of a linguistic sign. In technical communication, these eponymous combinations allow the receiver to activate and retrieve their expert knowledge via the proper name. Regarding this matter, Kalverkämper (1978: 225) states:

> Schon der Einsatz von Namen weist über den aktuellen Text hinaus. Der Name ist nämlich ein Appel an den Leser oder Hörer, sein Vorwissen in den Textverstehensprozess einzubringen. Namengebrauch entspricht daher einem Setzen von deutlichen Vorwissensmarkierungen.[5]

These onymic formations refer to a shared knowledge and reflect the dialogic character of the exchange of ideas. Hence, it is not surprising that these neologisms enjoy great popularity in blogs and social media where dialogic aspects of communication play an important role.

Ronneberger-Sibold (2009: 145) states with regard to confix formations in German:

> Eine neue reguläre Konfixbildung ist für ihre Adressaten wie ein reguläres Wortbildungsprodukt interpretierbar, das heißt transparent und motiviert. **Transparent** bedeutet, dass der Rezipient der Konfixbildung eine

> **Wortbildungsbedeutung** zuordnen kann. Dazu muss er in der Lage sein, erstens ihre Elemente zu erkennen und zweitens die Verbindung dieser Elemente im Sinn eines produktiven Wortbildungsmodells zu deuten. **Motivation** bedeutet, dass die so ermittelte Wortbildungsbedeutung zur **referentiellen Bedeutung** (**Gebrauchsbedeutung**, **Lexikonbedeutung**) des Wortes passt.[6]

In addition, Ronneberger-Sibold specifies that confix formations are intended for an audience versed in technical terminology which would be able to correctly interpret these formations. Along these lines, the following precondition for the structures analysed here can be postulated: exclusively an audience that possesses the necessary technical interest and has the technical terminology and encyclopaedic proficiency would be able to correctly interpret structures of the type <proper name> + -*(o)nomics*. Furthermore, the neologisms analysed here can be considered fully-fledged internationalisms, in the sense that they appear in all languages with the same meaning and in almost identical form and that they are interpretable regardless of the specific language. The following examples illustrate this point:

> English: "Russian President Vladimir Putin thinks he can enjoy political and military freedom in dealing with Ukraine without experiencing crippling economic costs from sanctions or the exit of multinational firms from Russia. Call this **Putinomics**."[7]
> French: "Tel que je l'ai déjà mentionné, le principal problème de l'Ukraine est la « **Putinomics** », pas Poutine comme tel "[8]
> Italian: "Dopo aver perso quasi metà del suo valore contro dollaro ed euro in tre mesi, il rublo rimbalza stasera dell'8,5%. Ma per la **Putinomics** le prospettive restano tragiche [...]"[9]
> Spanish: "Se muestra convencido que una recuperación lenta, pero continuada, demostrará la viabilidad del modelo «**Putinomics**» basado en la explotación de los recursos que tanto beneficia la burocracia. "[10]
> Portuguese: "Com a "**Putinomia**" (Putinomics, em inglês), a política econômica de Putin, a Rússia parecia ter encontrado um caminho próprio."[11]

The above indicates that the word formations of this type are in essence identical and transparent cross-linguistically. In individual cases some languages can display deviations. For example *Tsipranomics* in German and Italian, while in Modern Greek the formation *Tsipr**o**nomics* has been documented. As mentioned, the formation rule is relatively simple and the productivity of this formation type is quite high (cf. below).

5. Presentation of the Corpus Used for the Study

With regard to the corpus that has been used for this analysis it must be noted that gathering data was rather difficult. Usually the data base **FACTIVA** is employed for compiling a corpus of specialised economics literature. However, this data base does not allow a left-truncated search (for words ending with *-nomics*). FACTIVA allows a right-truncated search (e.g. for *Renzi**, i.e. the engine searches for all forms beginning with *Renzi-* and thus provides *Renzismo*, *renziano* etc.). In order to avoid this problem, a list of 250 politicians' names was compiled (including heads of governments, ministers of finance, governors of national banks) and, subsequently, those names were subjected to an online search to check whether they had been used as bases for formations with *-(o)nomics*. Since this study was to be restricted to technical business and commercial texts, we were equally restrictive when sampling the occurrences, i.e. only those that appeared in the press and books (online newspapers, book advertisements etc.) were used in the study. Cases originating in blogs and social media were rejected since there is the risk that they falsify the overall picture by potentially constituting occasionalisms (nonce words) and individual creations. For instance, for the formation *Pontanomics* (after the former Romanian prime minister Victor Ponta [2012 – 2015]) one single instance was found in a user comment in a blog of a Romanian journalist[12]. Consequently, this formation has to be considered an occasionalism.

For the quantitative analysis and data gathering in German, the DWDS-corpus was used (Digitales Wörterbuch der Deutschen Sprache, "Digital Dictionary of the German Language"; http://www.dwds.de/). In the core corpus ("Kernkorpus") and *Zeit*-corpus (after the German weekly newspaper; ranging from 1946 to 2015), both part of the DWDS-corpus, a left-truncated search was carried out for occurrences of formations ending in *-nomics* (dating from 20.6.2015).

The search in the core-corpus garnered 96 cases with *-nomics*, with two instances of *Reaganomics* in 1996. The results from the *Zeit*-corpus turned out to be more fruitful: 1192 cases were found. While the word *economics* itself accounted for the large majority of these cases, other frequently occurring forms are:

> *Reaganomics* (first instance documented: 1981): 129 cases
> *Abenomics*: 42 cases[13]
> *Clintonomics*: 6 cases
> *Sarkonomics*: 6 cases

Rubinomics: 3 cases
Rogernomics: 3 cases
Merkelnomics: 2 cases
Likonomics: 1 case
Kohlismus/Kohlonomics: 1 case
Obamanomics: 1 case
Thatchernomics: 1 case

Occurrences other than *economics* include numerous company names (ergonyms: *Asianomics*, *Metanomics*, *Epigenomics*, *Dragonomics*, *Nutrigenomics*, *Organomics*, *Genomics*, *Bionomics*, *Metanomics*) and word formations like *Enronomics*, *Pulchronomics*, *Vapornomics*, *Psychonomics*, *Rebellonomics* (3x), *Mammohanomics*, which will not be included in the study at hand.

6. Data Analysis

Considering the preliminary character of these analyses, this penultimate section will put forward preliminary hypotheses regarding the linguistic properties of the neologisms under investigation. The levels we want to incorporate in our discussion are phonetics, morphology, semantics, and pragmatics.

With regard to phonetics, cases with the splinter *-onomics* have to be distinguished from cases with the shortened form *-nomics*. It should be noted that the longer version could also be interpreted as <linking vowel *o* + *nomics*>; Fleischer and Barz (2012: 141) consider the vowel *o* in confix compositions as a characteristic linking vowel. Schpak-Dolt (2010: 141 and 2012: 134-136) consider *-o-* as "Übergangsvokal" (Engl.: "transition vowel") in Greek scholarly formations.

Generally, if the onymic basis ends with a consonant, the form *-onomics* is attached (*Chiraconomics*). If it ends with a vowel, then *-nomics* is attached (*Schäublenomics*, *Kutschmanomics*). However, there are numerous exceptions and, at best, tendencies can be formulated: if the name ends with a liquid (*l*, *r*), with *-n*, or with a sibilant, then often *-nomics*, without a linking vowel, is attached: *Merkelnomics, Waigelnomics, Hitlernomics, Kirchnernomics, Orbanomics, Fillonomics, Cameronomics, Chamberlainomics, Chaveznomics*. The silent final *-e* (*e muet* in French) is often elided (*Lafontainomics*, but *Hollandenomics*), while other final vowels (except *-o*) can be replaced with *o*: *Bersani – Bersanomics* (but: *Renzinomics*, *Prodinomics*).

An interesting fact is that factors related to syllable also play a role in these eponymous formations. In simple terms, based on the corpus, it can be said that formations with predominantly four syllables, five syllables at most, are common. Consequently, despite the sibilant we have *Glosonomics* (M. Glos), *Klausonomics* (V. Klaus), despite the liquid we have *Blaironomics*, despite *-n-* we have *Brownonomics*, in order to maintain a syllable count of four (but: *Häuplnomics*). Conversely, in order to maintain the syllable order of the series formation, reductions in the onymic element can occur. In other words, these formations violate the principle of Nübling et al. (2012), according to which proper names are left intact. Thus, we have:

Sarkozy – Sarkonomics
Zapatero – Zaponomics
Balkenende – Balkenomics
Erdoğan – Erdonomics (along with *Erdoganomics*)
Gusenbauer – Gusonomics
Topolanek – Topolanomics

The question remains to what extent these formations might result from hypernyms of the full variant of names, i.e. *Gusonomics* from *Gusi*, and *Sarkonomics* from the hypernym *Sarko*, and thus have a familiar or pejorative connotation to them. However, as mentioned, there are partly competing tendencies: forms like *Häuplnomics* or *Bushnomics* are attested but uncommon as mentioned above.

With regard to morphology, in Italian the formations with *-nomics* are feminine singular as the following examples illustrate:

> **DALLA MATTEONOMICS ALLA PADOANOMICS**. Come era prevedibile, Bruxelles ha riscritto le priorità **della Renzinomics** (per quel che se ne può capire), secondo i dettami **della Padoanomics** (che invece si conosce bene anche dalle analisi condotte all'Ocse). Siamo già davanti al dualismo che si è verificato più volte in questi anni (con Berlusconi e Tremonti, o con Letta e Saccomanni)? Chi ha a cuore le sorti del governo e ancor più quelle della ripresa economica italiana deve augurarsi che sia solo una impressione superficiale. (highlighted by FF and HW)[14]

> Questa stralun**ata** «**Berlusconomics**», attendista e rinunciataria, ha consentito all' Italia di sfilarsi momentaneamente dal girone infernale del Club Med.[15]

However, in German the formation can be treated both as feminine singular and plural, as well as with or without article. In cases that feature an article the plural form is more common; frequently these formations are put in quotation marks.

Usage with an Article:

Singular feminine:

Die «Reaganomics» stellt den faszinierenden Versuch dar, im Zeitalter der Massendemokratie die Mehrheit der Bevölkerung davon zu überzeugen, daß ein egalitärer Wohlfahrtsstaat sie auf Dauer arm macht (1056)[16]

Plural:

Seine so genannten «Abenomics» zeigen Wirkung (188)[17]

Die «Clintonomics» glauben, sie könnten sowohl die Staatsausgaben steigern als auch das Defizit reduzieren (895)[18]

Während die «Reaganomics» behaupteten, Steuersenkungen würden sich selbst finanzieren, verkünden die «Clintonomics», dasselbe leisteten öffentliche Ausgaben als «Investitionen». (896)[19]

Usage Without Article (more prototypical for proper names?)

Singular:

Bewertet man das Vorgehen nach der Treue zu den eigenen Regeln, dann wirkt «Merkelnomics» wie ein fortwährendes Taumeln, Wirtschaftspolitik im betrunkenen Zustand (128)[20]

Plural:

«Sarkonomics» sind flexibel, bündnisfähig und keiner Theorie verpflichtet, sondern der Fortdauer einer Wirtschaftsordnung (504)[21]

Concerning the semantics and pragmatics in the usage of these eponymous formations, it can be said that – in analogy to *-gate*-formations – there has been a development towards repetition, mainstream usage, and trivialization of the formation type. The elements formed in such a manner have found their way from the domain of economic policy to business language and common language. However, a converse shift for other formation types (*humanomics* and *neuronomics*) towards theoretical-scientific usage can also be detected.

In the language of journalism, the eponymous formations that have been investigated here are often prominently positioned in the headings (cf. *L'Espresso,* 22.7.2013: "Non dubitate della Abenomics"), while they are rarely found in the texts themselves and only play a marginal role. They command the prestige and connotation of technical terms. However, as mentioned, they are more frequently used in social media (blogs, etc.) than in journalistic writing. Finally, another tendency needs to be addressed, which ought to be confirmed by a more detailed contextual analysis: namely, that frequent eponymous formations derived from first names seem to carry a pejorative connotation, while formations based on family names appear more neutral, which might be illustrated with the following competing formations:

Obamanomics vs. *Barakonomics*
Renzinomics vs. *Matteonomics*

7. Conclusion

In conclusion, we wish to highlight that, to our knowledge, the formations on *-(o)nomics* we investigated had never been subjected to a linguistic analysis before (with the exception of Bauer 2005). Therefore, we have entered new territory. The next step will be to update and expand the corpus study. In doing so, it needs to be tested whether, on a morphological level, the shortening of the onymic bases follows the principles outlined here and according to which criteria (syllabic structure, consonant environment, etc.) the linking vowels *-o-* or *-i-* are being selected. Additionally, a more extensive study would show if the tentative conclusions regarding gender and number of *-(o)nomics*-formations can be confirmed. To that end, the grammatical behaviour of these formations in other Romance Languages needs to be investigated contrastively.

Moreover, with respect to the pragmatic dimension, a context-specific study of the usage of *-(o)nomics*-formations would yield an insight into whether there are semantic and connotative differences regarding the usage of either family names or first names (*Renzinomics* vs. *Matteonomics*). For this aspect, it might be relevant whether the selection of either the first- or the family name varies according to geographic region. In this regard, a preference for first names might be observable in South America (*Evonomics*, *Hugonomics*)

If the focus were on recipient perspective, instead of on the formation of these neologisms, studies regarding word reception and technical knowledge of the recipients could additionally clarify how meaning construal and connotation vary depending on country and cultural domain. An Italian citizen should have a more detailed concept of the measures taken in an economic policy labelled as *Renzinomics* than an Austrian or British person.

Another subject of investigation, which has been intentionally excluded here, could be the formations with *-(o)nomics* without a proper name (or its shortened version) but with confixes (such as *Neuro(eco)nomics*, *Humanomics*, *Wikinomics*) or appellative bases (such as *Soccernomics*, *Zombienomics*) respectively. In the former, the neologisms refer to more comprehensive and abstract concepts. See, e.g., Don Tapscott (*Wikinomics*, 2006) or the research done by Ernst Fehr (2003) on neuroeconomics. Furthermore, the above mentioned formations whose first element consists of an ergonym (brand name) should be worth a closer inspection (*Amazonomics*, *Applenomics*, *E-Baynomics* etc.).

References

Baldinger, Kurt. 1968. "Post- und Prädeterminierung im Französischen." In *Festschrift Walther von Wartburg zum 80. Geburtstag*, edited by Kurt Baldinger, vol. 1, 87–106. Tübingen: Niemeyer.

Bauer, Laurie. 2005. "The Borderline Between Derivation and Compounding." In *Morphology And Its Demarcations: Selected Papers From The 11th Morphology Meeting, Vienna, February 2004*, edited by Wolfgang U. Dressler et al., 97–108, Amsterdam; Philadelphia: John Benjamins.

Benson, Morton, Evelyn Benson, and Robert Ilson. 1986. *Lexicographic description of English*. Amsterdam et al.: Benjamins.

Cotticelli Kurras, Paola. 2012. "I nomi commerciali a cavallo di due secoli: continuità e innovazione." *QuadRIOn* 4: 321–347.

—. Forthcoming. "Des Kompositums seine Grenzen: Italienische Wortschöpfungen aus heutiger Sicht." In Festschrift zum 65. *Geburtstag von Elke Ronneberger-Sibold*, edited by Kerstin Kazzazi et al. Tübingen: Stauffenburg.

Dardano, Maurizio, and Pietro Trifone. 1997. *La nuova grammatica della lingua italiana*. Milano : Zanichelli.

Fehr, Ernst (ed.) (2003). *Psychologische Grundlagen der Ökonomie.* Zürich: Verlag Neue Zürcher Zeitung.

Flach, Susanne, Kristin Kopf, and Anatol Stefanowitsch. Forthcoming. "Skandale und Skandälchen kontrastiv. Das Suffix *-gate* im Deutschen und Englischen." In *Stiefkinder der Onomastik. "Sonstige Namenarten". Conference Proceedings*, edited by Rita Heuser and Mirjam Schmuck.

Fleischer, Wolfgang, and Irmhild Barz. [4]2012. *Wortbildung der deutschen Gegenwartssprache*. Berlin; Boston: De Gruyter.

Glück, Helmut, ed. [4]2010. *Metzler Lexikon Sprache*. Stuttgart; Weimar: Metzler.

Großmann, Maria, and Franz Rainer, eds. 2004. *La formazione delle parole in italiano*. Tübingen: Niemeyer.

Iacobini, Claudio. 2004. "Composizione con elementi neoclassici." In *La formazione delle parole in italiano*, edited by Maria Großmann, and Franz Rainer, 69–95. Tübingen: Niemeyer

Kalverkämper, Hartwig. 1978. *Textlinguistik der Eigennamen*. Stuttgart: Klett/Cotta.

Migliorini, Bruno. 1963. *Saggi sulla lingua del Novecento*. Firenze: Sansoni.

Nübling, Damaris / Fahlbusch, Fabian / Heuser, Rita. 2012. *Namen. Eine Einführung in die Onomastik*. Tübingen: Narr.

Panagl, Oswald. 1998. *Fahnenwörter der Politik. Kontinuitäten und Brüche*. Wien et al.: Böhlau.

Ronneberger-Sibold, Elke. 2004. "Warennamen." In *Namenarten und ihre Erforschung. Ein Lehrbuch für das Studium der Onomastik. Anlässlich des 90. Geburtstages von Karlheinz Hengst*, edited by Andrea Brendler, and Silvio Brendler, 557–603. Hamburg: Baar.

—. 2009. "*Thermodur, Blend-a-med, Sivitrex*: Konfixe in deutschen Markennamen: Typen – Geschichte – Funktionen." In *Studien zur Fremdwortbildung*, edited by Peter O. Müller, pp. 141–193. Hildesheim: Olms.

—. 2015 [=2015a]. "Word creation." In *Word Formation: an international Handbook of the Languages of Europe*, edited by Peter O. Müller et al., vol.1, pp. 485–499. Berlin; New York: de Gruyter.

—. 2015 [=2015b]. "Word formation and brand names." In *Word Formation : an international Handbook of the Languages of Europe*, edited by Peter O. Müller et al., vol.3, 2192-2210. Berlin; New York: de Gruyter.

Schpak-Dolt, Nikolaus. [3]2010. *Einführung in die französische Morphologie*. Tübingen: Max Niemeyer.

—. [2]2012. *Einführung in die Morphologie des Spanischen*. Tübingen: Niemeyer,

Schweickard, Wolfgang. 1992. *Deonmastik. Ableitungen auf der Basis von Eigennamen im Französischen. Unter vergleichender Berücksichtigung des Italienischen, Rumänischen und Spanischen*. Tübingen: Niemeyer.

—. 1995. "Morphologie der Namen: Ableitungen auf der Basis von Eigennamen." In *Namenforschung. Ein internationales Handbuch zur Onomastik*, edited by Ernst Eichler et al., vol.1, 431–435. Berlin; New York: de Gruyter.

—. 2001. "Ableitungen auf der Basis von Eigennamen (Deonomastik)." In *Lexikon der Romanistischen Linguistik*, edited by Günter Holtus, Michael Metzeltin, and Christian Schmitt, vol. I,1, 899–904. Tübingen: Niemeyer.

Serianni, Luca. 1989. *Grammatica italiana. Italiano comune e lingua letteraria*, Torino, UTET.

Wandruszka, Ulrich. 1980. "‚Post-‘ oder ‚Prädetermination‘ in den romanischen Sprachen? " In *Romanistisches Jahrbuch* 31: 56–72.

Notes

[1] The categorisation issues arising in formations with the element *-mane* and *-logue*, which reside in the grey area between composition and suffixation, is well-known. This unclear membership is reflected in strongly varying terminologies.

2 Among other things, the exogenous word formation units that are potentially active in forming words become in fact active units due to reanalysis and morphematization of segments of complex loanwords. (Fleischer and Barz 2012: 104).

3 In most cases, exogenous word formation units are Greek and Latin roots that often have found their way into German via other languages. (ibid.).

4 http://formiche.net/2014/03/06/padoan-inizia-riscrivere-la-matteonomics/ (accessed on 23.6.2015).

5 Simply the use of a name refers beyond the text at hand. The name is an appeal to the reader or listener to draw on their previous knowledge for the text interpretation. Using names corresponds to placing explicit markers for previous knowledge.

6 A new regular confix formation is as interpretable by the addressee as a regular word formation product, i.e. as transparent and motivated. Transparent means that the recipient can assign a word formation meaning to the confix formation. In order to be able to do that, they must, firstly, recognize the elements and, secondly, interpret the combination of these elements in terms of a productive word formation model. Motivation means that the thus determined word formation meaning is in accordance with the referential meaning (contextual meaning, enciclopaedic meaning) of the word.

7 http://www.washingtonpost.com/opinions/robert-j-samuelson-putinomics/2014/04/02/4af0e39e-ba84-11e3-96ae-f2c36d2b1245_story.html (accessed on 15.6.2015).

8 https://www.contrepoints.org/2014/05/08/165493-lukraine-est-lartisan-de-ses-malheurs-etatistes (accessed on 13.6.2015).

9 http://www.fanpage.it/il-rublo-interrompe-la-caduta-ma-putin-resta-sotto-pressione/ (accessed on 15.6.2015).

10 http://pagines.sytes.net:8801/txetxenia/index.php?option=com_content&view=article&id=739:russia-encallada-en-un-any-desdeveniments-i-pocs-canvis&catid=73:politica&Itemid=1&lang=es, (accessed on 9.6.2015).

11 http://revistaepoca.globo.com/tempo/noticia/2011/11/capitalismo-moda-russa.html (accessed on 08.06.2015).

12 http://www.petreanu.ro/2014/11/17/victor-ponta-demisia/, accessed on 23.06.2015.

13 Shinzo ABE, Prime Minister of Japan, 2006-2007, since 2012.

14 http://www.formiche.net/2014/03/06/padoan-inizia-riscrivere-la-matteonomics/ (23.6.2015).

15 Source: Massimo Giannini, La Repubblica, 13.2.2010.
16 «Reaganomics» constitutes the fascinating attempt to convince the majority of the population in the age of mass democracy that an egalitarian welfare state will impoverish them in the long run.
17 His so-called «Abenomics» show results.
18 The «Clintonomics» believe they could increase public spending and decrease the national deficit.
19 While the «Reaganomics» claim that tax cuts would finance themselves, the «Clintonomics» declare that public spending could do the same as «investments».
20 If one assesses the approach according to faith for one's own principles, then «Merkelnomics» appears like a perpetual stagger, economic policy in a drunk state.
21 «Sarkonomics» are flexible, capable to form alliances and not obliged to any theory but to the continuation of an economic order.

A NEW SUBCATEGORY IN COMMERCIAL PROPER NAMES: INTERNET PLAN NAMES IN RUSSIAN

SERGEY GORYAEV AND OLGA OLSHVANG

Abstract

The wide circulation of the Internet service for private users leads to an interesting onomastic phenomenon. Initially the consumer paid for the connection itself; the Internet connection for a household could be compared to that of other utilities (power supply, telephone, cable or antenna TV). However, the development of computer and economical technologies evokes an emergence of a new concept–an Internet plan. The linguistic consciousness of native speakers comprehends it as an object (ideal, of course) able to bear a special designation, which falls into the pattern of a usual trade name.

Introduction

The object of interest in this presentation is the names of the billing plans for Internet-connection, on Russian material. This study allows us to raise and, to some extent, to come close to solving two theoretical issues.

The first issue is a general onomastic and onomasiological one. This category of proper names allows us to trace and record in the mass public consciousness the emergence of the idea of a new, previously non-existent object, and this idea is so specific, clear and denotative, that it may and even should be indicated with a proper name. P. Tomasik is fair to say that "at the beginning of the 21st century, it became fashionable to call some services as products" (Tomasik, 2012: 54) and to designate these products with proper names. In this article, we show that it is not just a question of fashion, but also the formation of the relevant idea of a possible denoter of such a name in the public consciousness.

The second issue is a linguistic and technical one concerning all product names in general. This category of proper names allows us to consider the technical possibility of the language in the area of commercial naming. In this article we will look broadly at just one aspect–figurative or metaphorical as it has more to do with common language thinking and to a lesser extent–with a particular language, and therefore it can easily be translated.

Our observations are based on the corpus of about 300 names of the billing plans offered by 60 providers in the Russian city of Yekaterinburg at the beginning of 2015.

Extralinguistic background

Technological development, especially in the computer field, leads to the fact that the masses become familiar with scientific and technological advances. In particular, it happened to the personal computer, which, having originally been seen as an exotic device, has become an integral part of everyday life. Moreover, for some time after the wide expansion of computers, the connection to the Internet was still exotic.

In particular, with regard to the field of our material, that is the situation in Yekaterinburg, the largest city (with a population of almost 1.5 million people), in the second half of the nineties many people already had computers, but the permanent connection to the Internet was, for the most part, unavailable. Temporary connection used the dial-up technology, and the number of service providers was negligible.

In general, the non-occurrence of an Internet connection is not determined by the price but by the lack of networks' development. The networks develop gradually and the number of providers increases until there is full coverage of the city area. But the emergence of the concept of "billing plan" in relation to the Internet does not happen. From the perspective of an ordinary person, the fact of connecting to the Internet and the traffic consumption are subject to payment. And this perception of the Internet is superimposed on the existing stereotype: the Internet becomes one of the utilities, like connecting to the water supply, or electrical outlet. Thus, the Internet is perceived as a substance, the consumption of which shall be paid for.

In some cases, this situation has remained until now. Providers offering Internet access for businesses advertise it as the "Internet to the office", they do not create any billing plans and stipulate traffic costs. It is not common practice to charge for the possibility of connecting to the Internet in the city.

However, a small number of operators offer a so-called "Internet to the dacha"; it refers to the connection of a cottage in the suburbs, outside the coverage area of city networks. In this case, the possibility of the connection itself is subject to the advertising.

Thus, in these two situations, the Internet is a substance which has only two important qualities, from a consumer perspective,–the availability and price, which are subject to payment. In this situation only one proper name appears –"Internet" itself (for specificity of this proper name see Bergien 2003).

Denotative formation

The term "billing plan" appears along with the development of the market with regard to Internet access for individuals. Initially, it is only a supplement to the concept of the Internet; it is expressed in the language by the advertising phrase **"connect to the Internet on our billing plans."**

Such a notion is reflected in the names of billing plans which are "technical" by nature, most often they are based on the connection speed, such as an existing line of billing plans of an operator "*Speed of the external channel up to 3 Mb/s,*" "*up to 6 Mb/s,*" "*up to 10 MB/s,*" "*up to 15 MB/s.*" Such a name of the billing plan may include an indication of the price or the combined indication of price and speed: "*256 Kbit/s 600 rubles per month*", "*128 Kbit/s 500 rubles per month*", "*512 Kbit/s 650 rubles per month*", "*1 Mbit/s 750 rubles per month.*" (the example also contains a line of the billing plans of one operator).

Formally such names are recorded as proper names; they are written in quotation marks, often with a capital letter, which is a clear sign of a proper name in the Russian language. But for the inner form and often for the outer form as well, they are descriptions. The phrase containing such name is semantically and grammatically incomplete without the word "Internet".

However, the development of technologies, such as the computer or market ones, does not stand still, and billing plans become complicated. They differ not only by the speed of access and cost but also by a number of other aspects–the dependence of the speed on the time of the day, the connection between the speed and the amount of traffic, daily and monthly limits, etc. Thus, the consumer who chooses the billing plan does not pay for the Internet, a kind of substance which he gets on the wire, but a whole range of qualities. And in the consumer's mind a comprehensive concept of "billing plan" is gradually formed as a separate, independent entity, a separate independently conceivable item that is subject to the purchase and payment. In the advertising language it is expressed in the phrase **"buy our billing plans."**

This sentence is, to some extent, artificial in the Russian language due to the semantics of the word "план" (plan). Even the most recent explanatory dictionary of the Russian language provides only one, first meaning of this word, which can co-occur with the word "покупать" (buy): "*чертеж, изображающий в масштабе на плоскости местность, предмет, сооружение...*" (a drawing which shows in scale on the plan a territory, an object, a structure), other meanings such as "rules of procedure", "image scale", "point of view" (*Big Academic Dictionary* 2011: 9–10) do not assume such significance.

But this phrase really exists and is used in the advertisement of Internet providers and mobile operators. We shall point out that it is an example of how the advertising text affects the standard language norm, although this is not the subject of our article. In this case, we are interested in the following: the existence of such a phrase in the language indicates that in the minds of native speakers a new concept has been formed, a fragment of extralinguistic reality has got a terminological designation.

Onomastic exploration of new denotation

It should be noted that the question of the attribution of such verbal units (trade names in the broadest sense) to proper names is still debatable[1]. Without going into details, we note that at the theoretical level, we consider all of the following examples as undoubtedly proper names. But in terms of the mass language speaker, certain gradation is possible which, in some cases, is supported by the grammar of the Russian language, by the difference between nouns and adjectives[2].

Two examples will illustrate this thesis.

The question is whether we can consider the long nominations which are descriptive by their form as proper names. As an example, we take two names: the billing plan "Bezlimitny 690" (Unlimited 690) and the billing plan "Hit 699" (we picked up names with approximately the same figures, which refer to the monthly cost of the implied tariff in rubles).

There are two possible answers to this question. From the point of view of the onomastics theory these are undoubtedly proper names, as they refer to a specific single object. In fact, the function of the commercial name is just to select an object from a range of homogeneous objects. But in terms of everyday language consciousness, the first example is not a name, but a description; and the second example is a name, that is a proper name.

The first name expressed by an adjective refers to a noun "billing plan" and is a description. The second one does not have any semantic reference to the signified concept, and therefore can be considered as a proper name.

Thus, the onomastic exploration of the new concept of "Internet plan" by the language takes place in two stages.

The first stage: the names of the billing plans are semantically and often grammatically linked with the concept of a billing plan. They are designed to simplify the consumer's choice, and provide him with the necessary qualities for a billing plan as an independent entity. Examples are such names as "Pochtovy" (Postal), "Sutochny" (Daily), "Bezlimitny" (Unlimited), "Deti vi dome" (Children in the house),–the plans are chosen at different operators, or "Personalny" (Personal), "Domashny" (Home), "Semeyny" (Family), "Gostepriimny" (Friendly), "Rabochy" (Work), "Business" (the range of plans at one operator).

We consider two names separately. 1) "Everybody is at home". Semantically, the name is associated with the purpose of the tariff–for family use and for connecting multiple devices. But the external form refers to the spoken comic expression, "У тебя не все дома?" meaning "you're crazy", something like "he is not all there". 2) "uDachny" the word "udachny" means "lucky", but in this case two providers have used this adjective based on restructuring, one of them even stressed this graphically. This writing refers to the Russian word "dacha", as the tariff is designed for private houses in the suburbs.

Using the language game is evidence of the transition from the first stage to the second one.

The second stage is to create an undoubted proper name which does not carry any semantic load. In its pure form it is most clearly illustrated by the use of proper names of other categories to refer to the billing plan: place names "Olympus", personal names "Mashenka" (diminutive from the Russian version of the name Mary), "Jussi" (a borrowed woman's name), and a name from astronomy "Mercury".

These and similar names, grammatically drawn as nouns, are undoubtedly proper names from the point of view of an ordinary native speaker, and thus, there is a final onomastic development of new denotation "Internet plan".

At the same time, we note that the native speaker shall have a certain level of abstract thinking. The emergence of such names suggests that the idea of the billing plan has been finally formed as a kind of single conceivable object. Strictly speaking, this is natural in a situation of sale. Even in Roman law the concept of "res incorporales" was developed, which means an incorporeal thing. This is an item that cannot be touched, but which exists in legal terms and can be transferred, sold, paid, and so on.

Creative element as a sign of a proper name

It is quite easy to set the border between the name and the description intuitively. But it is difficult to put a theoretical basis for this distinction. We will use a recent concept proposed by R. Ratmayr who distinguished a "creative element" in the name: "advertising function is to appeal to the purchase; it is performed primarily by a creatively invented element of the full name" (Weiss, Zanodvorova, Issers et al. 2014: 301, our translation). Nevertheless, the strict definition of the "creative element" has not been proposed, so we will briefly add what we consider an undoubtedly proper name.

Roughly speaking, we obtain an undoubted proper name if we "cleanse" the name of the billing plan of the descriptive elements, leaving only one whose semantic relationship with the designation object does not result from the dictionary definition, but it is metaphorical in the broadest sense of the term.

So we will classify the aforementioned tariff "Bezlimitny" (Unlimited) as a descriptive name, and we refer the tariff "Semeyny" (Family) to figurative nomination due to, at least, the features of lexical compatibility of the word in the Russian language because it implicitly draws a vivid picture–a family who use the Internet.

With this approach, among the material in question there is a group of undoubted proper names. A variety of concepts is the source of metaphors. Let us consider 10 examples that we ranged by the degree of increase of unexpectedness of associations.

The most predictable cases are linked with the idea of speed: (1) *Скорость (Speed)*–by the name of one of the qualities of service provided, however, since no quantitative values of speed are specified, the name gives an opportunity for imaginative perception. (2) *Форсаж* (*Boost)*–the metaphor is also based on the idea of speed. (3) *Тифон (Typhoon)*–the idea of speed is connected with the idea of the elements sweeping everything.

Three following cases are presented by lexical items which come into a "core fund" to build commercial names, not only in the Russian language: (4) *Орбита (Orbit)*–this word was popular as a commercial name in the beginning of the space age, and remains popular to this day. Initially, we assumed that this name of the billing plan was for connecting via satellite, but we made a mistake, this is a common network connection. (5) *Олимп*

(Olympus) (6) *Титан (Titan)*–names that refer to ancient mythology, expressing the idea of power, superiority (remember the names of two sister-ships "Olympic" and "Titanic"), the metaphor is also clear in any European language.

The following names are also universal and as commercial names they may denote anything. (7) *Премьер (Premier)*, (8) *VIP*[3], (9) *Люкс (Lux).* They are united by the idea of luxury, and high quality. Interestingly, these three words have appeared in Russian language in recent years, but they are already widely utilized in naming.

Perhaps the most unexpected nomination is the following. (10) *Partisan (Partisan).* It should be clarified that the concept of a partisan in the Russian language has a mandatory aura of heroism, but in opposition to it, it also has an aura of irony. First, we would suggest that perhaps the name is associated with the peculiarities of the billing plan, for example, with unlimited speed at night, but the direct relationship was not found, although this billing plan suggests a complex relationship between the speed and the traffic volume.

Onymic microsystems

Microsystems are a few names of one operator which are built on a common creative base, but chosen to reflect the difference between the billing plans. They are interesting because a lexical item once chosen for a proper name brings to life a variety of names, and the emergence of a new name is not explained only by the author's free choice, but by the internal logic of onomastic system.

In our material we present three microsystems[4].

(M1) Sun–Mercury–Mars–Jupiter–Saturn–Uranus–Neptune

"Space" topic has already been present in the name of "Orbit", and here we see the names of the planets of the solar system. But the principles of the nomination within the microsystem are incomprehensible. The idea is supported only for the last three planets–the farther from the sun the greater speed and cost, there is no visible match for others according to the distance from the sun, nor the size of the planet, although knowledge about the structure of the solar system is included in the school curriculum and is generally known.

(M2) Pint–Gallon–Barrel

The metaphor is obvious, the Internet is compared with beer. Let us note that for the Russian language, these lexical items are exoticisms, matching the Anglo-American culture. Besides, in this microsystem, there is an idea of the Internet as a substance having a certain amount, but embodied at the metaphorical level.

In our opinion, the third microsystem is based on the most unexpected metaphor, the Internet is compared with dance music.

(M3) Bachata–Salsa–Samba–Twist–Rock 'n' Roll

Here the metaphor is sustained in its purest form. The names of the tariffs which differ (in ascending order) by the speed provided are presented by the names of dances, differing by the rhythm of the music (in the direction to a more frequent one). In this we shall note that the creation and interpretation of this metaphorical system requires special knowledge. In particular, the word *Бачата (Bachata)* is not recorded even in the latest standard dictionaries of the Russian language.

Thus, we see that in the corpus of names of the billing plans taken into consideration, there are pronounced proper names opposed to the descriptions on the principle of creation. In general, they occupy about half of the entire corpus, but a variety of lexical items is considerably smaller because one lexical item often builds the names for several tariffs, for example *Волна 3/6 (Wave3/6), Волна 5/10 (Wave 5/10), Волна 10/20 (Wave 10/20), Волна 54/27 (Wave54/27), Волна 50/100 (Wave 50/100).* The figures indicate the maximum day and night speed of the access. It is noteworthy that in this microsystem the differences in the quality of billing plans are transmitted in figures, so it is, rather, a method of terminological and not onymic nomination, on which we will dwell.

Onomastics and terminology

Most of the names also contain figures in addition to creative or descriptive components. Typically, the figures show the provided connection speed or the required monthly payment. It is a kind of a relic–remaining from the time when in the name of the billing plan the figures carried a main individualized and at the same time informing load and the consumer, getting acquainted with the offer, evaluated and selected for himself the connection corresponding to the number of parameters, but not the Internet plan as a single conceivable object.

There are several cases, when the figures are used in the nomenclature purposes, such as a range of billing plans from one provider *Optimal 1, Optimal 2, Optimal 3.* A serial number in this case shows that the tariffs somewhat differ quantitatively and life experience adds that it is probably the difference in price.

The use of figures as a part of the name is not typical for proper names in pure form. This is a sign of another kind of special language unit, – terminology, i.e. the sphere of language that is understandable only to specialists. Moving the term to the common lexis is not unusual. In fact, the phenomenon of transition of the word from terminology to common language is one of the trends of the twentieth century, and the transition of terms from the "computer sphere" is the twenty-first century trend.

But if we look at our material, we can see that the figures obscure rather than make the limitation of the concept easier. In most modern names the figures are not explicitly motivated, that is, in the name itself there is no indication what these figures represent. Moreover, for promotional purposes the creators of the names pick "non-round" numbers, so their appearance as part of the name can be motivated by the beautiful appearance of multidigit numbers, such as *Online 649, Online877*, or another series *888 RusCom*, *676 RusCom*, *454 RusCom*, where the alphabetic component is the provider's company name, but after a careful reading of the advertisements it is clear that the figures are a monthly payment.

Thus, the figures are a kind of coquetry of the person, who creates the name with one who receives it; it is an allusion to the general membership in the "mystery" of scientific and technical knowledge. Selecting numbers may not be due to scientific and technical requirements, but to aesthetic and advertising purposes. And among our examples, many are, by the method and purposes of creating, commercial proper names, disguised as technical designation.

Conclusion

In this article we considered the emergence of a new subcategory of commercial names–Internet plan names–in the Russian language. In essence, this is another kind of advertising name, "the name of any product in the broadest sense of the word" (Krukova 2004: 7). Our case is interesting because the emergence of a new advertising name is not associated with the emergence of a new product, as long as the act of connecting to the Internet, which is the product itself in this situation, does not require the designation with a proper name. We cannot say either that the emergence of proper names for the billing plans is due to advertising necessity, since there are still providers which focus their promotional efforts on the company name and billing plans themselves can be without individual names, and look like specification. The logic of the emergence of proper names, which we presented above, in brief is as follows: *description of specification of the product–description, compressed to one word/phrase–undoubted proper name.*

We hypothesize that commercial names and, broader, commercial relations play an increasing role in the life of a modern man who is not by chance called *homo oeconomicus*, whose life is largely determined by economic realities. And the technical concepts and ideas (such as, for example, the specification of the Internet connection), that are involved in the sphere of human economic relations are reinterpreted from the standpoint of the ordinary person, the average native speaker. As a result, in mass representation, firstly, there is a formation of incorporeal object, incorporeal thing, and secondly by analogy with other kinds of goods it receives a commercial proper name.

References

Bergien A. 2003. "Name oder Terminus? Kategorienwechsel im fachsprachlichen Bereich". In: *Namenkundliche Informationen.* #83/84, Leipzig: 55–66.

Большой Академический словарь русского языка. Т. 17. 2011. Москва, Санкт-Петербург. (*Big Academic Dictionary of the Russian language*. V. 17, 2011. Moscow, St. Petersburg).

Крюкова И. В. 2004. *Рекламное имя: от изобретения до прецедентности*. Волгоград (Krukova I. 2004. *Advertising name: from invention to precedentness*. Volgograd).

Langendonck, W. Van. 2007. *Theory and Typology of Proper Names*. Berlin, New York.

Розанова Н., Китайгородская М., Долешаль У., Вайс Д. и др. 2014. *Еда по-русски в зеркале языка*. Москва. (Weiss D., Zanodvorova A., Issers O., Kitaigorodskaya M., Rathmayr R., Rozanova N., Hoffmann E., with the participation of Dolechal U. 2014. *Russian Food through the Mirror of Language*. Moscow).

Романова Т. П. 2007. "Система способов словообразования рекламных собственных имен". В: *Вестник СамГУ* #5/2 (55): 204–214 (Romanova T.P. 2007. "The system of word formation methods for advertising proper names". In: *Samara State University Bulletin* #5/2 (55): 204–214).

Томасик П. 2012. "Находятся ли названия маршрутов городского транспорта в кругу интересов ономастов?" В: *Вопросы ономастики* #2(13): 53–62 (Tomasik P. Are city transport route names relevant to onomastics?" In: *Voprosy onomastiki* #2(13): 53–62).

Notes

[1] We shall briefly recall the two concepts, which insert the trade names in the realm of proper names: I. Krukova introduces the concept of advertising names and treats them as peripheral names, which, unlike the core names–personal names, do not always comply with the concept of a proper name (2004). W. Langendonck distinguishes a large category of non-prototypical proper names, where he also includes trade and brand names (2007).

[2] In Russian the adjectives have quite pronounced formal signs, though, of course, from the point of view onomastic theory "all proper names are nouns, whatever form they may have" (Romanova 2007: 205).

[3] The name is immediately written in Latin.

[4] Due to the fact that all lexical items used in the examples have a clear Russian-English equivalent up to the coincidence at transliteration level, we mostly provide only English translation of the Russian material.

NAMING AND MARKETING A JOB COACHING FIRM: MEANS AND STRATEGIES

KATHARINA LEIBRING AND ANNA SVEDJEDAL

Abstract

This paper focuses on the names of companies in the Human Resources (HR) sector, a field that hitherto has attracted little interest from onomasticians. Our study object are names of private job coaching firms in Sweden, establishments which were very rare before 2008 as the national public agency Arbetsförmedlingen (The Employment office) dominated the labour market support measures then. The Conservative government then launched a major project outsourcing tasks to private enterprises. The special mission for these so-called job coaches was to get unemployed persons back into work or further education. Since then, many new companies aimed at job coaching have been established. In this paper, a sample of the company names are examined. Their usage of different languages, linguistic and onomastic features in the names, and the semantic meanings they convey are investigated. As these job coaching firms are recent additions to the Swedish commercial advertising landscape, we also discuss some of the marketing strategies displayed on the companies' internet websites.

Introduction

Many studies of company names have focused on companies providing material products or services (e.g. car repairs, flower shops, restaurants), or offering well-established practical services, such as hair-dressers or beauty salons.[1] As far as we are aware, very few studies in ergonomics have discussed names of the new professions significant for the post-industrial and free-market service society, e.g. names among enterprises or firms operating in the area of human resources (HR). In this paper, we will make a tentative attempt at diminishing this lack of research by presenting a study of the names of job coaching firms in Sweden.

Our aim is to establish whether these ergonyms, alluding not to material but to hard-to-define “mental products”, differ from ergonyms connected with more tangible or physical products. To clarify this, several basic questions must be answered. Which languages are used? What linguistic elements do the names consist of? Are there mostly other names, proper words or more new-coined structures in the names? Can we observe any prototypical name elements among them?

This is a pilot study using a limited corpus of company names registered in Sweden as belonging to job coaching firms. We will look at the names from both a linguistic and a semantic perspective. As these firms seldom have physical shop windows, their Internet appearance is important; we will also study some of the marketing strategies found on selected websites.

Method and material

To achieve our aims, we will use Paula Sjöblom’s semantic model for categorizing company names, which she has developed in a series of papers (Sjöblom 2007; in Ainiala et al 2012). For the linguistic analysis, we will compare structures in company names as shown in papers by, among others, Angelika Bergien (2009, 2012a), where languages used and the proportions of onyms vs. appellatives are investigated.

Before we present the actual analyses, we find it important to define *coach* and *coaching* in this particular context. We will also give a short background to the origin of job coaches in Sweden, and say a few words on a particular Swedish employment project, and why so many firms in the labour market field of human resources (HR) suddenly started branding themselves as job coaches.

The name corpus has been collected from two different sources, mostly from a sub-provider to the Swedish public employment agency and some from internet websites. All companies have been checked against the Swedish official company directory (websites www.bolagsverket.se; www.allabolag.se) to establish that they classify themselves as offering job coaching. In total, our corpus consists of the names of 52 different enterprises having job coaching as one of their main descriptive elements. A majority of the companies are small and young, which in this context is defined as having been founded after 2008. Their business and legal form varies; some are registered as limited companies while others are trading companies or private firms. From the total corpus of 52 companies, ten were selected for study of their websites. One major parameter for selection here was a prominent display of the phrases "job coach" or "job coaching" on the website.

The Swedish job coach project – background

What is a coach and what is coaching? According to the International Coaching Federation's (ICF) website,[2] a coach belongs to the labour-market group of support professionals. Coaching is defined as

> partnering with clients in a thought-provoking and creative process that inspires them to maximise their personal and professional potential.--- This process helps clients dramatically improve their outlook on work and life, while improving their leadership skills and unlocking their potential.

Other members of this group include consultants and psychotherapists. Coaching should however, states ICF, be seen as distinct from therapy, consulting, mentoring, training, or athletic development. The ICF certifies people worldwide, and many of the coaches in our study are ICF certified on different levels. A coach has different responsibilities, which are summarized by the ICF in four points:

- to discover, clarify and align with what the client wants to achieve
- to encourage client self-discovery
- to elicit client-generated solutions and strategies
- to hold the client responsible and accountable

In many countries in the Western world, an abundance of coaches of different fields in the business market, as well as in the market of individual self-help, and as an aid to find employment, are found today. To illustrate this, in Sweden alone, over 500 companies have a registered name containing either the word *coach* or the word *coaching*.[3]

Around 2008, the phenomenon of job coaching, i.e. helping and motivating unemployed persons to find jobs or trainee posts, became an issue in Sweden. Earlier, most official help and support to unemployed persons was maintained through the Swedish public employment service (Arbetsförmedlingen), and private employment firms were not encouraged. In 2008, the conservative government allowed private entrepreneurs the right to start companies aiming at coaching and advising job-seeking people. A large job coaching project was initiated by the government in 2009, where Arbetsförmedlingen procured external actors to work as job coaches. The aim was that the external actors, often small firms, would encourage and help persons, often those recently unemployed, to find new jobs and get out of social security dependence. The unemployed persons eligible for this type of help, were given lists of names of job coaching companies from which they could select a coach. Thus the company names and the websites were important as criteria for choosing a certain coaching company.

This project operated for two years, and was followed by a similar project in 2011 which was subsequently closed down in 2013. By the time of closing, 750 coaching companies were engaged in the project, and ca 270 000 persons had been given coaching. The first procurement was assessed as having been moderately successful in helping people find new employment. The second, however, met with less success, and the remaining allotted money was, on account of a government decision in late 2013, re-directed at aiding people who were further away from the labour market, e.g. long-term unemployed or newly arrived immigrants. Many of the job coaching companies have kept on coaching people within other public or private projects. (Liljeberg, Martinson & Thelander 2012.)

Linguistic features

As has been shown in earlier studies, many ergonyms in many branches are created from, or contain, names from other parts of the onomasticon, especially anthroponyms. This is conspicuous in older ergonyms, however, in younger companies this group is smaller (see on this e.g. Bergien 2012a, Fahlbusch 2014, Leibring 2014, Sjöblom in Ainiala et al 2012: 230). A second big group of company names are created from words related to the product or service given. Newer names are often coined from quasiwords, language mixes, or made up of abbreviations.

Regarding the linguistic features of the ergonyms, we will thus first examine how big a part of the names of job coaching firms contain other types of names, e.g. personal names or place-names, and how these names (or parts of names) are positioned in the ergonyms. Many of these names are related to the owner's name and we will investigate what part(s) of the personal names are used. Second, in the ergonyms lacking connections with anthroponyms, we will study if these ergonyms contain other names, words found in the common language or if the name elements are new constructions. Third, we will look at the different languages found in the names. And fourth, we will try to identify some core words specifying this certain type of companies.

1. The name of the owner is in some way used in 22 (ca 40 %) of the company names. The distribution between the different name elements is shown in table 1. The anthroponymic parts are put in italics.

Type of name	**Number of occurrences**	**Examples**
Full name is used	3	CoachYou *Marie Lundgren*
Full family name is used	8	*Färnlycke* Konsult AB
First name or pet form is used	3	*Mely* Mångfald, *Nilla* AB
Part of owner's name is used	7	*TobRob* < first names *Tobias* and *Robert*; *Mörckta* AB < surname *Mörck*
Word-play based on owner's name	1	*Winnforce* Sweden AB < *Winnfors* (surname)

Table 1. Use of owner's name in company names.

Half of these company names (11) display the owner's family name, either on its own or in a name phrase with the first name. A first name is used in 6 cases, ranging from pet form (*Nilla* AB from *Pernilla*) to a combination of the first name and the family name (*Marie Lundgren*). No less than 7 names are new creations from some part of the owner's names. As these examples show, there is a rather high percentage of job coaching firms that use personal names, even higher than in my study of company names of five different trades, where 33% of the names contained personal names in 2009 (Leibring 2014: 406, 411). However, the figures are lower than in the findings by Angelika Bergien of company names in Magdeburg in 2006 (Bergien 2012a: 180). A majority of the personal names are placed in front (i.e. to the left) of the descriptive part in the company name, as in *Färnlycke Konsult AB*. Only two ergonyms have the personal name put after the descriptive part (e.g. *CoachYou Marie Lundgren*).

Place names are used in only 6 of the 52 names, around 12%. Two examples are *Smeden i Västerås AB* and *Coachgruppen Uppsala AB*. This rather low number could be explained by the fact that there is not much local feeling connected with the services provided. On the other hand, as Bergien (2012b) and Boerrigter (2007: 59f.) have shown, smallish companies often display local place-names or have local references in their names. As the job coaching firms are often rather small, the relative lack of place-names could be something typical for support professions in contrast to professions offering other types of services. More studies are of course needed to confirm or reject this hypothesis. All six place names are put after the descriptive part in the company name.

2. The company name does not use the owner's name. This is the case in 30 of the 52 names. Of these, 22 names are constructed from real words. In addition to nominal phrases, like *Du Kan Nu* (Engl. "You Can Now") and single words, like *Versal*, also ungrammatical word combinations can form names, such as *Avancera Coaching AB* and *Spira Rekrytering AB*. Eight names contain words or word formations that are not found in the ordinary lexicon: *Ametop Coaching - Consulting*, *Gapea Helhet–Utveckling–Resultat*, *Incluso AB*, *Informeria AB*, *Osobra konsult*, *Peopletransition*, *Pii kommunikation AB* and *Verto konsult AB*. Among these, two names include acronyms not related to the owner's name: *Gapea* and *Pii*. To both these acronyms explanations are given on the companies' websites, probably as a means of attracting client interest. In the case of Gapea, the explanation is rather strained: "att fylla GAP Effektivt och Anpassat" (Engl. "to fill gaps efficiently and adapted")

3. The languages used, when disregarding onyms, are Swedish and English. Latin elements, and quasi-language words occur as well. Swedish is the most common language with 23 tokens as single language. English only is found in 12 company names, and mixed with Swedish in 4 more (e.g. *Nearlife – samtal & utveckling*). The names *Incluso AB* and *InformeriaAB* contain Latin-sounding elements while the word *ametop* in *Ametop Coaching-consulting* is not found in any language known to me.

Well-known phenomena in ergonyms in other company sectors are the incorrect use of capital letters and lack of space between words. These features are present in this corpus as well, as in the names *InMovement*and *VarDagsrörelse*.

4. Some core words that reoccur in the names are *coach*, *coaching*, *consulting*, where the two first words can be used in either Swedish or English. Some more Swedish nouns found in several company names are *konsult*, *kommunikation* and *utveckling*, in English: "consult", "communication" and "development". All these words relate to the business idea of these companies, and they are all used in the descriptive texts on the companies' websites (see below).

Semantic description

As a theoretical background for the description of the semantic contents, we have used a model by Paula Sjöblom, most recently elaborated in the handbook of Finnish onomastics, *Names in focus* (Ainiala et al 2012: 241 f.). In her model, company names are divided into four different categories depending on the relationship between the name and its referent, in decreasing order from transparency to opacity. These categories are:

1. Direct meaning relationship
2. Indirect meaning relationship
3. Compressed meaning relationship
4. Disconnected meaning relationship

In group 1, where the direct meaning is expressed, e.g. that the relevant trade is spelled out, we find 20 examples among our corpus of names of job coaching firms. Two examples are *Confident Coaching AB* and *MentorJobbcoaching*. Among the 11 names expressing an indirect meaning relationship (group 2), we find both metonymic and metaphoric associations, as in the names *Gapea Helhet - Utveckling - Resultat* (Engl. transl. "(acronym) + totality–development–result") and *Mely Mångfald* (Engl. transl. personal name *Mely* + "multitude or manifoldness").

Two examples of names in group 3, where several semantic components are pressed together, are *Nearlife - samtal&utveckling* ("talks & development") and *Smiling Mountain Training & Coaching*. Only 6 names can be classified as belonging to this group. The last group (4), consists of names with no real connection to the referent's service. These names are often created from the owner's name or from words totally unrelated to the business idea. Some examples are *NillaAB* (pet form of owner's first name), *Frontways* and *Smeden i Västerås AB* ("the smith in Västerås"). We have found that 11 names of the 52 fit into this group.

As in all categorizing of names, there is a small sample of names that are either of unclear or of ambiguous meaning, thus could be placed into either of two groups. Among the names studied here, we find that 4 names could be placed in more than one group, or were hard to define. These ergonyms are *Du Kan Nu* ("you can now") *InMovement*, *Pii Kommunikation AB* and *Ståpäls AB* ("goose-bumps in a positive way").

The largest group is thus that of the names expressing a direct meaning relationship – they give clear information about the services the company renders. Even though most of these companies were founded during the last decades, and the direct meaning in many trades has been seen as diminishing (Sjöblom in Ainiala 2012: 230), this structure remains strong. Two possible explanations for the relatively high figures among job coaching firms could be that this type of service has become available only recently, and thus the need for direct information is still great, or that this is a typical attribute in names of companies in the hitherto onomastically unexplored HR-sector. Further studies are needed.

Marketing strategies on websites

As stated earlier, the websites of these companies are important selling points as potential clients choose their coach from them and from the company name. We made a small pilot study of ten companies where the words "coach" or "coaching" figured in prominent positions on their websites. Seven of the companies also give their own definition of what coaching is, and some refer to ICF. We then analysed the websites in relation to their attitude towards a prospective client. Is the client in focus, and if so, how is his or her attention attracted? What other ways of attracting interest are shown apart from direct focus on the client?

Our chosen companies are named respectively *Akleja Friskvård*, *Ametop Coaching - consulting*, *AvanceraCoaching*, *CoachYou Marie Lundgren*, *Du Kan Nu*, *Gapea Helhet - Utveckling - Resultat*, *Human coaching*, *InMovemen*t, *Nearlife - samtal & utveckling* and *Osobra konsult*. Only one of these firms incorporates the owner's name in its name, but the names of all owners are easily found on the website.

On these websites, three companies put questions in the active mode to a prospective client. One example is *AklejaFriskvård* where the prospective client is asked (in my translation): "What do you want from life? What are you prepared to pay to get it?" And the company answers: "Goal-focused coaching will give you what you want".

These firms are very focused on getting the client's attention through an active role. Some other companies are not asking direct questions but are nevertheless very client-orientated. Here, we find the company *Du Kan Nu*, which sports a large question mark and poses several complicated questions, e.g. "What are the reasons why certain individuals, groups and organizations are so successful in their life-changing choices, while others find this process more difficult?" As a pendant to the company name ("you can now"), the owner describes herself under the heading Vad Kan Jag? ("what can I?"). Six companies out of ten offer a presentation of the company's owner. These presentations include formal references, life achievements as well as private interests.

Some companies have websites that are more descriptive - the prospective client seems to be less in focus than is the main ideas of the company. The firm *Nearlife - samtalsterapi och coaching* uses a long written text. All the webpages contain long-winded information and their key concept seems to be "develop the art to lead yourself". Its name is not explained but I associate it with a perhaps unintentional pun on the phrase "near-death".

One website that stands apart from the majority is *InMovement*. This is the only website of the ten that is multimodal in that it contains not only written texts but sound effects and moving pictures as well. It is also the sole company to offer parallel texts in Swedish and English. No questions are put to the clients, the page is just descriptive. The company's slogan is "the company that sets people in motion". To move the body and use the intelligence of the body are the key concepts for achieving changes in people's lives, according to this company. Its name, *InMovement*, is thus very closely connected with the company's concept.

From what we have learned from this brief overview of some websites we can see that the term coaching is still not well-established as there is a need for presentation and definition on most of the websites. The owners and their CVs are also important factors for attracting interest. Many websites are directly orientated at prospective clients, thus giving the feeling of a close and intimate situation. The name of the company is sometimes explained, but the key terms and the person seem to be of more importance than the actual story behind the name.

Conclusions

Through this pilot study we have tried to pave the way for a larger study of ergonyms in the HR sector. We have found that the names of the companies are used as marketing factors in a few cases, but that many of the names contain direct descriptive elements, and that many of them include (parts of) the owner's name. Core words and phrases focusing on change and achievement are common both in names and on websites. Some prototypical elements are *coach(ing)*, *development* and *communication*, in both Swedish and English. The core words belong to the semantic fields of action, communication, changes, development, future and promote a positive attitude and outlook. On many websites, the focus is on the prospective customer or client, often through questions directed at him or her. We can also find that the person behind the company is important, that stories are told about the founder etc. Clients are important, but the owner or the company is as well. This direct approach could be typical for the marketing of HR services as the focus is on person to person.

As stated above, this is only a study of a limited name stock in one section of the HR sector. This is still a novel area for onomastics, and we would like to end this paper with some questions for future research on ergonyms in the HR sector.

Our questions are: how do these company names compare to names of companies providing material products? Are there more similarities to ergonyms used in other sectors where individual skills are valued, such as the beauty and health care sector, or in the learned professions, e.g. lawyers and accountants? Our hope is that scholars in different countries will find this subject interesting, so that in the future international comparisons can be made and our common knowledge of commercial names is broadened.

References

Ainiala, Terhi, Minna Saarelma, and Paula Sjöblom. 2012. *Names in Focus. An Introduction to Finnish Onomastics*. Helsinki: Finnish Literature Society.

Bergien, Angelika. 2012a. "Business names as indicators of tradition and innovation". In *Onomastic goes business. Role and relevance of Brand, Company and Other Names in Economic Contexts*. Edited by Holger Wochele, Julia Kuhn, and Martin Stegu, 177–84. Berlin: Logos.

—. 2012b. "Cultural and regional connotations of company names in local contexts." In *Names as language and capital*. Ed. by Reina Boerrigter and Harm Nijboer, 7–12. Amsterdam: Meertens Instituut.

Boerrigter, Reina. 2007. "Identity reflecting business names". In *Proceedings of the 21st International Congress of Onomastic Sciences, Uppsala 19–24 August 2002. 3*. Editors Eva Brylla, Mats Wahlberg in collab. with Rob Rentenaar, 53–61. Uppsala: Institutet för språk och folkminnen.

Boerrigter, R. and H. Nijboer, eds. 2012. *Names as Language and Capital*. Amsterdam: Meertens Instituut.

Fahlbusch, Fabian. 2014. "*Löhr Automobile*, *Autohaus Höptner*, *Willi Sommer*. Familiennamen in Unternehmensnamen". In *Linguistik der Familiennamen*, Hrsg. Friedhelm Debus, Rita Heuser, Damaris Nübling, 367–93. (Germanistische Linguistik 225–227). Hildesheim: Olms.

Kremer, L. and E. Ronneberger-Sibold, eds. 2007. *Names in commerce and industry: Past and present*. Berlin: Logos.

Leibring, Katharina. 2014. "Surnames in names of companies in Sweden – a diachronic study". In *Linguistik der Familiennamen*, Hrsg. Friedhelm Debus, Rita Heuser, Damaris Nübling, 395–417. (Germanistische Linguistik 225–227). Hildesheim: Olms.

Liljeberg, Linus, Sara Martinson, and Jonas Thelander. 2012. *Vad innebär det att bli coachad? En utvärdering av jobbcoachningen vid Arbetsförmedlingen*. (IFAU Rapport 2012:24). Uppsala: IFAU.

Sjöblom, Paula, 2007. "Finnish Company Names: Structure and Function." In *Names in commerce and industry: Past and present.* Ed. by Ludger Kremer and Elke Ronneberger-Sibold, 297–306. Berlin: Logos.

Sjöblom, P., T. Ainiala and U. Hakala, eds. 2013. *Names in the Economy. Cultural Prospects.* Newcastle upon Tyne: Cambridge Scholars Publishing.

Wochele, H., J. Kuhn, and M. Stegu, 2012, eds. *Onomastic goes business. Role and relevance of Brand, Company and Other Names in Economic Contexts*. Berlin: Logos.

www.aklejafriskvard.se
www.allabolag.se
www.ametopsweden.com
www.avanceracoaching.se
www.bolagsverket.se
www.coachfederation.org
www.coachyou.se
www.dukannu.se
www.gapea.se
www.humancoaching.se
www.inmovement.se
www.nearlife.se
www.osobra.se

Notes

[1] See e.g. the sections on company names in the proceedings from the four earlier symposias in the Names in the Economy series, cited as Kremer & Ronneberger-Sibold 2007; Wochele, Kuhn & Stegu 2012; Boerrigter & Nijboer 2012; Sjöblom, Ainiala & Hakala 2013.

[2] See: www.coachfederation.org/need/landing.cfm?ItemNumber=978&navItemNumber=567 where the two following quotations are found.

[3] See www.bolagsverket.se and www.allabolag.se for the exact figures.

CAR NICKNAMES AND THEIR RELATION TO THE BRAND

JANNE SEPPÄLÄ

Abstract

The neutral and simple title gives a false impression of simplicity around the topic, the structure of this presentation and the perspective through which the content is presented. A more descriptive "secret" subtitle for this contribution might be "what can an onomastician provide for marketing agencies". Having a doctoral dissertation (Seppälä 2013) as the background, this contribution might be seen as a scientific article. Rather than a scientific article, however, I am trying to provide new ideas and methods for applied, economy-influenced onomastics. After the introduction I will describe how car nicknames potentially can serve to interpret brands and measure their strength. From a simple measurement of the number of names I will proceed to the content and metaphors in the names and, last but not least, to an analysis of name formation, which can reveal brand strength as well.

Introduction–car brand nicknames as a phenomenon

Car brand nicknames–such as Bug, Mitsubitchy, Ashtray, Tin Lizzie and Chevy, or even Big Money Waste–exist in many languages, even though they have not been in the spotlight of research.

For this reason, my doctoral dissertation is a broad collection of texts around car nicknames, name giving, name-formation or name-structure, metaphors in names, motives for name-giving, name loans and alterations, and the multiple meanings of names. The material consisted of 3500 Finnish and 600 Estonian nicknames for cars, tractors and bicycles–mostly car nicknames. The nicknames were collected by interviewing people, by reading magazines and books and by browsing the Internet. N.B.: For simplicity, all this material will be called "car nicknames" in the rest of this text, even though there are other (non-car) names in the material as well. This will not greatly distort the results, because the structures and themes in all the names are mostly the same and the aim of this paper is not to give exact statistics but to provide new research ideas.

Nicknames and nickname-formation can be seen falsely as harmless word play. As Al Ries (2010) has written that nicknames serve a communication function. They indicate an emotional connection with the brand. Or in the case of a formal name, the lack of one. He sees that the Chevrolet owner who calls his or her car a "Chevy" is communicating some emotional connection with the brand–positive (more likely) or negative. Ries states that, of the six leading automobile brands, only Chevrolet has a nickname. In Finnish, most brands have, but some–the most neutral ones–tend to have the least names. The number of names will be discussed more thoroughly in § 1.

§ 3 consists of metaphor-based analysis of how cars are seen (metaphorical target domains) and § 2 contains an analysis of the motives for name-giving (what properties and parts are the most significant in cars). In my research concerning Finnish names, I have noticed that these target words tend to form groups: cars are metaphorically seen as humans, animals, boxes and machines, as shown later.

In order to make the reader familiar with the relevant terminology, I shall first concisely describe the mechanisms of nickname-formation. New names can be derived from official brand names; such nicknames are called *secondary forms* (Alfa Romeo → Alfa). New names can also be invented spontaneously based on a vehicle's appearance; such nicknames are called *primary nicknames* (VW Typ 1 → Hitler's revenge). Linguistically, the alteration that creates secondary-form nicknames can be categorized as alteration by phonological, morphological or lexical means (see Peter McClure's model concerning nicknames, McClure 1981: 65–67). While writing the dissertation, the model had to be reworked in order to profoundly analyze those nicknames I had collected. The main structure types are seen in the figure 1 (see appendix).

Even though they are called "nicknames", the tone or emotional content of many of the brand nicknames can be seen as neutral - or, more precisely - labile. A specific context, attitude, or tone of speech may be needed when trying to judge if, for example, "Chevy" is something positive or negative in a single speech act. Still, as seen in the pie chart, secondary names can be divided into two groups. A secondary name can either be a "neutral" hypochorism or carry an added meaning as the alteration Gorilla (from Toyota Corolla) does. Furthermore, in addition to these, there are alterations, which resemble some already existing word but never exactly get there - like Mitsubitchy. The connotations the nickname has, then, are mostly bound to the "target word" of alteration (bitchy). And if the car itself appears as bitchy, the perfect nickname has been found.

Names can, of course, consist of two parts as well, as does the name Wing Caddy. The word "caddy" does not have any common meaning in the Finnish language, so the latter part of the name is seen as a neutral hypochorism, actually a loan nickname. The first part of the name, "Siipi", refers directly to the wings (tailfins) of the '59 Cadillac. The varying prevalence of these name types among different brands is discussed in § 4.

As a terminological note, I have to clarify the words car brand, brand name, car model, model name and so on. In this contribution the word *brand* refers to a brand as a whole, containing everything from a brand name to colors, marketing phrases, company values and attitudes. A *brand name* refers to a name itself (like Mercedes-Benz) and a *model brand name* or a *model name* refers to a name of a car model or car model brand (like Corolla). It is also necessary to note that for some car brands, the different models are quite strongly and independently branded, while for other car brands, this is not the case. Mazda models with their numbers can be seen as a part of the Mazda family, while actual names such as Focus, Sierra, Cortina and Taunus can be used without a "family name". These "family ties" can also be seen in nicknames. In § 4, I will show one method for analyzing brand power by studying both car brand nicknames and car model nicknames, and by observing the prevalence of secondary forms of the brand name in nicknames. For example, Volvo models are seen as more independent (from "The Saint" to "The Coffin") as compared to "Classic Caddy", "Wing Caddy" and "Elvis Caddy", which all belong to a family by their names. In Finnish, the determinant goes almost always before the determined in compounds.

1. Number of nicknames as a measure for brand strength

Originating from historical-philological linguist Hans Sperber (1923: 45–49), the terms attraction, expansion and affect are quite well established. *Affect* refers to the richness of feeling, the amount of emotional load. As seen from an etymological point of view, affect appears in the vocabulary in a number of ways: affect can, for example, promote a phonetic motivation and cause overwhelming derivation when words are generated (Kulonen 2006: 324). *Attraction*, on the other hand, means that there is a concept, which has insufficient possibilities for linguistic expression, compared to the amount of emotional load attached to it (Hämäläinen, 1946: 261). A concept with a high attraction is so important and emotionally powerful that the existing words are not sufficient to express strongly enough, or to describe it well enough. Such concepts or themes (e.g. sexuality) around which a lot of vocabulary is concentrated are called *attraction points* or *attraction centers*. In addition to attraction points, there are *expansion points* and *expansions areas* as well. In practice, *expansion* means that a word is considered so attractive and expressive that it gets used more widely and its semantic field expands. There are many fields of concepts, which can easily give metaphorical expressions to other areas; for example, war-related vocabulary has been widely borrowed by sport jargon (Kuiri 2004: 35). In this section, the attraction points get the most attention, whereas expansion points have their place in § 3.

In this section, we go through some statistics based on my corpus: which car brands and which car models have the most names. The main idea is simple: the more names a brand or a model has, the more well-known and powerful it is. As is typical for statistics, the numbers of names must be interpreted wisely to avoid false impressions. At the end of the section, I will discuss some misleading points and evaluate the suitability of this method for brand research.

The number of car brand nicknames per car brand is presented in table 1.

Car brand	Number of nicknames	Car brand	Number of nicknames
Lada (VAZ)	104	Mazda	16
Skoda	35	Toyota	14
Peugeot	35	Trabant	13
Opel	34	Mitsubishi	12
Ford	29	Saab	12
Volvo	28	IFA	11
BMW	26	Buick	11
Cadillac	25	Pontiac	11
Chevrolet	20	Audi	10
Volkswagen	19	Dodge	10
Wartburg	19	Suzuki	8
Fiat	18	Bedford	8
Mercedes-Benz	18	Talbot	8
Nissan	17	Renault	8
Chrysler	16	*total*	605

Table 1. Number of car brand nicknames.

As can be seen, the Russian car brand Lada has the most nicknames and, therefore, should arouse the most emotions among the Finns. There are at least two main reasons for Lada's leading position. The most obvious one is the significance of the scary, imposing and strange Soviet Imperium, located right next to Finland. Names like Uralin Mersu "the Ural Mercedes" even sound a bit like taboo-names, expressing the country of origin without mentioning the USSR directly. The second reason is phonotactics in Finnish. The phoneme /d/ has come to the Finnish language quite late, and is therefore quite often replaced with /r/, /t/ or /ø/ in speech (at least lower-class speech). Alteration caused by phonotactics leads then easily to another kind of alteration (from Lada to Lara, from Lada to Laatokka "Ladoga"). Among the top ten, there are also some other brands whose official names do not adapt well to Finnish (e.g. Peugeot, BMW, Volkswagen). However, to be frequently nicknamed, a car brand does not need to have a name that is especially prone to alteration: most of the frequently nicknamed car brands here do have some kind of common reputation in Finland.

A further question arises, though. How to distinguish between the real strength of brand from the complexity strictly bound to a brand name itself, as a phonetic or linguistic entity? In the next table, table 2, the number of all nicknames (brand nicknames, model nicknames and nicknames for specific individual vehicles) is shown for each brand.

Car brand	Number of names	Car brand	Number of names
Ford	303	BMW	42
Lada	252	Cadillac	40
Volvo	158	Dodge	40
Volkswagen	155	Datsun	38
Saab	124	Mazda	31
Fiat	107	Chrysler	30
Opel	93	Renault	30
Toyota	91	Audi	29
Mercedes-Benz	76	Honda	29
Chevrolet	74	Vauxhall	26
Citroen	67	Mitsubishi	23
Skoda	61	Wartburg	23
Peugeot	48	Buick	20
Nissan	48	*total*	2127

Table 2. Number of car nicknames (all reference levels) per a car brand.

Unlike in table 1, Ford seems to have most nicknames in table 2. Even this surprising change has a very natural explanation: during the 20th century, Ford was sold for a longer time than Lada, and Ford has produced a great number of different models. Ford models have also had model brand names for a long time (like Taunus and Orion), and the number of hypochorisms based on model names lifts Ford higher on this "ranking list". Still, something affectuous can be seen in the top 5: Saab, Lada and Volvo are built in the countries neighbouring Finland.

I will not further analyze the differences in the popularity of the model nicknames, but will just briefly mention some top models and their numbers of names: Saab 96 (59), Ford Escort (50), Fiat 600 (28), Toyota Corolla (27), Ford Taunus (24), Citroen 2CV (24) and Volvo PV (22). A special characteristic of the car or a special brand seems to result in a heightened chance of nicknaming.

Disclaimers

The theory of affect, attraction and expansion is quite plausible, although in practice it is often misapplied: a word having a lot of synonyms (or the concept referenced by the word) is often interpreted as affective whether it really is or not. As stated, even a phonetic (and other) structure of a word or a name can lead to alteration. Another weakness of this method is that it does not take into account the number of referents in the real world (that is, the number of the existing cars of a specific brand, etc.). The results were calculated based on the number of names in the material only. It is quite natural that, for example, Volkswagen has more names than the Hummer, because a large variety of Volkswagen models has been on the market and Volkswagen cars have been imported to Finland for decades. The number of vehicles must be taken into consideration in order to better understand the strength of a brand. In addition, even the time line–both in names and vehicles–has to be taken into account: for example, some brands have been more popular in the past, and might be over-represented in the material from the present viewpoint. Still, the number of nicknames might be used to measure - as a simple method - the relative strength of brands.

2. What is noticed in cars, and what does it mean?

In this short section I will briefly show what motives for name-giving were found in the material - in other words, what is important or significant about the vehicles. In picture 2, I show how the various motives tend to form groups (groups can also be called *cognitive areas*). In car nicknames, many characteristics and special properties of the cars can be demonstrated. Names describe the form and color, age, usability, origins and so on. Even multiple motivations are possible, for instance, the Lada brand's nickname Tsernobiili refers both to the country of origin and the amount of smoke or pollution produced by the car, by referring metaphorically to the nuclear plant and disaster in Chernobyl. At the same time, the part biili refers to a spoken-Finnish word biili (derived from Swedish bil < automobil) meaning a car.

From the brand-researcher's point of view, what can the classical method of onomastic research – the analysis of name-giving motives – provide? An onomastician knows what is important enough in a vehicle so that it can be used when giving names. This information can be used when cars are branded and rebranded.

Name-giving motives are shown in the next spreadsheet (see appendix, fig. 2).

3. How cars are seen, and can a brand be seen in metaphors?

My approach is based on the idea that metaphors reveal both how people see cars and the kinds of emotions they attach to them. In this section, I aim to show which metaphorical source domains have been used in car nicknaming in my material. The analysis covers both primary names with metaphorical structures and secondary names with their partially false metaphors.

A specific metaphorical source domain, insects for instance, can be used to express different characteristics of cars. Let's take a look at the names Leppäkerttu “Ladybird”, Kirppu “Flea” and Espanjan ampiainen “Spanish wasp”. The name Leppäkerttu was used for a rusty van, and the metaphor was used in order to describe the van's rusty red color with dots. The name Kirppu simply refers to the small size of the car, whereas Espanjan ampiainen refers to the sound and the country of origin of the Montera-Brio motorcycle. Sometimes metaphorical structures can be very complex, and understanding them requires cultural knowledge. For instance, the beetle-form older Volkswagen models have a nickname - Katri Helena, which refers first to the Finnish artist, singer and songwriter Katri Helena. But what has Katri Helena to do with a car? One of the most famous songs sung by Katri Helena is *Minne tuuli kuljettaa* “Where the wind will take me”. Compared to newer cars, the Volkswagen Beetle was a light-weight car. Another example of complexity is the name for Daewoo cars, Mikroaaltouuni “Microwave oven”. One single metaphor is employed to express both the sound and the country of origin, and maybe also the small size and the form, modern plastic materials, as well as the fact that Daewoo surprisingly manufactures both cars and microwave ovens.

The schematic map of metaphors in car nicknames is shown in appendix, fig. 3.

Metaphors used in car nicknaming tend to form groups: schemes. The schematic generalizations on the highest level are “a car is a living organism”, “a car is a tool” and “a car is a container”, and there are, as the map shows, a large number of sub-schemes or lower-level generalizations. Cars tend to be seen as boxes, dishes and buildings (container-scheme), humans, plants and animals (living organisms), or as complicated technical apparatus. Real data examples are shown in color, and they have not been translated into English. As the schematic map shows, the three main schemes also interact with each other. Living organisms are perceived in our culture as containers as well, sometimes even as instruments or tools. On the other hand, many technical devices have container-like characteristics. The borders are blurry.

Official brand names have been found to derive their content from source domains such as (the fastest) animals, (famous) place names, astronomy, royalty and race courses (Lehrer 1992: 129-132). These themes can also be seen in nicknames, but in many cases they might have been used with sarcastic intent. When creating new brands, this is something that should be taken into account.

4. Does the referent's brand have effect on a name's structure?

In this section, I will discuss what the mechanism of name-formation can reveal, or, what a name's structure can tell about the brand and its strength. The pie charts reproduced in appendix fig. 4 show the structure types of names and the origin of the components of a name. These concepts (primary, secondary and so on) were briefly presented in the introduction, and a deeper understanding of name categorization is not a prerequisite for understanding the significance of this chart set; only the colors are essential here. The color green indicates that the name is produced based on the referent's properties (the so-called primary names), yellow indicates that the name is produced on the basis of the official brand name (i.e. secondary names), and red refers to the two-part names, which contain the official name in some form. Mixed colors depict those structure types that are somehow in between these groups. By observing the amount of these colors in the pie charts, it can be determined to what extent the official name is present in the informal brand and model names (yellowness and redness). This makes it possible to draw conclusions regarding both the strength of the brand-level brand and, on the other hand, the amount of affectivity in brands and models. Roughly it can be stated that the redness in a chart indicates the intensity of the brand-level brand, while green indicates the so-called affectivity, which in turn promotes name-creation based on the properties of the car. Rich yellowness and minimal redness in the model names indicate that the model is more strongly branded than the brand itself, and thus the model is first and foremost a representant of its model and less a representant of the brand-level brand.

Greenness

The graph presenting the brand names of Lada, Wartburg, Volvo and Mercedes-Benz is particularly green. These brands have, therefore, the highest number of names based on the properties of the referents (cars), i.e, these brands are particularly affectuous. These brands also carry various cultural connotations from, for example, the Swedish and Russian culture, ranging from high to low quality and from welfare to poverty. None of these cars are necessarily seen as particularly dynamic, either. Continuing to the charts where the numbers of model (nick)names of these brands are shown and when we compare the results, we see that the amount of the color green is less for Lada and Wartburg but greater for Volvo and Mercedes-Benz (as compared to green in the respective brand name charts). This reflects the fact that, in the cases of Lada and Wartburg, the affect is primarily linked to the car brand('s brand), while the Volvo and Mercedes-Benz models are apparently perceived as more individual. Models differing clearly from each other can be named based on their characteristics, for example, the Mercedes-Benz models *Lokinsiipi* “the gull wing” and *Väyrynen* (< a well-known politician Paavo Väyrynen; the name refers to the car’s headlights via the eyes and glasses -metaphor).

Greenness (name-giving based on the referent's properties) on the model-name level is common also with the brands Volkswagen, BMW and Skoda. In particular, the VW Beetle and a big Skoda from 1950 (so called Lahna-Skoda (< Lahna “bream”) are named according to their characteristic features. This is well illustrated by one informant's statement: only as an adult did he understand that the Beetle and VW belong to the same car brand.

Redness

The strength of the brand label can also be examined on the basis of the red colour in the graphs. Thus, red refers to a two-part name containing one name part, which is derived from a brand's or a model's official name. By far the most red on the model-nickname charts is seen for Cadillac, and a little less, for Toyota, Mercedes-Benz, Volvo, BMW and Lada. Red here indicates the strength of those brands, because the official name or its hypochorism has been included in an informal name as a part. For example, many of the nicknames for Cadillac models contain a brand name (*Elviscädi* "Elvis caddy", *Siipicädi* "Wing caddy", *Kääpiöcädi* "Dwarf caddy") and the same tendency can be observed for other labels named above (*Vauvamersu* "Baby Mercedes", *Remmivolvo* "Belt Volvo" and *Barokkibemari* "Baroque-BMW"). On the contrary, this two-part name type is not used for Peugeots at all. Peugeot officially gives numbers to its models, instead of names, which highlights the brand's brand as a whole and makes the individual models less independent.

Yellowness and light green

Yellow, then, refers to the so-called pure secondary names, i.e., the names derived from the official name and are neutral hypochorisms without any added meanings, e.g. Volkswagen → VW. The production of such neutral hypochorisms is a kind of indication that the referent is considered to be quite neutral–as mentioned–alteration can proceed a lot further than what would be phonotactically inevitable.

In the left column (the column for brand names) a large quantity of yellow can be seen in the charts of the brands BMW, Ford, Chevrolet, Cadillac, Volkswagen, Mercedes-Benz and Toyota. These are all brands, which have a relatively good reputation. In the right column (the column for the model names), the amount of yellow is significant for Chevrolet only, and Chevrolet has had some well-known, relatively independent and popular models (e.g. Corvette, Impala, El Camino).

The light green colour, then, refers to name type, which is derived from the official brand name but alteration has yielded a metaphorical name expressing some real or imaginative properties of the referent (as the name Gorilla (< Corolla) does. This name type is most typical for Peugeot and Opel nicknames and quite used in Nissan and Fiat nicknames as well. In such cases, the brand is strong but it seems to be commented on by naming or "re-naming". This commenting by name-giving can be pejorative or ameliorative and the line between them is not very clear.

Conclusion

In this paper I have tried to provide some examples of how some brands of cars might be analyzed by scrutinizing their nicknames. The number of names used can tell us something about affect and brand strength, but the name structures employed can reveal even more about brand strength and especially about the relationship between a car brand and a model brand. The analysis of metaphors and name-giving motives provides a more qualitative view. When creating new brands, the known alteration mechanisms and risks attached to them ought to be taken into account. The fact that most metaphoric Finnish car nicknames tend to belong to three schemes carries a meaning: it is likely that even new nicknames will belong to these groups. A brand-creator must then decide, whether he wants the car to be a passive container, a complicated apparatus or a vivid living organism with a personality. Name-giving motives reveal, in turn, what kind of properties are noticed in cars. Because a nickname can be crucial for the brand, properties like form, colour and special components should be considered from that point of view. For instance, round headlights resemble eyes, creating possible humans or animal associations. If then an official brand name is something, which can be altered towards an appellative animal or human meaning, a nickname is about to be created.

An onomastician studies names and name-giving. Familiarity with the tradition, both of official brand names and of nicknaming, makes it possible to either follow the tradition or to play with it.

References

Hämäläinen, Simo. 1946: "Suomalaisesta sotilasslangista." *Virittäjä* 50: 256–67. Helsinki: Kotikielen seuran aikakauslehti.

Kuiri, Kaija. 2004: *Semantiikan peruskurssi. Luennot ja harjoitukset.* Toinen, muuttamaton painos. Tampere: Tampereen yliopiston kieli- ja käännöstieteiden laitos, suomen kieli.

Kulonen, Ulla-Maija. 2006: "Eläimet ja affekti – etymologisia huomioita." *Virittäjä* 110: 322–335. Helsinki: Kotikielen seuran aikakauslehti.

Lehrer, Adrienne. 1992: "Names and naming: Why we need fields and frames." In *Frames, Fields, and Contrasts*, A. Lehrer and E. V. Kittay, 123–42. Hillsdales, NJ: Erlbaum.

McClure, Peter. 1981: "Nicknames and petnames: Linguistic forms and social contexts." *Nomina* 5: 63–76.

Ries, Al. 2010: "Marketers Lucky Enough to Have a Nickname Shouldn't

Abuse It." http://adage.com/article/al-ries/names/145225/

Seppälä, Janne. 2013: *Kulkine.net – tutkimus epävirallisista kulkineennimistä*. Doctoral dissertation, Jyväskylä University, dep. for languages. Available in http://www.kulkine.net.

Sperber, Hans. 1923: *Einführung in die Bedeutungslehre*. Bonn–Leipzig: Kurt Schroeder Verlag.

Appendix

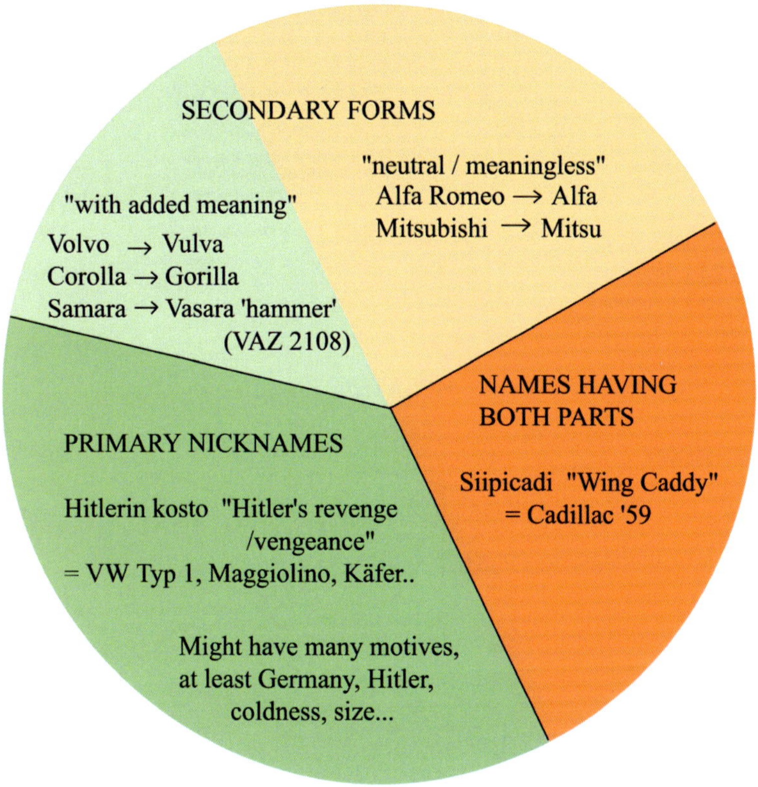

Fig. 1: Basic groups of names based on the type of name-formation.

WHAT IS IMPORTANT/NOTED IN CARS - BASED ON NAMES

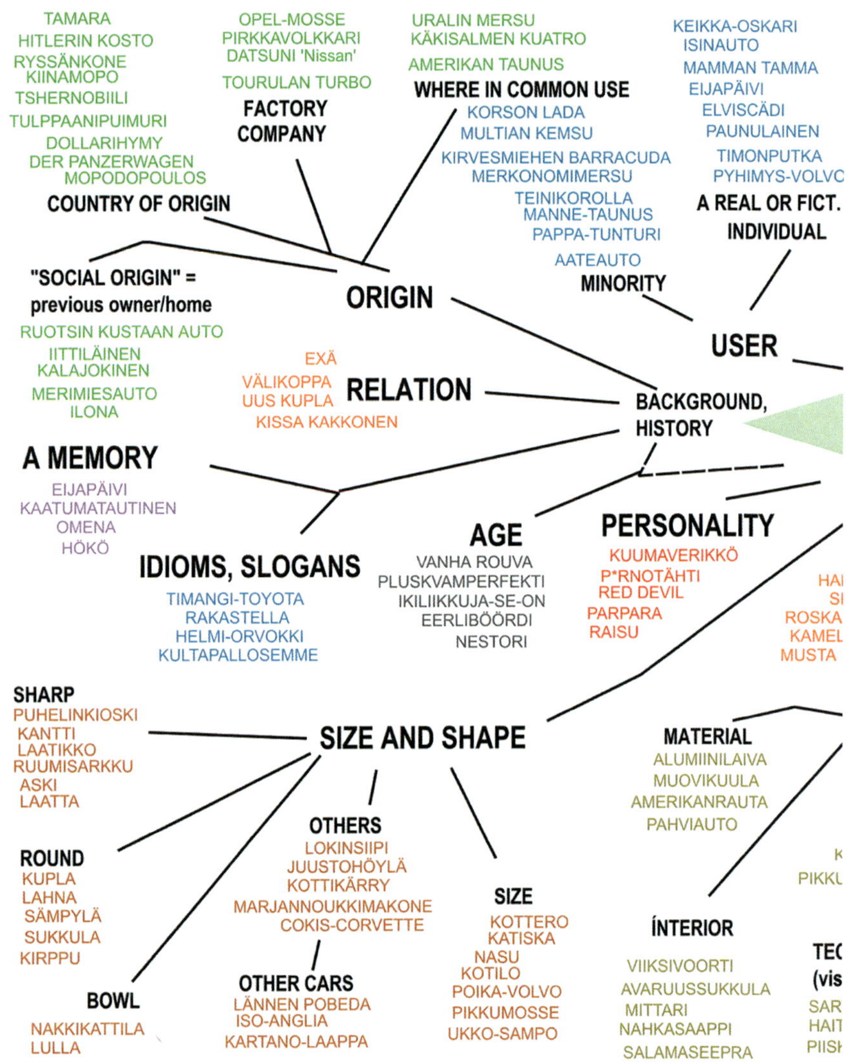

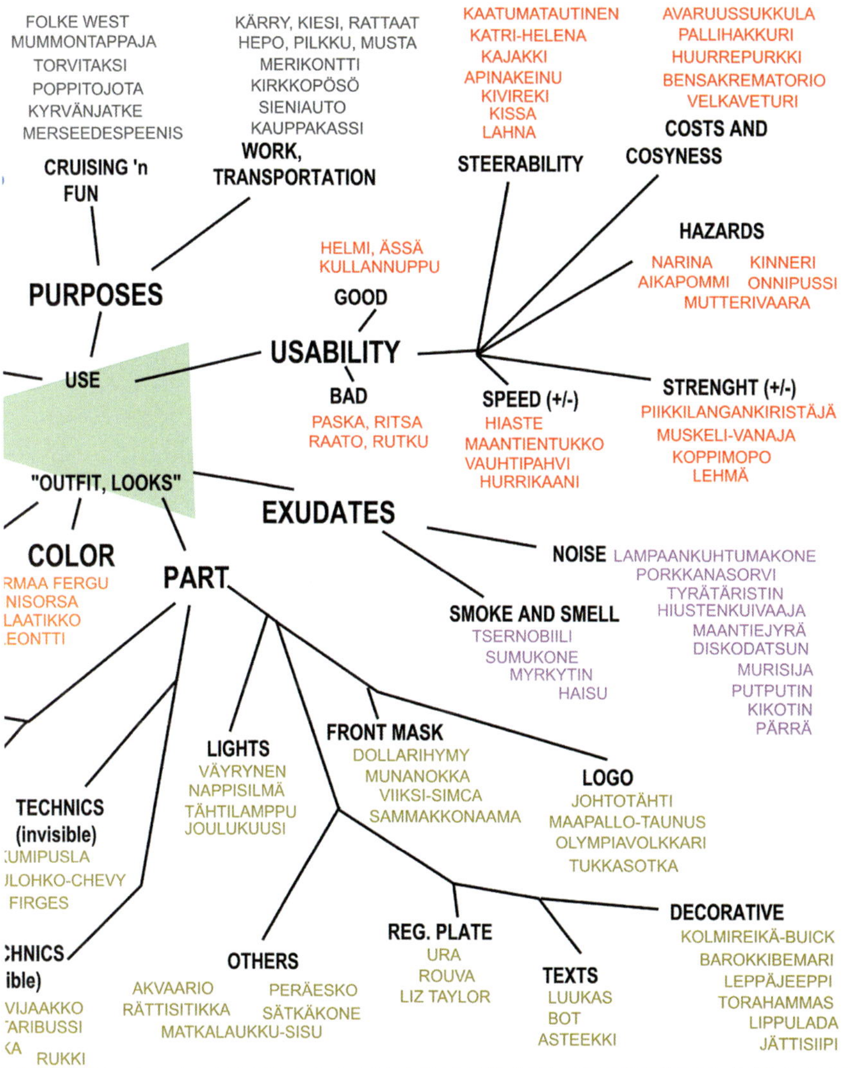

Fig. 2: Name-giving motives in cars.

METAFORIC SOURCES IN CAR NICKNAMES

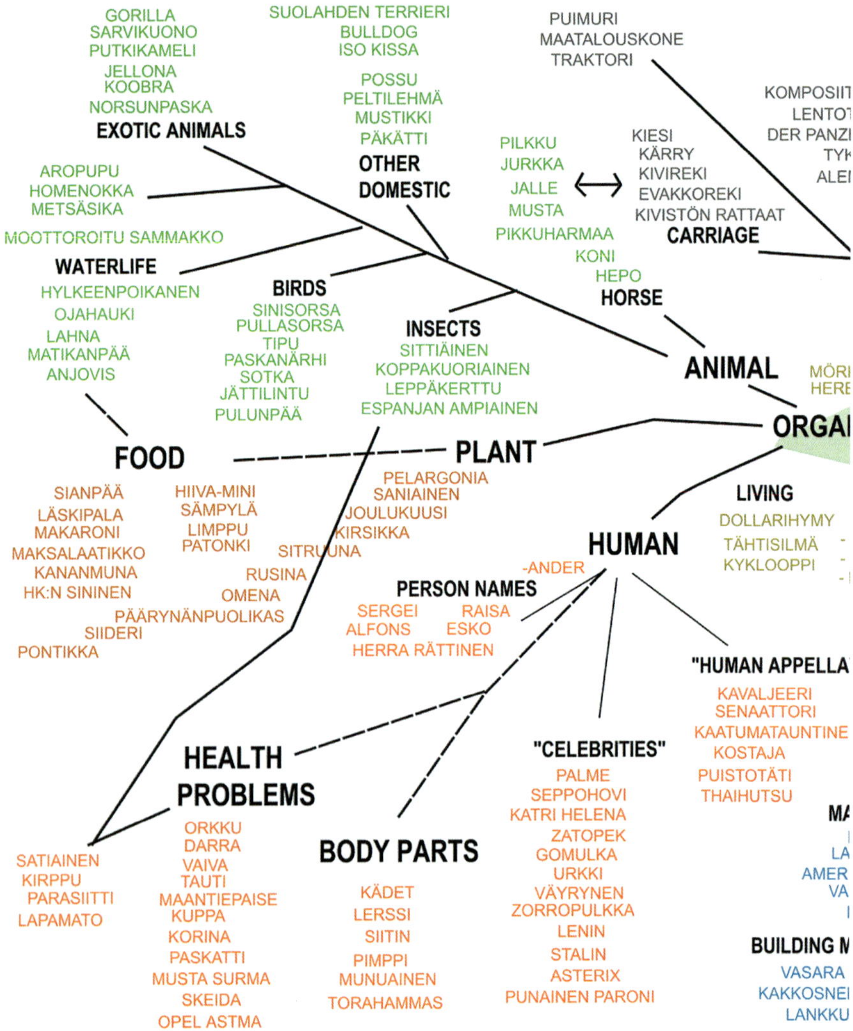

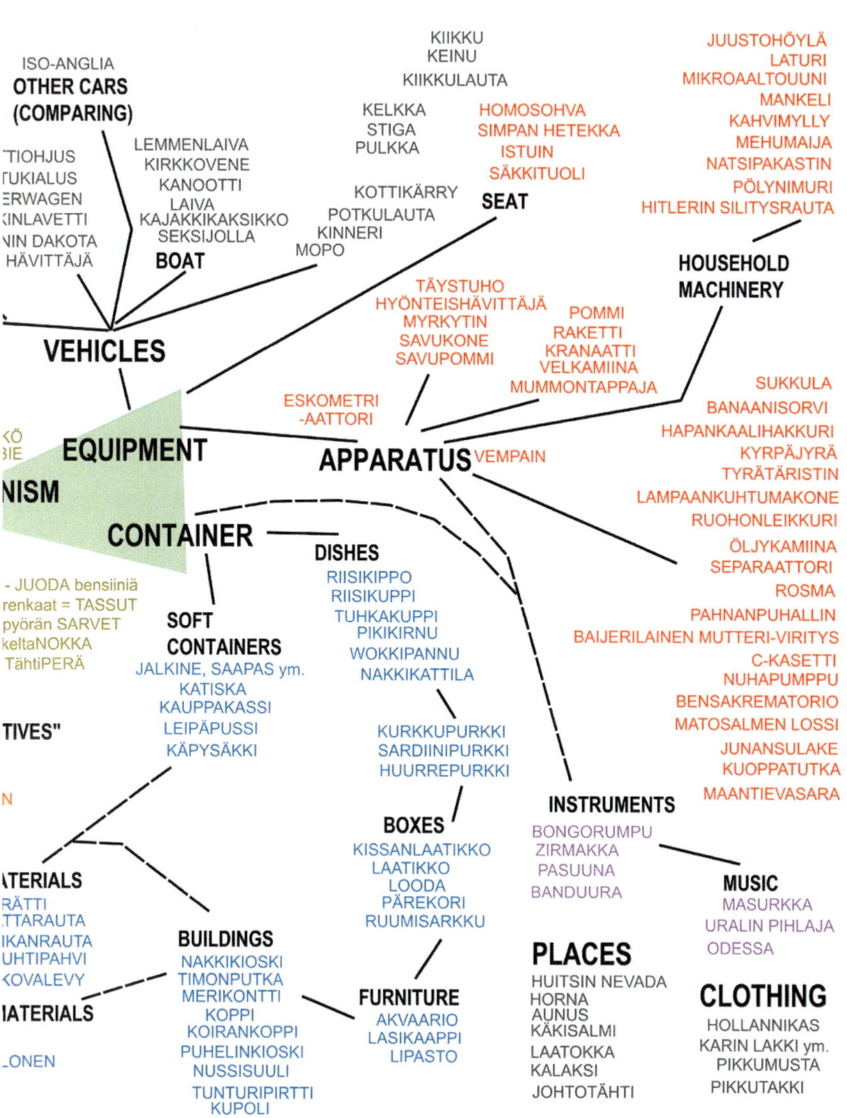

Fig. 3: The schematic map of metaphors in car nicknames.

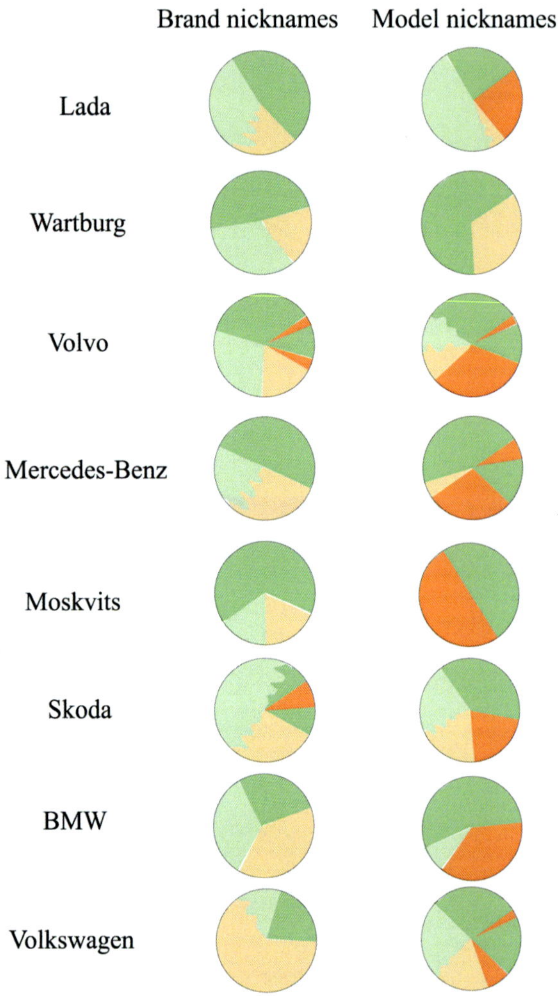
Brand nicknames
Model nicknames
Lada
Wartburg
Volvo
Mercedes-Benz
Moskvits
Skoda
BMW
Volkswagen

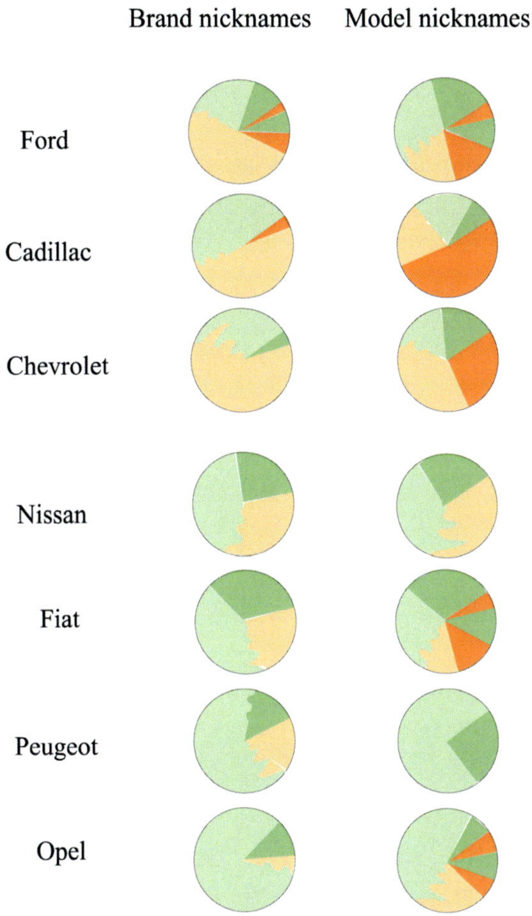

Fig. 4: Typical name-structures in brand nicknames and model nicknames.

Current Trends in Naming Romanian Travel Agencies

Adriana Stoichitoiu Ichim

Abstract

The aim of this paper is to identify the most frequent strategies and patterns in naming travel agencies in the contemporary Romanian economic environment. Starting from the premise that NTAs, like other names of companies, are conventional signs, motivated not only linguistically, but also economically, socially and culturally, the first section focuses – from a pragmatic perspective – on the impact of the relationship between the owner (as name giver) and the potential customer (as receiver and interpreter) in establishing successful naming formulas. In the second part of the paper we investigate – from an onomastic point of view – the two elements incorporated in an NTA.

Introduction

The aim of the present paper is to reveal – from a multidisciplinary point of view – the most frequent strategies and patterns of naming for travel agencies in the contemporary Romanian economic environment. In what follows, by the syntagm *travel agency* we designate "a company that arranges travel and / or accommodation for people going on a holiday / vacation or journey" (OALD: 575).

Our interest in this topic is primarily motivated by the fact that such names (henceforth referred to as NTAs) still represent a neglected area in Romanian onomastics despite their novelty and the large variety of this (sub)category of commercial names coined after the 90s, following the dissolution of the communist regime and the affiliation of both managers and customers to the values and lifestyle of the consumer society.[1]

Secondly, taking into account the strong impact of the various forms of tourism on the social, cultural, educational and economic sectors of the national societies, the topic under discussion might be of interest not only to onomasticians, linguists and lexicographers, but also to other professional categories (such as specialists or students in tourism management and services, marketing and advertising and – last but not least – to businessmen looking for a functional, memorable and catchy name for starting up a company).

In the meantime, given the growing interest of the general public in the field of tourism, an analysis of the onomastic practices and the underlying marketing strategies could reveal to the potential customer various "manipulative" techniques that have come into widespread use over the last two decades.

Although our analysis is mainly synchronic, it is worth mentioning that during the communist period, in the context of a tourism industry, which was underdeveloped and strictly controlled by the central administrative and political authorities, the only travel agencies operating in the Romanian public space were *Oficiul Național de Turism "Carpați"* ("Carpathian Mountains" National Tourism Office), abbreviated ONT, and *Biroul de Turism pentru Tineret* (Tourism Bureau for Youth), abbreviated BTT. As state-owned companies with subsidiaries in every district of the country, they promoted different types of domestic tourism (balneological, cultural, social) and provided travel packages just for Eastern communist countries. As can be easily noticed, both names are fully descriptive and stereotyped, including only Romanian words. They served solely to identify the company and its domain of activity, showing a total lack of interest not only in the communicative policy towards the potential customers, but also in the marketing strategies in their particular field.

By contrast, the large number of creative NTAs that have appeared since the downfall of the communist regime in December 1989 are very similar to those in other European countries, mainly as a consequence of the political openness towards Western Europe, but also due to some internal major mutations such as private property and free enterprise, or the rejection of any form of political intrusion in the commercial naming practices. Moreover, the offer of Romanian travel agencies has included new forms of tourism that have emerged over the last few years[2]: Rom. *turism activ* cf. Engl. *active tourism*, Rom. *turism de aventură* cf. Engl. *adventure tourism*, Rom. *turism culinar / gastronomic* cf. Engl. *culinary / gastronomic tourism*, Rom. *turism religios* cf. Engl. *religious tourism*, Rom. *turism medical* cf. Engl. *therapeutic / health tourism*, Rom. *turism rural* cf. Engl. *rural tourism*, Rom. *turism verde / ecologic* cf. Engl. *green / ecological tourism*, Rom. *turism științific* cf. Engl. *scientific tourism*, Rom. *turism pentru practicarea jocurilor de noroc* cf. Engl. *gambling tourism*, etc.

Theoretical and methodological considerations

Since the onomastic literature dealing with commercial nomenclature exhibits a great terminological variety – as proved by Sjoblöm (2013) especially – we find it necessary to distinguish between different partially overlapping terms related to commercial and economic activities, such as *chrematonyms*[3], *ergonyms*[4] or *commercial names*[5]. In Romanian onomastic bibliography there is also some variation in designating names of businesses by generic terms (*trade names*[6]; *commercial names*[7]) or by more specific expressions (*firm names* and *company names* considered as synonyms[8]).

Following Sjoblöm's classification of commercial names (2015), travel agencies are understood as trade and service companies identified by official denomination formulas, registered with *Oficiul Național al Registrului Comerțului* (ONRC)[9] and coined according to the regulations of the Romanian legislation concerning the names of companies and the right of intellectual property[10].

According to Romanian business legislation[11], companies and firms are free to choose their names, with no restrictions related to language, provided that the respective denominative formulas are available and distinctive (unique). The name of the owner and the field of activity are not compulsory. Yet, the use of offensive and misleading terms is forbidden, along with other words, such as *stat* "state", *guvern* "government" or *științific* "scientific", *academie* "academy", *universitate* "university", *școală* "school" and their derivatives. In the meantime, words involving any connection with the official name of the state or of an administrative area, as well as names of national authorities can be used solely in virtue of special permission from the Secretary General of the Government.

The corpus under investigation in the present paper consists of 315 NTAs located mainly in Bucharest but also in other large Romanian cities (Cluj-Napoca, Iași, Brașov, Timișoara, Constanța, Sibiu, Ploiești, Baia Mare, etc.), and gathered from specialized websites on the Internet. Since our study does not seek to be exhaustive, the focus will be on qualitative rather than quantitative results, attempting to enlighten some interesting characteristics of this (sub)category of commercial names.

The specific purposes of our investigation have led to a tripartite organisation of the current paper. Starting from the premise that NTAs, like other names of companies are conventional signs, motivated not only linguistically, but also economically, socially, psychologically and culturally, the first section focuses – from a pragmatic perspective – on their functions as linguistic and advertising signs, paying special attention to the role played by the relationship between the *owner* (as *name - giver*) and the potential *customer* (as *receiver* and *interpreter*) in establishing successful *naming formulas*. In the second part, we investigate the two functional parts incorporated in an NTA (the *specific* and the *generic components*) from an onomastic point of view. The third part of the paper aims to establish the *linguistic profile* of NTAs, which is further analysed from formal, etymological and semantic perspectives.

The pragmatics of NTAs

From a pragmalinguistic perspective, NTAs, just like other names of businesses (e.g., names of public houses, names of accommodation locations, shops, or other commercial entities) have been analyzed in Romanian onomastic literature[12] as results of a specific speech act, taking into account the three functions performed by such complex signs in a commercial context: locutionary (related to the phonetic, morphological, syntactic and semantic level), illocutionary (regarding the communicative intentions of the locutor – owner), and perlocutionary (aiming at the effects on the receiver / interpreter customer). As Felecan, D. (2011: 76) stated, a firm name must be seen as the result of an "implicit communicative consensus" between the name–giver and the receiver, since the former as owner is interested not only in identifying his business, but also in meeting the customer's needs and expectations. In other words, the act of naming and the selection of appropriate denominative practices should take into consideration both legal and marketing aspects. As a consequence, in addition to their basic functions (i.e. to reflect *identity* and *distinctiveness* in order to be registered and benefit from legal protection[13]), NTAs, as intentional signs, perform several other functions, identified by Sjöblom (2005: 268).

The *informative function* refers to the knowledge the Romanian customer can get of the touristic services[14] either directly, from "transparent" (motivated) NTA's (e.g. *Fortuna Business Travel, Adventure Travel*, *Scuba Diver, Vacanţe la Mare* "Holidays on the Seashore", *Roxy Travel Family*) or indirectly (implicitly) from partially motivated (e.g. *Avraam Travel* for a tourism agency proposing religious pilgrimages) or non-transparent (non-motivated) names (e.g. *Your Travel Company*, *Galaxy Travel, Arcadia Travel, Hello Holidays*);

The *persuasive / advertising function* is achieved *via* positive images and appreciative semantic connotations meant to attract the prospective customer and to sell the service / product by means of suggestive names (e.g. *Happy Holiday*, *Turism la Maxim* "Tourism at the Maximum", *Dream Tour*, *Carpe Diem Travel*).

The *socioculturally integrative function* is salient in a category of NTA's alluding to symbolic values and attitudes shared by the owner and his potential customers in a national and sociocultural environment (e.g. *Carpatia Dacia Nemuritoare* "Carpathian Eternal Dacia", *Karpaten Tourism*, *Danubius Travel*, *Transilvania Tourist*, etc.)[15].

The importance of naming strategies in today's marketplace, is reflected by a large number of (mostly American) websites focusing on linguistic tips given by professional namers to persons planning to set up a travel agency. One can mention, in this respect, *Tips on Good Names for a Travel Business*[16], *31 Good Catchy Tour Company Names*[17], *50 Good Names Suggestions for Your Travel Agency Business*[18] or *47 Catchy Travel Agency Company Ideas*[19]. A few examples for such tips of successful naming could be the following: "The name you choose for your business should not only be functional, but catchy and memorable as well"; "Setting up a travel agency? The first thing you have to do is to find a great name to attract customers"; "Consider a name that relates to the target demographic of your travel agency".

It is worth noting that a comparative approach between the most creative names recommended as being able to call the American public's attention to the touristic services[20] on the one hand, and Romanian NTA's on the other, will reveal significant similarities following the alignment of Romanian companies with the international marketing strategies. In addition to the borrowing of international stereotyped naming patterns, the choice of English names irrespective of the official language of a country relies on the status of lingua franca that Shakespeare's language has acquired in the field of tourism all over the world[21].

On the other hand, a comparative approach of NTAs and other names of service-related companies reveals a number of peculiarities in designating the different service-providers. From a cognitive point of view, quite a large number of NTAs show a lack of interest in the objective informative aspects such as the owner's identity, the location, the values of national or regional culture, or the profile of the specific business, which are generally designated by the borrowed appellative words *travel* and *tour(s)*. Since the commercial success is the main goal of the name – givers, their attention is primarily focused on the creative, symbolic, and expressive potential of the name, whose purpose is to evoke positive associations and emotions. As a consequence, descriptive names appear quite rarely, while allusive or even conventional non-transparent formulas displaying a cosmopolitan aspect are favoured.

An onomastic approach of NTAs

According to widespread opinion[22], company names are *complex nominal formulas* consisting of two functional components, which can be easily identified in the linguistic structure of NTAs as well.

The *generic component* (GC), called a "corporate identifier" (Sjöblom 2014: 95) or an "onomastic classifier" (Rateau 2013: 176), is not obligatory according to Romanian law. Nevertheless, most NTAs include such common nouns functioning as appellatives and indicating the form or branch of business.

From a historical point of view, the GCs can be grouped in two categories:

- An extremely brief list of Romanian noun phrases used during the communist regime: *agenție de turism* "tourism agency" (a phraseological calque rendering the Fr. *agence de tourisme* – cf. PR: 2642)[23], *oficiu de turism* "tourism office" and *birou de turism* "tourism bureau" are not listed as such in the most usual Romanian general dictionary (DEX_2), although the nouns *agenție* (< It. *agenzia*, Germ. *agentie*), *oficiu* (<Lat. *officium*, Germ. *offizium*, Fr. *office*) and *birou* (< Fr. *bureau*, Rus. *biuro*, Germ. *Büro*) are to be found in DEX_2 as parts of the common language.
- After the dissolution of the totalitarian regime in 1989, the category of appellatives under discussion was seriously modified (with respect to both quantity and quality). The three syntagms quoted above are not in active use any longer. Instead, one can notice a clear predominance of English GCs *travel (agency)* and *tour (operator)*, which are accounted for not only by their international character linked to the development of the international tourism industry in the context of globalisation, but also by the prestige of the source-language[24] and by subjective factors, such as fashion imitative and snobbish behaviour of both name-givers and customers[25]. Relevant statistics show that within a corpus of 204 Romanian NTAs, the word *travel(s)* occurs 72 times and *tour(s)* occurs 41 times (Rață and Petroman 2012a: 45).

Interesting semantic changes can be identified in both cases, since in Romanian NTAs *travel* and *tour(s)* are used stereotypically as synonyms, regardless of their definitions provided by English language dictionaries (cf. OALD: *1565*, 1575) or their specific collocations in English (cf. Rață 2012). More precisely, as GCs, *travel* and *tour* placed in post-position, designate a company (*travel agency*) or a shop / store (*travel agent*), in examples such as: *Alfa Travel*, *Europa Travel*, *Malta Travel*, *Nefertiti Travel*, *123 Travel*; *Pontic Tour*, *Ştefan Tours*, *Prestige Tours*, *Partner Tour*, *Paloma Tours*. Besides the lack of proper definitions in Romanian dictionaries, other sources of confusion might be the frequent use of the pseudo-anglicism *tour / tur-operator* in everyday language, as well as the formal and semantic resemblance between two partial false friends[26]: Rom. *tur* "a long journey including the visiting of a number of places in sequence" and Engl. *tour*, which has developed a technical divergent meaning in Romanian (cf. *Mariatur*, *Rogvaiv Tur*, *Vranceatour*, *Happy Tour*). As cases of inappropriate use, we can mention pleonastic NTAs such as *Activ Tours & Travels*, *Kalimera Holidays Tours & Travel*, *Ana Tour & Travel*.

In third position (according to the frequency in use) the GC may consist of the English word *tourism*, which is being used alternatively with its Romanian counterpart *turism*, instead of the noun phrases *tourism agency* or *agenţie de turism*: *Butterfly Tourism*, *Best Tourism*; *Horoscop Turism*, *Karpaten Turism*, *Simpa turism*.

It is noteworthy that our analysis regarding the use of *travel*, *tour* and *tourism* as GCs in Romanian confirms Rateau's statements on the international character of an onomastic classifier, which is

> à la fois linguistiquement, commercialement, touristiquement et géopolitiquement international/isé; il est ou bien peut être aujourd'hui emprunté à plusieurs langues au sein desquelles il a été déjà intégré, et être utilisé par la plupart des locuteurs des langues du monde (presque) entier, sans obligation spécifique d'emploi grammatical (ortographe, etc.) (Rateau 2013: 176).

The compulsory specific component (SC) represents the identifying part of an NTA, i.e. the name of the company, meant to make it unique, in an objective or allusive way, but also intended to be appealing, persuasive and marketable, even amusing or playful, without excluding manipulation.

The SCs that can be used separately as NTAs or included in the structure of Romanian NTAs are:

- Proper names:
  - the first name of the owner or a hypocoristic (*Christian Tour*, *Veronica Travel Agency*, *Cami Travel*, *Eddie's Travel*, *Bibi Tourism*);

- a domestic or foreign toponym (*Transilvania Travel*, *Oltenia Tour*, *Carpați Travel*, *Malta Travel*, *Europa Travel*, *Gibraltar Travel*, *Kussadassi*);
- famous names from mythology (*Dedal Tour*, *Icar Tours*, *Arcadia Travel*, *Adonis*, *Minerva*), from the Bible (*Avraam Travel*), from history (*Magellan Turism*, *Nefertiti Travel*), literature (*Mary Poppins*, *Ali Baba Tour*, *Gulliver Tours*);
- astronyms (*Sirius Turism*, *Vega Travel International).*

- Romanian, but mostly foreign (English, Italian, French) common nouns or adjectives onymized (used as proper names), indicating the location (*New Travel Muntenia*, *Paralela 45*), the profile of the company (*Adventure Travel*, *Scuba Diving*, *Vacanțe la Mare*) in an explicit manner or merely suggesting it (*Edelweiss Travel* – tour-operator specialized in voyages to Austria). They may also refer to the freedom of travelling (*Infinity Travel*, *Giro del Mondo*, *Mapamond*, *Globetrotter*) or emphasize the high quality of services (*Dream Holidays*, *Happy Holiday*, *Gold Holidays*, *Optimus Travel*, *Prestige Tours*, *Smart Tours*, *Turism la Maxim*, *Supertour*, *Turism Bon Voyage*).

The linguistic profile of NTAs

A formal classification of Romanian NTAs

Such a taxonomy is aimed to establish the most frequently used formation patterns, with respect to the syntactic and morphological peculiarities of NTAs[27]. Taking into account the number of words within an NTA, two classes of names appear to be relevant.

Very few *one–word NTAs* are to be found and they are made up of: a single Romanian common noun (*Maraton*, *Mapamond*), a foreign symbolic anthroponym (*Adonis*, *Euridice*, *Minerva*) or toponym (*Kusadassi*). The compounds included in this category are based on different types of blends[28], resulting from the association of: two common foreign nouns (*Travelart*, *Tourdesign*, *Travelmaker*), a truncated word in ante- or postposition and a full word (*Eurotravel*, *Eurotrip*, *Europoint*, *Touropa*, *Karpatour*, *Mariatur*, *Simpaturism*), or an international formative in prefix position, followed by a noun (*Neotour*, *Ecovoyage*, *Intertours*).

The overwhelming majority of NTAs consist of *multi-word formations* that can be grouped according to their syntactic structure. The largest group consists of *nominal phrases* including a head (as a SC) and a modifier (as a GC), the latter mainly situated in postposition, according to the English word order, which is not typical of Romanian[29]. The GC (*tour*, *travel*, *travel agency*) can be preceded–as a SC–by a foreign adjective (*Smart Tours*, *Pretty Travel*, *Best Travel*, *Happy Tour*, *Byron Travel Agency*), by a proper noun from the category of toponyms (*Atlantic Tours*, *Bavaria Tours*, *Madagascar Travel*, *Transilvania Travel*) or anthroponyms, mostly first names of the owners (*Christian Tour*, *Gregory Tour*, *Magda Travel*, *Eddie's Travel*[30]), by a foreign common noun (*Apple Tour*, *Butterfly Tourism*, *Family Travel*, *Mobby Tour*, *Prestige Tours*), by numerals (*123 Travel*), adverbs (*Always Travel*), international acronyms (*XXL Tours*, *SF Travel*) or greeting formulas (*Bye Bye Travel*).

In a small group of noun phrases the SC can be situated in postposition, according to the Romanian syntactic rules: *Travel Planet*, *Travel Expert*, *Travel Tips*, *Travel Time*, *Travel 4 Fun*, *Turism Bon Voyage*.

The third syntactic pattern (noun phrases including two SCs as modifiers, in ante- and postposition) occurs only accidentally, and cannot be considered as typical of the Romanian NTAs: *Alma Tour Romania*, *Q Travel Confort*, *Roxy Travel Family*.

One can also find a few NTAs represented by predicative phrases, with a very clear advertising potential: *Let's Travel*, *Explore Travel*, *Visit Romania*.

As regards the morphosyntactic structure of many NTAs analysed in the present paper, the most striking feature is their extra-grammatical aspect, given the fact that a large number of the quoted naming formulas contravene the norms of literary (standard) Romanian[31]. According to Rateau (2013: 173), such types of "international" company names reveal the effects of globalisation and the intention of name-givers to catch the attention of potential customers by using names with foreign acoustics, i.e. names capable of conveying prestige:

> Sur le plan grammatical, il arrive que l'on ne puisse plus, uniquement, parler de grammaire française, anglaise, zouloue...mais – de grammaire onomastique internationale, naturellement conventionnelle, c'est-à-dire sans convention spécifique oficialisée – la liberté du créateur onomastique est telle, et, sans aucun doute, tellement naturellement légitime que certains points de ces dites grammaires s'entremêlent très librement dans le tourbillon des actes de créativité.

In order to illustrate the category of NTAs that obey the morphological and syntactic norms of literary Romanian, we can mention: *Agenția de Turism Maori* "Maori Tourism Agency", *Vacanțe la Mare* "Holidays on the Seashore", *Clubul Vacanţelor* "The Holiday's Club", *Vacanţe de Vis* "Dream Holidays".

An etymological perspective on Romanian NTAs

From the etymological point of view, most NTAs are *hybrid multiple-term names*, incorporating words of different origins (cf. *Bon Voyage Tour & Travel*, *Edelweiss Travel*, *Mondo Travel*, *Boutique Travel*, *Sejour Tours*, etc.). As the number of foreign words from international languages is several times larger than that of the indigenous words, we can consider that this category of company names reflects the well-known openness (or "*hospitality*"[32]) of the Romanian language to loan words and its great force of assimilation. In our corpus, the most frequently encountered *source-language* is English, followed – at a great distance – by French, Italian and, occasionally, German, Spanish, Greek, and Latin[33].

The overwhelming majority of these fashionable loan words preserve their original spelling and pronunciation and, unlike genuine Romanian words, they are not subject to nominal inflection. In the field of company names, the unadapted borrowings are favoured for their "foreign connotations" associated with the so-called "mythe du mot étranger" (Etiemble 1964: 254), i.e. the prestige of the source–language[34], as well as for their novelty and expressiveness. In this respect, Constantinescu, Popovici, Ştefănescu (2002: 186) pointed out:

> In many cases the English form is preserved unchanged because it is considered technically necessary, fashionable or international. There is, then, nowadays a readiness of speakers for the *tale quale* acceptance of Anglicisms.

Within the large group of English loans, we have inventoried – from an onomastic perspective – some words and syntagms used as GCs (or categorial classifiers): *travel*, *tour(s)*, *travel agency*, *travel services*, *tours and travel*, *travel and tourism services*. The majority of the English unadapted loans are included in the structure of numerous NTAs as SCs, since they are considered more successful (in commercial terms) than their Romanian equivalents. It is interesting to point out that most of them are not mentioned by Romanian language dictionaries (e.g. DEX_2)[35] because they are not functionally or semantically motivated. As examples of such "superfluous (or luxury) anglicisms"[36], meant to convey positive connotations, which have turned into clichés by recurrent, stereotypical use in different NTAs, we can mention adjectives (*Active* Travel, *Funny* Travel, *Romantic* Travel, *Best* Travel, *Exclusive* Travel, *Fantastic* Tours,

Free Spirit, *Happy* Tour, *Maxim* Travel, *Smart* Tours), nouns (*Anchor* Travel, *Prestige* Tour, *Cocktail* Holidays, *Escape* Tour, *Hobby* Tour, *Leader* Tour, *Palace* Tour, *Paradise* Travel Agency, *Star* Travel, *Top* Travel), verbs (*Pack* and *Go*, *Visit* Romania) or colloquial greeting formulas (*Bye Bye* Travel, *Hello* Holidays).

The growing number of totally unadapted English loans and syntactic patterns clearly demonstrate, in our opinion, the deliberate promotion in the field of tourism of a hybrid idiom, respectively the so-called *Romgleza* (*"Romglish"*), a portmanteau word, obtained by combining *Româna* and *Engleza*, following the model of Etiemble's well-known *Franglais* (cf. Stoichițoiu Ichim 2003). Though less numerous, other unadapted borrowings occur as prestige markers according to the same business strategy. They were selected from French (*Boutique* Travel[37], *Soleil* Travel, *Bon Voyage* Tour and Travel, *Bonjour* Holiday, *Miniprix*discount Voyage, Rom*sejour* Travel), Italian (Mito *Viaggi e Vacanze*, *Mondo* Travel, *Unita* Tour, *Via* Europa, *Giro del Mondo*), German (*Edelweiss* Travel), Spanish (*Playa* Tour, *Paloma* Tours, *Estella* Travel), Greek (*Kalimera* Holidays Tours & Travel, *Alfa* și *Omega*), or Latin (*Amicus Qvo Vade*, *Omnia* Tours).

Nevertheless, it should be noted that, in many NTAs, there are foreign words that may have double or triple etymology since they were borrowed into Romanian from Romance languages (especially French, but also Italian) and / or from English: *Royal* Tour, *Prestige* Tours, *Cardinal* Travel, *Passion* Tourism & Travel[38]. Sometimes, a foreign or pseudo-foreign spelling is meant to catch the attention of the potential customer and to suggest a certain sociocultural or geographic context: *Albatross* Travel, *Tropikal* Tours, *Klass* Tour, *Leader* Tour (cf. the Romanian current spelling: *albatros*, *tropical*, *clasă*, *lider*).

As for the Romanian words included in a relatively small number of NTAs, there are mostly neologisms, associated to English words in asyntactic noun phrases: *Miraj* Sun Travel, *Ambasador* Tours & Travel, Travel *Confort*, Travel *Ideea*.

A semantic perspective on Romanian NTAs

As commercial names are always receiver/customer-oriented, aiming to catch his attention and to make him memorise and purchase the respective product or service, the analysis of the semantic level of both company and product names captured the attention of many Romanian and foreign researchers (such as Bugheșiu 2011, Cotticelli Kurras 2013,

Felecan D. 2011, Felecan, O. 2011, Sjöblom 2005 and 2014, Stoichiţoiu Ichim 2013 and 2014).

Following the criteria proposed by Cotticelli Kurras (2013: 261 – 265), concerning the semantic transparency of Italian product names analyzed from the view point of the consumer, we must notice important differences between the two components of an NTA, which make up a successful company name.

Since the function of the GC is to identify the field of activity (i.e. touristic services), the information is provided in a fully transparent way solely by the Romanian noun phrases (*agenţie de turism* or *birou de turism*). As to the English borrowings *travel* and *tour(s),* when analysed from a purely theoretic point of view, they may be either half-transparent to the English – speaking customers (due to a certain lack of semantic precision, which makes the two English borrowings to be used as synonyms in Romanian NTAs[39]) or opaque to the rest of the target audience. Actually, in the context of the strong influence of English in the field of commercial onomastics, we may consider that the English GCs display the suitable degree of transparency in relation to their referent, so that all customers could easily identify them.

A much more complex situation may be found when we focus on the *degrees of semantic acceptability* of the SCs, ranging from a totally transparent meaning to an entirely opaque one.

A small group of SCs, characterized by a *high degree of transparency* and *accessibility*, include descriptive, objectively motivated formulas, which consist of either Romanian and / or foreign common nouns (*Vacanţe la Mare* "Holidays on the Seashore", *Turist Club* "Tourist's Club", *Balneo Turism*, *Student Travel*, *Scuba Diver*, *Condor Hunting and Business Travel*), or a first name, denoting the owner(s) (*Christian* Tour, *Fabiola & Alex* Turism, Mr. *Peter* Company). Geographical names may locate the travel agency in space (*Transilvania* Tourist Service, *Transilvania* Travel Services, *Karpaten* Turism), or may emphasize a particular field of interest or a business target of the respective company (*Malta* Travel, *Gibraltar* Travel, *Delta* Best Turism, *Danubius* Travel).

The *lowest degree of transparency* (from both semantic and morphological perspectives) is illustrated by several categories of opaque SCs, such asemantic blends (*Rovial* Travel, *Camira* Turism, *Weco* Travel), or acronyms whose meaning remains obscure for the target – audience (*C&AE* Business Travel, *O.M.* Travel, *D. A.* Turism, *EXIM* Tour). As noticeable exceptions, we can mention here *DTS* Travel Agency (in which the acronym abbreviates the noun phrase *Dental Touring Services*) and

CND Turism (where *CND* < Rom. *Ce ne dorim* "what we want for ourselves").

The largest and the most interesting group of SCs include *connotative names* reflecting the name-giver free creativity. Such names can be considered opaque with respect to the objective naming criteria since they are irrelevant for the relation between the name, on the one hand, and the business and the owner, on the other. At the same time, such names display a particular type of transparency, due to their ability to function at an emotional level. Instead of conveying objective information, they are meant to evoke in the customer's mind positive associations and suggestive images, which are part of the collective imaginary related to touristic activities. As Sjöblom (2005: 272) pointed out, nowadays, quite many commercial names are no more connected to their referent:

> No longer did the name have an informative function, but rather its task was to produce positive images, to give a push to business (= persuading function). What these images are like depends on the name and the community, the historical time and culture.

A crucial role in achieving this marketing strategy is assigned to several *connotative (metaphorical) fields*, related to symbolic values that a customer may recognize and assume (see, on this subject, Cotticelli Kurras 2013: 262 – 265, and Balode and Bušs 2014: 21 – 23). The highly stereotyped connotative fields well represented in our corpus of Romanian NTAs are related to:

- nature, landscapes, and ecological lifestyle: *România Turistică* ("Touristic Romania"), *Fresh Holidays*, *Green Tour*, *Ecovoyage Tour*, *Paradise Travel Agency*, *Sunny Days Travel*, *Oasis Tour*, *Soleil Travel*;
- luxury, high quality and comfort: *Gold Voyage*, *Prestige Tours*, *Optimus Travel*, *Royal Tour*, *Perfect Tour*, *Travel Confort*;
- freedom, adventure, and fun: *Escape Tour*, *Funny Travel*, *Travel 4 Fun*, *1001 Adventures*, *Active Travel*, *Passion Tourism and Travel*;
- holiday, leisure activities, and social contacts: *Amiciția Travel* ("Friendship Travel"), *Hello Holiday*, *Bonjour Holiday*, *KissTravel.ro*, *Cocktail Holidays*, *Fantasy Travel*;
- reliability, affordable prices: *No Limit Ideal Travel*, *Smart Travel*, *Travel Tips*, *Miniprixdiscount Voyage*, *Travel Wise Office*, *Expert Tours*;
- religion, history, and mythology: *Avraam Travel*, *Getica Turism*[40], *Nefertiti Travel*, *Dedal Tour*, *Icar Tours*, *Phoenix Tour*;

- long–distance real or virtual voyages: *Mapamond*, *Galaxy Tours*, *Travel Planet*, *Mondo Travel*, *Giro del Mondo*, *World Tourism and Tours*;
- rare and/or exotic names from flora and fauna: *Edelweiss Travel*, *Kiwi Travel*, *Panda Travel Agency*, *Monkey Travel*, *Falcon Travel*, *Colibri*.

In the same category of creative NTAs – more or less connected with the respective business – one can range a few funny formulas aiming to catch the customer's attention by humour and clever wordplay[41] (for instance, based on homonymy: *Travel 4 Fun*), or by a naming formula imitating the specific patterns used on the Internet websites *(JollyTour.ro*, *KissTravel.ro*).

Concluding remarks

Taking all the aforesaid into consideration, it is obvious that the names of travel agencies (NTAs) represent an interesting area of investigation, not only from a legal and economic point of view, but also from onomastic and pragmalinguistic perspectives.

To sum up, our analysis underlined the novelty and the large variety of naming patterns displayed by this category of company names in the Romanian public space after the dissolution of the communist regime in 1989. Besides the alignment of both managers and customers to the values and marketing strategies of the Western consumer society, the growing influence of English as a *lingua franca* determined the tendency of present-day Romanian to adjust the naming patterns in accordance with those existing in other European countries.

A multidisciplinary approach allowed us to analyse NTAs as a special type of complex conventional signs in relation to their functions of identification, individualization, and advertising performed in the economic autochthonous environment. Particular attention has been paid, from a pragmatic perspective, to the implicit communicative consensus established between the owner (as name-giver) and a potential customers (as receivers and interpreters as well).

The onomastic investigation identified two segments of an NTA: the optional generic component (*travel*, *tour*, *tourism agency*) and the compulsory specific component, which aims not only to identify the company, but also to make the whole name persuasive and catchy.

From an etymological point of view, the most striking characteristic of both generic and specific components is the overwhelming proportion of totally unadapted English borrowings that enabled us to speak about a so-called "Romglish" of tourism.

The formal analysis of NTAs showed a large majority of noun phrases, including a head (as a specific component) and a postponed modifier (as a generic component), according to the English word order.

As regards the semantics of Romanian NTAs, the most common type is represented not by descriptive and transparent formulas, but by rather connotative and highly creative ones, meant to create a strong persuasive effect on the target audience. In view of achieving this objective, both proper names and onymized common nouns carrying positive associations (related to nature, ecological lifestyle, high quality of services and comfort, freedom, adventure, and leisure activities) are selected appropriately.

References

Avram, Mioara. 1993. "La créativité et l'«hospitalité» du roumain," *Revue roumaine de linguistique* XXXVIII, (1 – 3): 23 – 26.

Balode, Laimute, and Ojārs Bušs. 2014. "Two sketches on Latvian names in the economy." *Studii şi cercetări de onomastică şi lexicologie* VII (1-2): 13-24.

Bergien, Angelika. 2013. "From *Sollar Valley* to *Shadow Mountain*: Identity construction in location-based company names." In Felecan, and Bugheşiu (eds.), 106-119.

Bugheşiu, Alin. 2011. "The semiotics and pragmatics of trade names." In Zafiu, Uşurelu, and Bogdan Oprea (eds.), vol. 2, 33–42.

—. 2013. "Names of Transylvanian hotels in the context of globalization." In Felecan (ed.), 81–90.

Constantinescu, Ilinca, Victoria Popovici, and Ariadna Ştefănescu. 2002. "Romanian". In: *English in Europe*. Manfred Görlach (ed.), 168 – 194. Oxford: Oxford University Press.

Cotticelli Kurras, Paola. 2013. "Italian commercial names. Brand and product names on the globalized market." In Felecan, and Bugheşiu (eds.), 257-276.

Crystal, Davi.d 2000. *English as a global language*. Cambridge: Cambridge University Press.

Czopek-Kopciuh, Barbara. 2013. "Names of companies in Poland." In Felecan, and Bugheşiu (eds.), 120-130.

DCR_3 = Dimitrescu, Florica (ed.), Alexandru Ciolan, and Coman Lupu. 2013. *Dicţionar de cuvinte recente*, 3rd edition, Bucureşti: Logos.

DEX_2 = "Academia Română, and Institutul de Lingvistică "Iorgu Iordan –

Al. Rosetti".” 1998. *Dicţionarul explicativ al limbii române*. Bucureşti: Univers Enciclopedic.

Etiemble, René. 1964. *Parlez-vous franglais*? Paris: Gallimard.

Felecan, Daiana. 2011. “Observaţii referitoare la configuraţia semiotică a unor nume de firme (NF) din spaţiul public românesc actual.” In Zafiu, Uşurelu. and Bogdan Oprea (eds.), vol. 2, 63 – 76.

Felecan, Oliviu. 2011. “Tipologia numelor de firme din spaţiul public românesc actual.” In Zafiu, Uşurelu, and Bogdan Oprea (eds.), vol. 1, 249–258.

Felecan, Oliviu (ed.). 2013. *Name and naming: Proceedings of the second international conference on onomastics: Onomastics in contemporary public space: Baia Mare, May 9-11, 2013*. Cluj-Napoca: Mega / Argonaut.

Felecan, Oliviu, and Alina Bugheşiu (eds.). 2013. *Onomastics in contemporary public space*. Newcastle upon Tyne: Cambridge Scholars Publishing.

LTI = Stănciulescu, Gabriela, Nicolae Lupu, Emilia Ţiţan, Gabriela Ţigu, and Felicia Stăncioiu. 2002. *Lexicon de termeni turistici*. Bucureşti: Oscar Print.

NPR = *Le Nouveau Petit Larousse* (sous la direction de J. Rey-Debove et A. Rey). 2004. Paris: Dictionnaires Le Robert.

OALD = Hornby, A. S. 2005. *Oxford Advanced Learner's Dictionary of Current English*. Oxford: Oxford University Press.

Rateau, Michel A. 2013. “De la notion de grammaire dans l'acte de dénomination: le cas des sud-africains donnant des noms d'origine française à des lieux commerciaux.” In Felecan (ed.), 170–189.

Raţă, Georgeta. 2012. *Travel* collocations. In Raţă, Petroman, and Petroman (eds.), 75-80.

Raţă, Georgeta, and Ioan Petroman. 2012a. “English borrowings in the Romanian of tourism (Travel agencies).” In Raţă, Petroman, and Petroman (eds.), 43-48.

Raţă, Georgeta, and Ioan Petroman. 2012b. “English borrowings in the Romanian of tourism (Sites of travel agencies).” In Raţă, Petroman, and Petroman (eds.), 49-54.

Raţă Georgeta, Ioan Petroman, and Cornelia Petroman (eds.). 2012. *The English of Tourism*, Newcastle upon Tyne: Cambridge Scholars Publishing.

Roibu, Melania. 2014. “False friends: true ennemies in language?” *Studii şi cercetări de onomastică şi lexicologie* VII (1-2): 263-274.

Sjöblom, Paula. 2005. “The problem of meaning and function related to company names.” In *Proceedings of the 21st International Congress of*

Onomastic Sciences. Uppsala, August 19-24, 2002, vol. 1. Eva Brylla, and Maths Wahlberg (eds.), 264 – 276. Uppsala: Sprök-och folkminnesinstitutet.

Sjöblom, Paula. 2014. "Commercial names and unestablished terminology." In *Els noms en la vida quotidiana. Actes del XXIV Congrès International d'ICOS*, 92-98. Online: http://llengua.gencat.cat/ca/services/informacio_i_difusio/publicaciones_en_linia/btpl_col/actes_icos

Sjöblom, Paula, Terhi Ainiala, and Ulla Hakala (eds.). 2013. *Names in the economy. Cultural prospects*, Newcastle upon Tyne: Cambridge Scholars Publishing.

Stoichiţoiu Ichim, Adriana. 2003. " 'Romgleza': opţiune personală sau efect al globalizării?" In *Identitate românească şi integrare europeană*. Gabriela Gabor (ed.), 95-103. Bucureşti: Ars Docendi.

—. 2006. *Aspecte ale influenţei engleze în româna actuală*, Bucureşti: Editura Universităţii din Bucureşti.

—. 2013. "Restaurant names in the city of Bucharest: cross – cultural and sociolinguistic perspectives." In Sjöblom, Ainiala and Hakala (eds.), 89-105.

—. 2014. "Observaţii privind numele agenţiilor de turism din spaţiul public românesc." In *Cultura limbii. Omagiu doamnei profesor Domniţa Tomescu*. Gabriela Duda (ed.), 273–292. Ploieşti: Editura Universităţii Petrol–Gaze din Ploieşti.

Tomescu, Domniţa. 2003. "Noms commerciaux étrangers dans l'onomastique roumaine d'aujourd'hui." In *La langue et les parlants / Language and its users / Limba şi vorbitorii*. Tatiana Slama–Cazacu (ed.), 168-175. Bucureşti: Arvin Press.

—. 2011. "L'emprunt des noms commerciaux anglais dans l'onomastique roumaine actuelle." In *Proceedings of the international conference "Applied linguistics today – between theory and practice", Novi Sad, October 29 – November 1, 2009*. Snežana Gudurić, and Dušanka Točanac (eds.), 117-123. Novi Sad.

Walkowiak, Justyna B.2013. "Foreign branding in Poland: chrematonyms and anthroponyms." In Felecan (ed.), 218–227.

Zafiu, Rodica. 2003. "Sui prestiti recenti dall'inglese: condizionamenti morfologici e scelte culturali." In *Románia e Románia. Lingua e cultura romena di fronte all'Occidente.* Teresa Ferro (a cura di), 83 – 95. Udine: Forum Editrice Universitaria Udinese.

Zafiu, Rodica, Camelia Uşurelu, and Helga Bogdan Oprea (eds.). 2011. *Limba română: ipostaze ale variaţiei lingvistice*, vol. 1, 2. Bucureşti: Editura Universităţii din Bucureşti.

Online sources

(accessed March – June 2015)
http: // www.anat.ro/despre-anat/membri/lista-membrilor/
http: // www.agentiideturism.infoturism.ro
http: // www.infotravelromania.com/topagentii.php
http: // en.m.wikipedia.org/wiki/Brand_names
http: // en.m.wikipedia.org/wiki/Globalization
http:// en.m.wikipedia.org/wiki/Tourism
https://en.m.wikipedia.org/wiki/Franglais

List of abreviations

Engl.=English; Fr.=French; Germ.=German; It.=Italian; Lat=Latin; Rom.=Romanian; Sp.=Spanish.

I would like to thank my colleague, lecturer Melania Roibu, Ph.D at the University of Bucarest, for her assistance in reviewing the English version of this article.

Notes

[1] As noticeable exceptions in this respect one may mention Rață and Petrovan (2012a) and Stoichițoiu Ichim (2014).

[2] According to Wikipedia, such types of structures corresponding to the English "Adjective / Noun + *Tourism*" (rendered in Romanian by a "*Tourism* + Adjective" noun phrase or by a "*Tourism* + Prep. + Noun") are inventoried under the umbrella term. *Adjectival Tourism*.

[3] For Walkowiak (2013: 218), *chrematonyms* include names of companies and products or brands as well.

[4] In a restricted sense, *ergonym* designates only names of companies (Balode and Bušs 2014:13; Czopek-Kopciuch 2013:121). In a broader sense, it includes names of non-commercial institutions besides those of commercial business and products (Sjöblom 2014:92).

[5] As stated by Sjöblom (2014), *commercial name* (as a hyponym of *ergonym*) is an expression which refers to four different subcategories of names regulated by law and used in an economic context (company names, trademarks, product names and brands).

[6] Cf. Bugheșiu (2011).

[7] Cf. Felecan, D. (2011), Felecan, O. (2011), and Stoichițoiu Ichim (2014).

[8] Cf. Tomescu (2003), (2011).

[9] See https://portal.onrc.ro and
http://www.metacautare.ro/web?ts=go&q=firme+registrul+comertului.

[10] Legile 26/1990 and 31/1990, and Ordonanța Guvernamentală 72/2004.
[11] See http://www.monitorulexpres.ro/?mod=monitorulexpres&p=contabil_expres&_id=97740.
[12] See, among others, Bugheșiu (2011), (2013), Felecan, D. (2011), Felecan, O. (2011) and Stoichițoiu Ichim (2013).
[13] Cf. Bergien (2013:107).
[14] On this subject, see Bugheșiu (2011: 38–40), Ballode, and Bušs (2014: 14–15) and, especially, Sjöblom (2014:93), who highlights the fact that "a good name is a good way to show and sell things, because of the fact that the heart of a proper name is to identify its referent, to single it out, make it unique and distinguish it from all others".
[15] Despite their striking foreign (mostly English) names, all NTA's mentioned in the current paper denote travel agencies legally registered in the Romanian urban space. As other Romanian company names (for instance, those of public houses, hotels or shops), NTAs have been strongly influenced during the last two decades by English as a global language (cf. Tomescu 2011, Bugheșiu 2013, Stoichițoiu Ichim 2013).
[16] http://smallbusiness.chron.com/tips-good-names-travel-business-3298.html (accessed 2.05.2015).
[17] http://brandongaille.com/31-good-catchy-tour-company-names/ (accessed 2.05.2015).
[18] http://www.buggle.com/articles/good-name-suggestions-for-your-travel-agency-business.html (accessed 2.05.2015).
[19] http://brandongaille.com/47-catchy-travel-agency-company-ideas/ (accessed 30.04.2015)
[20] *Joy Tour & Travel*, *Let's Go Travel Agency*, *Liberty Travel*, *Fantasy Cruises*, *A Dream Come True*, *Bon Voyage!*, *Travel Fantasies*, *Two by the Sea* (for couples), *Golden Years Adventures* (for retirees), *Oh Solo Mio* (for singles), etc.
[21] Referring to tourism activities in the chapter *International travel* of this book, Crystal (2000: 95–97) pointed out: "If there is a contemporary movement towards English use, therefore, we would expect it to be particularly noticeable in this domain. And so it is." See, also, on this subject, Rață and Petroman (2012b) and the numerous English borrowings included in LTI (e.g. *camping*, *caravaning*, *charter*, *back-office*, *bed and breakfast*, *brunch*, *bungalow*, *cafeteria*, *catering*, *youth hostel*, *front-office*, *room-service*).
[22] Cf. Felecan, D. (2011: 64), Stoichițoiu Ichim (2013: 94–98) and (2014: 207), Sjöblom (2014: 95).
[23] Surprisingly, in a specialized dictionary (LTI: 14) the only listed structure is *agenție de voiaj* (cf. Fr. *agence de voyage*).
[24] Cf., in this respect, the concept of *foreign branding*, as presented in Walkowiak (2013); see, also, Tomescu (2003), (2011), and Rateau (2013).
[25] For a full picture of the English influence on the present-day Romanian language, see, especially, Constantinescu, Popovici, and Ștefănescu (2002), Zafiu (2003), and Stoichițoiu Ichim (2003, (2006).

[26] According to Rateau (2013: 178), they can be considered "termes empruntés au sens detourné". For a detailed discussion on false friends and some bordering phenomena, see Roibu (2015).

[27] In this respect, see also the typology of Italian brands established by Cotticelli Kurras (2013: 266–271).

[28] For a presentation of various blending patterns encountered in Polish company names, cf. Czopek – Kopciuch (2013: 122–124).

[29] The Romanian typical word order is "Noun+Adjective". On the problem of the word order inversion, see Constantinescu, Popovici, Ştefănescu (2002: 183-184): "The reverse of English has apparently started to influence Romanian word structure, especially within company names".

[30] The English synthetic Genitive, meant to connote the "Englishness", frequently occurs in names of Romanian public houses (see Stoichiţoiu Ichim 2013: 99) instead of the genitive of proper names marked in Romanian by a proclitic form of the definite article (*lui Eddie*).

[31] As a Romance or Neo-Latin language, Romanian has a rich nominal inflection, with the case indicated by noun endings and the agreement in gender, number and case between noun modifier and the noun they modify.

[32] For a detailed analysis on the correlative concepts of *hospitality* and *creativity*, see Avram (1993).

[33] According to Raţă and Petroman (2012a: 45–46), within a corpus of 204 Romanian NTAs inventoried in their article, 50% of the total number of words are English, 20% are Romanian, 4% are Italian, 2% are French, while Latin, Greek, German and Spanish words represent about 0,5% each.

[34] On this subject, see, among others, Bugheşiu (2013: 87), Walkoviak (2013: 220–223), Stoichiţoiu Ichim (2013: 99–101).

[35] We can mention as exceptions *lider* (< Engl. *leader*), *hobby*, *cocktail* and *star* (registered în DEX_2).

[36] Concerning the categories of *necessary* vs. *superfluous (or luxury) anglicisms*, see Constantinescu, Popovici, Ştefănescu (2002:172), and Stoichiţoiu Ichim (2006: 226–230).------------

[37] *Boutique* is registered in DCR_3 as a hotel-related word, since it designates a small, stylish establishement providing lodging in a friendly environment.

[38] The internationalisation of hotel and public houses' names has been discussed by Bugheşiu (2013), respectively Stoichiţoiu Ichim (2013).

[39] Cf. *supra*, p. 5.

[40] The ajective turned into noun. Getica is a derivative whose root is the ethnonym *Get* < Geto-Dacians, a term used to designate the inhabitants of antique Dacia.

[41] Cf. Balode and Bušs (2014: 20).

"OH LORD, WON'T YOU BUY ME A MERCEDES BENZ?" BRAND NAMES IN LYRICS AND MUSIC VIDEOS

SABINE WAHL

Abstract

Brand names traditionally form an integral part of the internal and external business and corporate communication of a company, e.g., of print advertisements and brochures, television and radio commercials, of the company's homepage and various microsites as well as of the packaging of a product. However, these are not the only contexts in which consumers encounter brand names in everyday life. Much money is spent to promote products in films, television series and video games, which is called product placement. Currently, it is discussed, whether another form of presenting a product to a large – and often international – audience may also be described as product placement: the promotion of brands in song lyrics. This paper aims at analysing a multilingual corpus of song lyrics in which brand names are included in the title and/or in the lyrics of a song. It focuses on the relative frequency of single products and product classes, the positive and/or negative contexts in which the brand names are mentioned as well as the possible influence of the music genre. Moreover, this study will also shed light on the diachronic development of this phenomenon. By including the respective music videos (if available), it will be demonstrated which artists have adopted a multimodal product placement strategy.

Introduction

The modern consumer encounters brand names not only in supermarkets where they are written on the packages of the respective packages and on the price marks on the shelves or in all kinds of advertising, ranging from print advertisements to radio and television commercials, out-of-home displays and online advertisements: They are also present as words in our lexicon, e.g., when we refer to all paper handkerchiefs with the brand names of the respective market leader *Tempo* (in Germany) and *Kleenex* (in England or Spain).[1] Brands and their names can also be encountered in television series, video games and films where they are presented visually and/or verbally[2]. This presentation of brands in the latter three contexts is referred to as product placement:

> Product placement means any form of audiovisual commercial communication consisting of the inclusion or reference to a product, a service or the trade mark thereof so that it is featured within a programme, in return for payment or for similar consideration.
>
> Product placement, in contrast to sponsorship messages, is, built into the action of a programme whereas sponsor references may be shown during the programme but are not part of the plot.
> (European Commission, Audiovisual and Media Policies)[3]

In Germany, all regulations concerning television and radio, including advertising and product placement, can be found in the so called *Rundfunkstaatsvertrag*[4] ("Interstate Treaty on Broadcasting and Telemedia – Interstate Broadcasting Treaty"). In this contract, it is stated that advertising and product placement must not have any influence on the content of the programme. Additionally, advertising must be separated from the programme content by acoustic, visual or audiovisual means. In some cases, it is also required to label programmes that contain product placement explicitly: "P" is inserted at the beginning and at the end of a programme for at least three seconds and for monetary support "Enthält Produktplatzierung" ("contains product placement") or for non-monetary support "unterstützt durch Produktionshilfe" ("supported by production help")[5]. All forms of product placement must not include a direct sales appeal. Moreover, the product placement must not be too apparent.[6] In addition, product placement in programmes with informative character and in children's programming is not allowed.

There is, however, yet another context in which consumers encounter brand names in everyday life. When they listen to music, they come across lyrics in which brand names are mentioned, as the following example shows:

Oh Lord, won't you buy me a ***Mercedes Benz****?*
My friends all drive ***Porsches****, I must make amends.*
Worked hard all my lifetime, no help from my friends,
So Lord, won't you buy me a ***Mercedes Benz****?*

These are the first lines of Janis Joplin's song *Mercedes Benz* (1970/1971)[7]. She prays for a *Mercedes Benz* because she wants to keep up with her friends all of whom drive *Porsches*.[8] In these first four lines of the song two luxury car brands are mentioned, one of them even twice.

Currently whether this form of presenting a brand to a large – and often international – audience in song lyrics may also be described as product placement is under discussion.[9] It is, in any case, a way of promoting brands by which associations with the artists as celebrity endorsers may be seen.

The media coverage regarding this topic[10] suggests that certain artists and brands are linked quite closely, e.g., the band *Run-DMC* were offered a contract to endorse *Adidas* sports shoes after their song „*My Adidas*" had been released. In other cases, it can be observed that mentioning a brand name in a song has an impact on the sales figures of the respective product or brand. For some artists, the connection between their art and this form of advertising is even closer: They have created their own products and promote them in their lyrics (*Jay Z* and his brand *Ace of Spades*)[11]. One artist (*Puffy*) has even founded an advertising agency (cf. Kaufman 2003).

The media coverage and studies also indicate that mentioning brand names in lyrics is often genre-specific (Gloor 2014: 53, Kimball 2014): This form of promoting brands is more common in hip-hop and rap songs. Moreover, there seems to be a preference for certain product classes, namely cars (*Mercedes* is often mentioned), luxury brands and alcoholic drinks.

A previous scientific study conducted in the area of business sciences has found that there is a relationship between brand attitude and the attitude towards the artist (van Vaerenbergh et al. 2011), which is comparable to other studies on the choice and influence of celebrity endorsers (cf. Pringle 2004, Wahl 2009). A second, musicological study (Gloor 2014) with a diachronic focus, analysed the Top 30 Billboard songs (1960-2010) and showed that the number of brand names in the lyrics of these highly successful songs increased over time.

This paper aims at analysing the situation in Germany. It will demonstrate that brand names are included in the title and/or in the lyrics of a song. The study focuses on the relative frequency of single brands and product classes, the positive and/or negative contexts in which the brand names are mentioned as well as the possible influence of the music genre. By including the respective music videos (if available), it will become obvious which artists have adopted a multimodal strategy by presenting the brands and their names verbally and visually.

Corpus

The corpus of this study consists of all songs that were listed among the MTV Top 100 in Germany in 2014. The lyrics of these songs were used in the version presented by the online platform www.songtexte.com. If the lyrics were not available on this platform www.azlyrics.com and www.songtextemania.com were consulted. As far as the respective music videos are concerned, the versions presented by MTV (m.mtv.de/charts/241-top-100-jahrescharts-2014) were analysed.

Brand Names in the German Top 100: Results and Interpretation

Brand names occurred in 15% of the lyrics of the most successful songs in Germany in 2014 (cf. Fig. 1):

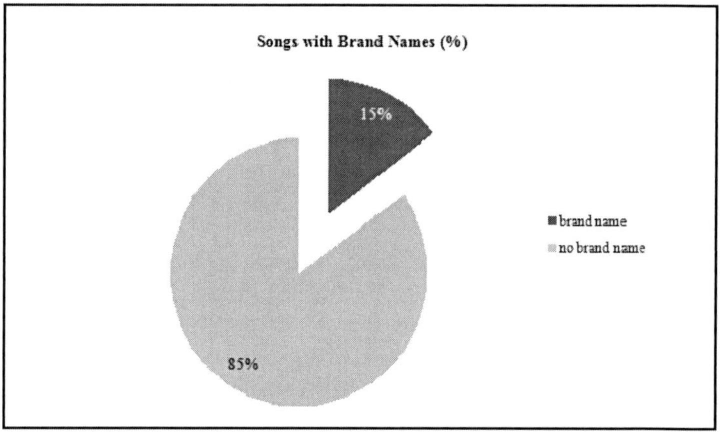

Fig. 1. Songs with brand names.

In the 15 Top 100 songs that contain at least one brand name, 31 different brand names are mentioned in the lyrics (types). The most common product classes are:

- cars: *Bentley, (Mercedes) Benz, Cadillac, Ferrari, Lamborghinis, Testarossa*[12], *Passat, (Rolls-) Royce* and the famous motorbike *Harley (Davidson)*
- luxury brands: all the luxury car brands mentioned above, *Alexander McQueen, Balmain, Louie sheets (Louis Vuitton)*
- alcoholic drinks: *Ace, Cris, D'USSÉ, Goose, Myx Moscato, Volí*
- computer and new media: *Instagram, Mac, Photoshop*

This result is in line with the media coverage cited above. *Cadillac, Instagram* and *Mac* are all named in two songs each. *American Apparel Underwear* is the name with the highest number of token: four in one song. This is because it is part of the refrain. *Cadillac* is named three times in two songs. *Barbie* (in one song), *Instagram* and *Mac* are mentioned twice each.

In all songs of the corpus, the brand is named in the main part of the lyrics and not in the title. There is only one song title that refers directly to Twitter, but by using the # symbol instead of the name: *#Selfie* by *The Chainsmokers* (number 93).

9 out of these 15 songs are by rap artists. Three more songs feature rappers. This result is also in line with the media coverage cited above.

In the 15% of the songs that contain a brand name, usually more than one type of brand name is mentioned. There is even a song that mentions seven different brand names: the song *King* (number 77) by the German rap artist *Kollegah*. He focuses mainly on luxury car brands (*Benz, Testarossa, Bentley-Emblem, Lamborghinis, Royce*), a computer brand (*Mac*) and a gun (*MAC-10*). With the compound *Bentley-Emblem*, he verbally refers to the logo of this brand. As the list of brand names in this song shows, it is not always the entire registered brand name that is mentioned, e.g., in *(Mercedes) Benz* or *(Rolls) Royce*. With these conventionalized short forms of the brand names, it is possible to refer to the same brand in one instead of 4 syllables and one instead of two syllables respectively. This strategy can be used to make the brands an artist wants to mention fit into the rhythmic pattern of the song.[13]

In these songs, brands usually are named in positive contexts. Only in *All about that bass* by *Meghan Trainor* (number 35), the brand names *Photoshop* and *Barbie* are used differently:

I see the magazines working that ***Photoshop***
We know that shit ain't real
Come on now, make it stop
[…]
Yeah, my momma she told me don't worry about your size
She says, boys they like a little more booty to hold at night
You know I won't be no stick-figure, silicone ***Barbie*** *doll*
So, if that's what's you're into
Then go ahead and move along
Because you know I'm all about that bass

For the linguistic field of onomastics, it is also interesting that brand names are not the only name category that is mentioned in this song.

Kollegah names the title of his album and song *Bossaura* and includes place names like *Costa Rica*, *Guantanamera* and *Rom* (German spelling for the Italian capital), as well as other names: *Abel, Julius Cäsar, Ku Klux Klan, Rambo-Mimik, Zeus*.

This song is not the only example in which additional name categories play an important role (cf. Fig. 2):

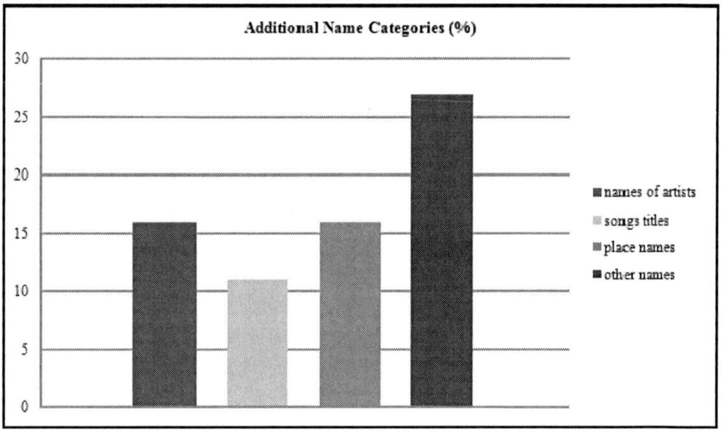

Fig. 2. Additional name categories.

In 16% of the German Top 100, the names of artists are mentioned. This includes cases of self-reference (see below). 11% of the songs include the title of other songs (see below). Place names are given in 16% of the songs and 27% of the songs include other names, e.g., of celebrities that are not working in the music business, of historically important persons, of film characters and films and of fictional characters (literary texts).

As artists and celebrities in general are often described as brands with a certain image, it could be argued that their names belong to the category "brand names" as well.[14]

A good example of this is the song *Lieder* by *Adel Tawil* (number 33). This song is basically a long list of song titles and artists that have influenced *Adel Tawil's* work and career. It is obvious that all these songs and artists are mentioned in a positive context. As it is his debut single as a solo artist, he mentions the band with whom he started his career.

The following list of hidden songs and artists mentioned in the lyrics was compiled by the audience of a radio station[15] and was adapted for this purpose (S.W.):

Original German Lyrics	**Hidden Song – Title**	**Hidden Song – Artist**
Ich ging wie ein Ägypter	*Walk like an Egyptian*	*The Bangles*
hab' mit Tauben geweint	*When Doves Cry*	*Prince*
...Voodoo-Kind	*Voodoo Child*	*Jimi Hendrix*
wie ein rollender Stein	*Like a rolling stone*	*Bob Dylan*
Im Dornenwald sang Maria...	*Maria durch ein Dornwald ging*	*Traditional German Christmas song*
ich starb in deinen Armen...	*Just Died in your Arms Tonight*	*Cutting Crew*
...Bochum '84	*Bochum*	*Herbert Grönemeyer*
ich ließ die Sonne nie untergehen	*Don't Let The Sun Go Down On Me*	*Elton John*
...wundervollen Welt	*What a wonderful world*	*Louis Armstrong*
Refrain:		
tanz' mit Tränen in den Augen	*Dancing with tears in my eyes*	*Ultravox*
Bowie war für'n Tag mein Held	*Heroes (Just for one day)*	*David Bowie*
EMF können es nicht glauben	*Unbelivable*	*EMF*
...lila Regen	*Purple Rain*	*Prince*
ich will ein Feuerstarter sein	*Firestarter*	*Prodigy*
Whitney wird mich immer lieben	*I will always love you*	*Whitney Housten*
Michael lässt mich nich' allein	*You are not alone*	*Michael Jackson*

...Willkommen im Dschungel	*Welcome to the Jungle*	*Guns'n'Roses*
Fremd im eigenen Land	*Fremd im eigenen Land*	*Advanced Chemestry*
...persönlicher Jesus	*Personal Jesus*	*Depeche Mode*
...im Gehirn total krank	*Insane in the Brain*	*Cypress Hill*
wann werd ich, werd ich berühmt sein	*When will I be famous*	*Bros*
...Rio mein König	*König von Deutschland*	*Rio Reiser*
Ende der Straße	*End Of The Road*	*Boys II Men*
war ein Verlierer, Baby!	*I'm a loser baby*	*Beck*
hielt ich ein Cover in der Hand, darauf ein Mönch, der in Flammen stand	Cover of the single *Killing in the Name Of*	*Rage Against the Machine*
Kurt Cobain sagte mir, ich soll kommen wie ich bin	*Come as you are* (+ guitar riff from this song can be heard in the background)	*Nirvana*
Refrain (see above)		
einer von fünf Jungs		*The Boyz* (Adel Tawil was a member of this band.)
„One Minute“	*One Minute*	*The Boyz*
Dann traf ich auf sie		With the pronoun *sie* (‚her‘), he refers to his partner Anette Humpe in the band *Ich + Ich*.
sie erinnerte mich	*Du erinnerst mich an Liebe*	*Ich + Ich* (+ reference to Anette Humpe)

vom selben Stern	*Vom selben Stern*	*Ich + Ich*
(Codo – DÖF)	A part of the song *Codo* by *DÖF* can be heard.	Anette Humpe was a member of the band *DÖF*

Table 1. Hidden Songs and Artists in *Lieder* by Adel Tawil.

This long list of references to artists and song titles is also partly included in the music video (see below).

Brand Names in Music Videos

Music videos are films that are produced to accompany the respective songs. Like all films, music videos can be described as multimodal artefacts:

> Multimodal texts[16] integrate selections from different semiotic resources to their principles of organisation. […] These resources are not simply juxtaposed as separate modes of meaning making but are combined and integrated to form a complex whole which cannot be reduced to, or explained in terms of the mere sum of its separate parts. (Baldry/Thibault 2006: 18)

The music video to the song *Lieder* is mainly set in a record store. *Adel Tawil* looks for the records he names and presents their covers to the viewers. Sometimes the covers even appear on his shirt. In both cases the pictures are synchronised with the lyrics – with the result that the names are presented multimodally, i.e., in the song text (the mode of language) and in the pictures. In the following example, *Adel Tawil* names the late *David Bowie* and his album *Heroes*, while he presents the cover of this album. Moreover, he names the band *EMF* whose cover is printed on his t-shirt:[17]

Image

Lyrics [BOwie WAR für'n TAG mein HELD und emF kann ES nich' GLAUben]

Fig. 3. Screenshot – Lieder.[18]

In the music videos accompanying the songs, there are generally three ways of presenting the brands: firstly, they can be presented verbally in the lyrics only. Secondly, they can be presented visually in the moving images alone, and thirdly, the artists can make use of this audiovisual format and present the brands multimodally.

In the German Top 100 the multimodal presentation of brand names rarely occurs. The only three examples are *Timber* by *Pitbull* (number 14), *All about that bass* by *Meghan Trainor* (number 35) and *King* by *Kollegah* (number 77).

Image

Lyrics [voLÍ]

Fig. 4. Screenshot – Timber.

The example is taken from *Timber*. The visual presentation of the brand is comparable to a packshot in a television commercial.

In all other cases, the sung brand names remain restricted to the lyrics. However, in 91% of the music videos, additional brands are introduced.[19] Cars (including *Mercedes*) and alcoholic drinks are often presented visually, but there are several product classes that get more attention here than in the lyrics: fashion and sports brands (e.g., *Adidas*, *Converse*, *Nike*, *N*), instruments (guitars and drums), recording equipment (hardware and software as shown on computer screens), and the headphone and loudspeaker brand *Beats* (*b*). This is due to the fact that the artists' (and other persons') dance moves, as well as the artists playing and recording their songs, are shown.

One example is the song *25* by the German hip hop band *Die Fantastischen Vier*. In this song, which was released to celebrate 25 years on stage, there is not a single brand name mentioned in the lyrics. The only names the audience hears are the names of the band members (*Thomas*, *Smudo*, *Andy*, *Michi*, in this order) and the nicknames of the band: *Die Vier* "the four" and *Die Fantas*. The first nickname is an ellipsis of the band name and is derived from the number of band members. The second one is a back-clipping[20] of the adjective *fantastisch* "fantastic"[21], converted into a noun with the plural ending *-s*. In this form, the name can be interpreted as referring to the lemonade brand. In the video, e.g., *MTV*, *Nike*, *Nokia*, and various beer brands can be seen.

That it is possible to create certain humorous effects by inconsistent multimodal presentations of brand names in the verbal and visual part of the music video, is shown by the following early example by *Die Fantastischen Vier*. Their song *MfG*[22] (1999) mainly consists of long lists of acronyms, including brand names.[23] When the car brand *BMW* in the German pronunciation [be:.ʔɛm.'ve:] is sung, a young man pointing to his necklace with a huge *Mercedes Benz* logo is presented in the music video:

[bmW]

Fig. 5. Screenshot – MfG.

This may be described as an imperfect fit between the verbal and the visual presentation of the brand which plays with the expectations of the viewers.

The acronyms that were selected to become part of the lyrics consist of three syllables and have their main accent on the last syllable, like *MfG* [ʔɛm.ʔɛf.'ge:] and the German pronunciation of *BMW* (see above). This is due to the fact that the words in the lyrics must fit into the rhythmic pattern of a song. In two cases, the pronunciation is changed because of the rhythm of the music:

TUI (Touristic Union International)
[tu̯i]
[te:.ʔu:.'ʔi:]

TÜV (Technischer Überwachungsverein)[24]
[tʏf]
[te:.ʔy:.'fa̯ʊ]

Instead of looking for other acronyms that fit into the rhythmic pattern, *Die Fantastischen Vier* changed the pronunciation of the two acronyms: The two monosyllabic reading acronyms become trisyllabic spelling acronyms.[25] This artistic freedom influences the sound shapes of the brand names with the result that it might be harder to understand them. However, understanding the brand names in the lyrics and music videos is a prerequisite for a possible advertising effect.

Conclusions

Brand names occurred in the lyrics of 15% of the German top 100 songs of the year 2014. In several of these songs more than one brand name was mentioned. Almost all of these songs are by rappers or feature rappers, which indicates that this phenomenon is genre-specific. Although it may be debated whether this can be described as a form of product placement, it is a form of celebrity endorsement that may lead to increased brand awareness. If artists were paid for naming certain brands (the contexts are mainly positive), it would be a form of product placement and thus, an additional way of making money in the music business.

The study has shown that other name categories are also important, e.g., names of other artists and their songs. If artists and celebrities may be regarded as brands (in a broader sense), there were even more brand names to be found in the lyrics.

Only a few artists make use of a multimodal presentation of brands in their respective music videos. But in most of the Top 100 music videos, a large number of additional brands are presented visually. Thus, in the music videos the genre factor is not as influential as in the lyrics.

The example of the song *MfG* has demonstrated that an intended "imperfect fit" of the verbal and visual brand presentation may be used to create a humorous effect.

This song has also shown that the pronunciation of brand names may be altered due to the rhythm of the music. It is often for the same reason that short forms of brand names are mentioned.

It would be interesting to study how many of the brand names mentioned can be identified and understood by the target audience, especially if they occur in altered forms, in English lyrics (on the German music market, cf. Wahl 2013) or if artists cite brands that are not as internationally famous as *Cadillac* or *Mercedes Benz*.

References[26]

Baldry, Anthony and Paul J. Thibault. 2006. *Multimodal Transcription and Text Analysis*. London: Equinox.

Baumgarten In this volume

European Commission, Audiovisual and Media Policies: https://ec.europa.eu/digital-agenda/en/audiovisual-commercial-communications-avmsd.

Gloor, Storm. 2014. "Songs As Branding Platforms? A Historical Analysis of People, Places, and Products in Pop Music Lyrics". *Journal of the Music & Entertainment Industry Educators Association*. Volume 14, Number 1: 39-60. http://www.meiea.org/Journal/Vol.14/Gloor-MEIEA_Journal_vol_14_no_1_2014-p39.pdf

Kaufman, Gil. 2003. "Push The Courvoisier: Are Rappers Paid For Product Placement?" http://www.mtv.com/news/1472393/push-the-courvoisier-are-rappers-paid-for-product-placement/

Kimball, Roger. 2014. "It's Grammy Time: Who's Belting out Name Brands?" https://www.truthinadvertising.org/product-placement-songs/

MTV Top 100 – 2014, Germany: m.mtv.de/charts/241-top-100-jahres charts-2014

Nicholson, Rebecca. 2015. "Brands and bands – product placement in pop is a betrayal of fans' loyalty" http://www.theguardian.com/commentisfree/2015/jun/08/brands-bands-pop-music-product-placement

Nübling, Damaris, Fabian Fahlbusch and Rita Heuser. 2012. *Namen. Eine Einführung in die Onomastik*. 2nd edition. Tübingen: Narr (Narr Studienbücher).

Pringle, Hamish. 2004. *Celebrity Sells*. Chichester.

Ronneberger-Sibold, Elke. 2010. "Word Creation: Definition – Function – Typology". In *Variation and Change in Morphology*, edited by Franz Rainer et al., 201-216. Amsterdam, Philadelphia: Benjamins (Current Issues in Linguistic Theory 310).

Ronneberger-Sibold, Elke and Sabine Wahl. 2012. "*Kinamic*, *Bolidon* und *Maikäferflugbenzin*: Wortbildung und -schöpfung in deutschen Markennamen. In *Il linguaggio della pubblicità italiano e tedesco:*

teoria e prassi – Italienische und deutsche Werbesprache: Theorie und Praxis edited by Paola Cotticelli Kurras, Elke Ronneberger-Sibold and Sabine Wahl, 313-334. Alessandria: Edizioni dell'Orso.

Ronneberger-Sibold, Elke and Sabine Wahl. 2013. "Preferred Sound Shapes of German Brand Names". In *Names in the Economy: Cultural Prospects* edited by Paula Sjöblom, Terhi Ainiala and Ulla Hakala, 232-249. Newcastle upon Tyne: Cambridge Scholars Publishing.

Shea, Erin. 2013. *Luxury brand endorsements in popular song lyrics may influence purchase.* http://www.luxurydaily.com/luxury-brand-endorsements-in-popular-song-lyrics-may-influence-purchases/

Yves van Vaerenbergh et al. 2011. "The Impact of Brand Name Placement in Song Lyrics on Brand Attitudes: Does the Attitude towards the Artist Matter?" In *Advances in Advertising Research (Vol. 2) Breaking New Ground in Theory and Practice* edited by Shintaro Okasaki, 21-33. Wiesbaden: Springer.

Wahl, Sabine. 2009. "Nike – die Marke der Sieger." In *Marke und Gesellschaft. Markenkommunikation im Spannungsfeld von Werbung und Public Relations* edited by Nina Janich, 207-225. Wiesbaden: Springer VS Research (Europäische Kulturen in der Wirtschaftskommunikation Bd. 15).

Wahl, Sabine. 2013. "'Hello Sunshine' – A Multimodal Analysis of a Volkswagen Television Commercial." In *The Multimodal Analysis of Television Commercials* edited by Barry Pennock-Speck and Maria Milagros del Saz Rubio, 137-156. Valencia: PUV (English in the World Series).

Wahl, Sabine. in print. "Doppelte Multimodalität in deutschen, englischen und spanischen Werbespots." In *Crossmediale Herausforderungen in der Unternehmenskommunikation* edited by Christopher M. Schmidt. Wiesbaden: Springer VS. (Europäische Kulturen in der Wirtschaftskommunikation).

http://www.azlyrics.com/lyrics/janisjoplin/mercedesbenz.html

http://www.die-medienanstalten.de/fileadmin/Download/Rechtsgrundlagen/Gesetze_aktuell/RStV_18.pdf

http://www.ffh.de/musik/hit-news/toController/Topic/toAction/show/toId/18421/toTopic/musikalisches-raetsel-geloest-adel-tawils-lieder.html

http://www.horizont.net/marketing/nachrichten/James-Bond-Das-gigantische-Werbe-Spectre-akel-fuer-Marken-Unternehmen-und-Drehorte-137088

https://en.wikipedia.org/wiki/Mercedes_Benz_%28song%29
https://www.tagesschau.de/kultur/janis-joplin-101.html
m.zdf.de/ZDF/zdfportal/xml/object/5297264
www.autobild.de/marken-modelle/ferrari/testarossa/512m
www.azlyrics.com
www.songtexte.com
www.songtextemania.com

Notes

1 The process that a (brand) name loses its status as name (partly or completely) and becomes a common noun is called deonymisation (cf. Nübling, Fahlbusch, Heuser 2012).

2 As the latest James Bond film indicates, a lot of money is spent to promote products in films, television series and video games (http://www.horizont.net/marketing/nachrichten/James-Bond-Das-gigantische-Werbe-Spectre-akel-fuer-Marken-Unternehmen-und-Drehorte-137088).

3 https://ec.europa.eu/digital-agenda/en/audiovisual-commercial-communications-avmsd.

4 http://www.die-medienanstalten.de/fileadmin/Download/Rechtsgrundlagen/Gesetze_aktuell/RStV_18.pdf.

5 m.zdf.de/ZDF/zdfportal/xml/object/5297264.

6 However, this is not specified in detail, e.g. by giving a maximum duration or a rule concerning close-ups.

7 http://www.azlyrics.com/lyrics/janisjoplin/mercedesbenz.html, https://en.wikipedia.org/wiki/Mercedes_Benz_%28song%29.

8 Janis Joplin herself owned a Porsche, which was sold at auction in 2015 (https://www.tagesschau.de/kultur/janis-joplin-101.html).

9 A similar discussion may be seen with regard to literary texts (cf. Baumgarten in this volume).

10 E.g. Kaufman 2003, Kimball 2014, Nicholson 2015, Shea 2013.

11 Cf. http://hubpages.com/entertainment/Rap-Music-and-Product-Placement.

12 *Testarossa* is a short form of *Ferrari Testarossa* (www.autobild.de/marken-modelle/ferrari/testarossa/512m).

13 *Louie sheets* is used instead of the much longer *Louis Vuitton sheets*.

14 Following a legal definition of the term “brand”, the categorization depends on the registration of the name as trade mark by a responsible intellectual property office (cf. Ronneberger-Sibold/Wahl 2012, 2013).

15 http://www.ffh.de/musik/hit-news/toController/Topic/toAction/show/toId/18421/toTopic/musikalisches-raetsel-geloest-adel-tawils-lieder.html.

16 The term *text* is used in a very broad sense here. In this paper the term *text* refers to language-only texts, whereas the term *artifact* is used for multimodal “texts” like films. For an overview of different definitions of the term multimodality see Wahl (in print).

[17] In this transcription the square brackets are used to show that these elements, i.e., the picture and the sung text, are presented simultaneously (see Wahl 2013 for details).

[18] http://www.universal-music.de/adel-tawil/videos/detail/video:330439/lieder. It is interesting that the presentation of the album here and in many other instances can be described as a kind of multimodal interaction with the viewers (cf. Wahl in print).

[19] In three songs only the instruments of the artists are presented. But these instruments can usually be identified as belonging to a certain brand.

[20] For a detailed description of this technique of word creation see Ronneberger-Sibold (2010).

[21] They had used this spelling even before it was introduced in the orthographic reform in Germany in 1996.

[22] This acronym means *Mit freundlichen Grüßen* ("Yours sincerely").

[23] This song, released in 1999, is just an example and not part of the main corpus of this study. Thus, the brand names are not included in the statistics.

[24] "German Association for Technical Inspection".

[25] For a detailed description of these techniques of word creation see Ronneberger-Sibold (2010).

[26] The online sources were last checked on 3 February 2016.

CONTRIBUTORS

MASSIMO ARCANGELI. Full professor of Italian Linguistics at the University of Cagliari. He cooperates with the "Istituto dell'Enciclopedia Italiana Treccani", the "Società Dante Alighieri" and several Journals and Newspapers.

ILIA BARANOV. Creative Director at Krique Advertising Agency, Moscow, Russia. His main interests are brand names efficiency in real business and cultural influences in brand names.

DOMINIK BAUMGARTEN. PhD, coordinator of the DFG-Research Training Group UbiCrypt at Ruhr-University Bochum, Germany. His research interests are advertising language, pictorial communication and product placement.

ANGELIKA BERGIEN. PhD habil, professor of English Linguistics at the University of Magdeburg, Germany. Her main research interests are pragmatics, socio-onomastics, cognitive linguistics and interdisciplinary approaches to all sorts of texts.

DAIANA FELECAN. PhD, full Professor Hab. at the Technical University of Cluj-Napoca, North University Centre of Baia Mare, Romania. Her main research interests are pragmatics, onomastics (proper name theories), sociolinguistics, history of the (literary) Romanian language, contemporary Romanian syntax, stylistics, literary theory.

FIORENZA FISCHER. PhD, associate professor of Italian Studies at the Institute for Romance Languages, Department of Foreign Language Business Communication, Vienna University of Economics and Business. Her main interests are Italian linguistics, onomastics, pragmatics (euphemisms and metaphors), language for special purposes, and interrelation between knowledge and language in economics.

SERGEY GORYAEV. PhD, ass. prof. at the Ural Federal University and Missionary Institute, Ekaterinburg, Russia. His main research interests are trade and company names, theory of onomastics, onomasiological approach to proper names.

OXANA ISSERS. Professor of Russian and General Linguistics at the Omsk F.M. Dostoevsky State University, Russia, chief editor of "Communication Studies". Her main research interests are verbal communication, pragmatics, brand names, advertizing.

MARJA KALSKE. PhD, university lecturer of Finnish language and literature at the University of Lapland, Finland. Her main interests in research are the values and attitudes found in names, animal names and place names.

ANTON KRYUKOV. PhD, chief editor at Cyrillica LLC, former assistant professor at Moscow State University of Civil Engineering, Russia. His main research interests are cultural linguistics and advertising name studies.

IRINA KRYUKOVA. PhD habil, professor of Linguistics Department of Volgograd State Socio-Pedagogical University, Russia. Her main research interests are pragmatics, socio-onomastics, functional stylistics.

KATHARINA LEIBRING. PhD, Associate professor in Scandinavian languages, Senior research archivist at the Institute for Language and Folklore, Uppsala, Sweden. Her main research interests include post-medieval personal names, socio-onomastics, animal names, and commercial names.

ANTJE LOBIN. PhD habil, professor of Italian and French Linguistics at the Johannes-Gutenberg-Universitaet Mainz. Her main research interests focus on brand name communication, media linguistics, discourse analysis and society related linguistic questions.

OLGA OLSHVANG. PhD, Head of the Department of foreign languages at the Ural State Medical University, Yekaterinburg, Russia. Her main research interests are methods of teaching foreign languages and ICT in teaching foreign languages.

SOLVITA POŠEIKO. PhD, university lecturer in Baltic Philology at the Rēzekne Academy of Technologies and researcher at the Institute for Regional Studies. Her main research interests are sociolinguistics, socionomastics, language acquisition, linguistic and semiotic landscapes.

MARIE ANTOINETTE RIEGER. Associate professor of German Linguistics at the University of Bologna, Italy. Her main research interests are colonial and postcolonial linguistics with a focus on covert racism in literature and advertising, onomastics (brand names and literary names), and valency theory.

JANNE SEPPÄLÄ. PhD, LL.M., D.Sc. (Tech.) candidate in Aalto University, School of Engineering, Department of Built Environment, Finland. His main interests are names of everyday common technological devices and alteration in names and naming.

TATIANA SOKOLOVA. PhD in Philology, Professor Assistant at the Kutafin Moscow State Law University (MSAL), Russia. Her main research interests are naming examination, creative speech activity, naming, urbanonyms, trademarks, trade names and interdisciplinary approaches at the interface of onomastics, linguistics and jurisprudence.

ADRIANA STOICHITOIU ICHIM. PhD, full professor of General and Romanian Linguistics at the University of Bucharest, Romania. Author of four books and 130 scholarly articles, reflecting her research interests in lexicology, semantics, terminologies, commercial naming, language of the law and media discourse.

ANNA SVEDJEDAL. Uppsala. BA in Spanish linguistics and interpretation from Stockholm University. Her main research interests are linguistic diversity and socio-onomastics.

SABINE WAHL. M.St., M.A., university lecturer in German Linguistics at the University of Bremen. Her research interests include the phonology and morphology of brand names, the linguistic and multimodal design of advertisements and commercials as well as language and music.

HOLGER WOCHELE. PhD, external lecturer at the Vienna University of Economics and Business and at the University of Vienna, researcher in Romance Studies (French, Italian, Rumanian, Spanish). His main interests are romance linguistics, morphology, onomastics, applied linguistics, folk linguistics and interrelation between language and economy.

LYAYSAN ZAMALETDINOVA. PhD student in Peoples' Friendship University of Russia (Moscow, Russia). Her main research interests include commercial names and speech creativity in naming.